OXFORD
BIBLE ATLAS

Student Volunteer Staff, with Supervisors, excavating at Tell el-Hesi, biblical Eglon, a Canaanite royal city taken by Joshua (Josh. 10.3, 34–35). See also p. 98 for another area of the tell, the first 'mound of many cities' to be excavated in Palestine (1890).

OXFORD
BIBLE ATLAS

Second Edition

Edited by

HERBERT G. MAY

with the assistance of

G. N. S. HUNT

in consultation with

R. W. HAMILTON

Formerly Keeper of the Department of Antiquities,
Ashmolean Museum, Oxford

LONDON
OXFORD UNIVERSITY PRESS
NEW YORK TORONTO

Oxford University Press, Walton Street, Oxford OX2 6DP

London Glasgow New York Toronto
Delhi Bombay Calcutta Madras Karachi
Kuala Lumpur Singapore Hong Kong Tokyo
Nairobi Dar es Salaam Cape Town
Melbourne Auckland

and associates in
Beirut Berlin Ibadan Mexico City Nicosia

Oxford is a trade mark of Oxford University Press

Hardback edition: ISBN 0 19 211556 1
Paperback edition: ISBN 0 19 211557 X

First published 1962
Second edition 1974
Seventh impression 1983

FILMSET BY BAS PRINTERS LIMITED, WALLOP, HAMPSHIRE
CARTOGRAPHY BY OXFORD CARTOGRAPHERS LTD
PRINTED IN GREAT BRITAIN
MAPS DRAWN AND PHOTOGRAPHED BY
OXFORD CARTOGRAPHERS LTD
AND PRINTED BY
COOK, HAMMOND, AND KELL, LONDON
TEXT PRINTED
AT THE UNIVERSITY PRESS, OXFORD
BY ERIC BUCKLEY
PRINTER TO THE UNIVERSITY

Foreword

ALMOST every reader of the Bible will realize that the Scriptures, from Genesis to Revelation, contain extensive historical materials and innumerable allusions to the geographical background of that history. The geographical references range eastward to the Tigris and Euphrates and beyond to Media, Elam, and Parthia—from which came some of those present at Pentecost—and even to India. Including Asia Minor, Egypt, Ethiopia, and Arabia, they reach westward beyond Greece and Rome as far as Spain, which Paul visited or hoped to visit, and where we are perhaps to find Tarshish, towards which Jonah started on his fateful voyage. Between these limits, the Holy Land itself, under its various names—Canaan, the land of Israel, or Palestine—with its immediate neighbours, is at the centre of the picture throughout.

It is not surprising, therefore, that an Atlas should be of great help to every reader of the Bible and particularly every student; but it must be a historical atlas, not only showing, by maps at the most convenient scales, the physical geography of the area concerned and of particular parts of it, but also, by successive maps of the same area, showing the historical changes which came about through the rise and fall of empires, the changes in geographical names, the appearance of new cities and villages and the disappearance of others, and similar historical developments. Moreover, it cannot be based on the Bible alone, but must make full use of modern archaeological knowledge which both illuminates and supplements the Bible text. Thus, there is mention in the Bible of Ur and Babylon in Mesopotamia, Hazor, Megiddo and Beth-shan in northern Palestine, Lachish and Debir in Judah, and many other places about which little, perhaps not even their exact locations, would be known were it not for archaeological data. Further, there are places very important historically, which do not happen to be mentioned in the Bible, but which must be shown on the maps of the region and taken into account by the student as part of the total historical and geographical background. Thus, there will be found in this Atlas such places as Mari on the Euphrates, Akhetaton (Tell el-Amarna) in Egypt, Ugarit in Phoenicia, Hattusa in Asia Minor, Serabit el-Khadim in Sinai, which are unfamiliar to most Bible readers but are none the less important. There are, too, names of whole peoples, such as the Hurrians in Mitanni, the Sumerians in the Tigris-Euphrates valley, or the Hittites, with their capital at Hattusa, which can be placed on the

map as a result of archaeological evidence. Few and obscure allusions to the Hittites in the Bible would give very little idea of their real importance. Such peoples as the Hittites are on the fringe of the Bible story but in a Bible atlas they must be shown as part of the total background. Nevertheless, in all the maps of this Atlas, the Bible is central, and their purpose is to throw light on it and relate it to its historical and geographical setting.

Because in many cases a map alone would not do this for the ordinary reader, an accompanying text has often been placed on the same page-opening as the map. This Atlas, therefore, is not a book with maps in it, requiring the user to turn from maps to text and back again, but basically an Atlas of maps, with accompanying text. Each text presents concisely the more important biblical and extra-biblical materials relevant to the map. The text relates the map to the biblical data, indicating specific biblical passages involved, and it often relates the map and the biblical data to wider historical backgrounds, using the archaeological sources in the way outlined above.

The *Introduction* provides a more general perspective of geographical and historical backgrounds, with relevant chronological charts, and supplements and correlates much of the data relevant to the individual maps. Here too are placed illustrations relevant to the Introduction itself, or to the maps and map-texts, which could not satisfactorily be included in the map section. Only a relatively small selection can be given of the great wealth of illustrative material now available as a result of archaeological discoveries: the reader or teacher will discover how to supplement this from other books, and, if possible, by actual sight of objects in museums.

The progress of knowledge about the geographical and material background of the Bible—not only the empires, cities, and villages but the daily life and everyday objects of biblical times—has been phenomenal, particularly in this century, and this has been primarily, if not entirely, due to archaeological research. The chapter on *Archaeology and the Bible* explains for the layman how the archaeologist's work can bring these results and what sort of knowledge can be expected to come from archaeological sources, and this too is illustrated with photographs.

The overall plan of the map section is set out in the Table of Contents: if this plan is studied briefly and borne in mind, the use of the maps themselves will be greatly assisted.

Acknowledgements

The Editors wish to express special thanks to the staff of the Cartographic Department of the Clarendon Press, particularly to Mr. David P. Bickmore and Mrs. Mary Denniston, whose interested concern for the Atlas and careful work are reflected in the arrangements and excellence of the maps. Valuable assistance in the preparation of the text and maps on pp. 48–49 has been given by Mr. Gordon Smith of the Department of Geography at Oxford University. The Vegetation map on p. 50 is based on a map in the *Atlas of Israel* published by The Department of Surveys, Ministry of Labour, and The Bialik Institute, The Jewish Agency in 1960. For the translation of the wording of this and other maps from the *Atlas of Israel* thanks are due to Mr. David Patterson, Lecturer in Post-Biblical Hebrew in the University of Oxford. Mr. E. W. Gray, Student of Christ Church, Oxford, and Tutor in Roman History, gave valuable advice on the mapping of the Roman provinces on pp. 88–91. Dr. Gerald B. Cooke of Oberlin College assisted Professor May in the preparation of a number of the facing-page texts. Miss Elizabeth Livingstone has given assistance in checking and collating the place-names and the locations of sites on various maps in this Atlas.

Acknowledgements for permission to reproduce illustrations are gratefully made to the persons and institutions mentioned in the list of Sources of Illustrations on p. 144. Thanks for generous assistance in obtaining illustrations are due especially to Miss Kathleen Kenyon and members of the staff of the University of London Institute of Archaeology, and to Professor D. J. Wiseman, Professor of Assyriology in the University of London, formerly of the Western Asiatic Department of the British Museum.

The Second Edition

Whereas the first edition was edited by Herbert G. May with the assistance of Robert W. Hamilton and Geoffrey N. S. Hunt, this revision is made, as the title-page indicates, by Herbert G. May and Geoffrey N. S. Hunt in consultation with Robert W. Hamilton. The phrase 'in consultation with' is in part an inadequate recognition of the large role played by Mr. Hamilton in the first edition, parts of which were his special responsibility and in which the maps profited from his expertise and experience in Palestinian archaeological and topographical research. Although he was not able to take part in the detailed work of revision, the other two editors were glad to be able to consult him and to retain, with only small revisions, the bulk of the work he did for the first edition.

Special appreciation is due to Professor H. Thomas Frank of Oberlin College, Ohio, for his assistance with the illustrations in this edition. Tribute is here paid to Mr. Wilbur D. Ruggles, New York, for his part in initiating the original project and his encouragement of this edition. The editors express thanks also to Miss Susan le Roux and Mrs. Susan Stenderup of Ely House, London, and to Colonel C. R. Bourne and Mr. Terry R. Hardaker of the Cartographic Department of the Clarendon Press, Oxford.

Contents

Abbreviations

OLD TESTAMENT

Gen.	Genesis	Eccles.	Ecclesiastes
Exod.	Exodus	S. of Sol.	Song of Solomon
Lev.	Leviticus	Isa.	Isaiah
Num.	Numbers	Jer.	Jeremiah
Deut.	Deuteronomy	Lam.	Lamentations
Josh.	Joshua	Ezek.	Ezekiel
Judg.	Judges	Dan.	Daniel
Ruth	Ruth	Hos.	Hosea
1 Sam.	1 Samuel	Joel	Joel
2 Sam.	2 Samuel	Amos	Amos
1 Kgs.	1 Kings	Obad.	Obadiah
2 Kgs.	2 Kings	Jon.	Jonah
1 Chr.	1 Chronicles	Mic.	Micah
2 Chr.	2 Chronicles	Nah.	Nahum
Ezr.	Ezra	Hab.	Habakkuk
Neh.	Nehemiah	Zeph.	Zephaniah
Esth.	Esther	Hag.	Haggai
Job	Job	Zech.	Zechariah
Ps.	Psalms	Mal.	Malachi
Prov.	Proverbs		

APOCRYPHA

1 Esd.	1 Esdras	Sirach (Ecclus.)	Ecclesiasticus or the Wisdom of Jesus son of Sirach
Tobit	Tobit		
Judith	Judith		
		1 Macc.	1 Maccabees
		2 Macc.	2 Maccabees

NEW TESTAMENT

Matt.	Matthew	1 Tim.	1 Timothy
Mark	Mark	2 Tim.	2 Timothy
Luke	Luke	Tit.	Titus
John	John	Philem.	Philemon
Acts	Acts of the Apostles	Heb.	Hebrews
Rom.	Romans	Jas.	James
1 Cor.	1 Corinthians	1 Pet.	1 Peter
2 Cor.	2 Corinthians	2 Pet.	2 Peter
Gal.	Galatians	1 John	1 John
Eph.	Ephesians	2 John	2 John
Phil.	Philippians	3 John	3 John
Col.	Colossians	Jude	Jude
1 Thess.	1 Thessalonians	Rev.	Revelation
2 Thess.	2 Thessalonians		

Other abbreviations, used especially in the Gazetteer, are listed on p. 120.

Introduction: Israel and the Nations

PART I: THE HOLY LAND

THE HEART of our concern in a Bible atlas is the Holy Land, a territory of insignificant size when compared with the total land area of the Mediterranean basin. On a map of Europe and North Africa it seems to be tucked away unobtrusively in a distant corner of the Mediterranean. And yet its geographical position in relation to the rest of the Near East is such that from earliest historic times to the present it has been intensively involved in the political, commercial, and cultural life of that region. It is not physical geography alone which accounts for this, for we must study it also in terms of human geography. Not only must the geography be related to political, cultural, and ethnic factors, but the creative initiative of individuals in many areas of human activity and thought must be considered a part of the complete picture. For instance, not the geographical position of Israel, but Israel as a creative people, with its kings, prophets, priests, and writers, and their insights, more adequately explains Israel's almost boundless influence. Here, in a special way, there was the hand of the God of Israel working creatively in history. The tradition which regarded Jerusalem as the very geographical centre of the world has its justification.

People do not live in a vacuum. The kind of houses they live in, the activities in which they engage, the tools they use, reflect their physical environment. Climate and soil determine their agricultural pursuits. Flora and fauna affect food habits. Commerce and industry depend on available raw materials and accessibility of markets. The fact that the irregular coastland of Phoenicia provided many harbours, in contrast with the coastline of Palestine, makes it easier to understand why the Phoenicians were carriers of the Mediterranean commerce, while the Israelites were not a sea-going people. The location of cities is not accidental; they were often placed at strategic cross-roads on trade routes over which went the national and international commerce. The topography of a country may influence the nature of civil administration. Even the forms of religious expression may reflect geographical and climatic conditions;

it is no accident that the great god of Egypt, Amon-Re, was a sun god, as was Marduk of Babylonia, while the great god of Canaan was Baal, the rain god.

The two names of the Holy Land with which we are most familiar are Canaan and Palestine. The name Palestine comes to us through the Greek from 'Philistia', the southern coastland of the Holy Land, named after its inhabitants, the Philistines. In other words, the name of a part of the country came to be applied to the entire country. The name Canaan seems most probably to have meant 'red-purple'. Wool dyed with the local red-purple (Tyrian purple) dye was an important export of the country. Before the name came to be applied to the country, it may have designated the traders in this industry. The word 'Canaanite' was still used in the Bible to mean 'trader' or 'merchant', as in Zech. 14. 21; Prov. 31. 24; Job 41. 6. Canaan might also include the Phoenician coastland. Ugarit in north Phoenicia was reckoned to be in Canaan, and in Gen. 10. 15, Canaan is the father of Sidon (cf. Isa. 23. 11, 12). 'Phoenicia' comes from the Greek word *phoinix*, 'red purple'. Less probably Canaan means 'the western lands' (= Amurru).

Climate and Geography
(Maps, pp. 49–53)

The territory occupied by the Israelite tribes in Palestine and Transjordan was roughly about 10,000 square miles, about the area of Vermont or about one-fourth larger than Wales. (See map, especially p. 61.) 'From Dan to Beer-sheba,' the proverbial limits of Palestine (Judg. 20. 1, &c.) was only about 145 air miles. 'From Geba to Beer-sheba' designated the area of the cities of Judah (2 Kgs. 23. 8), although the southern border of Judah was reckoned to extend to Kadesh-barnea, about forty-five miles south of Beer-sheba (Num. 34. 4). The northern limit of Israelite domination was the Entrance to Hamath (Lebo-hamath), the area between the Orontes and Leontes rivers, or a town

above: *The town of Safad in Upper Galilee, in an area of relatively high rainfall, among wooded slopes.*
below: *A view of the fertile Plain of Esdraelon (Plain of Megiddo, pp. 48, 49), with Mt. Tabor in the background.*

A scene in an area of very low rainfall; the road from Bethlehem to Jericho through the Wilderness of Judah (Judea).

(Lebweh) on the Orontes commanding the watershed between the rivers (Num. 34. 8; 1 Kgs. 8. 65). The Transjordan tribes occupied the territory between Mount Hermon and the Arnon (Deut. 3. 8), although Moab's northern border fluctuated between the Arnon and Wadi Husban. At times Israelite control included Moab and Edom, reaching to Ezion-geber on the Red Sea, enclosing the rich copper deposits of the Arabah and providing an important commercial outlet.

Palestine has a latitude roughly that of Georgia (U.S.A.), or southern Spain, or the Shanghai-Nanking area of China. Its climate is influenced also by the configurations of the land and its proximity to the desert. Although it possesses a variety of climate, in general it has two seasons: a winter which is the rainy season, and a rainless, bright, and sunny summer. The 'former' or early rains come in the autumn, and with them begins the agricultural year, for plowing can now be done on the rain-softened ground. Quite understandably the Israelites had an autumnal calendar; as in the modern Jewish calendar, the New Year occurred in the autumn, near the autumnal equinox. The heaviest rainfall comes in December to March. The 'latter' or spring rains are those of April and May, so important for the ripening of the crops (see Jer. 3. 3; Amos 4. 7).

Palestine lies between the sea and the desert, and the rains come from the westerly direction, from the sea. The rain clouds drop most of their moisture on the western slopes of Cis-jordan (Palestine west of the Jordan) and Trans-jordan, and a vastly decreased amount on the eastern slopes. (See map, p. 51.) In general the rainfall tends to become less from west to east, although this is counteracted by the fact that the rainfall may increase as one goes up the mountains. The average annual rainfall near Acco on the coast and at

Jerusalem up in the hills is around 24–26 inches. This is comparable with the annual rainfall in the London area (23·5 inches), Edinburgh (25 inches), or Victoria, British Columbia (27 inches); but in Palestine the rains are not scattered throughout the year and the summers are rainless. Inland on the plain north of Megiddo and Taanach, where the elevation is slight, it is a little less than 16 inches. The high Upper Galilee hills receive about 47 inches of rain (compare New York City, 41·6 inches), but south of Hebron only about 12 inches, illustrating how in general the rainfall also tends to decrease as one goes from north to south. In north Edom it may average about 11 inches.

The summers are hot on the coastal plains, but in the highlands it may be more pleasant. On the hills, as at Jerusalem, there may in occasional winters be snow, and frost is not uncommon. The average temperature at Jerusalem in January is about 48°F. (9° C.), but in August it is about 74° F. (23° C.). The summer nights there are cool. Even in the rainless summers moisture is not absent, for the dews are heaviest at this time. (Further statistics are shown on p. 50.)

East of Transjordan and south of the Negeb is the desert, where rainfall is minimal. Here rapid temperature changes may result in hot and dry winds which may be devastating in their effects on the Land of the Sown. More particularly these are the sirocco or *hamsin* winds which come in early autumn and late spring. The east wind from the desert became a natural symbol of the Lord's wrath in the Old Testament (Isa. 27. 8; cf. Ezek. 17. 10).

The rocks in Palestine are largely limestone, chalk, basalt, and sandstone. The central highlands, Galilee, and the Shephelah (see map, p. 49) are largely limestone, which makes good building stone. The Wilderness of Judea and the 'moat' that separates the central highlands from the Shephelah are chalk. Sandstone is found on the eastern edge of the Arabah (Jordan Valley). North and south-east of the Séa of Galilee basalt abounds, and particularly in northern Transjordan in the Bashan area. Cinder cones and plugs of volcanoes from which hot basalt once poured out may be seen in the Jebel Druze area. The basalt results in the un-relieved black landscape of Hauran, where even the cities are built of the same stone and blend into the dreary land-scape. To the east is the curious Leja (see pp. 48–49), a mass of congealed lava some 350 square miles in area, broken into cracks and fissures. The remnants of the ancient volcanic activity which produced the volcanic rock may be seen in today's hot springs, as at el-Hammeh by the Yarmuk in Transjordan and at Tiberias by the Sea of Galilee. Earth-quakes are most frequent and intense in the Jordan Valley, but violent earthquakes have also been recorded elsewhere in Palestine. There are copper ores in the Arabah south of the Dead Sea and in the Negeb.

Israel's own impression of the climate, topography, flora, and productivity of Palestine is best summed up in the words of Deut. 8. 7–9: 'For the Lord your God is bringing you into a good land, a land of brooks of water, of fountains and springs, flowing forth in valleys and hills, a land of wheat and barley, of vines and fig trees and pomegranates, a land of olive trees and honey, a land in which you will eat bread without scarcity, in which you will lack nothing, a land whose stones are iron and out of whose hills you can dig copper.' The allusion to 'stones of iron' may be to basalt, which was employed for various instruments and vessels. (For further details see pages 48–49.)

A Coastal Corridor

By virtue of its positions between the great civilizations of the Tigris-Euphrates and Nile river valleys and its location south of the kingdoms which flourished in Asia Minor, Palestine-Syria played a not insignificant role in the political history of the ancient Near East. (See map, pp. 54–55.) The armies and merchants of the Egyptians and of the Assyrians and Babylonians were often in this region. Hittites and Horites from Asia Minor infiltrated Palestine, and from this direction came the Hyksos; and through Asia Minor came the conquering Greek armies under Alexander the Great. The involvements of Palestine-Syria with Asia Minor in the Hellenistic and Roman periods were many, and the spread of the Christian church into Asia Minor is a most important aspect of the New Testament story (see pp. 88–91). The subsequent discussion will be concerned largely with the two great river-valley cultures.

It is particularly from the records of Egypt and Meso-potamia that much may be added to the history of Palestine-Syria as known from the biblical narratives. The caravans of trade and chariotry of war brought the Canaanites and Israelites into contact with the wider Near East. Despite the distinctive aspects of Canaanite culture, and even greater uniqueness of Israel's religion, Palestine was a part of a larger cultural area with which it had much in common. An understanding of the life and times of Israel's neighbours is essential to the full appreciation of Israelite religion and life.

As early as the end of the fourth millennium there was an intensive intermingling of cultures in the ancient Near East, and the influence of Mesopotamian culture on Egypt was already considerable, carried there through Syria and

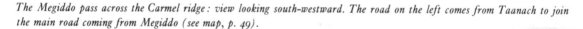

The Megiddo pass across the Carmel ridge: view looking south-westward. The road on the left comes from Taanach to join the main road coming from Megiddo (see map, p. 49).

The southern end of the Sea of Galilee and part of the Jordan Valley: view looking eastward towards the hills of Transjordan.

Palestine. Palestinian pottery of this period has been found in Egypt south of Cairo. The main routes of commerce (see pp. 48–49 and 66–67) were already well established. One of the great international trunk roads, later known as 'the Way of the Land of the Philistines' (Exod. 13. 17), and called by the Egyptians 'the Way of Horus', began at the fortress of Zilu near modern Qantara and then followed close to the coastline across the northern Sinai desert to Raphia, Gaza, Ashkelon, Ashdod, and Joppa; its northern extension crossed the Mt. Carmel range through the Megiddo Pass to the Plain of Esdraelon, whence it went on up to Damascus by fording the Jordan south of Lake Huleh at the point of today's 'Bridge of the Daughters of Jacob', or south of the Sea of Galilee at today's 'Bridge of Assembly'. Another route began as 'the Way to the Wilderness of Shur' (Gen. 16. 7), to cross the desert from Lake Timsah towards Kadesh-barnea (map, p. 59), whence it turned north through the Negeb to Beer-sheba, Hebron, Jerusalem, and Shechem, to come out also on the Plain of Esdraelon. A third route from Egypt crossed to Ezion-geber at the head of the Gulf of Aqaba, and then passed through Edom and Moab and up through Transjordan to Damascus; this is 'the King's Highway' of Num. 20. 17ff. (see p. 59).

Damascus was thus one of the most important cross-roads of the ancient orient. Traders and armies from Mesopotamia entered Palestine through it, or came down the Phoenician coast or through the Valley of Lebanon (Aven, Amos 1. 5), which divides the Lebanons into two ridges. Damascus was one of the more important smaller nations of the Near East, and often fought with Israel over the possession of northern Transjordan (see 1 Kgs. 22; 2 Kgs. 8. 28 ff.). David and Solomon controlled Damascus and the larger Syrian area, as also did Jeroboam (2 Sam. 8. 6; 2 Kgs. 14. 28), but the Syrian armies were often also in Israel (1 Kgs. 20; 2 Kgs. 6. 8; 13. 7, etc.) and even invaded Judah (2 Kgs. 12. 17 ff.). The relations of Israel and Judah with the Phoenicians were much more peaceful and largely commercial, as at the time of David and Solomon.

The History of Palestine in Perspective

No single geographical feature united Canaan. In contrast with the Nile and the Tigris-Euphrates, the Jordan in its deep gorge tended to divide, rather than unite, the countries on either bank. The rise of a native, over-all government in Canaan was also frustrated by the anxiety of Egypt and Mesopotamia to control this commercial corridor and buffer area. In Canaanite days the country was divided into innumerable city states, illustrated in the letters sent by Canaanite city kings to Egypt in the early 14th century B.C. Something of the material cultures of Canaan can be traced from the Pebble or Chopper culture of the Lower Paleolithic (Old Stone) Age, going back some 600,000 years. Dramatic evidence of early man comes from the Mount Carmel caves in Wadi el-Mughara (map, p. 94). Sickle flints, pestles and mortars evidence the beginnings of agriculture in the Mesolithic (Middle Stone) Age. Excavations at Jericho have disclosed in the lowest levels the pre-pottery period Neolithic (New Stone) city dwellers, going back into the seventh millennium B.C.* The Chalcolithic (Copper-Stone) Age was succeeded by the Early Bronze Age around 3100 B.C., although the introduction of bronze was gradual. The Hebrew patriarchs belong to the Middle Bronze Age (*c.* 2100–1550 B.C.), and it is at this time that the biblical scene moves from Mesopotamia to Canaan (maps, pp. 54–55 and 92–93). In the earliest part of this period Amorites, Semites from along the desert fringes, moved in to the Land of the Sown. Also from the north, probably from Asia Minor, were migrations of Horites or Hurrians, and in the latter part of this period the Hyksos peoples invaded Syria and Palestine and became the rulers of Egypt.

* See note on carbon-14 dating, p. 102

The River Jordan.

In its upper course, as here (left), at one of its sources in the region of Dan, where it issues from a number of strong springs ('Ain Leddan), the Jordan is a fast-flowing stream. In the deep valley between the Sea of Galilee and the Dead Sea, it meanders over the scrub-covered valley bottom, the Zor. *See p. 48.*

right: *The Wadi el-Mughara :
site of prehistoric caves.
Significant skeletal remains of the
Lower Palaeolithic (Old Stone)
period were discovered in the cave
where the debris from excavations
is evident (the 'Cave of the
Kids'). (See text p. 13)*

below: *Great stone tower of
walled city of Jericho in the
pre-pottery Neolithic period,
carbon date 6800 B.C., and still
standing to a height of 30 feet.
See p. 102. See also pp. 13, 92.*

Solomonic gateway at Gezer, looking from inside the city. There are guard rooms on each side of the road through the gate. Similar gateways were found at Hazor and Megiddo, which were also fortified by Solomon (1 Kgs. 9.15). See plans and p. 64.

The oppression of Israel and the Exodus from Egypt took place most probably under Rameses II (1301–1234), and Joshua's conquests (pp. 60–61) are to be placed in the last quarter of the 13th century, although some tribes of Hebrews had apparently entered Canaan earlier. The period of the Judges began with the Iron Age, *c.* 1200 B.C., around the time of the Philistine invasion, and lasted until the beginning of the reign of Saul, *c.* 1020 B.C. (map, p. 61). Saul made his headquarters at his city of Gibeah, where the excavations have uncovered a section of his citadel. The dates of the reigns of David and Solomon over the United Monarchy (pp. 64–65) are equally uncertain, but perhaps may have been between *c.* 1000 and 922 B.C. They mark the golden age of Israel's expansion in territory, commerce, and industry, and were years of significant political, religious, and literary development.

The Divided Monarchy has two main periods: the time of the co-existence of the kingdoms of Israel and Judah (922–721) (pp. 68–69) and the time of the kingdom of Judah after the fall of Israel (721–586) (pp. 72–73). The chronology of the kings of Israel and Judah presents many thorny problems, often insoluble despite the help given by contemporary data from Egypt and particularly from the Mesopotamian records. The chart on pp. 18–19 presents two of the more recent important chronological systems. The first date follows the reconstruction of Professor W. F. Albright and the second, in parentheses, that of Professor E. R. Thiele.

The general course of the Hebrew monarchies is indicated in the text (pp. 64, 68) and some relevant illustrations are given above and opposite. Israel was generally politically and economically more prosperous than Judah, despite violent disruptions which resulted in frequent changes in the ruling dynasties. Judah was often subservient to Israel. But it was Judah which was religiously more significant. Although the prophetic movement had its origins and much of its early growth (from Samuel to Hosea) in the territory of Israel, it reached its highest fruition in Judah. After the fall of the kingdom of Israel it was largely left to Judah to bear and bring to maturity the Hebrew heritage, although the importance of its development among the Samaritans must not be minimized. It was Judah which was carried into exile in 597 and 586 and returned from exile in 538 (pp. 76–77). These were the Jews, and the term 'Jew' means Judean, coming ultimately from the Hebrew *Yehudah*, Judah. The returning exiles were first under the governorship of Shesh-bazzar, who was succeeded by Zerubbabel, under whom the temple was rebuilt (520–515). Ezra returned to promulgate his law in 458 or (possibly) in 398 (see p. 30), and Nehemiah's first period of governorship began in 445. With the end of the Persian domination (pp. 78–79) Palestine submitted to the Greeks under Alexander the Great in 332. First the Ptolemies of Egypt and then the Seleucids of Syria ruled Palestine (pp. 82–83). At the end of the Hellenistic (Greek) period, independent Hasmonean rulers governed Palestine (142–63 B.C.), until the country came under the Romans, who remained its masters through New Testament times and beyond (pp. 84–91).

Some of the detail of this brief survey is filled in by the subsequent discussion of Egypt and Israel, Mesopotamia and Israel, Persia and Israel, the Greeks and Israel, and Rome and Israel. We shall see something of the role of the great powers in the affairs of Palestine and in the process glimpse the panorama of the history of the ancient Near East as reflected on the various maps and in the accompanying text pages.

Section of enclosure wall of the royal quarter at Samaria: the work of skilled (possibly Phoenician) masons employed by Kings Omri and Ahab. See p. 68.

The Siloam Inscription, from the wall of the tunnel of the water system at Jerusalem constructed by King Hezekiah (2 Kgs. 20.20). (See p. 114)

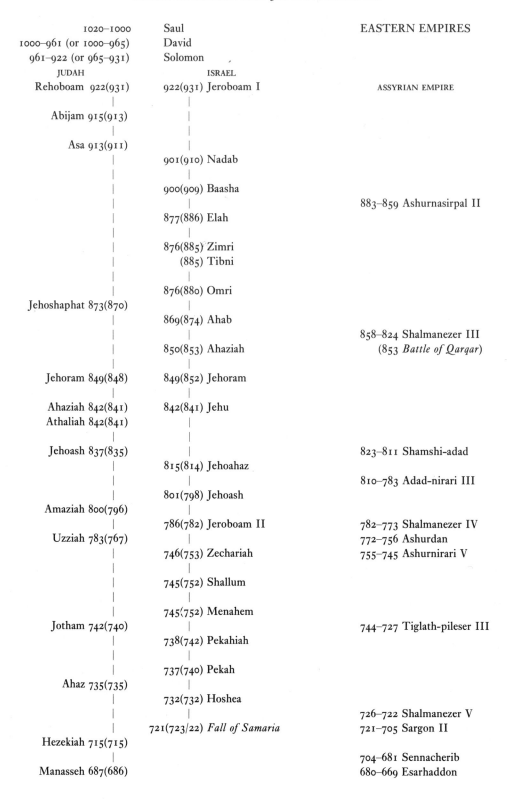

1020–1000	Saul	EASTERN EMPIRES
1000–961 (or 1000–965)	David	
961–922 (or 965–931)	Solomon	
JUDAH	ISRAEL	
Rehoboam 922(931)	922(931) Jeroboam I	ASSYRIAN EMPIRE
Abijam 915(913)		
Asa 913(911)		
	901(910) Nadab	
	900(909) Baasha	
	877(886) Elah	883–859 Ashurnasirpal II
	876(885) Zimri	
	(885) Tibni	
	876(880) Omri	
Jehoshaphat 873(870)		
	869(874) Ahab	
	850(853) Ahaziah	858–824 Shalmanezer III
		(853 *Battle of Qarqar*)
Jehoram 849(848)	849(852) Jehoram	
Ahaziah 842(841)	842(841) Jehu	
Athaliah 842(841)		
Jehoash 837(835)		823–811 Shamshi-adad
	815(814) Jehoahaz	810–783 Adad-nirari III
	801(798) Jehoash	
Amaziah 800(796)		
	786(782) Jeroboam II	782–773 Shalmanezer IV
Uzziah 783(767)		772–756 Ashurdan
	746(753) Zechariah	755–745 Ashurnirari V
	745(752) Shallum	
	745(752) Menahem	
Jotham 742(740)		744–727 Tiglath-pileser III
	738(742) Pekahiah	
	737(740) Pekah	
Ahaz 735(735)		
	732(732) Hoshea	
		726–722 Shalmanezer V
	721(723/22) *Fall of Samaria*	721–705 Sargon II
Hezekiah 715(715)		704–681 Sennacherib
Manasseh 687(686)		680–669 Esarhaddon

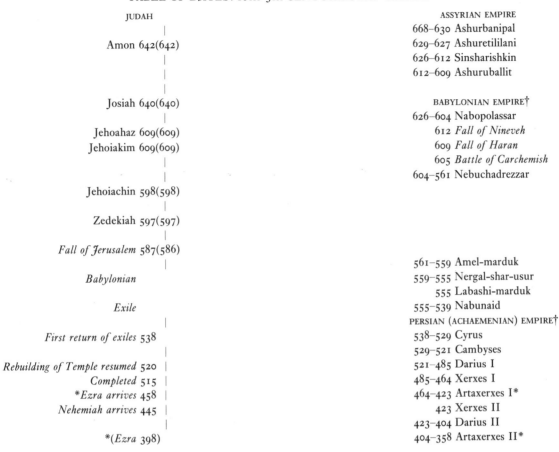

JUDAH	ASSYRIAN EMPIRE
	668–630 Ashurbanipal
Amon 642(642)	629–627 Ashuretililani
	626–612 Sinsharishkin
	612–609 Ashuruballit
Josiah 640(640)	BABYLONIAN EMPIRE†
	626–604 Nabopolassar
Jehoahaz 609(609)	612 *Fall of Nineveh*
Jehoiakim 609(609)	609 *Fall of Haran*
	605 *Battle of Carchemish*
	604–561 Nebuchadrezzar
Jehoiachin 598(598)	
Zedekiah 597(597)	
Fall of Jerusalem 587(586)	
	561–559 Amel-marduk
Babylonian	559–555 Nergal-shar-usur
	555 Labashi-marduk
Exile	555–539 Nabunaid
	PERSIAN (ACHAEMENIAN) EMPIRE†
First return of exiles 538	538–529 Cyrus
	529–521 Cambyses
Rebuilding of Temple resumed 520	521–485 Darius I
Completed 515	485–464 Xerxes I
Ezra arrives 458	464–423 Artaxerxes I*
Nehemiah arrives 445	423 Xerxes II
	423–404 Darius II
(Ezra 398)	404–358 Artaxerxes II*

† Babylonian and Persian dates are given here on the Accession-year system; beginning of first year of reign post-dated to the New Year following the accession.   * See Ezra 7. 1–7, and below, page 30.

The east gate of Shechem as reconstructed in the Late Bronze Age. Shechem, one of the more important political and cultic centres of the north, is associated with the patriarchs (Gen. 12.6, 33.18–34.31), and later Joshua assembled all Israel there (Josh. 24).

Sumerian writing. A schoolboy's tablet from Nippur, containing one of the earliest known word-lists: Sumerian on the left, Akkadian equivalents on the right.

Early writing from Serabit el-Khadim. Statuette of a sphinx with short inscription (dedication to a goddess) in early alphabetic script.

The Cradle of Civilization

Civilization's debt to the larger Near East cannot easily be adequately comprehended. Here was the cradle of three great religions of today—Judaism, Christianity, and Islam. From here comes the world's most treasured religious literature, the Bible. Here were the beginnings of agriculture and the earliest village life. Indeed, in the Near East lie the beginnings of literature, law and science. To the inhabitants of the southern Tigris-Euphrates valley, the Sumerians (pp. 54–55), must be credited the first real system of writing. The Sumerian stories of creation and the flood set the pattern for later accounts in widely scattered areas of the Near East. The Sumerians seem to have been the originators of certain forms of literature, such as the elegy or lament, and proverbs or wisdom literature. Dated around 3300 B.C., there comes from the city of Erech a small collection of documents which give groupings of birds, fish, domestic animals, plants, vases, personal names, &c., which may be called truly scientific records, perhaps intended to be teachers' handbooks. Among the Sumerians and their successors, the Assyrians (pp. 70–71) and Babylonians (pp. 74–75), are to be found the beginnings of medicine, mathematics, astronomy, geology, and metallurgy. To them is owed the sexagesimal system (counting by sixties or a fraction or multiple of sixty) reflected in our division of the circle into 360 degrees and the hour into 60 minutes.

The alphabet, our ABC, may be traced back to one of the several systems of writing used by the Canaanites before the entrance of the Israelites into Canaan. Although a few earlier examples of this alphabet have been found at Gezer, Shechem, and Lachish (see also pp. 94–95, 98), the most extensive early examples come from *c.* 1500 B.C., from Serabit el-Khadim in the Sinai Peninsula (see illustration and pp. 58–59, 92–93). It is difficult to estimate the importance and influence of this invention, for to it can be traced the alphabets of the Hebrews, Arabs, Greeks, Romans, and others. Significant architectural forms also had their origin in the Near East, including the so-called Ionic capital. Among the many artistic accomplishments of the ancient Near East is the development of music. Sumerian musical instruments from the early third millennium attest to an already high art. Canaanite musical instruments and musicians were popular even in Egypt. Hebrews and Greeks took over Canaanite melodies, and even the names of Canaanite musical instruments. Psalms in the Jerusalem temple were sung to Canaanite tunes.

Egypt and Israel

The life-blood of Egypt is the waters of the Nile which make it possible for man to live in a narrow ribbon of fertility set in the midst of the desert expanse of north-east Africa. The

An Egyptian landscape: the Pyramids at Gizeh, with the Nile, in flood, in the foreground.

Nile has its origins in two main branches, the White and Blue Nile, which join at Khartoum. The annual inundations of the Nile, with their deposits of rich soil brought down from the highlands of Abyssinia, bring to a practically rainless country the fertility that makes agriculture possible. This also forms the background of the development of the state in Egypt, through the necessity for an authority to control irrigation, the draining of swamps, and the construction of dams, dikes, and canals, all of which required co-operative effort. The Nile also provided the chief means of transport and communication, and so contributed to the unity of the country. Its reeds and brush supplied game and fowl, and its papyrus plant furnished the country's writing materials (see below) and gave us our word 'paper'. It is small wonder that the Nile was deified and that an Egyptian hymn describes it as 'the creator of every good thing'.

The Nile flows from south to north, so Lower Egypt (pp. 54, 58) is the spreading, flat Delta with its marshlands and with the branches of canals of the Nile running out to the Mediterranean; 'the waters of Egypt, their rivers, their canals, and their ponds', in Exod. 7. 19, refers to this area. Compare the references to the canals, the branches of Egypt's Nile, the reeds, and the rushes in Isa. 19. 6. The rest of Egypt to the First Cataract at Syene is Upper Egypt (p. 54). It is in Upper Egypt (Pathros) that one is most conscious of the desert. The desert sands at Thebes have preserved most of our evidence of Egypt's great past, as they have provided places for the burial of the dead and for the great temples (pp. 92–93). From Memphis at the foot of the Delta to Syene at the First Cataract is about 580 miles. The total extent of Egypt is designated 'from Migdol to Syene' (Ezek. 30. 6).

An unopened papyrus document as found at Elephantine (cf. p. 78), sealed and endorsed on the outside. This is a Jewish Aramaic papyrus of the 5th century B.C. Papyrus was thus used in Egypt throughout the biblical period.

Very naturally, because of its proximity, the Bible is more concerned with the Delta area. Here in the land of Goshen (map, pp. 58–59) the Israelites lived and were enslaved. Goshen is in the area of Wadi Tumilat. It is a fertile tract of land (cf. Gen. 47. 6), irrigated by a canal from the Nile, and lying between the Nile and Lake Timsah.

Egypt was geographically isolated, with deserts to the east and to the west. Its land connection with the rest of the Near East was a week's desert travel over the caravan routes across Sinai. Or its ships might take the sea route along the coast of Canaan. Yet Egypt could not permit itself to be isolated, for it needed Canaan both as a buffer state and as a communication corridor. Egypt's armies were often in Syria and Palestine, where the trade routes were the life-line of commerce. From earliest times Egypt traded with the Phoenicians, particularly through the harbour city of Gebal (pp. 55, 67). In the Middle Kingdom, the Twelfth Dynasty (c. 2000–1800), the Egyptians had a strong foothold in Syria and Palestine. Her traders and her products were prominent in the northern Phoenician city of Ugarit (pp. 55, 67), as well as elsewhere. In the patriarchal period Egypt was penetrated by the Hyksos, and in the 17th century Palestine was a part of Hyksos-controlled Egypt, which had its capital at Avaris. Egyptian power in the Eighteenth and Nineteenth Dynasties flourished in these areas. Thutmose I (1525–1495) penetrated to the Euphrates and set up his stele by its banks, and Thutmose III (1490–1436) made many campaigns here. Thutmose III lists 119 places in Canaan and lower Syria conquered by him in his first campaign. Egyptian amulets, scarabs, sculpture, and royal inscriptions found in Canaan witness Egypt's stake in this country in these dynasties.

The Tell el-Amarna letters, written to Egypt by the kings of Canaan, Phoenicia, Syria, and Asia Minor give further evidence of Egypt's involvement. The first non-biblical allusion to Israel occurs in the record of a king of the Nineteenth Dynasty, Merenptah. The bronze base of a statue of Rameses VI (1153–1149 B.C.) discovered in the Megiddo excavations evidences control of the Egyptians over their old Palestine dependencies in the early period of the Judges.

The interrelationships of Egypt and Palestine are abundantly illustrated in the biblical narrative. They begin with the story of Abraham's descent into Egypt. After the enslaved Joseph had become Egypt's 'minister of agriculture', Jacob and the brothers of Joseph entered Egypt, Echoes of the Hyksos movement have been found in these stories by some scholars. Israel, the people of the Lord, had its origins in Egypt, and Moses, the founder of the Hebrew faith, bore an Egyptian name. Joseph had married the daughter of an Egyptian priest, and an Egyptian princess was Solomon's chief wife (Gen. 41. 50; 1 Kgs. 3. 1; 9. 16). An important part of Solomon's trade was with Egypt (1 Kgs. 10. 28, 29, pp. 66–67).

Jeroboam I of Israel sought and received political asylum in Egypt (1 Kgs. 11. 40). Pharaoh Shishak invaded Israel and Judah in the reigns of Jeroboam of Israel and Rehoboam of Judah (1 Kgs. 14. 25 and Shishak's record). Judean and Israelite revolts against Assyria were encouraged by Egypt. Egypt was probably the instigator of the coalition against Shalmanezer III of Assyria at Qarqar in 853, an alliance in which Ahab of Israel participated. In 720 Sibe (O.T. So), Tartan (i.e. commander-in-chief or governor-general: 2 Kgs. 17. 4 'king') of Egypt, and Hanno, King of

Egyptian scarabs of the XVIIIth Dynasty.

A tablet from Tell el-Amarna: letter from a petty king to the King of Egypt. Such documents, found at Akhenaton's capital, give valuable historical information.

left: *Thutmose III, of the XVIIIth Dynasty. Fragment of a limestone relief from Western Thebes.*

right: *Akhenaton: head in quartzite from a sculptor's workshop at Tell el-Amarna.*

left: *Rameses II: basalt statue, probably from Karnak (Thebes).*

right: *Merenptah, of the XIXth Dynasty. An 'Osiride' figure, i.e. showing the Pharaoh as Osiris, in limestone, from Thebes.*

Gaza, set out together to defeat Sargon II, but met defeat. Egyptian intrigue in Philistia lay behind the revolt which brought Sargon into Philistia in 715 and 711. When Philistia revolted in 701 and Hezekiah joined the rebellion, the people of Ekron (map, p. 73) called on Egypt and Ethiopia for help against the Assyrians under Sennacherib, but the forces of Egypt and Ethiopia were defeated by the Assyrians. These and other reports of Egypt's activities in Palestine are documented in the Assyrian records (see also 2 Kgs. 18. 21–24). Now supporting the Assyrians against Babylonia, Pharaoh Neco marched through Palestine in 609 and slew Josiah at Megiddo (2 Kgs. 23. 29, pp. 72–73). In 605 the Egyptians were decisively defeated by Nebuchadrezzar at Carchemish (cf. Jer. 46). King Jehoahaz of Judah, who had been taken in bonds to Riblah before Neco and upon whom tribute had been imposed, was deposed and exiled to Egypt, and Neco put on the throne Jehoiakim, who taxed the land to pay silver and gold tribute to Egypt (2 Kgs. 23. 33–35). When Judah under Zedekiah revolted, the Egyptians in 587 tried in vain to give help to the besieged Judeans (Jer. 37. 5 ff.). To these and other evidences of Egyptian contacts in Palestine should be added the prophetic oracles on Egypt in Isaiah, Jeremiah, and Ezekiel. The role of Egypt in Palestine in the Hellenistic period is mentioned below (pp. 32–33).

The religious influence of Egypt on Canaan was minor when compared with its political and commercial contacts. It is very doubtful whether the near-monotheism of the religion of Akhenaton (c. 1370–1353) influenced the faith of Moses. The golden calf has a Canaanitish rather than an Egyptian origin. It has been plausibly assumed that an Egyptian work from some time after the 8th century, 'The Teaching of Amen-em-ope', has influenced Deuteronomy and the Psalms, with direct borrowing from it in Prov. 22. 17 – 23. 14, although an Aramaic original of the Egyptian work has been suggested. That Ps. 104 has been influenced by Akhenaton's Hymn to Aten or that Egyptian 'messianism' is reflected in Hebrew messianism is most dubious. The greater religious influence on Israel came from Mesopotamia.

Mesopotamia and Israel

'Mesopotamia', meaning 'the land between the rivers', is the Greek rendering of Hebrew *Aram-naharayim*, 'Aram of the (two) rivers', the area of the upper and middle Euphrates and Tigris, wherein lay Nahor and Haran (Gen. 24.10). The word came to mean the whole Tigris-Euphrates district. The two rivers join to become one through the marshland delta. It is questionable that the shoreline has shifted much within historic times. Despite the fact that it has a rainy season (about 8 inches annually) Babylonia depends on the river waters for its fertility. The Tigris and Euphrates have changed their courses in the Mesopotamian plain, the Euphrates having shifted westward to its present course. The pattern of ancient settlement can be seen in the hundreds of mounds containing buried cities which were located near a river or on a canal. The Tigris and Euphrates have

Nineveh: a view of Tell Quyunjiq, one of the two large mounds which mark the ruins of the ancient city of Nineveh.

above: *The ziggurat of Ur: the extant remains of the great artificial mound or temple-tower on which the god was worshipped. The man standing at the left shows the scale.*

below: *The ziggurat of Ur restored: drawing showing probable appearance, with steps and terraces.*

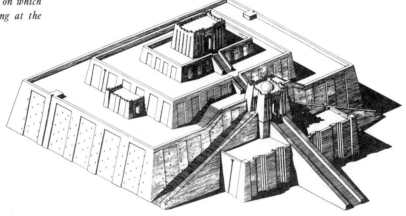

their origins in the high mountain regions of northern Armenia (Urartu) (p. 55). The annual inundations begin in the spring, and the receding waters leave their rich deposits. They occur with destructive force and lay waste the country-side. Ancient flood effects have been found in excavated cities, such as Kish, Ur, and Shuruppak, the last of these the home of the Mesopotamian flood hero. It is understandable that the story of the great deluge should have had its origin in this area. A Sumerian flood tablet excavated at Nippur (p.55) tells how Ziusudra built an ark and the flood swept over the land. Later flood stories give the name of the hero as Atramhasis (Atrahasis) and Utnapishtim. Their graphic descriptions of the flood were based on bitter experience.

It is obvious that water control was a necessary factor in the economy of the country. The area particularly from near ancient Eshnunna and modern Baghdad down to ancient Ur and Eridu (p. 55), a distance of over 200 air miles, could be irrigated. One of the most striking of public water works to the north was the aqueduct-bridge and its associated canal built north-north-east of Nineveh by Sennacherib, king of Assyria, to supply Nineveh with water, one of a succession of hydraulic works made by him.

Sumer and Akkad lay in the alluvial plain, Sumer to the south and Akkad to the north. This is the 'land of Shinar' of Gen. 11. 1 ff., a passage which refers to the early settlement in this area, and the story is reminiscent of the ziggurats or temple towers built by the Sumerians in their cities. The alluvial soil is naturally stoneless, and so the inhabitants had 'brick for stone'. Explorations have revealed that the early cities in Akkad were small and the area somewhat sparsely

A panel from the 'Black Obelisk' of Shalmanezer III: Jehu, king of Israel, prostrates himself before the Assyrian king, while behind him stand Assyrian guards. (For continuation see facing page.)

settled, in contrast with Sumer, which is what one might expect in the light of the earlier prominence of Sumer culturally and politically. The more extensive cultivation of Akkad did not begin until after 2000 B.C. with the construction of extensive irrigation waterways. The terms Sumer and Akkad continued to be used long after the Sumerian and Akkadian domination in the third millennium; Nebuchadrezzar was 'king of Akkad', and Cyrus, the Persian, called himself 'king of Sumer and Akkad'.

Assyria lay to the north of Babylonia. In contrast with the plain to the south, the mountains rise in northern Assyria to give it a climate comparable to that of western Europe and to provide minerals as well as stone for building. The two important tributaries of the upper Euphrates River are the Balikh and the Habor rivers (map, pp. 52–53). The Horite state of Mitanni lay in the area of the Balikh and Habor in the 16th to early 14th centuries (pp. 54–55). Frequently mentioned in the records are two tributaries of the Tigris, the Upper (Great) Zab and the Lower (Little) Zab, and below them are the Adhaim and Diyala tributaries, the latter reaching the Tigris below Baghdad.

The early geographical background of the Bible lies in the Tigris-Euphrates area. Two of the four rivers flowing from Eden were the Tigris and Euphrates (Gen. 2. 10–14), and the 'inundation' (usually rendered by 'flood' or 'mist') in Gen. 2. 6 that 'watered the . . . ground' belongs in this area. The ark rested on the mountains of Ararat (i.e., cuneiform,

Urartu). Babel (11. 9) is Babylon (pp. 54–55). Terah, Abraham, Lot, and Sarah came from the city of Ur and moved to Haran (11. 31). Nahor, the name of a grandfather and of a brother of Abraham, is also the name of a city in the Haran area, mentioned in the inscriptions from Mari on the Euphrates, which also refer to an Amorite tribe of Benjamin (Banu-yamina). Amorites at this time dominated Mesopotamia and Syria, ruling at Mari, Haran, Babylon, and elsewhere, and Abraham's group may have been among Amorite infiltrations into Canaan. The invasion of four kings from the east (from Shinar, Ellasar (Larsa), Elam, and Goiim—Gen. 14) may have been in part in the interest of controlling the trade routes through Transjordan and the mining areas of the Arabah. Isaac's wife, Rebekah, came from Aram-naharaim ('Aram of the Two Rivers', i.e., the Tigris and Euphrates), and here Jacob lived with his wives (Gen. 24 and 29). Jacob's marriage illustrates a marriage-form known in contemporary Mesopotamia. So also the household gods or teraphim in Gen. 31 have their analogy in a practice evident from cuneiform tablets found at Nuzi, according to which possession of the personal gods gave title to inheritance and family leadership.

The first judge, Othniel, rescued Israel from Cushanrishathaim, king of Mesopotamia (Aram-naharaim, Judg. 3. 7 ff.), whose name recalls that of a district in north Syria, Qusana-ruma. In contrast with Egypt, Mesopotamia did not

Continuation of the scene on the 'Black Obelisk': marshalled by Assyrian guards, Israelite porters bring tribute (see facing page: this is the adjacent panel on the right hand face of the stone).

interfere in the affairs of the young Hebrew monarchy in Palestine, and the power of David and Solomon extended to the Euphrates. The Assyrian king, Ashurnasirpal II (883–859), made an expedition to Carchemish and the Lebanons and reached the Mediterranean, taking tribute from Tyre, Sidon, Byblos, Arvad, and other Phoenician cities (see pp. 70–71). His son, Shalmanezer III, in 853 fought at Qarqar on the Orontes River against a coalition of twelve kings, which included, beside Ahab of Israel, the kings of Damascus, Hamath, Kue, Arvad, Ammon, and other cities and districts. This is not recorded in the biblical narrative, nor is the submission of Jehu of Israel to Shalmanezer in 841, when, after defeating Hazael of Damascus, Shalmanezer took tribute from Jehu. The event is recorded on the 'Black Obelisk', which depicts Jehu bowing down before the Assyrian king, while behind the prostrate Jehu come Israelites bearing tribute (see above). The saviour mentioned in 2 Kgs. 13. 5 had been plausibly identified with Adadnirari III (810–783), who campaigned against Damascus and Philistia in 805. His claim that Tyre, Sidon, the Land of Omri (Israel), Edom, and Philistia recognized his overlordship and paid tribute can have been only temporarily true.

Assyria's strong hand lay heavily on Palestine in the last half of the 8th century. Tiglath-pileser III (Pul) was the first of a succession of great kings who ruled during the century-long golden age of the Assyrian empire. Menahem

of Israel was forced to submit to his sovereignty, as we learn from 2 Kgs. 15. 19, 20 and Tiglath-pileser's own records, which also report tribute from Rezin of Damascus, Hiram of Tyre, and others. Menahem, he tells us, fled, but he returned him to his throne and imposed tribute on him. The foreshadowing of the end of the kingdom of Israel came when Ahaz purchased the help of Tiglath-pileser when Judah was attacked by Pekah of Israel and Rezin of Damascus (2 Kgs. 16; Isa. 7 and 8). After Tiglath-pileser had besieged and taken Damascus and put Rezin to death, Ahaz went to Damascus, presumably to give assurance of his vassalage. Tiglath-pileser invaded Israel; the territory east of the Jordan was turned into three Assyrian provinces, while Galilee became the province of Megiddo, with the province of Dor on the west. To the kingdom of Israel was left only Samarina, the capital city of Samaria and the territory south of it. In 724 Shalmanezer V, Tiglath-pileser's successor, began the siege of Samaria. The city fell to Shalmanezer's successor, Sargon, in 721. Sargon's own records are not consistent, and the claim for the destruction of Samaria in the first year of his reign comes from the final edition of his annals, found in the excavations of his capital city Dur-sharrukin (Khorsabad). It is thought by some scholars that not Sargon but Shalmanezer V, as the biblical text seems to imply (2 Kgs. 17. 1–6), conquered Samaria in 723/22; then in the second year of his reign (720) Sargon, in his first campaign, having quelled a rebellion in Syria and after conquering Gaza from Raphia to the brook of Egypt, turned to Samaria, which he conquered; he deported its inhabitants and rebuilt it as a centre of the new province of Samarina (Samaria).

All of Palestine was reckoned by the Assyrian king to belong to him. In 715 (or one or two years earlier) Sargon made a campaign to Philistia and the Egyptian border. In 711 (or 712) he invaded Philistia again. He conquered Gittaim, Gibbethon, Ekron, and Azekah, and he took Ashdod (see Isa. 20. 1 ff.). The archaeologists found there fragments of his victory stele. He made the area into the Assyrian province of Ashdudi (Ashdod). Sargon's successor, Sennacherib, in 701 invaded Philistia and Judah; he accepted the surrender of Hezekiah, who acknowledged his sovereignty (2 Kgs. 18 and 19, and the annals of Sennacherib). 2 Kgs. 19. 7 and 19. 36, 37 have sometimes been taken to mean that Sennacherib met his death at the hands of two of his sons shortly after his return to Assyria from his campaign against Hezekiah. Yet Sennacherib did not die until twenty years after his attack on Jerusalem in 701. Some scholars would explain this by presuming that two campaigns have been fused into one in the biblical account, and that shortly before his death Sennacherib made against Jerusalem a second campaign, of which there is no account in the Assyrian records. The reference to the attempted assistance by Tirhakah in 2 Kgs. 19. 9 has been taken as support for such a later campaign, for Tirhakah did not become king of Egypt until *c*. 689, although he may have been a general of Pharaoh Shabaka, or may have been king of Ethiopia, in 701, 2 Chron. 33. 10 ff. credits the next Assyrian monarch, Esarhaddon, with exiling Manasseh temporarily in Babylon. Esarhaddon himself tells of assembling ten kings of Cyprus and twelve kings from Phoenicia, Philistia, Edom, Moab, Ammon, and Judah, including Manasseh, to transport with their labourers timber from the Lebanons and stone colossi from the quarries for his palace at Nineveh. The last of the great Assyrian kings, Ashurbanipal, is probably mentioned as 'Osnappar' in Ezra 4. 10; the passage refers to Persians, men of Erech, Babylonians, men of Susa (Elamites), and others whom Osnappar deported and settled in the cities of Samaria and in the rest of the province Beyond the River.

As Assyria had been Israel's downfall, Babylonia was to

Sargon II, king of Assyria. Limestone relief from Khorsabad.

Tablet containing part of the Babylonian Chronicle. On this tablet is the chronicle recording the battle of Carchemish, 605 B.C.

Persepolis: extant remains of the portion of the city containing the palace of the Persian kings.

be Judah's nemesis. In the days of Sennacherib, Merodach-baladan of Babylonia had made advances to Hezekiah of Judah (Isa. 39; 2 Kgs. 20. 12–19). Not long after Nebuchadrezzar had defeated the Egyptians at Carchemish and in the district of Hamath in 605, Judah came under Babylonian domination (see pp. 74–75). Dan. 1. 1 may reflect the conquest of Judah by Babylonia at this time. The Babylonian Chronicle affirms that Nebuchadrezzar 'at that time conquered the whole of the Hatti-country [Syria and Palestine]'. In December of 604 Nebuchadrezzar sacked and destroyed Ashkelon, and in the same month the frightened Judeans proclaimed a fast (Jer. 36. 9). The revolt of King Jehoiakim in 601 (2 Kgs. 24. 1) is perhaps to be associated with an unsuccessful attack on Egypt by Babylonia. Jehoiakim's son, Jehoiachin, inherited the revolt, and Nebuchadrezzar marched to the Hatti-land in December 598. He encamped against Jerusalem, taking it on 16 March 597, carrying into exile the king, his mother, and others (2 Kgs. 24. 10 ff. and the Babylonian Chronicle). Inspired by Egypt, Judah under Zedekiah revolted in 589. After a long siege Jerusalem was taken and the city and temple destroyed (587 or 586), and more Judeans were carried into exile. Jer. 52. 30 reports another exile five years later. Nebuchadrezzar's son, Amel-marduk (the biblical Evil-merodach), elevated Jehoiachin above the kings who were with him in Babylon (2 Kgs. 25. 27–30; Jer. 52. 31 ff.). Palestine continued under Babylonian domination until the Persians took over the position of the dominant power in the Near East.

Persia and Israel

The land of the Medes and Persians lies east of Mesopotamia, protected by its mountain borders (map, pp. 78–79, see also pp. 52–53). It is a plateau of about a million square miles between the Tigris-Euphrates and the Indus Rivers, today occupied mainly by Iran, its eastern portion by Afghanistan and Baluchistan. On the north are the Alborz (Elburz) Mountains, which spring from the Armenian ranges and curve below the Caspian Sea, leading to the steppes of Khorasan, which greet the mountains coming from Afghanistan. Here east of the southern Caspian the mountains of Koppeh Dagh rise to almost 10,000 feet. On the south-west, also springing from the mountains of Armenia, are the Zagros Mountains and their extension running parallel to the Tigris-Euphrates and the Persian Gulf through Lorestan and Khuzestan; they then turn eastward to Baluchistan, to connect with the mountains in the east which become the Himalayas.

The Persian plateau is a land of mountains, deserts, and fertile strips. The great central desert, generally hour-glass in form, begins at the foot of the Alborz and extends south-

29

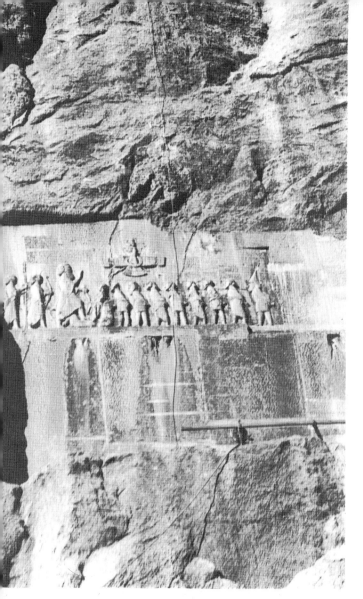

Rock-face at Bisitun showing, high above the ground, the relief representing king Darius receiving the submission of rebels, and, above and below this, the inscription recording his victory over them.

rebellions at the beginning of the reign of Darius I, depicted on the rock cliffs at Bisitun, there was intrigue in Judah to throw off the Persian yoke and make Zerubbabel, Jehoiachin's grandson, king, with the high priest Joshua beside him, but nothing came of it (Hag. 2. 23, Zech. 4. 1 ff., 6. 9 ff.). Tattenai, governor of the province Beyond the River, and his associates reported to Darius the rebuilding of the Jerusalem temple, suspecting that it involved a revolt. Cyrus's earlier permission was confirmed, and Darius issued a new directive on behalf of the Jews (Ezra 6).

Apparently in the earlier years of the reign of Artaxerxes I, an attempt to rebuild the walls of Jerusalem was temporarily frustrated by a letter sent by officials of Samaria and the rest of the province Beyond the River to Artaxerxes (Ezra 4. 7–23). Whether it was in 458/57, the seventh year of Artaxerxes I, or in 398/97, the seventh year of Artaxerxes II, that Ezra came to Jerusalem with a letter from the Persian king is uncertain (Ezra 7 ff.), although the former now seems more probable. It was in 445/44, the twentieth year of Artaxerxes I, that Nehemiah—himself a Jew—came from the Persian court with the king's authority to be governor of Judah and to rebuild Jerusalem's walls. He returned to Artaxerxes at Susa in 433/32, and later with the king's permission had a second period of governorship over Judah (Neh. 13. 6 ff.). The Elephantine Papyri from Syene in Egypt show that Nehemiah was succeeded as governor of the Persian province of Judah by a certain Bagohi—probably a Persian. But in the later period of Persian domination a considerable degree of local autonomy was granted to Judah, perhaps as a theocratic commonwealth. This is indicated by the discovery of coins stamped with the name Yehud (Judah) in Palestine, belonging to the late 5th and early 4th century. Pointing to the same conclusion are official seals stamped on jar-handles, bearing the same inscription. Despite the hardships of paying taxes or tribute to the 'Great King' (see Neh. 5. 1 ff.), the hand of the Persian government does not seem to have rested heavily on Judah. Persia found it wise to be lenient and at times generous with the Jews in Judah, and apparently won the support of a grateful people. But the sands of time were running out for the Persian Empire, and besides, another star was rising in the west in the form of Alexander, the son of Philip of Macedonia.

Not all the kings of the Persian empire appear in the biblical narrative. The list of the kings of Persia with their dates, in the tables on pp. 19 and 35, will be helpful in setting in perspective allusions to this period in the map texts, pp. 76 and 78–79.

east to the Makran ranges. There are swamps and dry saline areas in it, such as the major depression, the Dasht-e Kavir. The average height of the plateau has been estimated to be around 4,000 feet, with the greater elevation toward the rim. Rainfall is little, save in the Alborz Mountains. Iran has wide extremes of climate. The Medes played a significant role in Mesopotamian affairs in the period at the end of Assyrian domination. The Elamites, on the slopes of the plateau opposite Babylonia, were much involved in Mesopotamia's history from early times. But not until the time of Cyrus in the latter part of the 6th century did Israel in Palestine or in exile find influence from this direction a major factor in her life.

The meteor-like conquests of Cyrus over Media and Lydia and then Babylonia (see pp. 78–79) gave new impetus to the hope of the exiled Jews for return to Palestine. In the first year of his reign (538), after his conquest of Babylon, Cyrus issued a decree (Ezra 1. 2–4 and 6. 3–5), and the first group of Jews returned to Jerusalem and Judah. During the

above: *Soldier (with sword) and two attendants (in long garments) bringing gifts: from the frieze on the stairway of the palace at Persepolis.*

right: *A Persian courtier, from the frieze on the stairway of the palace at Persepolis.*

31

The Greeks and Israel—The Hellenistic period
(maps, pp. 77 and 82–83)

The involvement of Palestine in the international scene in the Hellenistic Period was, if anything, increased, although there is little direct reference to this period in the Old Testament outside the book of Daniel. In Daniel are specific allusions to the rise of the Greek kingdom under Alexander the Great, the division of his empire, and the struggles between the Ptolemies of Egypt and the Seleucids of Syria. In Zech. 9. 13 'Greece' (Javan) may refer to the Seleucid kingdom. Elsewhere 'Javan' usually refers to the Ionian coastland of Asia Minor or its adjacent islands. In Ezek. 27. 13 Javan is associated with Tubal and Meshech in Asia Minor as trading with Tyre. Isa. 66. 19 also associates Javan with Tubal and with Lud (Lydia). Joel 3. 6 accuses Tyre and Sidon of trading with the Greeks (Javan) in slaves from Judah and Jerusalem.

When Alexander the Great had defeated Darius III at Issus in 333, he took Damascus, conquered the island city of Tyre by building a mole to it from the mainland and by using ships, and moved south and took Gaza *en route* to Egypt. Alexander returned from Egypt to destroy Samaria to avenge the murder of his viceroy. In a cave in Wadi Daliyeh in the Wilderness of Judah were found papyrus documents brought by refugees from Samaria. A non-Palestinian type of fortification at Samaria (the round towers) in the Hellenistic period, and the rebuilding of Shechem in the late 4th century after a long gap of occupation, and other data have elicited the suggestion that after Alexander's destruction of Samaria the city was resettled by the Macedonians, and the Samaritans returned to Shechem to establish there a new capital.

After Alexander's death in 323 there followed the abortive rule of his half-witted half-brother, Philip; Alexander's infant son Alexander II, born after his death, was also hailed as king. There was a period of chaos and warfare. Alexander's kingdom went to his generals (see Dan. 8. 8, 22; 11. 4). Ptolemy I assumed the kingship of Egypt. He took possession of Palestine and Phoenicia, but he lost it, in 315, to Antigonus, the ruler of Phrygia, who besieged and took Tyre and left his son, Demetrius, in command at Gaza. In

Alexander the Great: Roman copy of a good Greek bust.

312 Ptolemy fought a decisive battle against Demetrius at Gaza, and legend (in Josephus) reports that Ptolemy entered Jerusalem with his army on the Sabbath when the inhabitants refused to fight. The exile of many Jews into Egypt by Ptolemy at this time is reported in the Letter of Aristeas. In 306 Antigonus unsuccessfully invaded Egypt, and many of his ships were wrecked in a storm at Raphia.

Seleucus, another general of Alexander, established himself as master in Babylonia, the year 312/11 (or 311/10) marking the beginning of the Seleucid Era. After the defeat of Antigonus in the battle at Ipsus in Phrygia in 301, Seleucus was given Coele-Syria (Palestine). He possessed the northern part of Syria and made Antioch his capital, but Palestine was to remain under the Ptolemies of Egypt until the reign of Antiochus the Great, after a series of wars between the two kingdoms. Much of the subsequent history

The city of Tyre: along the mole built by Alexander a neck of land has grown up joining the former island city to the mainland.

Hellenistic round tower at Samaria, and, adjoining it to the right, wall with substructure of masonry of the Israelite monarchic period.

of this period is reflected in the historical outline in Dan. 11, where 'the king of the south' refers to the various Ptolemaic rulers, and 'the king of the north' to the Seleucid kings, Seleucus I and his successors. See the table of dates on p. 35.

In the first Syrian war in 276 Ptolemy II invaded southern Syria, but was forced back by Antiochus I. In the second war Antiochus II took all of Phoenicia north of Sidon. The third Syrian war (c. 246–241) was the Laodicean war, fought against Seleucus II by Ptolemy III, who was outraged at the murder of Berenice, wife of Antiochus II and daughter of Ptolemy II, and her son (Dan. 11. 5–9). The fourth Syrian war was under Antiochus III (the Great), whose first two attempts to invade Palestine failed and who was severely defeated in the battle at Raphia in 217 by Ptolemy IV (Dan. 11. 10–12). However, weakness in Egypt under the child-king Ptolemy V offered another opportunity to Antiochus, culminating in his conquest of Palestine from Egypt through the victories at Gaza in 200 and at Paneas in 199 (Dan. 11. 15–16). In fear of Rome, Antiochus III married his daughter Cleopatra to Ptolemy at Raphia (Dan. 11. 17). His foray into Greece was frustrated by Rome, and he was defeated at Magnesia 'ad Sipylum' (in the Hermus valley in Asia Minor) by the Roman Scipio and died in Elymais (Susiana) (Dan. 11. 18–19).

The Jews in Palestine were favourably treated by Antiochus III, who remitted certain taxes and who made payments to them for sacrifices. Onias II, the high priest, refused to pay his taxes to Ptolemy IV—twenty talents of silver. Joseph of the house of Tobias was given tax-collection rights as 'tax farmer' for all of Palestine. When Palestine came under Antiochus the Great, tax farming remained in the Tobaid family, which became powerful and wealthy and was in bitter rivalry with the house of Onias. Antiochus III was succeeded by Seleucus IV, whose chief minister, Heliodorus, went to Jerusalem to seize the temple treasury (Dan. 11. 20). Onias III went to Seleucus IV to secure help in quieting riots in Jerusalem. Seleucus IV was murdered by Heliodorus, and Antiochus IV (Epiphanes) became king in 175 (Dan. 11. 20 ff.). In the absence of Onias, Jason, the brother of Onias, bribed Antiochus to give him the high priesthood. He was a Hellenist, in favour of accommodating the Jewish faith to Greek religion and culture, but after three years a larger bribe was offered to Antiochus by a layman, Menelaus, who now became high priest. He was an

Both sides of a silver tetradrachm (coin worth 4 drachmas) minted at Antioch, with head of Antiochus IV; the Greek inscription on the reverse reads:
BASILEŌS ANTIOCHOU THEOU EPIPHANOU, meaning '(of) King Antiochus, a god (or God) made manifest'.

33

Portrait-mask of a Seleucid king, probably Antiochus IV, discovered by Sir Aurel Stein.

his sons, described in the text on p. 76 (see Dan. 11. 21 ff.). The detailed story is recounted in 1 Maccabees. As a result of the victories of Mattathias' son, Judas, the temple, which had been desecrated by the 'abomination of desolation' in December 168, was rededicated in December of 165 (1 Macc. 4. 54). Another son of Mattathias, Simon, became independent ruler, and the high priesthood was vested in him and his descendants. (His brother Jonathan had earlier been designated high priest by Demetrius II.) They are known—after an ancestor Hasmon—as the Hasmonean rulers. See table of dates opposite.

The early days of the Maccabean revolt had witnessed the appearance of the congregation of the Hasidim, composed of Jews faithful to the law and opposed to Hellenization (1 Macc. 2. 42). From them both the Pharisees and the Essenes may have developed. It was perhaps during the rule of Jonathan (died 145 or 142) or his brother, Simon (died 135 or 134), that the 'Teacher of Righteousness', who founded the Essenes (the Qumran sect), arose, and Simon is perhaps the 'Wicked Priest' of the Scrolls. Simon's son, John Hyrcanus (135/34 to 104) was followed by his son, Aristobulus (104–103), the first Hasmonean to assume the kingship. In the reign of his brother, Alexander Janneus (103–76), there was civil war; the rebels hired the help of the Syrian king Demetrius III, who defeated Alexander Janneus at Shechem, but could not follow up his victory. This Demetrius III is mentioned in the Dead Sea Scrolls. The Hasmonean rule came to an end with the conquest of Jerusalem by Rome in 63 B.C., which leads us to the final section of our narrative. See illustrations, pp. 36–37.

Names and dates of most of the kings who reigned over the Seleucid and Ptolemaic empires are given in the table opposite. The list is not complete but includes the kings mentioned above and in the map texts.

unscrupulous Hellenist, who instigated his own brother to steal the temple vessels and who secured the murder of Onias at the sanctuary of Daphne near Antioch.

The tensions and conflicts, political and religious, came to a climax when Antiochus in 169 was forced by the Romans from Egypt and decided to compel the Jews in Palestine to accept Hellenization, intent on imposing unity on his kingdom through a common culture and religion. This led to the Maccabean rebellion under Mattathias and

Statuette of a Seleucid war-elephant seizing an enemy with its trunk, with driver and 'tower' on its back (cf. 1 Macc. 6. 30, 37).

WESTERN EMPIRES	PALESTINE	EASTERN EMPIRES
		PERSIAN (ACHAEMENIAN) EMPIRE
		358–337 Artaxerxes III
KINGDOM OF MACEDON		337–335 Arses
Philip		335–330 Darius III
Alexander		333 *Battle of Issus*

333 — EMPIRE OF ALEXANDER — 323

PTOLEMAIC EMPIRE	*(315 Antigonus takes Tyre)*	SELEUCID EMPIRE
323–283 Ptolemy I	*(312) Ptolemy takes Palestine)*	312 Seleucus king at Babylon
	HIGH PRIESTS	301–280 Seleucus king at Antioch
285–246 Ptolemy II	AT JERUSALEM	280–262/1 Antiochus I
		261–247 Antiochus II
246–221 Ptolemy III		247–226 Seleucus II
221–203 Ptolemy IV	Onias II	226–223 Seleucus III
		223–187 Antiochus III (the Great)
203–181/0 Ptolemy V	*(200/199 Antiochus takes Palestine)*	
	Onias III	187–175 Seleucus IV
181/0–145 Ptolemy VI	Jason	175–163 Antiochus IV (Epiphanes)
	HASMONEAN RULERS	163–162 Antiochus V
	166/5–160 Judas Maccabaeus	162–150 Demetrius I
	160–142 Jonathan	150–145 Alexander Balas
145–116 Ptolemy VII	142/1–135/4 Simon	(145–139/8 Demetrius II
	135/4–104 John Hyrcanus I	(145–142/1 Antiochus VI
116–108/7 Ptolemy VIII		139/8–129 Antiochus VII
	104–103 Aristobulus I	129–126/5 Demetrius II (restored)
	103–76 Alexander Janneus	(125–96 Antiochus VIII
		(115–95 Antiochus IX
88–80 Ptolemy VIII		
(restored)	76–67 Alexandra	
	66–63 Aristobulus II	
	(63 Pompey takes Jerusalem)	
	63–40 Hyrcanus II	
	40–37 Antigonus	
51–30 Cleopatra	HERODIAN RULERS	
(31 Battle of Actium)	37–4 Herod the Great	
ROMAN EMPIRE	(4 B.C. kingdom divided:)	

WESTERN EMPIRES	JUDEA	GALILEE	ITURAEA, &c.
27 B.C. Augustus			
–A.D. 14	4 B.C.–A.D. 6 Archelaus	4 B.C. Antipas	4 B.C. Philip
A.D. 14–37 Tiberius	(6–41 Roman governors)	–A.D. 39	–A.D. 34
A.D. 37–41 Gaius (Caligula)	(26–36 Pontius Pilate)		37–44 Agrippa I king
A.D. 41–54 Claudius	41–44 Agrippa I king over Judea, Galilee, and Perea		
	(44–66 Roman governors)		50–100 Agrippa II:
A.D. 54–68 Nero	(52–60 Felix)		50–53 king of Chalcis
	(60–62 Festus)	from 56 (or 61) Agrippa II king over parts of Galilee and Perea	
A.D. 68–69 Galba/Otho/Vitellius	66 *Jewish Revolt*		53–100 king of former
A.D. 69–79 Vespasian	70 *Fall of Jerusalem*		tetrarchies of Philip
A.D. 79–81 Titus			and Lysanias;
A.D. 81–96 Domitian			

above left: The excavated community site at Khirbet Qumran on the western shore of the Dead Sea.

below, left: An aerial view of the complex of buildings.

right: Entrance to Cave 4 at Qumran, in which a wealth of MSS was discovered.

below: Part of the great Isaiah Scroll (1Q Isa^a) from Qumran. The text, in Hebrew, runs from right to left and this shows the last three-and-a-half columns of the book.

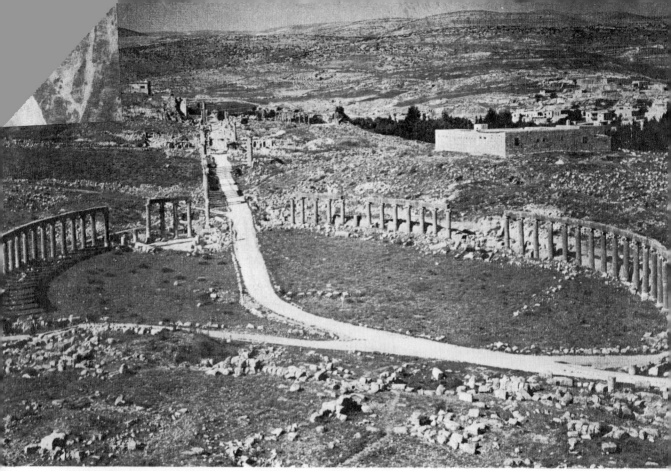

The forum of Gerasa (Jerash), one of the cities in and around Palestine which were re-founded on the Greek model and equipped with buildings in the Greco-Roman style.

Rome and Israel
(maps, pp. 85–87)

In 63 B.C. Pompey laid siege to the temple at Jerusalem, and on the Day of Atonement the temple area was breached. Some twelve thousand Jews are reported to have fallen. Jerusalem and Judea came under the power of Rome, with Gadara, Hippos, Scythopolis, Gaza, Joppa, Dor, and Strato's Tower made free cities. After a revolt of Alexander, the son of Aristobulus II, in 57 B.C., Judea was divided into five districts (i.e., Jerusalem, Gadara, Amathus, Jericho, and Sepphoris) under Gabinius, proconsul of Syria. Antipater, the governor of Idumea, controlled Hyrcanus, who had been made high priest and ethnarch of the Jews. Antipater cleverly played his politics, first supporting Pompey and then, after Pompey's death, supporting Julius Caesar. When Caesar invaded Egypt, he came to Caesar's help with three thousand armed Jews; he persuaded the Arabs and Syrians to assist Caesar and himself aided him in the capture of Pelusium. Antipater was made procurator of Judea by Caesar. He became virtual ruler of Palestine, and appointed one of his sons, Phasael, prefect of Judah, and another, Herod, prefect of Galilee.

Antipater was poisoned in 43 B.C., and Antigonus, son of Aristobulus II, the last of the Hasmoneans, was prevented by Herod from conquering Judea. Mark Antony made Phasael and Herod tetrarchs of the Jews. Antigonus, with the help of the Parthians who had invaded Syria, was now successful; the imprisoned Phasael committed suicide, Hyrcanus was exiled to Babylonia, and Antigonus ruled as king and high priest from 40 to 37. But Herod, having placed his family at Masada, went to Rome via Egypt and Rhodes to secure help from Antony, and the Roman Senate appointed him king of the Jews. He returned to Ptolemais, took Joppa, and recovered Galilee. Three years after he became king, he married Miriamme, granddaughter of Aristobulus II and Hyrcanus II. He took Jerusalem with the assistance of the Roman legions in 37 B.C., and ruled as king until 4 B.C. He is, of course, 'Herod the King' of the New Testament birth-stories of Jesus (see pp. 84–85).

Herod was one of the many client or allied kings (*reges socii*) of the Roman Empire. There was a series of such kingdoms on the east and south of the Empire, often bordering on imperial provinces. In Herod's day Cleopatra was a client queen, and she had provided a ship for Herod when he went to Rome to secure his kingship. There were, for instance, client kings in Asia Minor in Paphlagonia, Cappadocia, Pontus, Galatia, Armenia, etc., and Thrace was a client kingdom. The Nabataean kings were also such native rulers. These kings held their titles with the approval of Rome. They were appointed or replaced and their territories changed or enlarged at Rome's pleasure. Earlier the replacement was in the same royal line, but Herod's appointment was the beginning of a change in this respect, for he, an Idumean, replaced the Hasmonean house, of which Antigonus was the last king. The client kings were personally bound to the emperor, often through marriage alliances. The emperor sometimes brought up their children with his own or appointed guardians for their children. These client kings were relatively independent in the internal rule of their kingdoms. They might issue coins, as did Herod, although he was restricted to copper coinage. They were expected to provide military assistance for Rome and keep order on the boundaries of the empire. It has been well said that they were inexpensively serviceable to the empire.

The Jews bitterly disliked the covetous Herod, who despoiled the wealthy for his own gain and who slew with abandon his enemies and even members of his own family. He executed Alexandra, his mother-in-law, his brother Joseph, and Miriamme his wife, who was accused of infidelity. Miriamme was the second of ten wives of Herod.

In 31 B.C., Antony was defeated in the battle at Actium by Octavian, and in the following year Antony and Cleopatra committed suicide. Octavian now ruled the Roman Empire, and Herod went in haste to Rhodes to meet him. Herod gave to Octavian the loyal friendship and support he had given to Antony. Octavian was much impressed, and replaced on Herod's head the crown which Herod himself had removed, and so Herod's kingship was re-confirmed. In 27 B.C., Octavian was given the title of Augustus by the Roman Senate. Augustus was to reign until he was succeeded by Tiberius (A.D. 14–37), who was, in turn, followed by Caligula (A.D. 37–41) (see table on p. 35).

Herod's building activities were extensive both in Palestine and elsewhere. They included temples, palaces, and other public buildings at Rhodes, Nicopolis in Greece, Antioch in Syria, Tyre, Sidon, Damascus, and other places. He rebuilt and refortified the city of Samaria, naming it Sebaste, the feminine form of *sebastos*, the Greek equivalent of 'Augustus', and the name is still reflected in the modern village at the site, Sebastiyeh. Here the archaeologists have uncovered the ruins of the magnificent temple erected by Herod to Zeus Olympius in honour of Augustus, with its great forecourt some 250 feet square, and also the forum and stadium. Herod built Caesarea and constructed its port, and the excavated theatre, the aqueduct, and other Herodian works are visible today. Jerusalem was transformed with a magnificent new temple, a splendid palace, and fortifications which included the Tower of Antonia, a citadel at the northwest of the temple area. (See pp. 96–97.) Remains of his constructions can also be seen today at Ashkelon, Masada, Herodium, Machaerus, Hebron, and elsewhere. At Herodian Jericho where Herod had a winter palace a gymnasium has been excavated. The remains of his desert fortress retreat at Masada are most spectacular. (See illus. pp. 40–42.)

Antony (Marcus Antonius), Augustus's rival, defeated in 31 B.C.

Augustus Caesar: he was in theory only 'Princeps' or 'first citizen', but is shown in commanding pose as befits the ruler of the Roman world.

Caesarea, the coastal city which was the seat of the Roman governors of Judea. above: *the Roman theatre (now partly reconstructed for use as an auditorium)* ;
left: *Ruins of the ancient seaport, with fallen columns of the Roman period.*

above: *The site of Machaerus, originally fortified by Alexander Jannaeus, refortified as a desert retreat by Herod the Great, and used also by Herod Antipas. According to Josephus the place where John the Baptist was put to death.* (see maps, pp. 85 and 87).

below: *Monumental stairs at Samaria leading to the temple dedicated by Herod the Great to Augustus, with ruins of an altar at the foot of the stairs. Nearby was found the base of a statue of an emperor (probably Augustus).*

Masada. Impregnable rock fortress and refuge of Herod the Great, and last stronghold of the Jews after the fall of Jerusalem in A.D. 70 in the war against Rome. Excavations of 1963–65 by Professor Yigael Yadin have revealed the casemate wall, storehouses, administrative palace, the splendour of Herod's three-tiered palace villa, a synagogue, and other structures above the sheer rock cliffs, and mute evidence of the last tragic days of the dramatic defence of the stronghold by the Zealots in A.D. 73.

On Herod's death the rule went to his three sons, his will having designated Antipas as tetrarch of Galilee and Perea, Archelaus as king of Judea, and Philip as tetrarch of Trachonitis, Batanaea, and Gaulanitis. The Jews of Judea were very unhappy with Archelaus, and raised a clamour against him, and the horsemen of Archelaus slew 3,000 Jews at the Passover, following the death of Herod. Archelaus visited Rome, and while he was away revolt broke out in Judea, spreading to Galilee, Idumea, and Perea. The revolt was put down by Varus, the governor of Syria, and Josephus reports that 2,000 Jews were slain at this time. Archelaus was designated ethnarch of Judea, not king, by Augustus, and

ruled from 4 B.C. to A.D. 6, when he was exiled and his kingdom of Judea was made a Roman province which included Samaria, Judea, and Idumea (see map, pp. 86–87).

Herod Antipas ruled as tetrarch of Galilee and Perea from 4 B.C. to A.D. 39. He built the city of Tiberias and made it the capital of Galilee. It was he whom Jesus called 'that fox' (Luke 13.32). He was a man of considerable abilities, careful in handling his friendship with Rome, at the same time trying not to offend the religious scruples of the Jews. He met defeat at the hands of the Nabataean king Aretas. Agrippa I, who in A.D. 37 was made king over the tetrarchy of Philip, accused Antipas of revolting against the emperor

42

(Caligula), and Herod Antipas was exiled to Lugdunum Convenarum in Gaul and his tetrarchy added to Agrippa's kingdom.

Philip (4 B.C.–A.D. 34) was tetrarch of Ituraea, Trachonitis, Batanaea, Auranitis, Gaulanitis, and Paneas. He built Caesarea Philippi (Paneas) as his capital. He enlarged and improved the city of Bethsaida on the Sea of Galilee, calling it Julias after Augustus's daughter Julia. He was a person of moderation and justice. When he died without heir, his tetrarchy was added to the province of Syria.

After Archelaus had been exiled in A.D. 6, Judea was ruled by Roman governors. The first was Coponius (A.D. 6–9). At the beginning of the rule of Coponius, Quirinius (Cyrenius), the governor of Syria, took a census for taxation purposes in connection with the establishment of the province, and Zealots under the leadership of Judas of Galilee revolted in protest; Judas was killed (Acts 5. 37). The best known of the governors is Pontius Pilate (26–36), the fifth governor, under whom Jesus was crucified. He was not a good administrator, and he incensed the Jews by setting up in the palace of Herod votive shields which had on them the names of the emperor and the donors. He slew many Samaritans, and the Samaritans sent an embassy to the Roman legate, Vitellius. Pilate was ordered to Rome to answer before the emperor, and he was removed from office.

A grandson of Herod the Great, Herod Agrippa I was appointed at the death of Tiberius by the mad emperor Gaius (Caligula) as king (37–44) over the former tetrarchy of Philip. Agrippa was able to persuade Caligula to give up a project of setting up a statue of himself as god in the Temple at Jerusalem. When Claudius (41–54) succeeded the murdered Caligula, Judea and Samaria were added to Agrippa's territory. Thus he gained all the territory that had belonged to his grandfather, Herod the Great. Agrippa began to build a wall around the north suburb (Bezetha) of Jerusalem, probably near the point of the present north wall (see map, p. 96), but he was ordered by Claudius to cease. It was Agrippa who slew James (Acts 12. 1, 2) and imprisoned Peter (Acts 12. 3–19). It was under Claudius that the Jews were banished from Rome, and among those expelled were the Jewish Christians, Aquila and Priscilla (Acts 18. 2).

Agrippa died quite unexpectedly in 44. His kingdom was again made a province ruled by Roman governors, seven of them ruling between 44 and the beginning of the Jewish revolt in A.D. 66. The first was Cuspius Fadus (A.D. 44–46). Fadus ordered that the robes of the high priest be placed in the Tower of Antonia under Roman charge. The matter was referred to the emperor, and Claudius decided in favour of the Jews. Herod Agrippa I's only son, Agrippa, had remained in Rome after his father's death, and in A.D. 50 he was appointed king of Chalcis, in the Lebanon district (map, p. 91). Three years later Claudius transferred him to Philip's tetrarchy and to the tetrarchies of Abilene and Noarus, and here he ruled as king over a kingdom largely pagan. He is, of course, Herod Agrippa II. Following Claudius' death Nero gave him the toparchies of Tiberias

and Taricheae in Galilee and also the two southern toparchies of Perea, namely Julias and Abila. His capital was at Caesarea Paneas, renamed by him temporarily as Neronias, in honour of Nero. He was granted the right to appoint the High Priest at Jerusalem and supervise the Temple and the sacred funds.

M. Antonius Felix (A.D. 52–60), one of the governors and in whose reign the Sicarii or 'Assassins' arose among the Zealots, was the governor before whom Paul was tried at Caesarea (Acts 24). Felix married the sister of Herod Agrippa II, Drusilla (see Acts 24. 24). After Felix was recalled by Nero, he was succeeded by Porcius Festus (A.D. 60–62). Paul was brought by Festus from prison at Caesarea to appear before him (Acts 25. 1 ff.). Festus proposed that Paul be tried at Jerusalem, but Paul appealed to Caesar, and his case was laid before Herod Agrippa II by Festus. Agrippa asked to hear Paul, and Paul made his famous appearance before Agrippa and his sister Bernice (Acts 25. 23 ff.). Later, under the governor Gessius Florus (A.D. 64–66), Bernice appealed to Florus, interceding for the Jews and asking him to adopt a more conciliatory attitude toward them. There had been demonstrations against Florus in Jerusalem, and he had marched against the city and many Jews were killed. Agrippa II, who investigated the situation, urged submission to the government of the procurators and to Rome. At his suggestion the arrears in tribute were collected and the temple colonnades repaired. But the Jerusalem Jews soon turned against Agrippa and stones were hurled against him, and he left the city.

The relationship of the government to the Jews in Palestine had been deteriorating steadily. The revolt of the Jews in Palestine against Rome began in 66. The priests, lead by Eleasar, stopped the sacrifices made in behalf of the emperor, and the war was on. Nero selected Vespasian to put down the revolt. Vespasian conquered Galilee, and John of Gischala and his Zealots fled to Jerusalem. Vespasian became emperor in 69, and his son, Titus, arrived at Jerusalem with his Roman legions in April of the year 70. The siege lasted from April to September. On the 9th of Ab (in August) the gates were burned, and the Temple was also burned, despite the orders to the contrary given by Titus. In Herod's palace on the western hill, John of Gischala held out, but the entire city was in the hands of Titus on the 8th of Elul, in September. The war itself dragged on until 73, when Masada fell to Titus. On the arch at Rome Titus commemorated his victory with pictures of the temple treasures carried in procession. Vespasian (69–79) was succeeded by his son, Titus (79–81). It was under Domitian (81–96), in his last years, that the persecutions of the Christians occurred which gave rise to the book of Revelation.

The names and dates of Roman emperors down to Domitian, and of the three governors of Judea mentioned in the New Testament are given in the table on p. 35, and will be helpful to the reader in keeping in mind the succession of events we have been describing. A full list of

Relief on the Arch of Titus in Rome showing captured treasures, including the seven-branched lampstand, from the temple at Jerusalem, being carried in triumphal procession.

the governors of Judea between the rule of Archelaus and Herod Agrippa I is as follows:

	(dates A.D.)
Coponius	6–9
M. Ambivius	9–12
Annius Rufus	12–15
Valerius Gratus	15–26
Pontius Pilate	26–36
Marullus	36–37
Herennius Capito	37–41

Those between the rule of Herod Agrippa I and the Jewish Revolt were:

	(dates A.D.)
Cuspius Fadus	44–46
Tiberius Alexander	46–48
Ventidius Cumanus	48–52
M. Antonius Felix	52–60
Porcius Festus	60–62
Clodius Albinus	62–64
Gessius Florus	64–66

The Diaspora and the Spread of Christianity
(maps, pp. 88–91)

About forty years before the fall of Jerusalem the Church had been founded. It had at first centred around Jerusalem. The movement began to spread in Palestine. After the death of Stephen, Philip went down to an unidentified city of Samaria, and to Gaza, Azotus, and Caesarea, and Peter visited Lydda, Joppa, and Caesarea (Acts 8–10). Those who

were scattered because of the persecution that arose over Stephen carried the gospel exclusively to the Jews in Phoenicia, Cyprus, and Antioch (Acts 11. 19). Some of the Christians of Cyprus and Cyrene preached to the Greeks in Antioch of Syria (Acts 11. 20). It was in Antioch in Syria that the term 'Christian' was first used. The gospel also reached Rome, perhaps through some who had heard Peter at Pentecost. Paul was able to build on these foundations. From his missions at Damascus he went up to Jerusalem and then into the regions of Syria and Cilicia, where he settled at Tarsus for some time. Barnabas went from Antioch to Tarsus and persuaded Paul to work with him in Antioch. It was from Antioch that Paul and Barnabas started out on the first missionary journey, and with John Mark they set sail from Seleucia, to begin the great period of the expansion of the Church. To understand the success that Paul had we should review briefly the Jewish Diaspora (Dispersion).

It has been conservatively estimated that there were in the 1st century two million Jews in the Roman Empire outside Palestine, and some sober historians place the number at four millions. In Acts 2. 5–13 there is a list of Jews, devout men from every nation under heaven, also described as Jews and proselytes, who were in Jerusalem at Pentecost. The list may be taken as an indication of some of the places where there were Jewish communities in the Diaspora, i.e., Parthia, Media, Elam, Mesopotamia, Cappadocia, Pontus, Asia, Phrygia, Pamphylia, Egypt, Libya belonging to Cyrene (Cyrenaica), Rome, Crete, Arabia. One may compare 1 Macc. 15. 22–23 where there are listed the rulers and countries to whom the Roman Senate appealed in the time of Simon on behalf of the Jews, and where there were

44

diaspora 1. ~~Exiled~~ scattered Jews after the exile

2. Jewish Christians of apostolic age living among the heathen

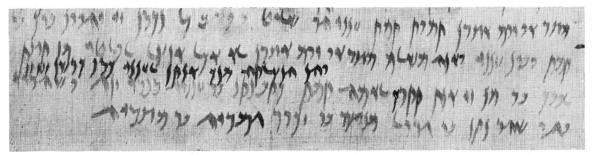

Some lines from an Aramaic papyrus from Elephantine: a Jewish marriage contract (cf. Tobit 7.14) dated 449 B.C.

therefore Jewish communities: Demetrius of Syria, Attalus of Pergamum, Ariarthes of Cappadocia, Arsaces of Parthia, and Sampsames, Sparta, Delos, Myndos, Sicyon, Caria, Samos, Pamphylia, Lycia, Halicarnassus, Rhodes, Phaselis, Cos, Side, Aradus, Gortyna, Cnidus, Cyprus, and Cyrene (see maps pp. 82–83, 88–89).

The exiles of 597 and 586 B.C. had been carried from Jerusalem to Babylon by Nebuchadrezzar. Some Jews had also gone into Egypt after the fall of Jerusalem (see Jer. 42–44). Aramaic papyri from Elephantine at Syene (Aswan) in Upper Egypt illuminate many facets of the life of a Jewish community of the Egyptian Diaspora of the 5th and the beginning of the 4th centuries B.C. After Alexander the Great there was a large Jewish community in Alexandria (it has been estimated at two-fifths of the total population), and for its Greek-speaking Jewish citizens a translation of the Pentateuch into Greek was made before 100 B.C. and was followed by the rest of the Jewish Scriptures, to make the Greek version of the Old Testament known as the Septuagint. (Compare the preface to the book of ben Sira (Sirach or Ecclesiasticus).) Philo of Alexandria illustrates the best Hellenistic Jewish scholarship and culture of the 1st century in Egypt.

Only a very small portion of the Babylonian exiles had returned to Palestine. There were important Jewish centres in Babylonia in New Testament times, the most important being at Nehardea and Nisibis on the lower Euphrates. An analysis of the biblical manuscripts among the Dead Sea Scrolls points to the probability that it was the Jews in Babylonia who were responsible for developing the early form of the Hebrew text which became the standard (Masoretic) text of Scripture used in the synagogue. The Dead Sea Scrolls include an early form of the tale of the madness of the Babylonian king in Dan. 4 as it circulated first in Babylonia, relating it to Nabonidus rather than to Nebuchadrezzar. The presence of Jews in the 1st century in Adiabene, east of the Tigris River between the Upper and Lower Zab, is evident from the account of the conversion of the royal house of Adiabene to Judaism. Here King Izates, his sister Helena, and his mother Helena became proselytes to Judaism. Queen Helena made a pilgrimage to Jerusalem and lived there for many years and Izates sent five of his sons there to be educated. Queen Helena was buried north of the city in the tomb known popularly today as 'the tomb of the kings'. The adoption of Judaism by the royal house doubtless encouraged the growth of Jewish settlements there, and

The so-called 'Tomb of the Kings' at Jerusalem, the burial-place of the royal family of Adiabene (1st century A.D.):
left: *the vestibule;* right: *to the left in the vestibule is the entrance to the tomb chamber, showing the rolling stone rolled back from the opening.*

Ruins of the synagogue at Capernaum (Kefar Nahum, Tell Hum): dating from the 3rd century A.D., this building may stand on the site of an earlier synagogue and represents the architecture of synagogues of the early Christian era.

Josephus records that Adiabene was one of the places where his work *The Jewish War* was read in Aramaic before it was put into Greek. The language spoken in this area was Eastern Aramaic or Syriac. It was perhaps in Adiabene during the days of its Jewish kings that, in the middle of the 1st century, parts of Scripture, first the Pentateuch, were translated into Syriac. There were Jews also in Edessa in Mesopotamia, and to this area Christianity came very early, the Syriac-speaking Christians here claiming a 1st-century origin. Josephus also mentions Parthians, Babylonians, and Arabians reading his work in Aramaic, and must refer to the Jews in these lands.

There were also many Jews in Syria, Greece, the islands of the Mediterranean, and Asia Minor. When Jason had been deposed from the high-priesthood in 168 B.C., he had fled to Sparta, where he knew that he would find a Jewish community. Paul was a native of Tarsus, the chief city of Cilicia, and belonged to a Jewish community there and later preached there to the Jews.

The Adiabene account just mentioned was not an isolated case of proselytism, for it was a common phenomenon in the Hellenistic period and the 1st century. Matt. 23. 15 reports that the Pharisees traversed sea and land to make a single convert. Jewish merchants were doubtless one source of the spread of Judaism. Phoenician colonies around the Mediterranean provided ground for new converts. The age was receptive to the kind of enlightened religion represented by Judaism, for many were tired of and disillusioned by the old gods. Josephus related how the people of Damascus in the time of Nero and governor Florus distrusted their own wives 'who, with few exceptions, had all become converts to the Jewish religion'. Palestine had earlier witnessed forcible conversion of Gentile peoples, as when the mixed population of northern Galilee and the Ituraeans had been converted to Judaism by Aristobulus I, and John Hyrcanus had forced the Idumeans to be circumcised. The Septuagint translators had coined a new term, *prosēlytos*, to render the Hebrew word *ger* (sojourner) for the religious convert found (in the 'P' source) in the Pentateuch, perhaps in part influenced by the phenomenon of proselytism in their day.

Besides the proselytes there were many who were attracted to Judaism but who did not find congenial the burden of the law. These were the 'God-fearers' (*phoboumenoi ton theon*) of Acts 10. 2 and 13. 16, 26, or the 'devout men' (*sebomenoi*) of Acts 13. 43; 17. 4, 17. They believed in the God of the Jews and attended the synagogues. The

Hellenized Jews of the Diaspora and the proselytes and the God-fearers were regarded by Paul as a primary source of possible converts, and the proselytes and God-fearers were doubtless the more easily convinced, for they welcomed a release from the requirements of Jewish law. At Thessalonica Paul argued for three weeks in the synagogue regarding the Scriptures, and 'some of them were persuaded, and joined Paul and Silas; as did a great many of the devout Greeks, and not a few of the leading women' (Acts 17. 2–4). Typical of Paul's procedure is the statement regarding Paul's activity in Corinth in Acts 18. 4: 'And he argued in the synagogue every sabbath, and persuaded Jews and Greeks.' It is not difficult to understand how important was the Jewish Diaspora in the history of the expansion of the early Church.

But, although Paul made it his practice to take his message first to the Jews and the adherents of the synagogue, when he was rejected he 'turned to the Gentiles' (Acts 13. 46–48), and so there came to be increasing numbers of Christians who had not belonged to the synagogues but came direct from paganism (Gal. 4. 8). In such ways a new, Christian, 'Diaspora' (1 Pet. 1. 1) was formed, sharing the Jewish monotheistic faith, and honouring the Jewish scriptures.

The sack of Jerusalem and the destruction of the Temple in A.D. 70, with its dramatic aftermath at Masada (see illustration, p. 42), marked the end of an age. The Second Revolt under ben-Kosibah (bar-Kokhba) in A.D. 132–5, vividly illustrated by the discovery of his dispatches (see p. 119) was also unsuccessful. Elsewhere the Jewish diaspora and the growing Christian community flourished. Christian meetings for worship, necessarily held in private houses, have left little trace, though in Rome some archaeological evidence of these house-churches has been discovered; the Church also possessed burial-places, notably the catacombs; and excavations of 1940–49 under St. Peter's in the Vatican City have revealed remarkable finds, among which was a 2nd-century aedicule, or memorial monument, built at the site of what was believed to be the last resting-place of the body of Peter, martyred in the persecutions of A.D. 64–5.

Of particular interest, too, are the earliest manuscripts of the New Testament and other Christian writings which survived on papyrus in Egypt. These include a small but important fragment of the Gospel of John in the John Rylands Library belonging to the first half of the second century; and several others of the late second or early third century, such as the Bodmer Papyri of the Gospel of John (containing chapters 1–14), and of those of Luke and John containing 102 out of 144 pages of the original codex (see illustration). Non-biblical, but of also great importance to scholars, are the Coptic papyri found in 1947 at Nag Hammadi (Chenoboskion) (see map p. 92). Dated to the early 4th century, they go back to 2nd and 3rd century Greek originals. It has been maintained that one of them, the Gospel of Thomas, originated in the Christian community of Edessa in the mid 2nd century. They have opened

A page from one of the earliest Christian manuscripts, the Bodmer Papyrus containing the Gospel of Luke and the Gospel of John. (See text.) This is a codex (leaves folded and stitched together like a modern book) not a roll like the Jewish scriptures: this page contains Luke 16. 9–21.

wide the question of the origin and nature of Gnosticism, a problem not unrelated also to the Qumran scrolls, and having a possible bearing on the date of the Gospel of John. Thus in the course of the 20th century A.D. new evidence for the study of the Biblical and post-Biblical worlds continues to come to light.

Palestine: Natural Regions

Palestine and Transjordan fall into five main natural regions which extend from north to south: (1) the **Coastal Plain**, (2) the **Western Hills** which are the central highlands of Palestine, (3) the **Rift Valley** or Arabah, (4) the **Eastern Hills** or plateau of Transjordan, (5) the **Desert** into which the eastern hills gradually merge. In the south, the area is bounded by (2a) the **Negeb**, and in the north-east it borders the distinct regions of (4a) the **Damascus Plain** and (4b) the **Leja**.

(1) The Coastal Plain. At the Ladder of Tyre the limestone hills of Upper Galilee reach the coast, forming cliffs and dividing the Plain of Phoenicia from the Plain of Acco. The former is only a few miles wide, but the irregular coast contains many suitable harbours. At the foot of the great limestone promontory of Mt. Carmel the plain is only a few hundred feet wide, and to the south is the Plain of Dor, which widens beyond the Wadi Zerqa into the marshy, luxuriant Plain of Sharon, once thickly covered with oak forests. The Plain of Sharon extends to the Valley of Aijalon, which reaches the sea near Joppa. South of this is Philistia, densely populated in biblical days, which has gentle hills and rolling vistas, where there could be grain fields of barley and wheat, although the rainfall decreases toward the south and the plain merges into steppe and desert. The straight coastline south of Mt. Carmel provides few natural harbours.

(2) The Western Hills (the Central Highlands of Palestine). In the Lebanons to the north this range rises to over 6,000 ft. above sea level. The highest peak in Palestine is Jebel Jermaq in Upper Galilee (3,962 ft.). Lower Galilee consists of a number of east-to-west ridges, none rising above 2,000 ft., with some fertile valleys leading to the coastal plain and the Jordan. The plains of Megiddo and Jezreel, divided by the watershed near Jezreel, form an important break in the central highlands providing a low and easy route. The Plain of Megiddo, with the Plain of Acco, is drained by the Kishon River, which in the rainy season becomes a torrent (Judg. 5. 21). It is one of the most fertile plains of Palestine. The Plain of Jezreel drops quickly below sea level and merges into the Plain of Beth-shan, part of the Arabah or Jordan valley.

The Hill Country of Ephraim is a broad limestone upland within which are fertile valleys and small plains, such as those of Lebonah, Shechem, and Dothan. On the hill slopes are olive, fig, and other fruit trees, while wheat and vines are cultivated in the valleys. The city of Shechem sat between the shoulders of Mt. Ebal (3,083 ft.) and Mt. Gerizim (2,889 ft.), where the road from the coastal plain and the north-south trunkline met. East of the watershed the land falls rapidly to the Jordan valley and forms an eroded wilderness, though not as desolate as the Wilderness of Judah to the south. No well-defined geographical feature marks the boundary between the Hill Country of Ephraim and the Hill Country of Judah, but the hills in Judah are a monotonous mass of more forbidding aspect, with sparse vegetation and stony outcrops. Between the Hill Country of Judah and Philistia is the Shephelah, a foothill region separated from the central highland by north-south tributary valleys and extending from Aijalon to Debir and southward. East-west valleys (Aijalon, Sorek, Elah, and Qubeiba) provide routes from the coastal plain into the hills and in the Shephelah are wider and more fertile. It is a country of grains and vines, and its trees are olive and sycamore (1 Kgs. 10. 27).

(2a) South of the Valley of Beer-sheba—Valley of Salt division in the central highlands is the **Negeb**, a barren steppe with the desert encroaching on it. In the central Negeb are limestone and sandstone ridges trending from north-east to south-west, and in the east is the steep descent to the Arabah, while in the west are sand dunes and loess hills. It is not an empty wilderness, and there were sedentary settlements here in the days of Abraham and of the later Judean kings, and in Nabataean and Byzantine times, the inhabitants tilling the soil where possible, caring for flocks, and gaining a living from the commerce carried along the caravan routes.

(3) The Rift Valley. This is depressed between two great geological faults. In its northern part lie the Orontes and Leontes rivers in the plain between the Lebanon and Anti-Lebanon Mts. Further south, it contains the valley of the Jordan, which is fed by springs at the foot of snow-capped Mt. Hermon (9,232 ft.). The word Jordan means 'that which goes down', and between Lake Huleh and the Sea of Galilee (695 ft. below sea level) it drops rapidly, continuing downward to the Dead Sea, which is 1,285 ft. below sea level and whose bottom is another 1,300 ft. lower. The narrow flood plain (the Zor) is covered with dense thickets of thorn scrub and tamarisk, the 'jungle of the Jordan' (Jer. 12. 5) (see illus. p. 14). The Zor is separated from the higher Ghor, or rift valley floor, by badlands of soft grey saline marls. The Jordan's winding course between the Sea of Galilee and the Dead Sea is three times the air mileage.

(4) The Eastern Hills (Transjordan). The Transjordan tableland is cut by four important rivers, the Yarmuk, Jabbok, Arnon, and Zered. Because of its height it receives considerable rain and is thus fertile, but the rainfall decreases eastward and the transition from steppe to desert is rapid. The fertile belt is widest in Bashan, noted for its grain and cattle (Deut. 32. 14), but narrows southward in Moab, which might produce food crops when there was famine in Judah (Ruth 1. 1). Gilead produced grain, vine, and olive, and was famed for its oak and pine.

(4a) From Mt. Hermon and anti-Lebanon flow the rivers that water the great irrigated oasis or garden region round **Damascus**.

South-east of this, and east of Bashan, is (4b) **The Leja (Trachonitis)** a great mass of dark basalt hills.

(5) The Desert. The Transjordan plateau slopes quickly down to the long, shallow depression of Wadi Sirhan and the wastes of the Syrian Desert. *See page 51.*

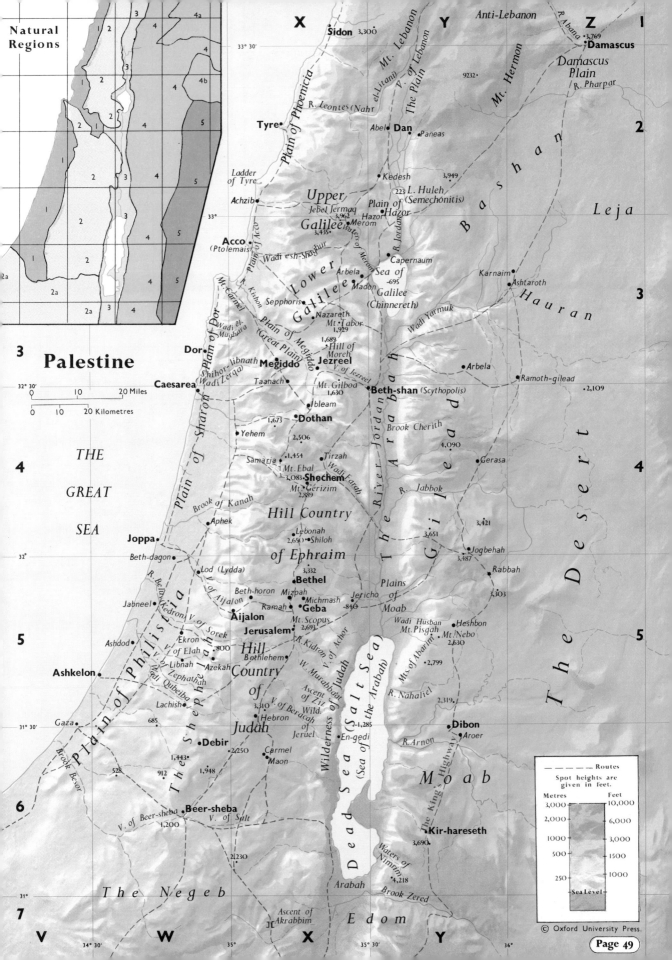

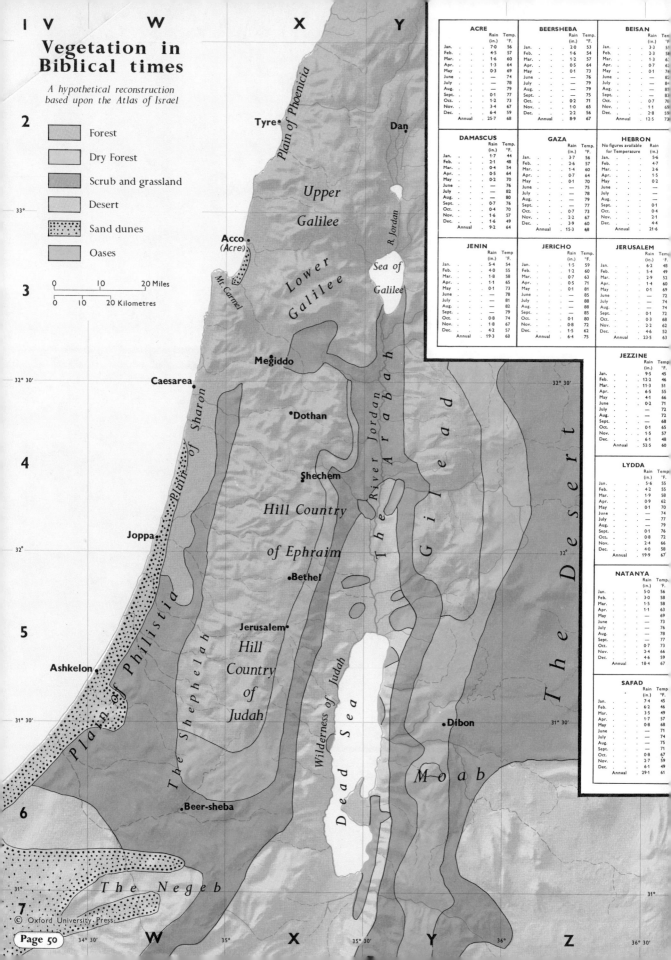

Vegetation in Biblical times

A hypothetical reconstruction based upon the Atlas of Israel

Legend:
- Forest
- Dry Forest
- Scrub and grassland
- Desert
- Sand dunes
- Oases

0 — 10 — 20 Miles
0 — 10 — 20 Kilometres

ACRE	Rain (in.)	Temp. °F.
Jan.	7.0	56
Feb.	4.5	57
Mar.	1.6	60
Apr.	1.3	64
May	0.3	69
June	—	74
July	—	78
Aug.	—	79
Sept.	0.1	77
Oct.	1.2	73
Nov.	3.4	67
Dec.	6.4	59
Annual	25.7	68

BEERSHEBA	Rain (in.)	Temp. °F.
Jan.	2.0	53
Feb.	1.6	54
Mar.	1.2	57
Apr.	0.5	64
May	0.1	73
June	—	76
July	—	79
Aug.	—	79
Sept.	—	75
Oct.	0.2	71
Nov.	1.0	65
Dec.	2.2	56
Annual	8.9	67

BEISAN	Rain (in.)	Temp. °F.
Jan.	3.3	59
Feb.	2.3	58
Mar.	1.3	62
Apr.	0.7	67
May	0.1	76
June	—	82
July	—	84
Aug.	—	85
Sept.	—	83
Oct.	0.7	78
Nov.	1.1	69
Dec.	2.8	59
Annual	12.5	73

DAMASCUS	Rain (in.)	Temp. °F.
Jan.	1.7	44
Feb.	2.1	48
Mar.	0.4	54
Apr.	0.5	64
May	0.2	70
June	—	76
July	—	82
Aug.	—	80
Sept.	0.7	76
Oct.	0.4	70
Nov.	1.6	57
Dec.	1.6	49
Annual	9.2	64

GAZA	Rain (in.)	Temp. °F.
Jan.	3.7	56
Feb.	2.6	57
Mar.	1.4	60
Apr.	0.7	64
May	0.1	70
June	—	75
July	—	78
Aug.	—	79
Sept.	—	77
Oct.	0.7	73
Nov.	2.2	67
Dec.	3.9	60
Annual	15.3	68

HEBRON (No figures available for Temperature)	Rain (in.)
Jan.	5.6
Feb.	4.7
Mar.	2.6
Apr.	0.2
May	—
June	—
July	—
Aug.	—
Sept.	0.1
Oct.	0.4
Nov.	2.1
Dec.	6.4
Annual	21.6

JENIN	Rain (in.)	Temp. °F.
Jan.	5.4	54
Feb.	4.0	55
Mar.	1.8	58
Apr.	1.1	65
May	0.1	73
June	—	78
July	—	81
Aug.	—	82
Sept.	—	79
Oct.	0.8	74
Nov.	1.8	67
Dec.	4.2	57
Annual	19.3	68

JERICHO	Rain (in.)	Temp. °F.
Jan.	1.5	59
Feb.	1.2	60
Mar.	0.7	63
Apr.	0.5	71
May	0.1	81
June	—	85
July	—	88
Aug.	—	88
Sept.	—	85
Oct.	0.1	80
Nov.	0.8	72
Dec.	1.5	62
Annual	6.4	75

JERUSALEM	Rain (in.)	Temp. °F.
Jan.	6.2	48
Feb.	5.4	49
Mar.	2.9	52
Apr.	1.4	60
May	0.1	69
June	—	72
July	—	74
Aug.	—	74
Sept.	0.1	72
Oct.	0.3	68
Nov.	2.2	62
Dec.	4.6	52
Annual	23.5	63

JEZZINE	Rain (in.)	Temp. °F.
Jan.	9.5	45
Feb.	12.2	46
Mar.	11.3	51
Apr.	6.5	55
May	4.1	66
June	0.2	71
July	—	72
Aug.	—	72
Sept.	—	68
Oct.	0.1	65
Nov.	1.5	57
Dec.	6.1	48
Annual	52.5	60

LYDDA	Rain (in.)	Temp. °F.
Jan.	5.6	55
Feb.	4.2	55
Mar.	1.9	58
Apr.	0.9	62
May	0.1	70
June	—	74
July	—	77
Aug.	—	79
Sept.	0.1	76
Oct.	0.8	72
Nov.	2.4	66
Dec.	4.0	59
Annual	19.9	67

NATANYA	Rain (in.)	Temp. °F.
Jan.	5.0	56
Feb.		
Mar.	1.5	58
Apr.	1.1	63
May	—	69
June	—	73
July	—	76
Aug.	—	78
Sept.	—	74
Oct.	0.7	73
Nov.	2.4	66
Dec.	4.6	59
Annual	18.4	67

SAFAD	Rain (in.)	Temp. °F.
Jan.	7.4	45
Feb.	6.2	46
Mar.	3.5	49
Apr.	1.7	57
May	0.8	63
June	—	71
July	—	74
Aug.	—	75
Sept.	—	71
Oct.	0.8	67
Nov.	2.7	59
Dec.	6.1	49
Annual	29.1	61

Map labels: Plain of Phoenicia, Tyre, Dan, Upper Galilee, Acco (Acre), Mt. Carmel, Lower Galilee, Sea of Galilee, R. Jordan, Megiddo, Caesarea, Dothan, Plain of Sharon, Shechem, The River Jordan, Gilead, The Arabah, Hill Country of Ephraim, Joppa, Bethel, Plain of Philistia, Jerusalem, The Shephelah, Hill Country of Judah, Ashkelon, Wilderness of Judah, Dead Sea, Dibon, Moab, The Desert, Beer-sheba, The Negeb

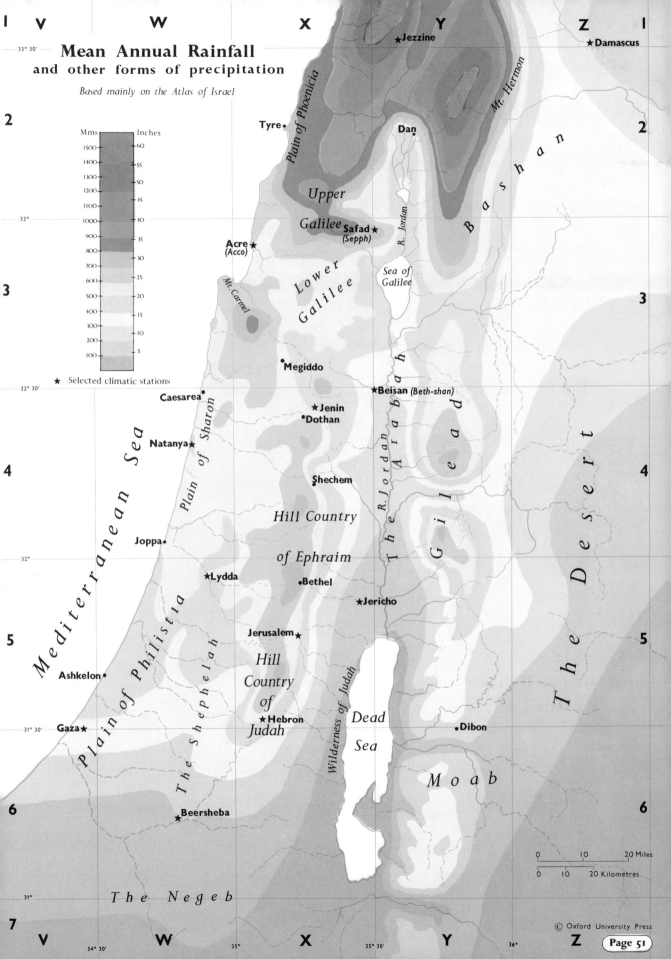

Mean Annual Rainfall
and other forms of precipitation

Based mainly on the Atlas of Israel

Mms		Inches
1500		60
1400		55
1300		50
1200		45
1100		40
1000		40
900		35
800		30
700		25
600		25
500		20
400		15
300		10
200		5
100		

★ Selected climatic stations

Jezzine ★

★ Damascus

Plain of Phoenicia

Mt. Hermon

Tyre •

Dan •

Upper

Galilee

Safad ★
(Sepph)

Bashan

Acre ★
(Acco)

R. Jordan

Lower

Galilee

Sea of
Galilee

Mt. Carmel

Megiddo •

Beisan (Beth-shan) ★

Caesarea •

★ Jenin
• Dothan

The R. Jordan

Arabah

Gilead

Natanya ★

Plain of Sharon

Mediterranean Sea

Shechem •

Hill Country

of Ephraim

Joppa •

Lydda ★

• Bethel

Jericho ★

Jerusalem ★

The Desert

Hill
Country
of

Ashkelon •

The Shephelah

Wilderness of Judah

Dead
Sea

• Dibon

Gaza ★

★ Hebron
Judah

Plain of Philistia

M o a b

★ Beersheba

0	10	20 Miles
0	10	20 Kilometres

The Negeb

© Oxford University Press

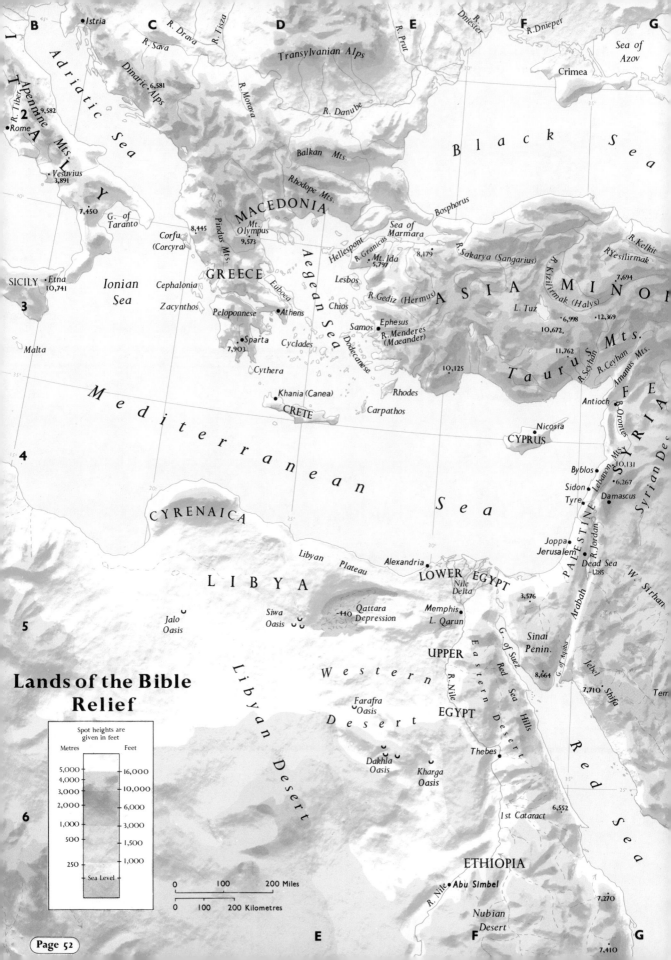

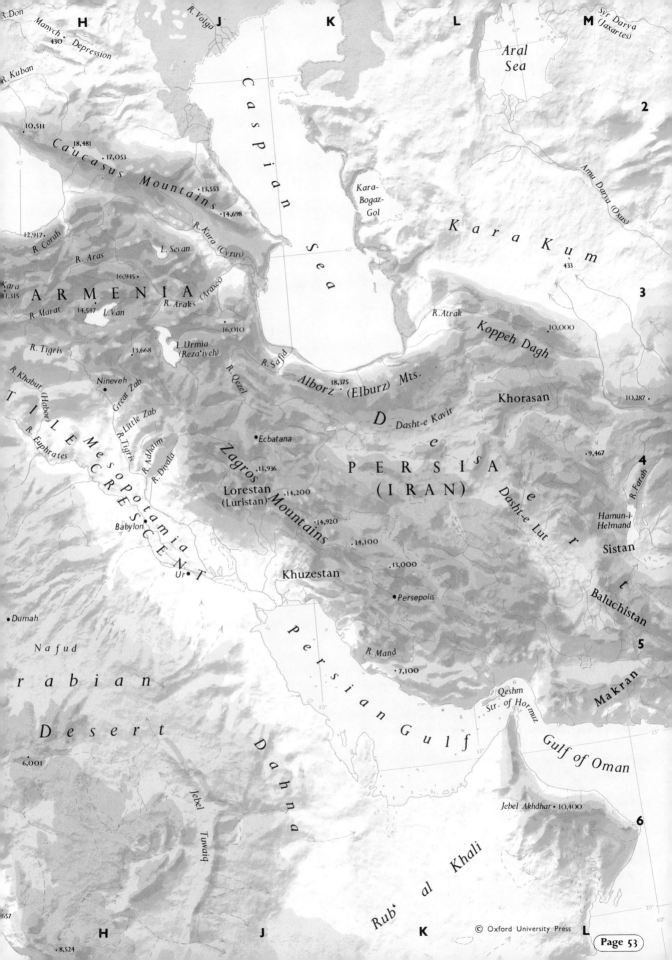

R. Don

R. Kuban

R. Volga

Syr Darya (Jaxartes)

Manych Depression 430

H **J** **K** **L** **M**

Aral Sea

·10,511

Amu Darya (Oxus)

·18,481

Caucasus Mountains ·17,053

·13,553

Kara Kum

·14,698

433

Caspian Sea

R. Coruh 12,917·

R. Kura (Cyrus)

L. Sevan

R. Aras

Kara-Bogaz-Gol

R. Atrak

Koppeh Dagh

·10,000

16,945·

R. Kara 11,315

ARMENIA

R. Murat 14,547

L. Van

R. Araks (Araxes)

16,010

R. Safid

Alborz · (Elburz) Mts.

18,375

Khorasan

10,287·

R. Tigris

13,668·

L. Urmia (Reza'iyeh)

R. Qezel

D

Dasht-e Kavir

R. Khabur (Habor)

Nineveh

Great Zab

R. Little Zab

·9,467

R. Tigris

4

E

Ecbatana

R. Adhaim

Zagros

·11,936

P E R S I A

R. Farah

R. Diyala

(I R A N)

R. Euphrates

Lorestan (Luristan)

·14,200

e

Hamun-i-Helmand

T I L E

·14,920

Dasht-e Lut

Sistan

M e s o p o t a m i a

·14,100

r

t

Babylon

·13,000

Baluchistan

C R E S C E N T

Ur·

Khuzestan

·Persepolis

·Dumah

5

N a f u d

D a h n a

P e r s i a n

R. Mand

·7,100

Makran

r a b i a n

Qeshm

Str. of Hormuz

D e s e r t

6,001·

G u l f

Gulf of Oman

Jebel Tuwaiq

Jebel Akhdhar ·10,400

6

657

Rub' al Khali

H **J** **K** **L**

·8,524

The Ancient Near East before the Exodus

Genesis is set against a wide geographical background. These pages deal in outline with the earliest history of this region over many centuries; the map refers mainly to the period 16th to mid-13th centuries B.C.

Mesopotamia. Excavations at Tell Hassuna below Calah, Tell Halaf, Tell el-'Ubeid near Ur, Erech, and other towns reveal the developing civilization of the prehistoric period, before c. 2800 B.C. The Sumerians, a non-Semitic people who perhaps came from the east (see Gen. 11. 2) around 3300 B.C., flourished in the lower Tigris-Euphrates valley from Nippur to Ur and Eridu. Before the end of the fourth millennium picture-writing which later developed into the wedge-shaped (cuneiform) script appears on clay tablets found at Erech. Here also was one of the earliest ziggurats, an artificial mountain on which the god dwelt. A Sumerian list of long-lived kings before the flood places kingship first at Eridu. The same list has the first dynasty after the flood at Kish, the next at Erech, and the third at Ur. This is the Classical Sumerian Period (c. 2800–2370 B.C.). The apex of Sumerian material culture is illustrated by objects found in the royal tombs at Ur. The enlightened King of Lagash, Urukagina, instituted social reforms and tax revisions. Lugal-zaggisi, who conquered Lagash and ruled as king of Erech and Ur, claimed dominion from the Lower Sea to the Upper Sea. He was defeated by Sargon of Agade, who established an Akkadian dynasty and whose rule extended to Syria and southern Asia Minor, also to the Upper Sea. In the late 23rd century barbarian Gutians from the Zagros Mts. brought Akkadian domination to an end. In the 21st century there was a revival of Sumerian power and culture. Gudea ruled at Lagash and soon Ur-nammu, who made the earliest known code of laws, established the Third Dynasty of Ur, and literature and art flourished.

In the 20th century Ur fell to Elam. Late in the same century King Lipit-Ishtar of Isin issued a Sumerian code of laws. Perhaps contemporary in origin are Akkadian laws of Eshnunna. In the First Dynasty of Babylon (c. 1890–1530) ruled the greatest lawgiver of them all, the Amorite king Hammurabi, both conqueror and administrator. A contemporary of his was Zimri-lim, king of Mari; thousands of clay tablets found there throw light on the period of the Patriarchs, as do inscriptions from the Hurrian city of Nuzi. *See page* 56.

Asia Minor. During the 16th century the Hittites ruled Asia Minor and part of Mesopotamia from their capital at Hattusa. This was followed by the rise of Mitanni, a Hurrian (Horite) kingdom which was forged by a ruling class of Indo-Aryans with horse-drawn chariots. The period of the supremacy of the New Hittite Empire in the 14th and 13th centuries was initiated by King Suppiluliumas, whose campaigns led him to the borders of Babylonia and to the Lebanon Mountains.

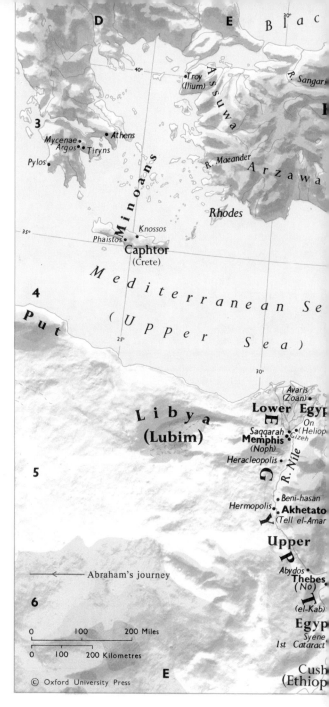

Egypt. During the Proto-dynastic period (c. 2900–2600) Upper and Lower Egypt were united by Menes of the 1st Dynasty. Already the hieroglyphic script was in use. In the Old Kingdom (c. 2600–2100), particularly in the 3rd and 4th Dynasties, Egypt rose to great power. To the 3rd Dynasty belongs Djoser's step pyramid at Saqqarah, and the great pyramids at Gizeh to the 4th Dynasty. From the 5th and 6th Dynasties come the pyramid texts, illuminating Egypt's religion. After a period of decline (7th to 11th Dynasties) Egypt revived in the 20th and 19th centuries, led by Amenemhet I of Thebes, who instituted the 12th Dynasty (the Middle Kingdom), and control over much of Syria-Palestine was reasserted. A large and varied literature of high merit comes from this period. The Egyptian state disintegrated (13th and 14th Dynasties), and during the

15th and 16th Dynasties Egypt was under the Hyksos, who *c.* 1750 invaded Syria-Palestine and infiltrated Lower Egypt. Memphis was their capital at first, but Avaris became the centre of their rule.

The New Kingdom (18th and 19th Dynasties) was the golden age of Egyptian expansion and power. Thutmose III at the battle of Megiddo, *c.* 1468, defeated a revolt headed by the prince of Kadesh, and his armies reached the Euphrates. At Akhetaton (Tell el-Amarna), were found letters from the kings of Babylonia, Assyria, the Hittites, Mitanni, Cyprus, Cilicia, Syria, and Canaan. There were letters from Ugarit, Gebal, Berytus, Sidon, Tyre, Acco, Damascus, Megiddo, Ashkelon, Jerusalem, Shechem, etc. To the same general period at Ugarit belongs a Canaanite temple library from which many mythological texts have

been recovered. Rameses II (*c.* 1301–1234) of the 19th Dynasty was the Pharaoh of the oppression, succeeded by Merenptah, in one of whose inscriptions occurs the earliest non-biblical allusion to Israel.

Genesis. The early biblical stories have a Mesopotamian background; see the Tigris (Hiddekel) and Euphrates in Gen. 2. 14; and the tower of Babel (the ziggurat of Babylon) in Gen. 11. Abraham moved from Ur to Haran and thence to Canaan (11. 22 ff.) and the wives of both Isaac and Jacob came from Paddan-aram (24, 29). With Joseph the scene shifts temporarily to Egypt, including a mention of On (Heliopolis) (39 ff.).

The Land of Canaan
Abraham to Moses

Abraham's Journeys. Abraham, at first called Abram, migrated from Haran to Canaan (Gen. 11. 31; 12. 4, 5). Coming to Shechem he built an altar there to the Lord who had appeared to him. He moved on and pitched his tent on a mountain with Bethel on the west and Ai on the east, where he built another altar. He journeyed southward into the Negeb (Gen. 12. 6–9). After a sojourn in Egypt, he returned to the Negeb and then to his earlier encampment between Bethel and Ai. To avoid strife between the herdsmen of Abraham and Lot, the two of them separated; Lot chose the Jordan Valley, settling at Sodom, while Abraham dwelt in Canaan west of the Jordan Valley, dwelling at Mamre near Hebron (Gen. 13). The vassal kings of Sodom, Gomorrah, Admah, Zeboiim, and Zoar rebelled against Chedorlaomer of Elam and gathered in the Valley of Siddim. The five sites are mentioned in the Ebla tablets, in the same order. Chedorlaomer and allied kings subdued Ashteroth-karnaim, Ham, Shaveh-kiriathaim, the Horites in Mr. Seir (Edom), the country of the Amalekites, and the Amorites in Hazazon-tamar. Sodom and Gomorrah were plundered, and Lot was captured. Abraham and his allies pursued the enemy north to Dan (Laish) and even beyond Damascus, defeating Chedorlaomer and recovering the spoils (Gen. 14). Later Abraham journeyed through the Negeb and sojourned in Gerar, where he encountered King Abimelech (Gen. 20). While in the Negeb Sarah bore Abraham a son, Isaac. God tested Abraham, commanding him to take Isaac to the land of Moriah (near Jerusalem?) and offer him as a burnt offering (Gen. 22. 2). Sarah and Abraham died, and were buried in the cave of Machpelah east of Mamre (Gen. 25. 7–10). Isaac, like his father, went to Gerar. He dug a well in its vicinity, and also in other places, including Rehoboth and Beer-sheba (Gen. 26).

Jacob's Journeys. After deceitfully procuring Isaac's blessing, Jacob left Beer-sheba to go to Paddan-aram for a wife, and *en route* he had a dream at Bethel (Gen. 28. 10–17). Returning home after twenty years with two wives and much wealth, he met the angels of God at Mahanaim (Gen. 32. 1–2). At the River Jabbok he wrestled with an angel and named the place Penuel (Gen. 32. 22, 30). After a friendly meeting with Esau, he went to Shechem by way of Succoth, while Esau returned to Edom (Gen. 33. 16–18). Rachel died and was buried near Bethlehem (Gen. 35. 19). Jacob came to Mamre to his father Isaac, who died and was buried by his sons Esau and Jacob (Gen. 35. 29). The Joseph story relates how Jacob sent Joseph to his brothers, who had been pasturing their flocks near Shechem, but had moved on to Dothan (Gen. 37. 17), and they sold him to a caravan of Ishmaelites who had come from Gilead (Gen. 37. 25–28). After Jacob's death in Egypt his embalmed body was brought back to Canaan and buried in the cave at Machpelah (Gen. 50. 4–14).

Judah and Tamar. Judah did not keep his promise to give his son Shelah, born in Chezib, as husband to Tamar. At Enaim, as he was on the way to Timnah with a friend from Adullam, Judah was seduced by Tamar and became

the father of Perez and Zerah (Gen. 38), founders of two important Judean tribal families (Num. 26. 20–21).

The Conquest of Transjordan. After the Exodus the tribes were led by Moses through the desert to Kadesh in the Wilderness of Zin (Num. 20). They defeated the king of Arad (a town or state?) at Hormah. By-passing Edom, they made camp in the Valley of Zered and on the other side of the Arnon (Num. 21. 3, 10–15). They moved on to Beer, Mattanah, Nahaliel, Bamoth, and the region of Mt. Pisgah (Num. 21. 18–20). Sihon refused them passage along the King's Highway, and a battle was fought at Jahaz and Sihon was slain. Israel seized his territory from the Arnon to the Jabbok, including the city of Heshbon (Num. 21. 21–25). Sihon had earlier driven out the Moabites north of the Arnon, destroying them from Heshbon to Dibon, including the area of Medeba (Num. 21. 27–30). Israel next moved north against Bashan, defeating Og at Edrei (Num. 21. 33–35; Deut. 3. 4). So the land was subdued, from Mt. Hermon to the Arnon (Deut. 3. 8). When Israel was encamped in the Plains of Moab east of the Jordan from Beth-jeshimoth to Abel-shittim (Num. 33. 47–49; 22. 1), King Balak of Moab vainly called upon Balaam to curse Israel (Num. 22–24). Ammon, whose capital was at Rabbah, was not molested, for it belonged to Lot's descendants (Deut. 2. 19). The tribes of Gad and Reuben and the half tribe of Manasseh chose to remain in Transjordan. Gad and Reuben built Dibon, Ataroth, Aroer, Atroth-shophan (about 9½ miles NE. of Ataroth), Jazer, Jogbehah, Beth-nimrah, Beth-haran, Elealeh, Kiriathaim, Nebo, Baal-meon and Sibmah (Num. 32. 34–37), and they occupied part of Gilead and southward to the Arnon, with the Jordan and the Sea of the Arabah as western boundary (Deut. 3. 16–17). The rest of Gilead and all Bashan, all the region of Argob, went to Manasseh, including the villages of Havvoth-jair (Deut. 3. 13–14; Num. 32. 41). Bezer in Reuben, Ramoth-gilead in Gad, and Golan in Manasseh were designated cities of refuge (Deut. 4. 43). Moses established the boundaries of Canaan (Num. 34. 1–10). He commanded the people to renew their covenant obligations to the Lord at Mt. Gerizim and Mt. Ebal after they entered Canaan (Deut. 11 and 27). From Mt. Nebo's summit, on Mt. Pisgah, the Lord showed Moses all the Promised Land, Gilead and as far as Dan, all Naphtali, the land of Ephraim and Manasseh, all the land of Judah, bounded by the Western Sea, the Negeb, and the Valley of Jericho (the Jordan Valley) as far as Zoar (Deut. 34. 1–6).

Additional Note. Archaeological finds from the late 20th century B.C. include numerous fragments of bowls and jars which had been ritually smashed, after they had been inscribed with names and designations of the local and foreign enemies of Egypt, among which appear Jerusalem and Ashkelon. From the late 19th century B.C. come figurines of bound captives with similar execration inscriptions on which there may be recognized the names of Jerusalem, Shechem, Helam, Pehel (Pella), Aphek, Achshaph, Rehob, Hazor, Ijon, Ashtaroth, Tyre, Acco, and other towns, including also Shutu, the ancient name of Moab. 18th-century tablets from Mari illumine Hazor's primacy (see Josh. 11. 10).

The Land of Canaan
Abraham to Moses

GAD, etc.   Tribes of Israel
EDOM, etc   Kingdoms encountered by the Israelites in the 13th century, B.C.

Cities mentioned in Numbers and Deuteronomy, but not in Genesis.

0   10   20 Miles
0   10   20 Kilometres

THE
GREAT
SEA

(The Western Sea)

• Damascus

I V   V   W   X Sidon•   Y   Z   I

A R A M
(S Y R I A)

Mt. Lebanon

Mt. Hermon
(Sirion, Senir)

• Ijon

Tyre• • Uzu   Abel•   Laish•
                          (Dan)•
• Kanah   •Aduru

MAACAH

• Kedesh

Achzib•   GESHUR   ARGOB

                Hazor•   BASHAN
Janoah•   •Merom
Beth-anath•

Acco•   Chinnereth•   Sea   •Karnaim
Achshaph•   Madon•   of   Golan• •Ashtaroth
         Hannathon•   Chinnereth
Mt. Carmel

Shimron•   Beth-yerah   •Yanoam   • Edrei
  •Japhia   (Philoteria)•
Jokneam•   HAVVOTH-JAIR •Ramoth-gilead
                Anaharath•
Dor•   Megiddo•   Shunem•   • Ham

Aruna• •Taanach Beth-shean•
Beth-haggan•   •Ibleam   Rehob•   Pehel
(En-gannim)   Dothan•   (Pella)•
Migdal•
Arubboth•
Gath of• •Yehem
Sharon •Socoh
                •Tirzah
                •Mt. Ebal   Succoth•   •Penuel   •Mahanaim
              •Mt. **Shechem**   •Jabbok
              Gerizim

Aphek•   •Jazer   •Jogbehah

Joppa•   •Ono
Beth-dagon•   Beth-nimrah•   **Rabbah**
     Lod•
          Bethel•   Plains
          (Luz)•Ai   Jericho• Gilgal• of Abel-shittim
Beth-horon•   (Shittim)•
Gezer• Aijalon•   Moab•   •Elealeh
     Gibeon•   Mt. **Heshbon**   •Bezer
Ekron• Beth-shemesh•   **Jerusalem**   Pisgah• Mt. Nebo•
Ashdod•   (Salem?)   Beth-• Medeba•
     Timnah•   •Bethlehem   jeshimoth   Baal-meon
Ashkelon•   Socoh•   (Ephrath)   (Beon)•
       Chezib• Adullam•   R. Nahaliel   •Kedemoth
          •Keilah   Ataroth•   •Mattanah
     Lachish• Mamre•   •Kiriathaim
Eglon• Beth-tappuah• **Hebron**   •Dibon
Gaza•   (Kiriath-arba)   R. Arnon •Aroer
Beth-eglaim• Debir•
(Eglaim)   • City of Moab
Yurza• Gerar• Gath?•
Sharuhen•
                Bab ed-Dra'•   • Ar
     •Moladah   ARAD?
Rehoboth• •Beer-sheba   M O A B
     Hormah• Arad?•
          •Aroer   Numeira•
The N e g e b
          Ziph•   es-Safi•
   Ascent of   Zoar•   Brook Zered
   Akrabbim   E D O M
(Khanazir)• Feifa•
Hazazon-tamar
(30° 48'N)

Plain of Sharon

Hill Country of Israel

The Shephelah

Hill Country of Judah

N

A

C

G I L E A D

M A N A S S E H

A M O R I T E S

R E U B E N

A M M O N

The Arabah

Jordan River

R. Jabbok

Mts. of Abarim

Salt Sea
(Sea of the Arabah)

33° 30'
33°
32° 30'
32°
31° 30'
31°

34° 30'   35°   35° 30'   36°

Possible location of the cities of Sodom, Gomorrah, Admah, Zebuiim, and Zoar in the Valley of Siddim.

© Oxford University Press

Page 57

The Exodus

The Exodus from Egypt. The Israelites dwelt in the land of Goshen, also called 'the land of Rameses', and as slaves they built for Pharaoh (Rameses II) the store cities of Pithom and Rameses (Ex. 1. 1–11). The latter was the capital city, and Moses, found in the Nile by Pharaoh's daughter, was brought up there. Grown to manhood, he fled to Midian (Ex. 2). While keeping Jethro's sheep he came to Mt. Horeb (Sinai), where he was called to rescue his people (Ex. 3). When the Israelites left for Canaan, they did not go by the Way to the Land of the Philistines (Ex. 13. 17), which led from the frontier fortress at Zilu to Raphia. They journeyed from Rameses to Succoth and Etham, and encamped before Pi-hahiroth between Migdol and the sea, in front of Baal-zephon, which is perhaps identical with Tahpanhes. The name translated 'Red Sea' (lit. 'Sea of Reeds') later referred to the Gulf of Aqaba, as in 1 Kgs. 9. 26 (see also Num. 21. 4; Deut. 2. 1). In the Exodus story it does not refer to a northern extension of the Gulf of Suez, whose water level was the same then as now. The place of crossing may have been the southern extension of Lake Menzaleh. The Israelites went 'the way of the wilderness by the Red Sea,' according to a possible interpretation of Ex. 13. 18.

The Way of the Wilderness. The traditional route leads southward to the southern end of the Sinai Peninsula. Two more direct northerly routes have been proposed: one leads along the sandy bar that narrowly separates Lake Sirbonis from the Mediterranean, Baal-zephon being identified with Mons Casius; the other goes eastward towards Jebel Helal, one of several possible identifications for Mt. Sinai in this area. Crossing the sea, the Israelites entered the Wilderness of Shur, and then later the Wilderness of Sin (Ex. 15. 22; 16. 1; Num. 33. 11). Some locate Dophkah (Num. 33. 12, 13) at Serabit el-Khadim, an Egyptian copper- and turquoise-mining centre where some of the earliest alphabetic inscriptions have been discovered. On the third new moon the Israelites came into the Wilderness of Sinai and encamped before Mt. Sinai where the Law was given (Ex. 19. 1 ff). They travelled through the Wilderness of Paran to Kadesh-barnea, which was also in the Wilderness of Zin, for desert boundaries are indefinite (Num. 10. 11, 12; 12. 16; 13. 26; 20. 1). From Kadesh spies were sent out and went into the Negeb to Hebron (Num. 13. 21 ff.). Edom refused Moses' request for permission to pass along the King's Highway, the trunk travel route from Ezion-geber through Edom and Moab to Damascus (Num. 20. 14–21).

From Kadesh to Canaan. From Kadesh-barnea the Israelites went to Mt. Hor, where Aaron died, and they defeated the king of Arad at Hormah (Num. 20. 22–21. 3). Num. 33. 41 traces the route from Mt. Hor to Zalmonah, to Punon, to Oboth, to Iye-abarim in Moab, while according to Num. 21. 4 they went by way of the Red Sea to go around the land of Edom, i.e., via Ezion-geber (see Deut. 2. 8). Whether they went north again by way of the Arabah or to the east of Edom is uncertain. The line of fortresses which protected the eastern boundaries of Edom and Moab has been revealed by modern explorations.

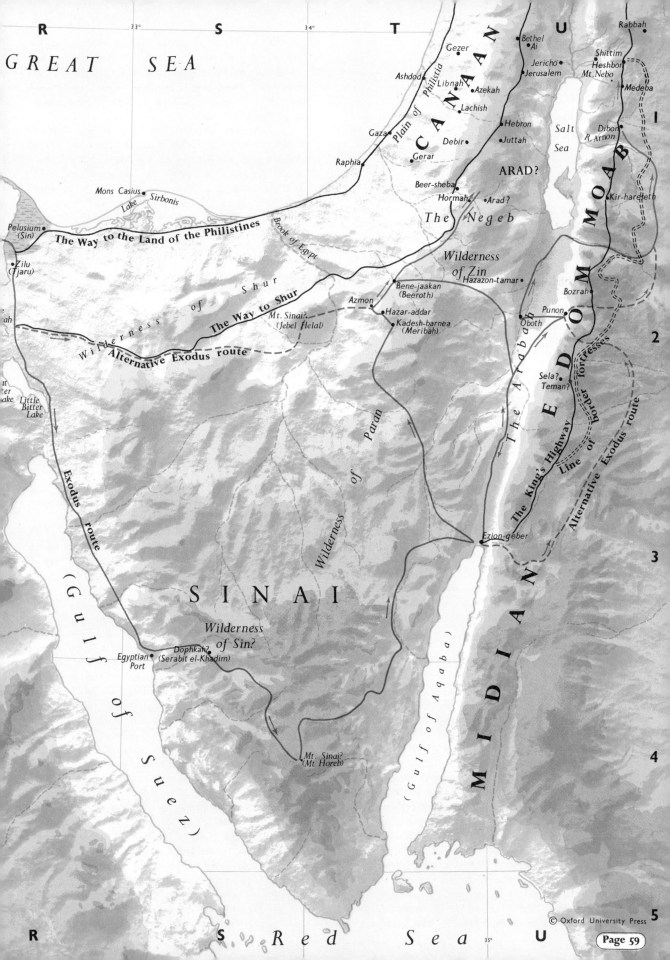

GREAT SEA

R   33°   S   34°   T   U

Rabbah

Bethel
Ai
Gezer

Jericho   Shittim
Jerusalem   Heshbon
Mt. Nebo

Ashdod
Libnah   Medeba
Philistia
Azekah
Lachish
Dibon
R. Arnon
Gaza   Hebron
Gerar   Debir   Juttah   Salt
Sea   Kir-hareseth
Raphia
Beer-sheba
Mons Casius Sirbonis   Hormah   Arad?   ARAD?
Lake
Pelusium   The Negeb
(Sin)
Zilu
(Tjaru)   The Way to the Land of the Philistines   Brook of Egypt
Wilderness of Zin   Hazazon-tamar
Wilderness   of   Shur   Bozrah
The Way to Shur   Azmon   Bene-jaakan   Punon
Mt. Sinai?   (Beeroth)   Hazar-addar   Oboth
(Jebel Helal)   Kadesh-barnea
Alternative Exodus route   (Meribah)

Little
Bitter
Lake   Sela?   Teman?

Wilderness   of   Paran

Exodus   route

S I N A I   Ezion-geber

Wilderness
of Sin?

Dophkah?
Egyptian   (Serabit el-Khadim)
Port

Mt. Sinai?
(Mt Horeb)

R   S   Red   Sea   35°   U

Israel in Canaan
Joshua to Samuel and Saul

(See also pp. 62–63 for some of the sites mentioned here.)

Conquest of Canaan. The people of Israel set out from Shittim, and when the waters of the Jordan were cut off between Adam and the Salt Sea they crossed into Canaan and encamped at Gilgal (Josh. 3–4). Jericho was utterly destroyed (Josh. 5–6). After Achan had been put to death in the Valley of Achor (Josh. 7. 24–26), Ai, east of Bethel, was attacked and left a heap of ruins (Josh. 8). The kings of Jerusalem, Hebron, Jarmuth, Lachish, and Eglon made war on Gibeon, which had a covenant with Joshua (Josh. 9. 3–15). Joshua defeated and pursued them down the pass of Beth-horon and as far as Azekah and Makkedah (Josh. 10. 1–42). In the north the kings of Hazor, Madon, Shimron, and Achshaph were the centre of another coalition against Joshua, which was defeated at the Waters of Merom (Josh. 11. 1–15).

Joshua is credited with taking all the land, the hill country, the Negeb, the land of Goshen, the Shephelah, the Arabah, from Kadesh-barnea and Mt. Halak in the south to Baal-gad below Mt. Hermon in the north (Josh. 10. 40, 41; 11. 16, 17). But much remained to be possessed, including Philistia with its five key cities, Gaza, Ashdod, Ashkelon, Gath, and Ekron (Josh. 13. 2–3; see Judg. 1. 1–26). In many cities, such as Beth-shean, Taanach, Dor, Ibleam, Megiddo, Gezer, Nahalol, Acco, Aphik, Bath-anath, Rehob, etc., the Canaanites were not driven out (Judg. 1. 27–36).

In the allotment of the land, Transjordan, from the River Arnon northwards, went to Reuben, Gad, and half the tribe of Manasseh (Josh. 13. 1–32). Lots were cast at Gilgal for the inheritance of Judah, Ephraim and Manasseh (Josh. 14–17). At Shiloh the remaining territory was allotted to Benjamin, Simeon, Zebulun, Issachar, Asher, Naphtali, and Dan (Josh. 18–19). Forty-eight cities were allotted to Levi from among the other tribes (Josh. 21. 1–42). Six cities of refuge were appointed (see map, and Josh. 20. 1–9). Joshua reaffirmed the covenant at Shechem (see illus. p. 112), which lay between Mt. Gerizim and Mt. Ebal (Josh. 24. 1–28; see 8. 30 ff.), and was buried at Timnath-serah (Josh. 24. 30).

The Judges. Othniel, who had taken Kiriath-sepher from the Canaanites (Judg. 1. 12, 13), rescued Israel from Cushan-rishathaim of Mesopotamia (Judg. 3. 7–11). Ehud from Benjamin slew Eglon, king of Moab (Judg. 3. 12–30). Shamgar, son of Anath, as his name indicates, was from Beth-anath (Judg. 3. 31). Deborah's commander Barak from Kedesh gathered his forces on Mt. Tabor and defeated Sisera, who was from Harosheth, by the River Kishon at Taanach near Megiddo, and the fertile plain of Megiddo was gained for Israel (Judg. 4. 6, 7; 5. 19–21). Gideon, with a force recruited from Manasseh, Asher, and Zebulun, encamped beside the Spring of Harod, and the Midianites were encamped north of them by the Hill of Moreh in the valley of Jezreel (Judg. 7. 1). Gideon pursued the Midianites into Transjordan toward Zarethan (Zererah), Abel-meholah, and Tabbath (Judg. 7. 22). Without help from

Succoth and Penuel (Judg. 8. 5–9) he went on east of Nobah and Jogbehah to Karkor in Wadi Sirhan and captured the Midianite kings (Judg. 8. 10–12). Gideon's son Abimelech became king at Shechem, which later revolted and was destroyed, and Abimelech was killed while attacking Thebez (Judg. 9).

Jephthah, who had fled from his brothers and was dwelling in the land of Tob (Judg. 11. 4), led the men of Gilead against the Ammonites, who claimed the territory held by the Israelites between the Arnon and the Jabbok. Jephthah smote the Ammonites from Aroer to Abel-keramim (Judg. 11. 33). He fought the men of Ephraim who had crossed to Zaphon, and slew those who tried to re-cross the fords of the Jordan (Judg. 12). Samson, whose father was from Zorah, married a Philistine girl from nearby Timnah (Judg. 13. 2; 14. 1). He consorted with a harlot from Gaza and was undone by Delilah, who was from the Valley of Sorek (Judg. 16. 1, 4). He was imprisoned at Gaza where he died violently, and was buried between Zorah and Eshtaol (Judg. 16. 21–31). There were also minor Judges, such as Tola of Issachar who lived at Shamir in the hill country of Ephraim, Jair whose thirty sons had thirty towns in Gilead called Havvoth-jair, and who was buried in Kamon, Ibzan of Bethlehem in Zebulun, Elon of Zebulun who was buried at Aijalon, and Abdon of Pirathon (Judg. 10. 1–5; 12. 11–15). Two supplementary stories tell how the Danites found a new home for their tribe at Laish (Judg. 17–18), and how Benjamin was attacked by the other tribes (Judg. 19–21). It was also in the period of the Judges that Ruth returned with Naomi from Moab to Bethlehem.

Samuel and Saul. Samuel was born to Hannah and Elkanah of Ramathaim-zophim and grew up in the sanctuary at Shiloh (1 Sam. 1–3). Shiloh may have been destroyed in the war between Israel and the Philistines (1 Sam. 4). A plague accompanied the presence of the captured ark at Ashdod, Gath, and Ekron, and it was returned by way of Beth-shemesh and was taken to Kiriath-jearim (1 Sam. 5–6). Samuel judged Israel from Ramah and made a yearly circuit to Bethel, Gilgal, and Mizpah (1 Sam. 8. 16, 17). Saul of Gibeah, who had been anointed by Samuel, mustered Israel against the Ammonites to relieve Jabesh-gilead, and then he was officially made king at Gilgal (1 Sam. 9–11). Spearheaded by an attack on the Philistine garrison near Michmash by Jonathan and his armour-bearer, the Israelites struck down the Philistines from Michmash to Aijalon (1 Sam. 14). Goliath was slain while the Philistines were encamped between Socoh and Azekah in Ephes-dammim, and the Israelites in the Valley of Elah; and the Philistines were pursued as far as Gath and Ekron (1 Sam. 17). David, fleeing from Saul, went to the priest at Nob, to Achish king of Gath, and then to the cave of Adullam (1 Sam. 21. 1, 10; 22. 1). After defeating the Philistines at Keilah (23. 1–12), he fled to the wilderness of Ziph, Maon, En-gedi, and Paran (23. 14, 24; 24. 1; 25. 1). He married Abigail, the wife of Nabal of Maon, who had refused to pay tribute (1 Sam. 25–26). David was given Ziklag by Achish (1 Sam. 27. 6). After consulting the 'witch' (medium) of En-dor (28. 7), Saul died in battle against the Philistines on Mt. Gilboa. The men of Jabesh-gilead rescued the bodies of Saul and his sons from the wall of Beth-shan, and buried them in honour at Jabesh (1 Sam. 31).

Israel in Canaan
Joshua to Samuel and Saul

ASHER, etc.   Tribes of Israel
●   Cities of Refuge
■   Philistine cities

0   10   20 Miles
0   10   20 Kilometres

THE

GREAT

SEA

Sidon

Damascus

Mt. Lebanon
Valley of Lebanon
Baal-gad
Mt. Hermon

Ahlab
Tyre
Dan (Laish)
Beth-rehob

Misrephoth-maim
Abdon
Achzib
Yiron
Kedesh
Hazor

Merom
Beth-anath
Waters of Merom
R. Jordan

Acco
Rehob
Achshaph
Aphik
Cabul
Chinnereth
Sea of Chinnereth
Ashtaroth
Golan

Nahalol
Madon
Rimmon
BASHAN

Hannathon
Bethlehem
Shimron
Hammath

Harosheth-ha-goiim
Mt. Tabor
Lakkum
HAVVOTH-JAIR

Naphath-Dor
Jokneam
Hill of Moreh
En-dor
ISSACHAR

Dor
Megiddo
R. Kishon
Shunem
Beer
Kamon
Edrei
Tob

Jezreel
V. of Jezreel
Ramoth-gilead

Taanach
Beth-shean

En-gannim (Beth-haggan)
Mt. Gilboa
Jabesh-gilead

Ibleam
Hepher
Bezek
Abel-meholah
Tabbath

Socoh
Thebez
Zarethan (Zeredah)
Zaphon

Tirzah
Mt. Ebal
Succoth
R. Jabbok

Pirathon
Shechem
Mt. Gerizim
Penuel

Baal-shalishah
Arumah
Ataroth
Adam

Gath-rimmon
Aphek
Tappuah
Lebonah
Shiloh

Joppa
Asor
Ramathaim-zophim
Jogbehah

Beth-dagon
Timnath-serah
Ephron (Ophrah)
Naarah
Betonim
Beth-nimrah
Rabbah

Upper Beth-horon
Bethel
Ai
Rimmon
Beth-peor

Lower Beth-horon
Beeroth
Mizpah
Gilgal
Jericho
Shittim
Abel-keramim

Gibbethon
Gibeon
Michmash
Heshbon

Jabneel
Shaalbim
Gezer
Aijalon
Chephirah
BENJAMIN
Gibeah
Anathoth
Bezer

Mount Baalah
Baalah
Shikkeron
(Kiriath-jearim)
Zela
Jerusalem (Jebus)
Beth-peor
Mt. Pisgah
Medeba

Baalath
Sorek
Zorah
Beth-shemesh
Middin
Mt. Nebo
Beth-baal-meon

Ekron
Timnah
Lehi
Secacah
Beth-jeshimoth

Makkedah
Jarmuth
Etam
Nibshan
Kedemoth

Ashdod
Libnah
Azekah
Bethlehem
Beth-zur

Socoh
Adullam
Giloh
Zereth-shahar

Ashkelon
Keilah
Mareshah
En-gedi
Kiriathaim

Lachish
Hebron
Dibon

Eglon
Jezreel
Ziph
Arnon
Aroer

Gaza
Debir
Maon
Eshtemoa

Gerar
Gath?
Anab
Goshen
Madmannah
Jattir

Ziklag
Bethul (Bethuel)
Kabzeel
ARAD?

Ashan
Beer-sheba
Hazar-shual
Arad?

Brook Besor
Hormah
Adadah (Aroer)

The Negeb

Ziph

Ascent of Akrabbim

EDOM

MOAB

Sea of the Arabah (The Salt Sea)
Brook Zered

R. Arnon

Karkor (37° 36'E)

Mt. Carmel

ASHER
NAPHTALI
ZEBULUN
MANASSEH
EPHRAIM
DAN
PHILISTINES
The Shephelah
SIMEON
JUDAH
Hill Country of Judah
BENJAMIN
GILEAD
REUBEN
AMMON
The River Jordan
The Arabah

V. of Achor
V. of Elah

© Oxford University Press

Page 61

33° 30'
33°
32° 30'
32°
31° 30'
31°

34° 30'
35°
35° 30'
36°

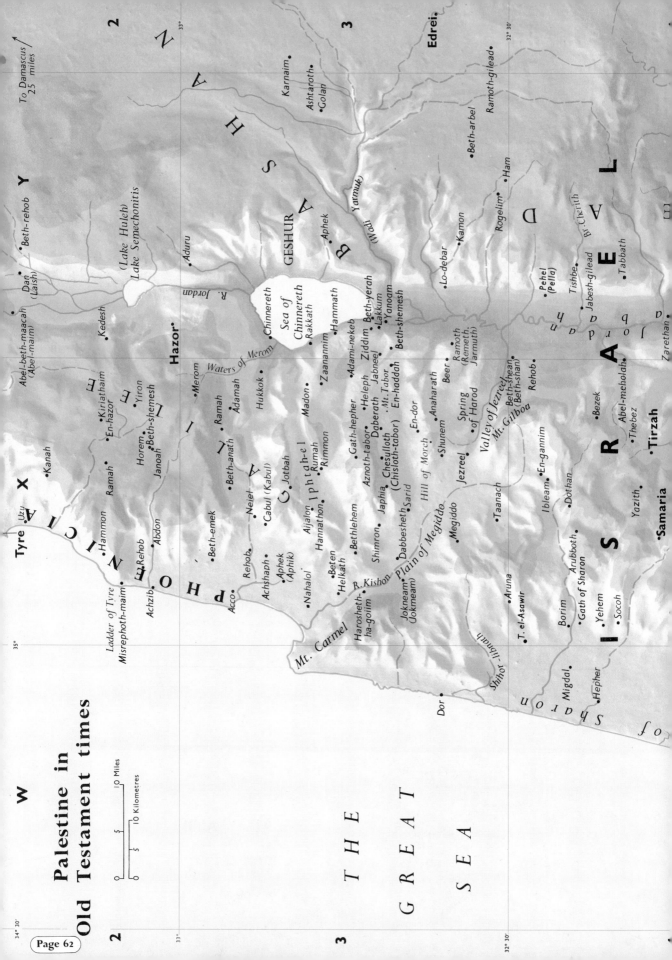

Palestine in
Old Testament times

W

10 Miles

0   5   10 Kilometres

0   5   10

THE
GREAT
SEA

To Damascus
25 miles

Y

Beth-rehob

Abel-beth-maacah
(Abel-maim)

Dan
(Laish)

Kedesh

(Lake Huleh)
Lake Semechonitis

Aduru

R. Jordan

GESHUR

Aphek

(Wadi) Yarmuk

N A S H E S

Karnaim
Ashtaroth
Golan

Edrei

Beth-arbel

Ramoth-gilead

Ham

B A

Hazor

Chinnereth

Sea of
Chinnereth
Rakkath

Hammath

Lo-debar

Kamon

Rogelim

Br.Cherith

D

Tishbe

Jabesh-gilead

Pehel
(Pella)

Tabbath

Waters of Merom

Merom

Adamah

Hukkok

Madon

Zaanannim

Adami-nekeb

Ziddim Beth-yerah
Lakkum
Jabneel
Beth-shemesh

En-haddah

Ramoth
(Remeth)
Jarmuth

Beer

Spring
of Harod

Beth-shean
(Beth-shan)

Rehob

Bezek

E

A

Zarethan

J o r d a n

R

A

E

L

Tyre

X

Uzu

Kanah

Ramah

Hammon

Rehob

Abdon

Achzib

Ladder of Tyre
Misrephoth-maim

Acco

Kiriathaim

En-hazor

Yiron

Horem

Janoah

Beth-shemesh

Ramah

Beth-anath

Beth-emek

Neiel

Rehob
Aphek
(Aphik)

Achshaph

Nahalol

Beten
Helkath

Cabul (Kabul)

Jotbah

Aijalon

Hannathon

Bethlehem

Shimron

Japhia

Dabbesheth

Sarid

R. Kishon

Harosheth-
ha-goiim

Jokneam
(Jokmeam)

Plain of Megiddo

Megiddo

Taanach

Ibleam

En-gannim

Dothan

Aruna

T. el-Asawir

Arubboth

Gath of Sharon

Yehem

Socoh

Borim

Yazith

Samaria

En-dor

Anaharath

Shunem

Jezreel

Valley of Jezreel

Mt. Gilboa

Abel-meholah

Thebez

Tirzah

I S R A E L

Rumah

Rimmon

Gath-hepher

Heleph

Daberath

Chesulloth
(Chisloth-tabor)

Aznoth-tabor

Mt. Tabor

Yanoam

Hill of Moreh

Mt. Carmel

Dor

Migdal

Hepher

Shihor-libnath

Sharon

of

Kanah

E

L

A

G

I

P h t a h - e l

P H O E N I C I A

THE
GREAT
SEA

2

3

The United Monarchy
David and Solomon

Development of the United Monarchy under David. At Saul's death his son Ish-bosheth (Ish-baal) was made king over Israel at Mahanaim, and David was anointed king of Judah at Hebron (2 Sam. 2. 1–4, 8–11). Their two armies clashed at the pool at Gibeon, and the defeated Israelites re-crossed the Jordan to Mahanaim (2 Sam. 2. 12–32). Abner covenanted with David at Hebron to betray Ish-bosheth, but was slain by Joab (2 Sam. 3). Two men from Beeroth of Benjamin slew Ish-bosheth and brought his head to David at Hebron (2 Sam. 4), and Israel accepted David as king. After seven years' rule at Hebron David captured Jerusalem (Jebus) and made it his capital (2 Sam. 5. 1–10). Lying between Judah and Benjamin, it provided a site immune from tribal jealousies. David's transfer of the ark to Jerusalem (2 Sam. 6) marks the beginning of its future as the Holy City.

David's conquests expanded the kingdom. He subdued the Philistines, who at the death of Saul had extended their power to Beth-shean. They invaded the Valley of Rephaim SW. of Jerusalem, and David's defeat of them at Baal-perazim, followed by a second victory in the valley and pursuit of them from Geba to Gezer, removed the Philistine threat to his kingdom (2 Sam. 5. 17–25). He defeated the Edomites in the Valley of Salt and put garrisons in Edom, so that his domination reached to the Red Sea (2 Sam. 8. 13, 14; 1 Kgs. 11. 15, 16). In Transjordan Moab was defeated and made subject (2 Sam. 8. 2). The alliance of Ammon with the Syrians of Beth-rehob and Zobah, the king of Maacah, and the men of Tob, was broken up by Joab, and David defeated the Syrians at Helam and put garrisons in 'Syria of Damascus' (2 Sam. 8. 3–8; 10. 6–19). Ammon was ravaged, its capital Rabbah besieged, and the Ammonites subdued and enslaved (2 Sam. 11. 1; 12. 26–31). David made favourable alliances with Toi of Hamath and Hiram of Tyre (2 Sam. 5. 11; 8. 9–11). A standing army, with a core of mercenary soldiers (Cherethites, Pelethites, and Gittites—2 Sam. 8. 18; 15. 18) made this possible. David took a census for military purposes, beginning at Aroer and 'the city that is in the midst of the valley', i.e., beginning at the Arnon River, and going northward through Gad and up to Kadesh (on the Orontes?), and around to Dan, and from there to the Tyre and Sidon area and down through Canaan to the Negeb of Judah at Beer-sheba. The totals given are 800,000 men in Israel and 500,000 in Judah (2 Sam. 24).

Dissension under David. Absalom's servants had slain his brother Amnon at Baal-hazor, and Absalom had fled to Geshur. With the help of a woman from Tekoa. Joab interceded for him, and Absalom returned and later had himself proclaimed as king at Hebron. David fled over the Mt. of Olives, and through the wilderness across the Jordan to Mahanaim (2 Sam. 13–17). He was befriended by men from Rabbah, Lo-debar, and Rogelim (2 Sam. 17. 27–29). After the battle of the Forest of Ephraim Absalom was killed, and Judah was asked to bring David back to Jerusalem (2 Sam. 18–19). Embittered Israel revolted under Sheba from Benjamin. Joab, after slaying his rival Amasa at Gibeon, besieged Sheba in Abel-beth-maacah, and the kingdom was saved (2 Sam. 20). When David was on his death-bed. Adonijah's attempt to secure the kingship was frustrated, and Solomon was anointed king at the spring Gihon (1 Kgs. 1, see also page 81).

The Reign of Solomon. Soon after Solomon's accession Abiathar was banished to Anathoth, and Adonijah and Joab were killed, as also was Shimei when he was on his way to Gath after runaway slaves (1 Kgs. 2). At the great high place of Gibeon Solomon asked for wisdom (1 Kgs. 3). Through strict administration, a state monopoly in trade, a forced-labour policy, and political marriages, Solomon brought peace, wealth and glory to the monarchy. The kingdom was divided into twelve administrative districts, sometimes deliberately divergent from the older tribal divisions. Listed as tribal and as city-states units, they comprised the following: (I) hill country of Ephraim; (II) Makaz, Shaalbim, Beth-shemesh, Elon, Beth-hanan; (III) Arubboth, including Socoh and the land of Hepher; (IV) Naphath-dor—the coastal area around Dor; (V) Taanach, Megiddo, Beth-shean, Abel-meholah, Jokmeam; (VI) Ramoth-gilead, including Havvoth-jair, Argob (Bashan); (VII) Mahanaim; (VIII) Naphtali; (IX) Asher, Bealoth; (X) Issachar; (XI) Benjamin; (XII) Gilead and the land of Sihon between the Arnon and the Jabbok (1 Kgs. 4. 7–17). (See numbers on map opposite; apart from the description of the districts in 1 Kgs., there is no information on the exact extent of each.) Judah seems to have been excluded, but there was one officer also over the land of Judah (4. 19).

Solomon glorified Jerusalem with magnificent public buildings, such as the temple and palace. Outside Jerusalem he built the cities of Hazor, Megiddo, Gezer, Lower Beth-horon, Baalath, and Tamar (1 Kgs. 9. 15–18). Particularly at Hazor and Megiddo the excavations have disclosed the extent and nature of his city-building. The fortified gateways at Gezer, Hazor, and Megiddo reflect the work of the same master architects. Solomon had store-cities and cities for his chariots, horses, and horsemen (1 Kgs. 4. 26; 9. 19; 10. 26), and imported for sale horses and chariots from Egypt and Kue (see p. 66). Extensive installations at Megiddo, thought to be for stabling horses, belong more probably to the period of Ahab, and even their use has been questioned. Solomon's copper mining in the Arabah was a government monopoly, as was his Red Sea commerce, initiating at Ezion-geber. Hiram, king of Tyre, provided Solomon with cedars and cypresses, and as part payment for his services Solomon ceded to Hiram twenty cities in a district of Galilee called the land of Cabul (1 Kgs. 9. 10–13).

During his reign Solomon had as adversaries Hadad of the royal house of Edom, Rezon of Zobah who became king at Damascus and ruled over Syria, and Jeroboam, an Ephraimite from Zeredah. The last of these was encouraged by Ahijah of Shiloh to revolt, but had to flee to Egypt (1 Kgs. 11. 14–40).

The Davidic Dynasty. The United Monarchy could not be maintained after Solomon's death, but the line of David was to continue to rule over Judah on the throne at Jerusalem, and the prophets were to look for the restoration of the United Monarchy under a king of David's line.

The United Monarchy

ISRAEL, JUDAH Hebrew kingdoms
ASHER, etc. Israelite tribes
SYRIA, etc. Non-Israelite peoples
■ Places fortified by Solomon
I–XII Solomon's administrative
districts (1 Kgs. 4. 7–19)

0   10   20 Miles
0   10   20 Kilometres

1°
2°
33° 30'
33°
32° 30'
32°
31° 30'
31°

V   W   X   Y   Z

↑ZOBAH

Sidon
•Damascus

SIDONIANS
Mt. Lebanon
BETH-REHOB
S Y R I A (A R A M)

Abel-beth-maacah
Dan
•Beth-rehob
Mt. Hermon

Tyre•
MAACAH
B A S H A N
ARGOB

Hazor ■
R. Jordan
GESHUR

Acco•
Merom•
IX
VIII

Cabul•
Sea of Chinnereth

THE
Mt. Carmel
ZEBULUN
ISSACHAR
X

G R E A T
Jokneam (Jokmeam)
R. Kishon
Lo-debar•
HAVVOTH-JAIR
Helam•

Dor•
IV
Megiddo ■
Jezreel•
V. of Jezreel
VI
Tob•

S E A
Taanach•
Mt. Gilboa
Beth-shean•
Rogelim•
Ramoth-gilead•

I S R A E L
Sharon
III
Arubboth•
Abel-meholah•
Jabesh-gilead•
G I L E A D

•Hepher
•Socoh
•Thebez
Zarethan•
VII

M A N A S S E H
Mt. Ebal
Shechem•
Succoth•
Mahanaim•
A M M O N

Plain of
Pirathon•
Mt. Gerizim
R. Jabbok

•Gath-rimmon
I

Joppa•
Zeredah•
•Shiloh
Jazer•

E P H R A I M
•Baal-hazor
XII
•Rabbah (Rabbath-ammon)

Bethel•
•Ephraim

Beth-hanan•
Beeroth•
Gilgal
Heshbon•

Lower Beth-horon ■
Upper Beth-horon•
XI Jericho

Gezer ■
Shaalbim•
Geba•
Medeba•

Baalath ■
Elon•
Gibeon•
B E N J A M I N

Makaz•
II
Kiriath-jearim•
Gibeah•
Anathoth•

Ashdod•
Ekron•
Sorek•
High Place
•Jerusalem

Ashkelon•
Beth-shemesh•
M O A B

Libnah•
Bethlehem•
•Netophah

•Adullam
Tekoa•
R. Nahaliel

Gaza•
Giloh•
S a l t   S e a (Sea of the Arabah)

P H I L I S T I N E S
The Shephelah (Lowland)
J U D A H
Hebron•
Dibon•

•Debir
Carmel•
•Aroer
R. Arnon

Gerar•
Ziklag•
Wilderness of Judah

Gath?•
The Negeb
•Kir-hareseth

Kabzeel•
•Arad

Brook Besor
Beer-sheba•
Valley of Salt

A M A L E K
Brook Zered

E D O M

Tamar (30° 48'N) ■

© Oxford University Press

34° 30'   W   35°   X   35° 30'   Y   36°   Z

Israel and Ancient Trade Routes

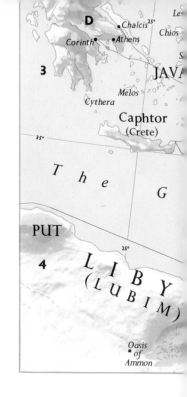

The Bible and Trade. The writers of the Bible and their editors were not primarily interested in the economic position of Israel, so that they did not say much about commerce and trade. Still, to maintain their independence as a nation for three or four centuries amongst powerful neighbours, Israel and Judah both relied largely on wealth brought in by the advantageous position of their country.

As the map opposite shows, Palestine, small as it is, happens to lie on a part of the coast of Asia through which all merchandise carried by camel or donkey between Egypt or Arabia and Mesopotamia or Asia Minor had to pass. Some of the more energetic of the Judean and Israelite kings, notably Solomon, were able to profit by this geographical fact, either trading themselves or taking a share of the value of goods that passed through their territory.

Some passages in the Bible speak clearly of this trade; others only mention it in passing, like the story in Gen. 37. 25–28 of the Ishmaelites who were carrying spices down to Egypt from Gilead, and stopped to add Joseph to their cargo. Other passages, again, only hint at trade relations, as when the writer of 1 Kgs. 16. 29–31 states that Ahab married the daughter of the king of the Sidonians, and leaves us to guess that some commercial understanding lay behind that marriage.

We cannot build up an exact picture of Israel's trading relations, nor distinguish clearly between the times when trade flourished and those when it slackened off. This map, therefore, is not related to any single period of time or any particular book of the Bible. But it tries to show the principal trade routes that were in use between the time of King David and the Exile, or even later, and the principal towns or tribes with which Israel or her immediate neighbours may have had trade relations. Some of the names, especially in Arabia, appear in the Bible as personal names, like the descendants of Abraham through Keturah in Gen. 25. But when we see that Keturah simply means 'incense', and remember that Arabian incense was one of the greatest sources of wealth in ancient times, it becomes obvious that names like Zimran, Jokshan, Medan and Midian, Keturah's sons, represent not individual persons but well-known peoples or tribes connected with the incense trade. Many of those names we cannot place on the map, but a few of them like Sheba (the Sabeans of Job 1 and of Roman times) or Nebaioth (the eldest son of Ishmael, Gen. 25. 13, and a pastoral tribe, Isa. 60. 7) can be identified with peoples known from other sources, and so located with fair confidence.

Solomon was a national figure, so his ventures in commerce were thought a fit subject for record. In 1 Kgs. 5. 10–11 and 9. 11 he sells wheat, oil and some land to the king of Tyre in return for gold and cedar of Lebanon. In 10. 28–29 he becomes the middleman between Egypt and the kings of N. Syria (the Hittites) for the exchange of Cilician horses and Egyptian chariots. (In this passage Cilicia is called 'Kue' (N.E.B. 'Coa'): the Hebrew text was misunderstood by most translators.) In 1 Kgs. 10 the Queen of Sheba (in S. Arabia) brings Solomon presents of gold and spices, the two great exports of Arabia to the Mediterranean world, and takes back a cargo of unspecified Israelite products ('whatsoever she asked'); this was the prelude to Solomon's profitable traffic with the spice merchants and 'all the kings of Arabia' mentioned in 10. 15. South Arabian spices destined for Egyptian and Syrian markets were normally carried overland by camels; the Red Sea was difficult to navigate and

there was no Suez Canal. Solomon and his partner Hiram (9. 26–28 and 10. 11, 22) decided to break the monopoly of the Midianites and other Arabian owners of camels by building ships at Ezion-geber on the Red Sea, so that the goods could be landed there direct from Arabia and thence be carried on by land under Solomon's own control, thus saving the heavy transit dues and protection money levied by the tribes besetting the Arabian land routes. This astute move could only have succeeded by an understanding with the Queen of Sheba who controlled the ports of origin. The same ships plying between Ezion-geber and S. Arabia would also call every three years at some remote African port, or in Punt (? Ophir), at the southern edge of the map, to take on ivory, silver, gold and apes (10. 11, 22).

Later Jewish Kings, lacking Solomon's diplomacy, were not so successful; and Jehoshaphat (1 Kgs. 22. 48–49), refusing the competent Phoenician mariners whom Ahab's son Ahaziah through his affinity with Tyre could have furnished, lost the whole fleet in a total disaster.

No doubt it was the Phoenicians who excelled in trade and nautical enterprise. Ezek. 27 gives a summary of their widespread traffickings. Some place-names in the map are taken from that chapter. Although Ezekiel names them as trading specially with Tyre, they were well-known to Jewish readers, and Israelite merchants would probably have done business with many of the same peoples at one time or another in the past.

Other names in the map are supplied from Assyrian or Egyptian records; and some are of ancient sites that have been recovered by archaeological exploration. All these sources may be used together to build up a picture of the commercial world to which Israel and Judah belonged before they were obliterated by the power of Assyria and Babylon.

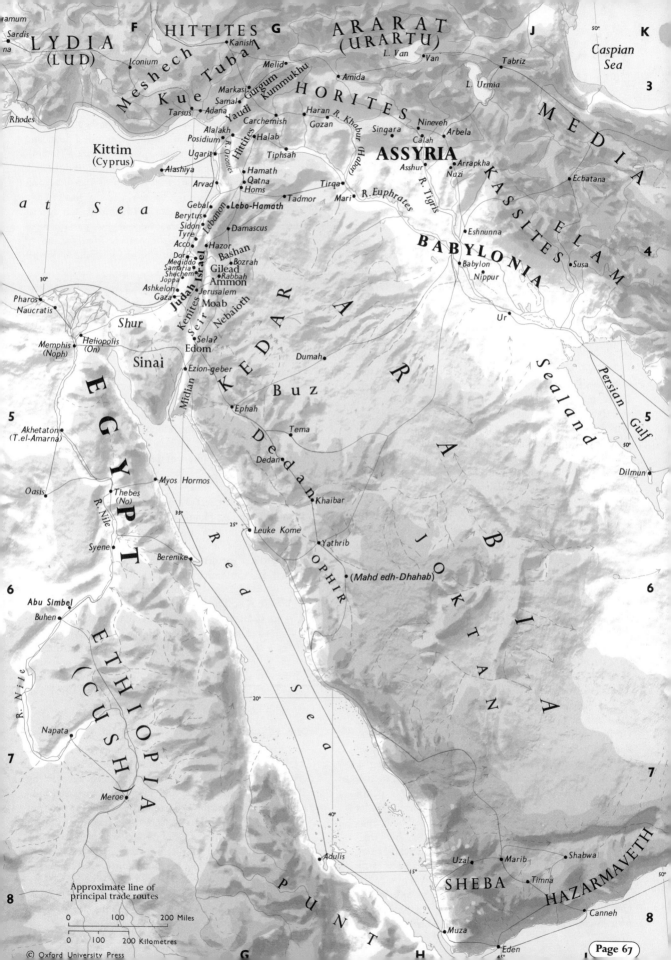

LYDIA
(LUD)

amum
Sardis
na
Rhodes

F   HITTITES   G   ARARAT   J   K
(URARTU)

Iconium   Kanish
Melid   L. Van
                 Van   Tabriz
                 L. Urmia

Meshech Kue Tubal Gurgum Kummukhu HORITES MEDIA
Tarsus Adana Yaudi Markasi Amida
Alalakh Carchemish Haran R. Khabur Singara Nineveh Arbela
Posidium Hittites Gozan Assyria Calah
Ugarit Halab   ASSYRIA Asshur Arrapkha
Alashiya Tiphsah   Nuzi
Hamath   Tirqa   R. Euphrates R. Tigris
Arvad Qatna   Mari
Homs   Tadmor
Gebal Lebo-Hamath   R. Euphrates   Eshnunna
Berytus Lebanon   Babylon
Sidon Damascus   BABYLONIA Nippur
Tyre   Hazor
Acco   Bashan   Susa
Dor   Bozrah
Megiddo Gilead   Ur
Samaria Shechem Rabbah
Joppa Ammon
Ashkelon Jerusalem
Gaza   Judah Israel Moab
Kenites Seir Nebaioth
Pharos Shur
Naucratis

Kittim
(Cyprus)

at   Sea

Memphis Heliopolis   Sela?
(Noph) (On)   Edom
        Sinai   Ezion-geber   Dumah

EGYPT Midian KEDAR Buz
                     Dedan Tema
Akhetaton   Ephah
(T.el-Amarna)
Oasis   Thebes Myos Hormos   Dedan
        (No)   Khaibar
Syene   R. Nile
        Berenike   Leuke Kome
Abu Simbel   Yathrib
Buhen   OPHIR   (Mahd edh-Dhahab)

ETHIOPIA (CUSH)   A R A B I A   J O K T A N

Napata   Red   Sea

Meroe

Approximate line of
principal trade routes
0   100   200 Miles
0   100   200 Kilometres
© Oxford University Press

PUNT

Adulis   Uzal Marib Shabwa
                Timna
        SHEBA   HAZARMAVETH
                Muza
        Eden   Canneh

The Kingdoms of Israel and Judah (c.922–721 B.C.)

Division and Conflicts. Rehoboam, Solomon's son, was accepted as king of Judah and went to Shechem where Israel had gathered. Jeroboam returned from Egypt and led the assembly of Israel in its demands for a less oppressive government (1 Kgs. 12. 1–5). When Rehoboam refused, Israel made Jeroboam king. Shechem was built as the capital, and Dan and Bethel, in the north and the south of the kingdom, were made national religious centres. In Transjordan Penuel was rebuilt (1 Kgs. 12. 25–33). Early in Jeroboam's reign the capital seems to have been moved to Tirzah (1 Kgs. 14. 17). In the fifth year of Rehoboam Shishak of Egypt plundered Jerusalem (1 Kgs. 14. 25, 28). (See illustration, p. 103.) In his own record he gives the names of conquered towns, including Raphia, Aijalon, Beth-anath, Adummim, Beth-horon, Socoh, 'the Field of Abraham', Gibeon, Beth-tappuah, Kedesh, Megiddo, Shunem, Taanach, Beth-shan, Rabbah, Mahanaim, and others. According to 2 Chr. 13. 19, Abijah, Rehoboam's son, took Bethel, Jeshanah, and Ephron from Jeroboam. Nadab, Jeroboam's son, was slain by Baasha when Nadab's army was laying siege to Gibbethon (1 Kgs. 15. 27). In his war with Judah, Baasha fortified Ramah, five miles north of Jerusalem, but Asa of Judah hired Ben-hadad of Damascus, who invaded Israel and conquered Ijon, Dan, Abel-beth-maacah, and all of Chinneroth (the region round Chinnereth), and all of Naphtali. Judah strengthened her boundary, re-fortifying Mizpah and Geba (15. 16–23). Asa defeated Zerah the Ethiopian in the Valley of Zephathah at Mareshah, and pursued him to Gerar (2 Chr. 14. 9–15). Elah, son of Baasha, was slain in Tirzah by Zimri. The news of this came to the Israelite troops under their commander Omri at Gibbethon. Omri came to Tirzah and took the city, and became king of Israel (1 Kgs. 16. 8–19).

The House of Omri. Omri established an important dynasty: in the Assyrian documents Israel became known as 'the land of Omri'. After six years' rule from Tirzah, Omri built the city of Samaria for his capital (1 Kgs. 16. 24). His son Ahab married Jezebel, the daughter of the Sidonian (Phoenician) king of Tyre (16. 31), and built a temple for Baal in Samaria. Jericho and other cities were rebuilt (16. 34). Elijah of Tishbe in Gilead opposed Jezebel's paganism. During the famine he dwelt by the Brook Cherith and at Zarephath (17. 5, 9). He confuted Jezebel's prophets on Mt. Carmel and slew them by the Brook Kishon (1 Kgs. 18). The city of Jezreel seems to have served as a second capital, and here Naboth had a vineyard beside Ahab's palace (1 Kgs. 18. 45; 21. 1 ff.). Ben-hadad of Damascus attacked Israel at Samaria and at Aphek, but was defeated both times (1 Kgs. 20). The Syrians held Ramoth-gilead, and Ahab was unable to take it, despite the assistance of Jehoshaphat of Judah, who had come up to Samaria. Ahab died in battle at Ramoth-gilead, and was buried at Samaria (22. 1–40).

Omri had subdued Moab, and after Ahab's death Mesha, king of Moab, successfully revolted (2 Kgs. 3. 4, 5). Mesha's own inscription found at Dibon tells of his conquest of Ataroth and Jahaz and of building the towns of Aroer, Bezer, Medeba, Beth-baal-meon, Beth-bamoth, and others, and making a highway in the Arnon valley. Jehoshaphat of Judah tried unsuccessfully to revive the southern trade connections of Solomon via Ezion-geber and the Red Sea (see p. 66). Jehoram, Ahab's son, and Jehoshaphat made a punitive expedition against Moab by way of Edom, and attacked Kir-hareseth (2 Kgs. 3). Under Jehoram (Joram), son of Jehoshaphat, Edom revolted, as also did Libnah (8. 20–22). The Elisha narratives describe Syrian attacks on Dothan and Samaria (2 Kgs. 6–7). Elisha instigated a regicide in Damascus. Jehoram of Israel made war against Hazael of Damascus at Ramoth-gilead, but was wounded and returned to Jezreel to be healed. Ahaziah, son of Jehoram of Judah, went down to see Jehoram in Jezreel (2 Kgs. 8. 28, 29).

The House of Jehu. Anointed king at Elisha's instigation, Jehu, Jehoram's army commander, made his famous ride from Ramoth-gilead across the Valley of Jezreel to Jezreel. He slew Jehoram of Israel, and Ahaziah of Judah was wounded at Ibleam and fled to Megiddo to die (2 Kgs. 9). Samaria and the rest of Israel fell to Jehu, but the Israelite territory east of the Jordan from Aroer by the Arnon and north through Gilead and Bashan was subdued by Hazael of Damascus (10. 32, 33). Hazael penetrated as far as Gath in Judah and even threatened Jerusalem, but was bought off by Jehoash (Joash), son of Ahaziah (12. 17, 18). After Hazael's death, Jehoash, grandson of Jehu, recovered the Transjordan lands (13. 25). Jehoash also fought with Amaziah of Judah, who had conquered the Edomites in the Valley of Salt and had taken Sela (14. 7). Jehoash defeated Amaziah at Beth-shemesh and plundered Jerusalem (14. 11–14).

Jehoash's son Jeroboam II restored the ancient boundaries of Israel from the Entrance to Hamath to the Sea of the Arabah, as predicted by Jonah from Gath-hepher (2 Kgs. 14. 25). His son Zechariah reigned only six months and was slain by Shallum at Ibleam, bringing to an end the house of Jehu (2 Kgs. 15. 10). In Judah Uzziah took Elath on the Red Sea and fought the Philistines, conquering Gath, Jabneh, and Ashdod, and was victorious against Ammon (2 Chr. 26. 6, 9, 10; 27. 5). In the days of Jeroboam II, Amos of Tekoa prophesied in Israel and Hosea began his prophetic career. In the year Uzziah died, Isaiah received his call. Inscribed sherds from Samaria increase our knowledge of 8th-century contemporary Israelite towns.

The Last Days of Israel. After a month's reign Shallum was struck down in Samaria by Menahem of Tirzah (2 Kgs. 15. 14). Menahem sacked Tappuah and its territory from Tirzah on (2 Kgs. 15. 16). His son Pekahiah was slain by Pekah in Samaria. Rezin and Pekah of Israel conspired against Ahaz of Judah, who had met defeat at the hands of Edom and the Philistines (2 Chr. 28. 16–18). Ahaz bought the aid of Tiglath-pileser III of Assyria, who took Damascus and captured Ijon, Abel-beth-maacah, Janoah, Kedesh, Hazor, Gilead, and Galilee, and turned the conquered territories into Assyrian provinces (2 Kgs. 15. 29; 16. 9). Pekah's successor Hoshea revolted against Assyria; Shalmaneser V came up against Samaria, and the city was taken by his successor Sargon in 721 (see pp. 70–71).

The Assyrian Empire

Earlier Conquests. Tiglath-Pileser I, who ruled around 1100 B.C., called himself 'king of the world, king of Assyria, king of the four rims of the earth', and claimed conquests from the Lower Zab to the Upper Sea. He marched against the Nairi countries, cut cedars from Lebanon, and took tribute from Gebal, Sidon, and Arvad. He crossed the Euphrates twenty-eight times. His army reached Lake Van. He controlled all of north Babylonia and conquered the city of Babylon. But this period of glory was short-lived, and dark centuries followed. A second epoch of domination followed with the brutal Ashurnasirpal II (883–859). From Bit-adini he crossed the Euphrates, took Carchemish, overran north Syria (Hattina), and washed his weapons in the Great Sea, taking tribute from Tyre, Sidon, Arvad, and other cities, and ascended the Amanus Mountains. His successor Shalmaneser III (858–824) greatly expanded Assyria's borders and boasted of reaching the sources of the Tigris and Euphrates. He marched against Akkad (Babylonia) and entered Babylon, Cuthah, and Borsippa. To the north he reached Lake Van. In 853 he invaded Syria; Aleppo submitted, but at Qarqar on the Orontes he met a coalition of twelve kings, which included the forces of Ahab of Israel, Hadad-ezer of Damascus, and detachments also from Hamath, Kue, Musri, Arvad, Arabia, and Ammon. In 841, crossing the Euphrates for the sixteenth time, he defeated Hazael of Damascus, and received tribute from Tyre, Sidon, and Jehu of Israel.

The Ascendency of Assyria. Assyria had been weakened by revolts and the encroachments of Urartu, but Tiglath-pileser III (744–727) broke Urartu's advance. He captured Arvad, invaded Philistia, and received tribute from Kummukhu (Commagene), Milid (Melitene), Kue, Samal, Damascus, Tyre, Gebal, the queen of Arabia, and other sources, including Menahem of Israel. He reached but could not conquer Turushpa in Urartu. Bribed by Ahaz to counter the attacks of Israel and Damascus on Judah (2 Kgs. 16. 5–9; Isa. 7–8) he conquered Damascus, incorporating it in his empire, and annexed all of Israel save the district of Samaria. He put Hoshea on Israel's throne, but soon after Shalmaneser V (727–722) became king of Assyria, Israel revolted. Shalmaneser invaded Judah, imprisoned Hoshea, and besieged Samaria. Sargon II (721–705) completed its subjugation, deporting 27,290 Israelites to Halah, to the Habor (the river of Gozan), and to Media. He rebuilt Samaria, importing aliens from Babylon, Cuthah, Avva, Hamath, and Sepharvaim (Sargon's annals and 2 Kgs. 17–18). Hanno, king of Gaza, and Sibe (or So, cf. 2 Kgs. 17. 4) of Egypt were defeated at Raphia. In 711 Azuri, king of Ashdod, withheld tribute, and the revolt spread. Without waiting to assemble his full army, Sargon invaded the coastland, conquering Gath, Ashdod, and Asdudimmu. (See p. 73.) Sargon conquered Babylonia which was under Merodach-baladan. He built a new capital at Dur-sharrukin. His son Sennacherib (704–681) met with revolt in Phoenicia and Philistia, encouraged by Merodach-baladan and Egypt (2 Kgs. 20. 12 ff.; Isa. 39). He marched against Hatti; the Phoenician cities capitulated, and Moab, Edom, Ammon, and others sent tribute. An Egyptian-Ethiopian force was defeated at Eltekeh, and Ekron was assaulted and taken. Judah was invaded and Jerusalem forced to capitulate (Sargon's annals and 2 Kgs. 18; Isa. 36). Babylonia fell to Sennacherib in 689, and Babylon was ruthlessly laid waste. See pp. 27–28.

Climax and Decline of Assyria. Sennacherib was slain at Nineveh in a conspiracy by his sons, the elder brothers of Esarhaddon (680–669). Esarhaddon pursued them to Hanigalbat west of the Upper Tigris, and they escaped to 'the land of Ararat', i.e. Urartu (see 2 Kgs. 19. 36, 37). After preliminary failure in Egypt, Esarhaddon entered Egypt, and conquered Memphis, and Egypt was brought within

Approximate extent of Assyrian domination
in the latter part of the 8th. century.

(Later, under Esarhaddon (680-669), Assyria conquered Egypt.)

```
0        100        200 Miles
0    100    200 Kilometres
```

the Empire, although defeated Tirhakah, king of Egypt,
escaped to Napata. Esarhaddon even claimed the conquest
of Ethiopia (Cush). He called himself 'king of Assyria,
governor of Babylon, king of Karduniash (Babylonia), king
of Egypt, Paturisi (biblical 'Pathros', Upper Egypt), and
Ethiopia'. On his way back Ashkelon submitted. Perhaps for
participating in the revolts in this part of the Empire or for
withholding tribute, Manasseh of Judah was exiled to
Babylon (2 Chr. 33. 10 ff.). On his north-west border
Esarhaddon defeated Teushpa, king of the Cimmerians
(Gimarrai), 'trampled on the necks of' the people of
Khilakku, and temporarily stopped the advance of the
Scythians.

Ashurbanipal (668–630) made a first campaign into
Egypt, taking Memphis and occupying Thebes, and in a
second campaign he defeated Tandamane, Tirhakah's
successor, and sacked Thebes. He is mentioned in Ezra 4. 10
as 'the great and noble Osnappar' Under Ashurbanipal
Assyria reached the peak of her cultural development,
reflected in the royal residences and library excavated at
Nineveh. But Egypt and Babylonia broke from Assyria's
grip, and after Ashurbanipal's death the decline was rapid.
Babylonia under Nabopolassar gained independence in 626
after an unsuccessful Assyrian attack on Babylon. Asshur
fell to the Medes in 614, and Nineveh was destroyed by the
Medes and Babylonians in 612 (cf. the Book of Nahum).
Ashuruballit assumed rule over Assyria in Haran, and in 610
retreated to Syria when the Medes and Babylonians captured Haran.

The Kingdom of Judah
after the Fall of Samaria
(721–586 B.C.)

Judah's Struggle to Survive. Israel had fallen in 721, and the Assyrian yoke was heavy on Judah. Hezekiah, king of Judah, rebelled against Assyrian domination, and also smote the Philistines as far as Gaza (2 Kgs. 18. 7, 8). He instituted religious reforms, and 2 Chr. 30 reports that he summoned the people from the whole land between Beer-sheba and Dan, from even as far north as Asher and Zebulun, to come and keep the passover at Jerusalem. Sargon of Assyria attacked Ashdod in 711, and made it an Assyrian province. Probably it was at this time that Micah prophesied against Philistia and the cities of this area, including Gath, Beth-ezel, Moresheth-gath, Achzib, Mareshah, and Adullam (Mic. 1. 10–15). Hezekiah strengthened Jerusalem's defences (2 Chr. 32. 5). For his waterworks at Jerusalem, the 'Siloam' pool and tunnel (2 Kgs. 20. 20; 2 Chr. 32. 30), see pp. 80–81. The fortifications were extended to enclose part of the western hill within the city walls. (See p. 80.)

Under Sennacherib, Sargon's successor, Assyria swept westward, and in 701 took the fortified cities of Judah. Isaiah pictures the invader coming down from the north upon Jerusalem, leaving Rimmon and coming to Aiath, passing through Migron, storing his baggage at Michmash, and lodging at Geba for the night; his route carries him past Ramah, Gallim, Laishah, Anathoth, Madmenah, and Gebim, and their inhabitants fear and flee; from Nob he shakes his fist against the hill of Jerusalem (Isa. 10. 27–32). (Some scholars associate this Isaiah prophecy with an earlier Assyrian invasion.) Sennacherib's own annals, which supplement at many points the account in 2 Kgs. 18–19, record how Sidon, Acco, Achzib, and other Phoenician cities submitted, and how he besieged and conquered Joppa, Beth-dagon, Bene-berak, Ekron, Eltekeh, and Timnah. His capture of Lachish is depicted on an Assyrian relief, and he used the city as a base for his operations against Jerusalem. Hezekiah seems to have capitulated, for Sennacherib exacted heavy tribute, including silver, gold, rich furnishings, and even daughters of Hezekiah (so Sennacherib's Annals; see 2 Kgs. 18. 14–16).

Perhaps from a time of Arab invasion from the desert into Moab comes the oracle in Isa. 15–16 (cf. Jer. 48), picturing the desolation of Ar, Kir (Kir-heres, Kir-hareseth), Dibon, Heshbon, Elealeh, Jahaz, Zoar, Sibmah, and Jazer.

Revival, Reformation and Decline. After the long reign of Manasseh and the two-year reign of his son Amon, Josiah ascended the throne in 640. In the eighteenth year of his reign a book of the law was found in the Jerusalem temple. The temple was cleansed of its paganism, and Josiah effected religious reforms from Geba to Beer-sheba (2 Kgs. 23. 8), and even in areas formerly belonging to Israel, which he controlled perhaps as a nominal vassal of Assyria. He destroyed the shrines in Bethel and in the cities of Samaria (2 Kgs. 23. 15, 19) and in the territories of Manasseh, Ephraim, and Naphtali (2 Chr. 34. 6, 7). He was killed at Megiddo in 609 by Pharaoh Neco (2 Kgs. 23. 29), who had come up from Egypt along the coastal trunk route and through the Megiddo pass, and was on his way up to the Euphrates. In his days royal potteries or storehouses for collecting taxes were established at Hebron, Ziph, Socoh, and 'Memshath' (see illustration p. 100, and Gazetteer under 'Memshath'). Josiah's son Jehoahaz became king. After a three months' reign he was put in bonds at Riblah by Neco and then taken to Egypt. His brother Jehoiakim was made king (23. 31–34).

The prophet Jeremiah of Anathoth (Jer. 1. 1) warned his people of invasion by a foe from the north, calling them to blow the trumpet of alarm in Tekoa and raise a signal on Beth-haccherem (6. 1). He seemed to hear from as far away as Dan the snorting of the approaching war-horses (Jer. 8. 16). He contrasts the perpetual snow of Lebanon and of the crags of Sirion (Mt. Hermon) with the inconstancy and disobedience of the people (Jer. 18. 14–15). For Judah's faithlessness the Jerusalem temple and city would suffer the fate of Shiloh (7. 12–14). Though the house of the king of Judah was 'as Gilead' or the summit of Lebanon to the Lord, it would become like a desert or an uninhabited city (Jer. 22. 6). When Jeremiah was brought to trial, the elders recalled the oracles of Micah of Moresheth (Jer. 26. 17, 18). For uttering oracles like those of Jeremiah, the prophet Uriah of Kiriath-jearim was put to death by Jehoiakim (26. 20–23).

The Fall of Jerusalem. Jehoiachin succeeded his father Jehoiakim and on 16 March 597 (dated by Nebuchadrezzar's own Chronicles) Nebuchadrezzar conquered Jerusalem and took Jehoiachin and the leading men of Judah into exile, setting up Zedekiah as king. Jeremiah advised the kings of Edom, Moab, Ammon, Tyre, and Sidon, as well as Zedekiah, to submit to Nebuchadrezzar (Jer. 27–28). Ezekiel pictured Nebuchadrezzar casting lots at the crossroads where signposts pointed to Rabbah of Ammon and to Jerusalem; the lot fell on Jerusalem (Ezek. 21. 18–23). In 589 the Babylonians again invaded Judah. Jeremiah gave the oracle in Jer. 34. 1–7 at the time when they had taken all the fortified cities except Lachish, Azekah, and Jerusalem. To this period belong the inscriptions on potsherds (the Lachish Letters) found in the excavations at Lachish. One of the letters refers to the fire-signals of Lachish, but adds that the signals of Azekah could not be seen, perhaps because by this time the city had fallen. In 587 or 586 the city of Jerusalem was captured and burned, and 'Judah was taken into exile out of its land' (2 Kgs. 25). Jeremiah, who had been taken in chains with other captives to Ramah, was released and elected to remain in Judah (Jer. 40. 1–6). Gedaliah, whom Nebuchadrezzar placed as governor over Judah, was murdered at Mizpah, the seat of his government, by Ishmael, who had been commissioned by Baalis of Ammon (2 Kgs. 25. 22–26; Jer. 40. 14; 41. 1–3). Ishmael slew all but ten of eighty men who had arrived from Shechem, Shiloh, and Samaria, bringing offerings and incense for the temple at Jerusalem (Jer. 41. 4–8). Johanan came on Ishmael at the great pool at Gibeon, but Ishmael escaped to Ammon (Jer. 41. 12–15). Near Bethlehem, against Jeremiah's advice, decision was made by Johanan and his associates to flee to Egypt (Jer. 41. 17 ff.).

The Babylonian Empire

© Oxford University Press

Beginning of the Neo-Babylonian (Chaldean) Empire. The Babylonians were intimately involved in the fate of Judah and were the object of many a prophetic oracle (e.g., Jeremiah, Ezekiel, and Isa. 40–55). Clay tablet texts of the chronicles of the Chaldean kings now provide information of the period which witnessed the end of the Assyrian empire, the rise of Babylonia, the fall of Jerusalem, and the exile of the Jews. After the Assyrians were beaten at Babylon in 626 B.C. (cf. p. 71), Nabopolassar was officially enthroned on 23 November 626. Gods of Susa which the Assyrians had deposited in Erech were returned to their city, evidence of the independence of Elam. In the war with Assyria, Nabopolassar marched up the Euphrates; Sukhu and Khindanu submitted and towns in the Balikhu area were plundered. East of the Tigris a town in the Arrapkha area was raided and the Assyrians pursued to the Lower Zab. An unsuccessful attack on Asshur was made. In 614 the Medes captured Asshur, Nabopolassar arriving after the city had fallen, and in 612 the Medes and Babylonians together took Nineveh (cf. p. 71). Sinsharishkun, brother of Ashuretililani and the second son of Ashurbanipal to sit on Assyria's throne, perished in the fall of the city.

The Babylonian armies marched several times to the upper Euphrates, reaching Nisibis, and in 610 with the help of the Medes and Scythians they took Haran. The Egyptians had made common cause with dying Assyria, and a combined attempt to recapture the city in 609 failed. Josiah of Judah had been killed as Neco of Egypt was *en route* to the Euphrates in this year (see p. 72). Nabopolassar's expeditions led him to the border of Urartu. The Egyptians had captured Quramati and Kimukhu south of Carchemish, and in 605 the crown prince Nebuchadrezzar defeated the Egyptians at Carchemish, setting fire to the city (cf. Jer. 46. 1–12). He took over Hatti (Syria and Palestine) as far as the Egyptian border, and Jehoiakim submitted.

Nebuchadrezzar's Reign. At the death of Nabopolassar, Nebuchadrezzar (604–561 B.C.) became king. His armies were frequently in Hatti to maintain control and collect tribute. In December 604 he marched against Ashkelon, turning it into a heap of ruins. In 601–600 he marched to Egypt, fighting an inconclusive, fierce battle (cf. Jer. 46. 13 ff.). Jehoiakim, with Egypt's encouragement, revolted, and in December 598 Nebuchadrezzar marched to the 'Hatti-land', and besieged Jerusalem. Jehoiakim had died on 8 December, and Jehoiachin had become king. Jerusalem fell on 16 March 597, and Nebuchadrezzar 'appointed a king of his own choice'—Zedekiah; Jehoiachin and others were exiled to Babylon (see 2 Kgs. 24 and Jer. 52. 28). Tablets found at Babylon dated 595–570 mention captives and skilled workmen from many nations, and include Jehoiachin and his five sons, the sons of Aga king of Ashkelon, and workmen, mariners and musicians from Tyre, Gebal,

Arvad, Elam, Media, Persia, Ionia, Cilicia, and Lydia. Captives from Pirindu and Khume resident in Babylon imply that Nebuchadrezzar had campaigned in Cilicia, perhaps around the time when Media under Cyaxares and Lydia under Alyattes were at war. The Medes and Lydians met at the Halys River in the famous Battle of the Eclipse on 28 May 585, and the Halys was established as the border between the two empires.

When Judah revolted in 589 the Babylonian armies invaded the land. In 588 the siege of Jerusalem began. An Egyptian army which came to Judah's help was defeated. When Jerusalem fell in July 587 or 586, Zedekiah was taken for judgment before Nebuchadrezzar at Riblah in the land of Hamath (2 Kgs. 25. 20–21). Rebellious Tyre underwent a

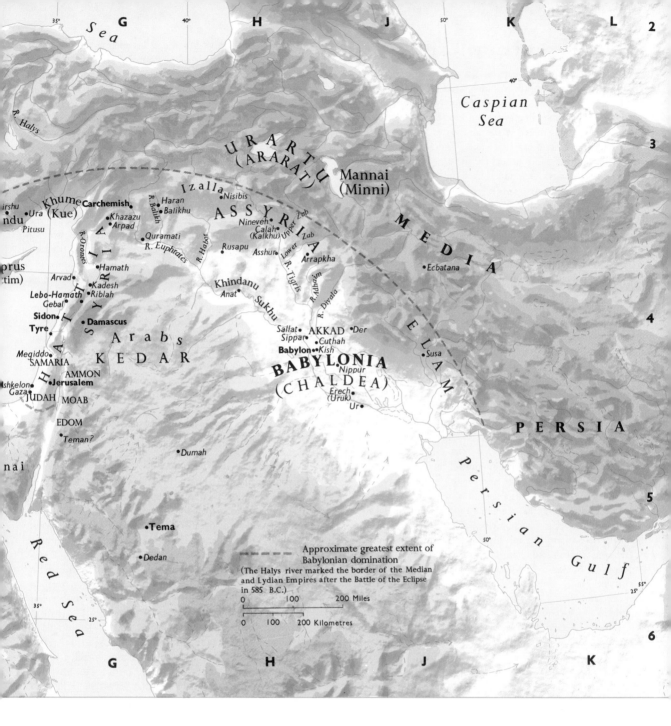

Approximate greatest extent of
Babylonian domination
(The Halys river marked the border of the Median
and Lydian Empires after the Battle of the Eclipse
in 585 B.C.)

0   100   200 Miles

0   100   200 Kilometres

thirteen-year siege, beginning 588–587.

Nebuchadrezzar's Successors. Nebuchadrezzar's son, Evil-merodach (Amel-marduk, 561–559; 2 Kgs. 25. 27–30) was followed by Nergal-sharezer (Neriglissar, Nergal-sharusur, 559–555), who had been present at the siege of Jerusalem (Jer. 39. 3, 13). He restored temples at Babylon and Borsippa (see p. 78), and in 557–6 campaigned against Appuashu of Pirindu, who entered Khume to plunder and take captives. He was pursued to Ura and Kirshu, and the island Pitusu was overrun. Sallune was burned. After the few days' reign of Labashi-marduk, Nabonidus became king of Babylonia (555–539). Of priestly lineage, he and his mother had been taken captive by Nebuchadrezzar at

Haran in 610. King Nabonidus carried on warfare in Syria and Lebanon, and his army was in Khume. Concerned for the caravan routes from South Arabia, he attacked the oasis city of Tema and made it his royal residence. He invested his son Belshazzar with the kingship at Babylon. Meanwhile Cyrus, king of Anshan, became king of the Medes and Persians, conquering Astyages, king of Media, and capturing Ecbatana (550). In an encirclement of Babylonia, he attacked Lydia, and after an indecisive battle at the Halys River, Sardis fell in 546. Northern Mesopotamia was taken and western Arabia invaded. The Babylonian army was defeated at Opis on the Tigris, and Sippar was taken. In October 539 Cyrus' general Gobryas entered Babylon with his troops, and Nabonidus was made prisoner.

Palestine after the Exile

The Return and Restoration. In 538 B.C. the exiles in Babylonia began to return to Judah, after Cyrus had issued a decree (Ezra 1. 2–4; 6. 3–5). Encouraged by Haggai and Zechariah, the rebuilding of the temple began in earnest in 520. Jerusalem's ruined walls and gates remained unrepaired for nearly a century longer. Ezra, returning with another group of exiles in 458 (or 398?), promulgated the law he had brought back and carried out marriage reforms (Ezra 7–10; Neh. 8–9).

In 445 Nehemiah came from Susa to rebuild the walls of Jerusalem (Neh. 1–2). He drew workers from Jerusalem and nearby towns, including Jericho, Tekoa, Gibeon, Mizpah, Zanoah, Beth-haccherem, Beth-zur, and Keilah (Neh. 3). He was opposed by Sanballat, the governor of Samaria, Tobiah of Ammon, the servant (i.e. official), and Geshem the Arab (Neh. 2. 19; 4. 7). Tobiah seems to have been governor of Ammon, ruling over central Transjordan; his family home was at modern 'Araq el-Emir, where there is a rock-cut tomb which has the name 'Tobiah' deeply incised in the rock. Geshem is mentioned on an inscription found at Dedan in Arabia, and his son Qainu calls himself King of Kedar on a silver bowl inscription found at Succoth in Egypt; Geshem apparently ruled with imperial Persian backing over a territory which included the Land of Goshen, Sinai, south Palestine, Edom, and north Arabia. These enemies of Nehemiah tried in vain to lure him out to one of the villages of the plain of Ono (Neh. 6. 1, 2). Among Nehemiah's reforms was prohibition of intermarriage with women of Ashdod, Ammon, and Moab (Neh. 13. 23–31).

Neh. 11. 25–36 contains a list of towns outside Jerusalem settled by the Jews, the people of Judah in Dibon, Jekabzeel, Kiriath-arba, Jeshua, Moladah, Beth-pelet, Hazarshual, Beer-sheba, Ziklag, Meconah, En-rimmon, Zorah, Jarmuth, Zanoah, Adullam, Lachish, and Azekah, and the people of Benjamin in Geba, Michmash, Hazor, Ramah, Gittaim, Hadid, Zeboim, Neballat, Lod, and Ono. In Ezra 2. 2–70 and Neh. 7. 6–73 are parallel lists of returning exiles, perhaps a fifth-century census of the Jewish community, and included are men from Gibeon, Bethlehem, Netophah, Anathoth, Beth-azmaveth (Azmaveth), Kiriath-jearim, Chephirah, Beeroth, Ramah, Geba, Michmash, Bethel, Ai, Nebo, Harim, Jericho, Lod, Hadid, and 'Ono.

The Maccabean Revolt. Alexander the Great (d. 323 B.C.) and his successors fostered the spread of Greek culture (Hellenism). Until the reign of the Seleucid king Antiochus III (the Great) (223–187), the Ptolemies of Egypt controlled Palestine and Phoenicia. The attempt of Antiochus IV (Epiphanes) (175–163) to force Hellenism on the Jews brought about the Maccabean revolt. Antiochus IV wreaked vengeance on Jerusalem, desecrating the temple. On 25 Chislev (December) in 168 (or 167) swine were offered on the altar of Zeus erected over the altar of the Lord. Heathen altars were built in the cities of Judah (1 Macc. 1). The aged priest Mattathias, of the family of Hasmon, refused to sacrifice a pig to Zeus at Modein and fled with his sons to the mountains (1 Macc. 2). After his death (167–166), his son Judas Maccabeus (i.e. Judas the Hammerer) led the rebels. They defeated the enemy under Apollonius and drove Seron and his men at the Ascent of Beth-horon into the land of the Philistines (1 Macc. 3. 1–24). Near Emmaus the king's army was routed and pursued to Gazara and into the plains of Idumea and to Azotus and Jamnia (1 Macc. 3. 38–4. 25). The next year a larger army was defeated at Beth-zur (Beth-sura) (1 Macc. 4. 26–35). The Jews gained a peace treaty and the removal of prohibitions against Jewish religious practices. After cleansing the temple and re-dedicating it on 25 Chislev, 165 (or 164), Judas fortified Jerusalem and Beth-zur (1 Macc. 4. 60 ff.). He defeated the Idumeans at Akrabattene and took Jazer and the neighbouring villages in Ammon (1 Macc. 5. 3–8). With his brother Jonathan he went to the assistance of the persecuted Jews at Dathema in Gilead, while his brother Simon went to the help of the Jews in Galilee and pursued the enemy as far as Ptolemais, taking the Jews of Galilee and Arbatta to Judea (1 Macc. 5. 9–23). Judas and Jonathan took Alema, Chaspho (Casphor), Maked, Bosor and other cities of Gilead. Carnaim and Ephron were subdued. In a campaign against Idumea, Hebron was taken. (1 Macc. 5. 24–68).

After the death of Antiochus, Judas attacked the Syrian garrison in Jerusalem, but was defeated at Beth-zechariah, and Beth-zur surrendered to the enemy (1 Macc. 6. 18–63). The Seleucid king Demetrius I appointed Alcimus as High Priest. Nicanor was sent to quell Judas' opposition, but was slain in the battle of Adasa (1 Macc. 7. 26–50). Later when Demetrius sent an army under Bacchides, Judas fell in the battle at Elasa (near Beth-horon) in 161 (or 160) (1 Macc. 9. 5–22).

The Hasmonean High Priesthood and Kingship. Jonathan now assumed leadership, and he and his followers lived for a while as freebooters in the Wilderness of Tekoa. He was attacked by Bacchides, who fortified Jericho, Emmaus, Beth-horon, Bethel, Timnath, Pharathon, Tephon, Beth-zur, and Gazara (1 Macc. 9. 32–53). Eventually peace was made, Jonathan ruling from Michmash (1 Macc. 9. 70–73). Demetrius I permitted Jonathan to fortify Jerusalem. He received appointment as High Priest (1 Macc. 10. 1–21). In the reign of Demetrius II Jonathan was cast into a dungeon at Ptolemais, and was later killed at Baskama in 145 (or 142?) (1 Macc. 12. 44–48; 13. 23–24).

Simon, Jonathan's brother and successor, fortified Joppa, Beth-zur, and Gazara (1 Macc. 14. 32–34). He drove the enemy from the citadel (the Acra) at Jerusalem. The high priesthood was established in his family (1 Macc. 14. 41–47). He and his two sons were murdered at Dok, but a third son, John Hyrcanus, who was at Gazara, escaped to rule as High Priest and to bring the Jewish state to the height of its power under the Maccabees, ruling from 135 (or 134) to 104 (1 Macc. 16. 11–24). Hyrcanus' son Aristobulus (104–103) was the first Maccabean ruler to assume the kingship. After him ruled Alexander Janneus (103–76), the widow Alexandra (76–67), and Aristobulus II (66–63). In the year 63 Pompey entered Jerusalem and the Romans took control.

Essenes. In the latter half of the second century B.C. the community of Essenes which was to produce the Dead Sea Scrolls was established at Khirbet Qumran and 'Ain Feshkha, where it existed until destroyed by the Romans *c.* A.D. 68. (See map p. 95.)

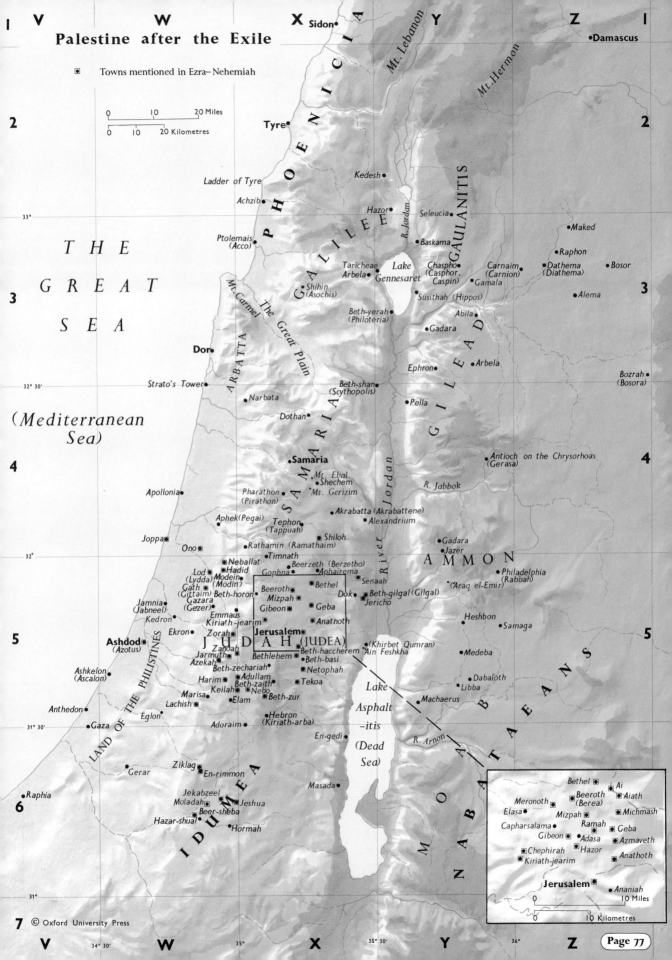

Palestine after the Exile

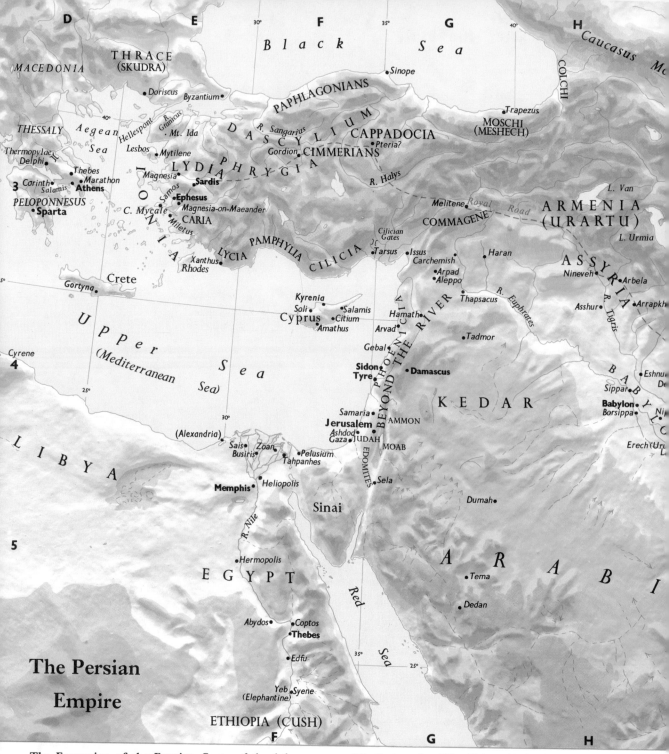

The Persian Empire

The Expansion of the Empire. Cyrus, of the Achaemenid family, brought into being the vast Persian (Achaemenian) Empire, which extended from Sogdiana in the north-east to the Aegean Sea in the west, and included the whole of the former Babylonian Empire. Cyrus issued from Ecbatana the decree freeing the exiled Jews (Ezra 6. 1–5). His son Cambyses (529–521) invaded Egypt, was victorious at Pelusium, took Heliopolis and Memphis by siege, and marched up the Nile. Libya and Cyrene submitted. Aramaic papyri discovered at Elephantine (Yeb), show that Cambyses found there a Jewish military colony.

Darius I (521–485) commemorated victories over his enemies in a huge inscription (in Persian, Elamite, and

Akkadian) on the cliff at Bisitun. Darius built Persepolis as his capital, and subdued western India, which became the satrapy of Hindush. Horsemen in relays along the Royal Road linked communication across the vast stretches of the Persian Empire. In 513 he traversed Thrace and crossed the Danube into Scythia: Thrace and Macedonia submitted to him. Miletus led an Ionian revolt, but was taken and sacked to avenge the burning of Sardis. In 490 a Persian expedition which landed at Marathon was defeated by the Athenians. Xerxes (485–464) made a full-scale invasion of Greece, defeated the Spartans at Thermopylae, and occupied Athens, but met severe defeat in the naval battle of Salamis, and Greece remained free.

Revolts and Downfall. Artaxerxes I (464–423) repulsed revolts in Bactria and Egypt. In his reign Ezra and Nehemiah (Ezra 7, Neh. 2. 1) came to Jerusalem. Darius II (423–404), who followed the forty-five-day reign of Xerxes II, quelled rebellions in Media and Lydia, but Egypt was lost. A letter of his sent in 419 to the Jews of Elephantine, directing the proper celebration of the feast of unleavened bread, is extant. Cyrus, the younger brother of Artaxerxes II (404–358), contested the throne with the help of 13,000 Greek mercenaries, but was defeated at Cunaxa in 401. Xenophon tells the story of the march of the 10,000 Greeks through hostile country, 400 of them reaching the sea at Trapezus. Artaxerxes III (358–337) reconquered Egypt,

lost and regained Phoenicia, and made an alliance with Athens against Philip of Macedon. Darius III (335–330), following Arses (337–335), lost and recaptured Egypt. Alexander 'the Great' of Macedon in 334 crossed the Hellespont, defeated the Persians at the Granicus, forced the surrender of Miletus, and won the crucial battle at Issus in 333. Alexander conquered Phoenicia and Egypt, and on the plain of Gaugamela between Nineveh and Arbela, Darius again lost to him. Alexander went on to Susa and Persepolis, which submitted, and pursued Darius to Ecbatana, Rhagae, and on into Hyrcania, where Darius was slain by his own men.

Jerusalem in Old Testament times

The Site. Modern Jerusalem has vastly outgrown all earlier phases in its physical development, and it is no longer easy to visualize the city of the Old Testament in relation to the present town. We may, however, use the extant medieval Turkish walls as a convenient point of reference. The area of these walls straddles an indented rocky plateau, having a general slope from north to south, and divided into two unequal ridges by a deep re-entrant valley curving up into it from the south. The eastern and western slopes of the plateau are defined by two more deep valleys, the Kidron on the east and the Hinnom on the west, which trace bold convex curves to meet the central valley some few hundred yards to the south of the city. The western ridge is both higher and broader than the eastern; but the lower, eastern ridge overhangs the only strong spring of perennial water, known in ancient times as the Gihon. Both ridges, in their general slope from north to south, are barred by re-entrant gulleys, which form saddles, or define summits, convenient for large-scale building. A second, but less useful, source of water, En-rogel, exists not far below the junction of the valleys.

The City of David. The first walled city, about 1800 B.C., was on the lower, eastern ridge. Here stood the 'stronghold of Zion' (2 Sam. 5. 7), which David captured from the Jebusites. The eastern wall was some two-thirds down the slope, just above the Spring Gihon. On the steep slope, terraces were supported by a series of retaining walls, which held the rock-fill in place and formed artificial platforms. This may be the Millo or 'Filling' of 2 Sam. 5. 9; 1 Kgs. 9. 15, etc.; or the Millo may be a fortified tower defending the gap between the city and the sacred area to the north. A sloping passage, a vertical shaft, and a rock-cut tunnel which brought the waters of Gihon to the foot of the shaft, provided the city with access to water and David's Joab with access to the city (2 Sam. 5. 6–8, RSV). The general line of the northern wall of the city can be traced.

Solomon built the house of the Lord, his own house, the Millo, and the wall of Jerusalem (1 Kgs. 9. 15). He extended the city to encircle the area where the rocky summit is enclosed in the famous Muslim Dome of the Rock which is often presumed to be the site of Solomon's altar. Here was the temple, and perhaps in the same area the royal quarters (1 Kgs. 6, 7). The Solomonic extension of the eastern wall apparently began at the edge of the summit of the ridge where evidence of a casemate wall has been found. The course of the wall is still quite conjectural.

The Monarchy. Under the later kings the population spread beyond the Solomonic City (cf. 2 Kgs. 22. 14). The walls were maintained and greatly extended during the period of the monarchy; Jehoash, king of Israel, demolished a stretch of walling along the north side of the city 'from the Ephraim Gate to the Corner Gate', 400 cubits or about 200 yards (2 Kgs. 14. 13). Uzziah fortified the Corner Gate and Valley Gate with towers, and Jotham 'did much building on the wall of Ophel' (2 Chr. 26. 9; 27. 3). Hezekiah and Manasseh are credited with work on the walls (2 Chr. 32. 5; 33. 14). It was probably Hezekiah who first extended the city to the western hill, where an excavated segment of a wall some 25 ft. thick prompts the suggested reconstruction. It postdates 9th- to 8th-century (royal?) tombs found in the Central Valley, and may be 'the other wall without' of 2 Chr. 32. 5. Hezekiah immensely strengthened Jerusalem by hewing a conduit (tunnel), re-discovered in 1880, to bring water from the Gihon Spring to a reservoir in the Central Valley (2 Kgs. 20. 20), within the walls of the extended city. A second unprotected earlier conduit can be traced from the spring-head, the Upper Pool of Isa. 7. 3, discharging through a short tunnel behind a dam built across the mouth of the Central Valley. This was the Old Pool of Isa. 22. 11, later re-sited or enlarged by Hezekiah into the 'reservoir between the two walls' designed to take the overflow of his new tunnel. Manasseh built an outer line of walling to defend the eastern flank of the city.

After the Exile. By the time of the Maccabees Jerusalem had spread right across the western hill, and according to some reconstructions it spread up the Central Valley to include the area within Wall II on map p. 96. But the newly-discovered Hezekiah wall seems to exclude the larger part of the western hill from the walled area of the pre-exilic city, and it was not rebuilt in the post-exilic period. The present evidence suggests the 'blue' wall here is no earlier than the Maccabean period, and thus Nehemiah's wall will simply have encircled the area of the eastern hill. Nehemiah's wall on the east of Ophel followed the crest of the hill, where remains of it have been found.

The Maccabean (Hellenistic) Period. The Greek king Antiochus Epiphanes (1 Macc. 1. 33) occupied and fortified the city and laid waste the Temple. When the Maccabees counter-attacked, there was a citadel which enabled the Greek garrison to keep a footing in Jerusalem until Simon was strong enough to expel them (1 Macc. 13. 49–50), but its situation is a very vexed question. As a counterpart to the Greek citadel the Maccabees themselves re-fortified the Temple hill, of which the strong point was a castle (Baris) north of the Temple, perhaps the same as the Tower of Hananel mentioned by Jeremiah (31.38). Here John Hyrcanus, as High Priest, took up residence and stored the priestly robes under guard (Josephus, *Antiquities* xviii. 4. 91); and here later Herod the Great was to build the Antonia Tower. Among the achievements of John Hyrcanus was the building of the walls of Jerusalem, reported written in the chronicles of his high-priesthood (1 Macc. 16. 23). By the time of Pompey's victory over Judah in 63 B.C. the south-west hill had been occupied. The location of the southern wall of the Maccabean city is made uncertain by the presence of Maccabean tombs (which must have been outside the city) and by the probability that a wall following a direct line from the lower end of the southwestern end of the city to the southern end of the City of David was first built by Herod Agrippa I (A.D. 41–44). *See further*, p. 97.

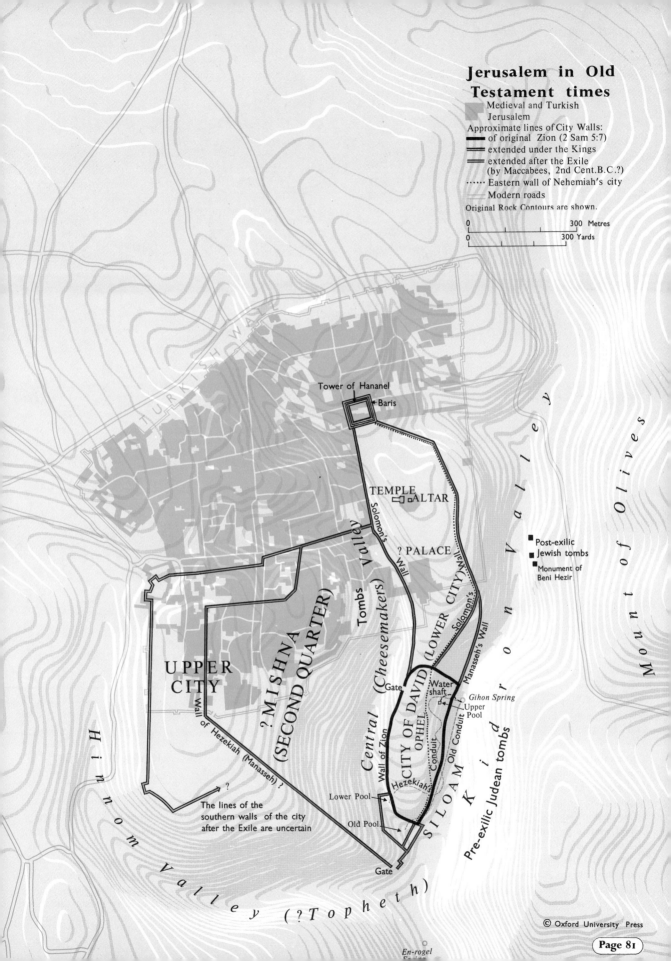

Jerusalem in Old Testament times

Medieval and Turkish Jerusalem
Approximate lines of City Walls:
of original Zion (2 Sam 5:7)
extended under the Kings
extended after the Exile (by Maccabees, 2nd Cent.B.C.?)
Eastern wall of Nehemiah's city
Modern roads
Original Rock Contours are shown.

0   300 Metres
0   300 Yards

TURKISH WALL

Tower of Hananel
←Baris

TEMPLE ALTAR

? PALACE

Post-exilic
Jewish tombs
Monument of
Beni Hezir

Solomon's Wall

Tombs

Central (Cheesemakers)

? MISHNA (SECOND QUARTER)

UPPER CITY

(Gate)

Wall of Zion

CITY OF DAVID
OPHEL
(LOWER CITY)

Solomon's Wall

Manasseh's Wall

Water shaft
Gihon Spring
Upper Pool
Old Conduit
Conduit

Wall of Hezekiah (Manasseh) ?

Hezekiah's

?

The lines of the
southern walls of the city
after the Exile are uncertain

Lower Pool

Old Pool

SILOAM

Kidron Valley

Mount of Olives

Pre-exilic Judean tombs

Gate

Hinnom Valley (?Topheth)

En-rogel

The Hellenistic Period
Ptolemaic & Seleucid Empires

Alexander's Successors. Alexander left in his wake many new or rebuilt cities, including Alexandria near Issus, Alexandria in Egypt, and many Alexandrias in the eastern provinces, all the way to the Jaxartes and the Indus rivers. He died at Babylon (323). From the subsequent confusion and warfare Ptolemy secured Egypt, Cyrene, Cyprus, and Palestine, and the Ptolemaic dominion extended to Lycia, Ionia, and the Aegean. Antigonus held Asia Minor, Lysimachus Thrace, Cassander Macedonia and Greece, and Seleucus Babylonia. After Antigonus' defeat at Ipsus (301), Seleucus secured Syria and was given Palestine, but Ptolemy had gained control of Palestine (called Coele-

syria) and Phoenicia. Seleucus later gained Asia Minor. His capital was at Antioch.

Ptolemaic and Seleucid Conflicts. After the death of Seleucus I (305–280) a long series of wars began between the Ptolemies and Seleucids. Antiochus II (261–247) drove the Egyptians out of Ionia, Cilicia, and Pamphylia, and took all Phoenicia north of Sidon. In 252 Antiochus II married Berenice, daughter of Ptolemy II (285–246), but Ptolemy III (246–221) went to war when Seleucus II (247–226), son of Laodice, became king; Berenice and her infant son were murdered. The Bactria-Sogdiana satrapy and Parthia

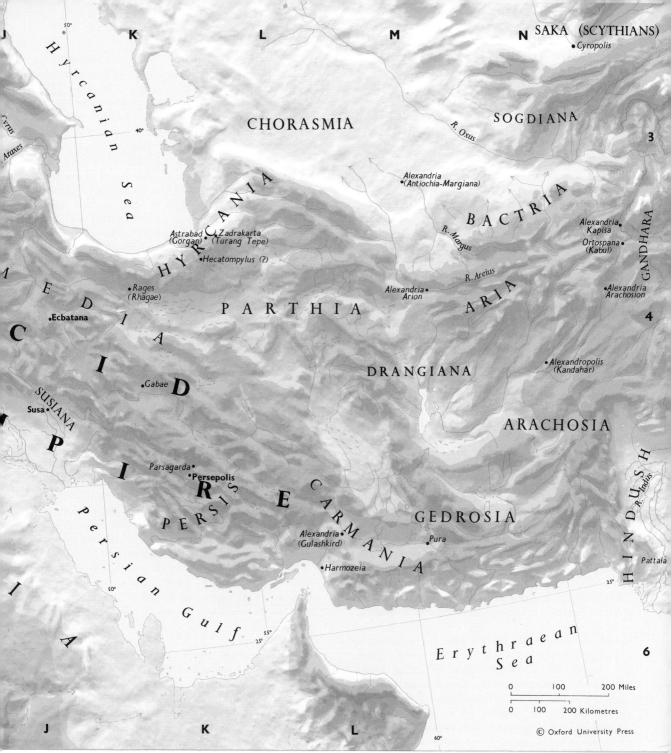

became independent. The Parthian kingdom was established in 247 B.C.

Seleucus III (226–223) was followed by Antiochus III (the Great; 223–187). After victories in Palestine and Transjordan, Antiochus III was defeated by Ptolemy IV (221–203) at Raphia in 217, but Antiochus was victorious at Gaza (200) and Paneas (199), and Palestine now belonged to the Seleucids. Antiochus was defeated by Rome at Magnesia (190), and so lost Asia Minor. His son Seleucus IV (187–175) was followed by Antiochus IV (175–163; see p. 76), called Antiochus Epiphanes, who became the arch-persecutor of the Jews and their faith. He had resided at Rome,

and he usurped the throne with the help of the king of Pergamum (see Dan. 11. 21). In his first campaign in Egypt (170/69) he captured Pelusium and reached as far as Memphis. In 168 he entered Memphis again, but in a suburb of Alexandria was ordered out of Egypt by a Roman legate. The Ptolemaic and Seleucid rivalries are noted in Dan. 11. The last strong ruler of the Seleucid dynasty was Antiochus VII (139/8–129). Simon (the Maccabee) was the first Hasmonean ruler free of Seleucid domination, and was recognized by the Romans and Spartans.

Palestine under the Herods

(c.40 B.C. to A.D. 6)

(For the period after A.D. 6, also dealt with in this text, see the map on pp. 86–87)

Herod the Great. In 63 B.C. the Roman general, Pompey, entered Jerusalem as conqueror, ending the rule of the Hasmonean dynasty (see pp. 76, 83). For his services to the Romans, Antipater, an Idumean, was made ruler of Galilee, and his sons Herod and Phasael wielded power. After a period of strife, and the deaths of Antipater and Phasael, Herod was recognized by the Romans in 40 B.C., and confirmed in 30 B.C. as king of the Jews, ruling over the whole of Jewish territory including Judea, Samaria and Galilee, together with the district east of the Jordan called Perea (from the Greek word for 'beyond') and lands east and north-east of Galilee (Auranitis, Trachonitis, Batanaea, etc.). It was bounded on the north by the Province of Syria (under the rule of a Roman governor) and on the south and south-east by the Nabataean Kingdom (capital, Petra, see p. 89). To the east and north-east lay the Decapolis, a league of self-governing cities; most of these, e.g., Scythopolis, Pella, and Philadelphia, were outside Herod's kingdom; the free city of Ascalon, and for a certain period Gaza and Joppa, were also excepted. Before the death of Herod (which occurred in 4 B.C.) Jesus was born in Bethlehem (Matt. 2. 1). Of non-Jewish descent, Herod was a Jew by religion but went as far as a Jew could in aligning himself with the power of Rome and the ways of the pagan world: he was responsible for many large public works in the Greco-Roman style such as a harbour at Caesarea (the former Strato's Tower, which was developed as a port), and public buildings at Jerusalem and Samaria; the latter he re-named Sebaste after Caesar Augustus (Greek 'Sebastos').

Herod's Successors. On Herod's death his kingdom was divided between three of his sons: Archelaus received Judea and Samaria, Herod Antipas Galilee and Perea, Philip Ituraea and Trachonitis (cf. Luke 3. 1). The last two took capitals which they named, in honour of Rome, respectively Tiberias (for Tiberius, emperor A.D. 14–37) and Caesarea Philippi. Archelaus reigned in Jerusalem (Matt. 2. 22) until A.D. 6, when he was deposed, and Judea (with Samaria) placed under the rule of a Roman governor, an official responsible to the emperor; the holder of this office A.D. 26–36 was Pontius Pilate. The governor was supported by Roman troops and had his headquarters at Caesarea, but there was a praetorium or Roman headquarters also in Jerusalem (see Mark 15. 16 and p. 97).

The Ministry of Jesus. Nazareth, where Jesus was brought up and lived till about the age of thirty, was a very humble village, unmentioned in the Old Testament or Jewish literature. The first three Gospels describe his activity in Galilee, centred particularly on Capernaum (Mark 2. 1), and also journeys into 'the region of Tyre and Sidon' (Mark 7. 24) and across the Sea of Galilee to the territory of certain cities of the Decapolis ('Gerasa' in some texts, 'Gadara' and 'Gergesa' in others; see Mark 5. 1, Matt. 8. 28, Luke 8. 26, and margins). Hearers flocked to him also from Perea, from Judea and Jerusalem, and even from Idumea in the south (Mark 3. 7). St. John's Gospel adds information about the visits of Jesus to Jerusalem and Judea, where he was baptized by John the Baptist and called his first disciples, talked with Nicodemus, and taught in the Temple. Sometimes he passed 'through Samaria' (John 4. 4) but on his last journey south he seems to have skirted Samaria (Luke 17. 11) and passed through Perea, recrossing the Jordan to pass through Jericho (Luke 19. 1) and so to Jerusalem where he was betrayed, crucified and buried. It was in and near Jerusalem that the risen Jesus was seen by Mary Magdalene (John 20. 14), by the two disciples walking to Emmaus (Luke 24. 13–32) and by the assembled disciples (Luke 24. 33–49), and that the Ascension took place; but, as he had promised (Mark 14. 28; 16. 7), Jesus also appeared in Galilee, linking the Resurrection appearances with the scenes of his ministry (John 21, Matt. 28. 16–20).

The Surroundings of the Ministry. Apart from Jerusalem, the places associated with Jesus in the Gospels were not important in the secular geography of Palestine. Cities such as Sepphoris, the most important town of Galilee, only four miles from Nazareth, or Tiberias, which gave its name to the Sea of Galilee (John 6. 1), play no part in the Gospel story, nor does Caesarea, the capital of Roman Palestine, nor Samaria-Sebaste (the Gospels mention only Samaria as a district). Jesus probably avoided such places because of their non-Jewish character (compare Matt. 15. 24): yet all around him and the disciples was their vigorous life with their Hellenistic and pagan ways, typical not of Judaism but of the wider east-Mediterranean world of the time. The life and teaching of Jesus, so closely linked in faith and thought with the Jewish religion and the Old Testament Scriptures, were set geographically in close relation with the great gentile world.

Palestine and the Early Church. The mission of the apostles and of the earliest church was centred, not on Galilee, but on Jerusalem (the scene of the Crucifixion and Resurrection) and reached outward to 'all Judea and Samaria and to the end of the earth' (Acts 1. 8). Rejected by the Jerusalem leaders, Christian teachers, including Apostles, went to Samaria (Acts 8. 4–5, 14) and the coastal cities from Gaza and Azotus to Caesarea (Acts 8. 26–40): the Christian 'Way' spread to Lydda and Joppa (Acts 9. 32, 36) and to Damascus (Acts 9. 2). These were the beginnings of an expansion which was to carry Christianity far beyond the borders of Palestine (see pp. 88/89); yet, till A.D. 70 at least, Jerusalem and the church in Judea retained a unique position, as is shown both in Acts (11. 1; 15. 1–6; 20. 16; 21. 15 ff.) and Epistles (1 Cor. 16. 3, 1 Thess. 2. 14, etc.). In A.D. 66 the fiercely-fought revolt of the Jews against Rome broke out, ending with the siege of Jerusalem and its capture and destruction in A.D. 70. In the former Herodian fortress of Masada (see illus. p. 42), members of the Jewish resistance against the Romans made a desperate last stand (A.D. 73).

Palestine under the Herods

- ▪▪▪ Boundary of Herod's kingdom at its greatest extent
- – – – Divisions, A.D. 6-37
- ▪ Fortresses

0   10   20 Miles
0   10   20 Kilometres

I · V · W · X Sidon• **Y · Z · I**

33° 30'

Damascus• (a city of the Decapolis)

Sarepta•

PROVINCE OF SYRIA

ITURAEA · ABILENE

•Bathyra?

Tyre

Paneas• (Caesarea Philippi)

R. Leontes

TRACHONITIS

33°

Ullatha

BATANAEA

Ptolemais•

GAULANITIS

•Raphana (a city of the Decapolis)

Chorazin•
Capernaum•
Gennesaret•
Taricheae• (Magadan)
Sea of Galilee

Bethsaida-Julias•

R. Jordan

GALILEE

Mt. Carmel
Sepphoris•

•Gamala

AURANITIS

Gabae• (Hippeum)
•Nazareth

Hippos•

•Dion?

The Great Plain

Yarmuk
Wadi• Gadara
Abila•

Dora•

HEROD

32° 30'

Caesarea• (Strato's Tower)

Scythopolis•

•Pella

Plain of Sharon

DECAPOLIS

OF

Sebaste• (Samaria)

•Amathus

•Gerasa

Neapolis•
•Mt. Ebal
•Mt. Gerizim

MARE INTERNUM (Mediterranean Sea)

SAMARIA

R. Jabbok

Apollonia Sozusa•

Alexandrium▪

Antipatris•

32°

Joppa•

Phasaelis•

•Gadara

PEREA

River Jordan

Thamna•

KINGDOM

Lydda•
Gophna•

Archelais•

Philadelphia• (Rabbah)

Jamnia•

Emmaus• (Nicopolis)

Jericho•
Cyprus▪

Betharamphtha•

Gazara•

Jerusalem•
•Bethany

Azotus•

JUDEA

Hyrcania▪

•Medeba

Bethlehem•

(Kh. Qumran: settlement of Dead Sea sect)

Ascalon• (Free city)

Herodium▪

Betogabri•
∴ Marisa

Wilderness of Judea

Callirrhoe•

Agrippias• (Anthedon)

•Hebron

Lake Asphaltitis

Machaerus▪

•Gaza

Adora•

31° 30'

IDUMEA

Engaddi• (En-gedi)

R. Arnon

(Dead Sea)

•Raphia

Masada▪

KINGDOM

Bersabe• (Beersheba)
•Malatha

31°

•Mampsis

NABATAEAN KINGDOM

© Oxford University Press

Page 85

7 · V · W · X · Y · Z · I
34° 30'   35°   35° 30'   36°

Palestine in New Testament times

A.D. 6-70

- - - - - Political boundaries A.D. '6-34

JUDEA, etc., Political units

- ● Places mentioned in the New Testament
- ▲ Cities of the Decapolis
- ▲ Cities of the Decapolis mentioned in the New Testament
- ■ Fortresses

10 Miles

10 Kilometres

Tyre

PHOENICIA

PROVINCE OF SYRIA

Caesarea Philippi (Paneas)

TETRARCHY OF PHILIP

AURANITIS

GAULANITIS

Ulatha

Abelane

Daphne

L. Semechonitis (Lake Huleh)

Thella

Seleucia

Sogane

R. Jordan

Bethsaida-Julias

Chorazin

Capar Canaeoi

Cadasa

Gischala

Jamneith

Sepph

Meroth

Achcabare

Capernaum

Ginnesar (Gennesaret)

Sea of Galilee

Gamala

Dion?

Abila

DECAPOLIS

Capitolias

Arbela

Gerasa

Hippos (Susithah)

Gergesa ?

Taricheae (Magadan, Dalmanutha)

Yarmuk

Emmatha

Gadara

GALILEE

Baca

Bersabe

Saab

Selame

Chabulon

Sogane

Jotapata

Cana

Rumah

Garis

Arbela

Bethmaus

Tiberias

Ammathus

Sennabris

Beth-yerah (Philoteria) Wadi

Pella

Scythopolis

Salim

Aenon

Herod

Brook Cherith

Asochis

Besara

Sepphoris

Nazareth

Japha

Sigoph

Dabaritta(Dabira)

Itabyrium (Tabor)

Exaloth

Nain

Agrippina

V. of Jezreel

Mt. Gilboa

Ginae

Bemeselis

Gabae (Hippeum)

Simonias

The R. Kishon

The Great Plain (Esdraelon)

Narbata

Gitta

Yishub

Sebaste (Samaria)

SAMARIA

Ladder of Tyre

Ecdippa (Achzib)

Ptolemais

Mt. Carmel

Gabata

Plain of Sharon

Sycaminum

Bucolon Polis

Dora (Dor)

Crocodilon Polis

Caesarea

MEDITERRANEAN

SEA

Tetrarchy of

Galilee

I S
I S

Philadelphia ▲
(Rabbah)

P E R E
A

Antipas)

•Zia
•Gadara

•Betharamphtha
(Livias Julias)

•Esbus

•Medeba (Madaba)

N A B A T A E A N   K I N G D O M

•Areopolis
(Rabbathmoab)

R. Nahaliel
•Callirrhoe

Machaerus ▪

R. Arnon

R. Jordan
•Coreae
•Alexandrium

•Phasaelis
•Archelais

Jericho
Taurus•
Cyprus•

(Kh. Qumran:
settlement of
Dead Sea sect)

Lake

Asphaltitis

(Dead Sea)

Judea

of

Hyrcania ▪
Kidron

Wilderness

W. Murabba'at

Engaddi
(En-gedi)

•Masada ▪

•Acrabbein
Mahnayim•
•Anathu Borceaus

Selo (Shiloh)•

Mt. Gerizim
•Pharaton
•Arus

•Tephon

•Thamna (Timnath)
•Ilon

Berzetho
•Gophna
Ephraim
(Aphairema)
•Bethel
•Berea   •Aialon?

Adasa•
•Capharsalama
Anathoth•
Bethphage•
Mt. Scopus   •Bethany
Gabath Saul•
Gabaon•   Amasa
Colonia Amasa
(Emmaus?)

Bethlehem•
•Beth-bassi
•Etam   Herodium▪

Thecoa
(Thekoa)

Terebinthus (Mamre)•

•Aristobulias

I D U M E A

•Capparetaea
•Capparsaba

Tower of
Aphek

Rathamin
(Arimathea?)
•Adida
•Modein

Pl a i n

Gazara•

Cariathiareim•

Bethletepha•
•Beth-zechariah
•Capharabis
Gemmaruris•

Betogabri•

Bethsura
(Beth-zur)•
•Alulos

Capharsaba•

Caphartobas•
•Adora

•?Caparorsa

Mampsis
Malatha▪

31° 01′ N

Lydda•

Accaron
(Ekron)•
Kedron•

Jamnia
R. Belus   (Kedron)

(Wadi Qubeiba)

Joppa

Apollonia•
Sozusa•

Brook Antipatris•
(Pegai)

R. Kanah

Adasa•
Sappho•
Lower Beth-horon
Upper Beth-horon

Emmaus•
(Nicopolis)

U   **Jerusalem**

U D E A

J

D

(under

Roman

administrat

•Bersabe
(Beersheba)

I D U M E A

W

X

To Province of Syria

Ascalon•(Free city)

Maiumas Ascalon
(Baths of Ascalon)

Agrippias
(Anthedon)

Gaza•

Brook Besor

Iamnitarum Portus•
(Jamnia Harbour)

•Azotus

5Azotus Paralius•
(Azotus-on-Sea)

© Oxford University Press

5

6

32°

32°

36°

31° 30′

35° 30′

35° 30′

35

34° 30′

34° 30′

The Background of the New Testament

Rome and the East

The Roman Empire. According to Luke 2. 1 Augustus Caesar ruled 'the whole *oikumenē*' (inhabited world). Caesar Octavianus, who put an end to the civil wars and brought the Roman and Hellenistic worlds welcome peace by the victory of Actium in 31 B.C., was declared 'Augustus' in 27 B.C. and lived till A.D. 14. His successors Tiberius, Gaius (Caligula), Claudius, and Nero, ruled till 69 over an area roughly bounded by the Atlantic, Britain (invaded A.D. 43), the Rhine, Danube, and Euphrates, and the Arabian and Sahara deserts. Apart from the war of the Jewish revolt against Rome (66–70), brief civil wars in 69, and certain frontier wars, the whole area was at peace throughout this period, permitting unrestricted travel; and as far west as Rome, and even in southern Gaul, Greek was widely spoken. Provinces were governed by proconsuls or legates, responsible to the Senate in peaceful areas (e.g. Gallio in Achaia, Acts 18. 12) or to the emperor personally in military and frontier provinces like Syria (Luke 2. 2). Client kingdoms, under native kings appointed and controlled by Rome, were used in backward and difficult areas not considered ripe for provincial status; such were the kingdoms of Herod the Great and Herod Agrippa II (a largely gentile area under a Jewish king: see p. 91) and the 'Kingdom of Antiochus' in Commagene and Cilicia Trachea. The eastern frontier was garrisoned against the nations beyond, especially the Parthians, who had destroyed a Roman army at Carrhae in 53 B.C., but throughout the New Testament period the Syrian frontier was quiet, so that, for example, Jews and others from Parthia, Media, Elam (Elymais), and Mesopotamia, as well as Roman provinces in Asia Minor and north Africa, could all be found at Jerusalem (Acts 2. 9–11).

The First Expansion of the Church recorded in Acts 2–11, under the leadership of Peter and others (see p. 90), reached as far as Antioch (Acts 11. 19), the chief city of the province of Syria. This was an important base for further expansion. Eastward lay Edessa and Mesopotamia (including Babylon where there was a large Jewish colony). The New Testament records (in Greek) the very important spread of Christianity through Greek-speaking provinces of the Empire to Rome; but there was also an expansion in Syria and eastward among those who spoke Syriac: Syriac-speaking Christianity centred on Edessa.

Paul was born of Jewish parents (his father being a Roman citizen) at Tarsus, a Greek-speaking city, was trained under the Rabbi Gamaliel at Jerusalem, and converted near Damascus (where there were already Christians). After a retreat to 'Arabia' (Gal. 1. 17) and a visit to the Apostles at Jerusalem, he went to his home province of Syria-Cilicia. (Gal. 1. 18–20.) Brought from Tarsus to Antioch by Barnabas (Acts 11. 25, 26), he began his great series of missionary journeys northwards and westwards, by which he 'fully preached the Gospel of Christ' 'from Jerusalem and

as far round as Illyricum' (Rom. 15. 19): Acts and other epistles give many details of this activity as it concerned the provinces of Cyprus, Galatia, Asia, Thrace, Macedonia, and Achaia (see pp. 90–91). Throughout, Paul kept in touch with the mother church at Jerusalem, but after his visit there in A.D. 57, he intended to extend his activity to Rome and to Spain (Rom. 15. 28).

In Jerusalem, owing to Jewish hostility, Paul was arrested; he spent two years at Caesarea, and then, having appealed to Caesar, was taken under a Roman escort by sea, via Myra in Lycia (Acts 27. 5), along the south coast of Crete, and towards Italy; shipwrecked at Malta, he continued, still as prisoner, by sea via Syracuse to Puteoli and thence to Rome (Acts 28. 14), where he remained two years under house-arrest. The sequel is not known but he may have been

released (see p. 90) and resumed his missionary work.

In Rome when Paul arrived, there was already a strong church, to which he had written his epistle. Its existence shows how Christianity had expanded, in ways not mentioned in Acts, by the agency of other apostles (cf. 1 Cor. 9. 5, Rom. 15. 20) and by the private migrations of individuals. Thus the expulsion of the Jews from Rome (Acts 18. 2) by Claudius (A.D. 41–54) is said by Suetonius to have been due to disturbances caused by 'one Chrestus': this may indicate that Christianity was already causing divisions among the Jewish community. Aquila and Priscilla, natives of Pontus, expelled from Rome at this time, came to Corinth (Acts 18. 2). All tradition, and early writings outside the New Testament, point to Peter as the co-founder with

Paul of the church in Rome. 'Babylon' from which 1 Peter was written (1 Pet. 5. 13) probably means Rome (the heathen, conquering city). Paul's two-year activity in Rome (Acts 28. 30–31) must have strengthened the church there. In A.D. 64 Christians were numerous enough in Rome for Nero (54–68) to fix on them the responsibility for the disastrous fire in that year, and, although widely believed to be innocent, many were put to death by his orders, including, according to reliable tradition, Peter and Paul. The church in Rome continued as the chief centre of Christianity in the West: St. Mark's gospel was almost certainly written there, and possibly also Hebrews. Christians from Italy (Heb. 13. 24) doubtless spread the faith on their travels, but details are unknown. In 2 Tim. 4. 10 there may be a reference to Gaul ('Gallia', also called 'Galatia' in Greek).

The Cradle of Christianity

The Eastern Mediterranean

The Area shown on this map was especially important in the growth of the Church in New Testament times.

Palestine and Syria. Christianity was carried from Jerusalem to Phoenicia, Cyprus, and Antioch (Acts 11. 19). From Antioch, capital of the province of Syria-Cilicia and a cosmopolitan city, the Pauline mission to the gentiles began. In Judea the persecution of Herod Agrippa I (king 41–44) was brief; Paul showed great respect for the church of Judea and Jerusalem; but the Jewish Revolt and war with Rome (66–70) leading to the sack of Jerusalem (70) and flight of the Christians to Pella, ended the importance of Jewish Christianity.

Asia Minor and the Aegean. These Greek-speaking countries, predominantly gentile but with Jewish colonies and synagogues in many cities, were the area of St. Paul's missionary journeys (*see insets*):

(1) From Antioch (Acts 13. 1) with Barnabas to Salamis in Cyprus, overland to Paphos, and then by sea to Perga in Pamphylia, thence inland to Antioch in Pisidia, Iconium, Lystra, and Derbe, and back through the same cities to Attalia, thence by sea to Syrian Antioch. The churches of Pisidian Antioch, etc., thus founded in southern Galatia, are probably those addressed in the Epistle to the Galatians.

(2) From Antioch (Acts 15. 35, 36) with Silas, overland to Derbe and Lystra (home of Timothy, who joined Paul here) through 'Galatian Phrygia' ('the region of Phrygia and Galatia', Acts 16. 6), then northwards as far as 'opposite Mysia', and to the coast at Troas, and thence, in response to a vision, to Macedonia, where the churches of Philippi and Thessalonica were founded, and to Beroea. Paul went via Athens to Corinth (18. 1), where, joined by the others, he stayed eighteen months, founding the local church. He sailed to Palestine, visited Jerusalem, and returned to Antioch (18. 22).

(3) From Antioch again through Galatian Phrygia (18. 23, the same area as 16. 6) and 'the upper country' to Ephesus. Here Paul spent two-and-a-quarter years (1 Cor. 16. 8, Acts 19. 8–10) and founded this important church; from it Christianity spread to Colossae (Col. 1. 1–2, the home also of Philemon) and Laodicea (Col. 4. 16) and to the hinterland generally. At Ephesus Paul kept in touch, by messengers (1 Cor. 1. 11, 2 Cor. 7. 6) and at least one personal visit (2 Cor. 1. 23–2. 1), with Corinth. He then travelled through Macedonia to Achaia where he spent three months, returned to Philippi, and sailed with the delegates of the churches for Jerusalem. At Miletus he called the elders of the Ephesian church to him, and took his farewell of them. At Jerusalem Jewish hostility resulted in Paul's arrest and removal to Rome (see pp. 88–89). According to tradition, he was released from his first Roman imprisonment, and so made further journeys in this area, visiting again Troas, Miletus, and Corinth (2 Tim. 4. 13, 20), leaving Titus in Crete (Tit. 1. 5) and intending to spend a winter at Nicopolis (Tit. 3. 12).

Churches in Bithynia, Pontus, and Cappadocia are addressed in 1 Pet. 1. 1. About A.D. 112 Pliny, the governor of Bithynia, found many Christians there, some converted over twenty years before. Under Domitian (81–96) John was banished to Patmos and wrote his letters to the Seven Churches of Asia (Rev. 1–3). Ephesus was the centre of activity of the apostle John and the Epistles of John were written to churches in the neighbourhood.

Alexandria was the home of Paul's helper Apollos (Acts 18. 24 ff.): the church there probably originated in New Testament times; but by what means is unknown.

Euxine Sea (Pontus Euxinus)

Mesembria

Sinope

Amastris · Amisus

Heraclea

PONTUS
BITHYNIA AND

PAPHLAGONIA

GALATIAN

Side

Bosphorus

Doriscus · Egnatian Way

Byzantium · Calchedon
Nicomedia · Claudiopolis
Nicaea
Prusa

Propontis

Gangra

Amasea
Comana
Pontica

R. Sangarius

Ancyra

Tavium

PONTUS

abros · Abydos
espont · (Alexandria)Troas
lesbos · Adramyttium
tilene

MYSIA

Dorylaeum

Gordium

Pessinus

GALATIA

R. Halys

Caesarea (Mazaca)

os

★ Pergamum

Cotiaeum

★ Thyatira

Appia

Amorium

Archelais

CAPPADOCIA

3

R. Hermus
Smyrna · ★ Sardis
★ Philadelphia

PHRYGIA

Antioch
Galatian
PHRYGIA

LYCAONIA

Comana
Cappadociae

Samos
Trogyllium

Hierapolis
Laodicea
Magnesia · Colossae
R. Maeander

Apamea

Iconium

Lystra

Mts.
R. Saros

R. Pyramos
Germanicea

COMMA-
GENE

Patmos
Didyma

Miletus

ICARIA

PISIDIA

Derbe

Cilician
Gates

CILICIA

R. Orontes

Halicarnassus

Tarsus · Issus

Cnidus

Rhodes

LYCIA

Xanthus

PAMPHYLIA
Perga
Attalia

KINGDOM OF
ANTIOCHUS

Taurus

Soli

Alexandria

AND SYRIA

Rhodes
Patara · Myra

CILICIA
TRACHEA

Seleucia
(Free city)

Seleucia
Pieria

Antioch

r r a n e a n   S e a

I n t e r n u m)

CYPRUS

Salamis

Citium

Laodicea

Apamea

Epiphania

Paphos

Emesa

Tripolis

To Herod
Agrippa II

PHOENICIA

Arca

Heliopolis

4

Berytus

Chalcis

Abilene

Sidon

Damascus

Tyre

Caesarea
Philippi

Kingdom of
Herod Agrippa
II

Ptolemais

Tiberias
Gadara
Scythopolis

Decapolis

Bostra

Caesarea
Sebaste
(Samaria)
R. Jordan
Joppa

Pella
Gerasa

Philadelphia

Judea

Jericho
Jerusalem

To Herod
Agrippa II

Insets (Paul's Journeys):

Paul's 1st Journey — Antioch, Iconium, Lystra, Derbe, Attalia, Perga, Paphos, Salamis, Antioch

Paul's 2nd Journey — Beroea, Thessalonica, Philippi, Neapolis, Troas, Athens, Cenchreae, Corinth, Ephesus, Antioch, Iconium, Lystra, Derbe, Antioch, Caesarea

Paul's 3rd Journey — Philippi, Troas, Assos, Mitylene, Chios, Corinth, Samos, Ephesus, Miletus, Cos, Rhodes, Patara, Antioch, Tyre, Ptolemais, Caesarea, Jerusalem

Boundaries of Provinces of
Roman Empire A.D. 65

ASIA, etc.   Roman Provinces

★   "Seven Churches" of Asia
(Rev. 1-3)

Selected Roman routes

0 · 50 · 100 Miles
0 · 50 · 100 Kilometres

30°

Canopus
Alexandria
Sais
Naucratis

Gaza

Raphia

Pelusium

NABATAEAN KINGDOM

© Oxford University Press

E G Y P T   F

The Near East
Archaeological Sites

The Ancient World. This map shows the principal sites in western Asia at which ancient remains excavated by archaeologists, or studied above the ground, have contributed to a knowledge of antiquity or have helped in particular to illuminate the background of the Bible. The map covers a wider field than the Bible narratives alone might be thought to require. But that is for a good reason. The Bible relates the story of people who did not live in a vacuum, but moved on a broad and well-populated stage. The ancient world, for all the difficulties and dangers of travel, was never divided by absolute frontiers; nor was its history in time so divided. Dynasties rose and fell; cities were built, grew in size and fame, dwindled, or were destroyed, but always succeeding generations inherited something from the past, and contemporaries knew something of their neighbours. The explorer of antiquity must therefore recognize the continuity of events both in space and in time; and the biblical student must extend his interest beyond the geographical and temporal limits of Israel's particular story.

The places shown on this map cover all periods of known human existence, from the hearths of stone-age man to the castles of the Crusades—but only where digging has taken place. It is therefore an archaeological not an historical map.

The Beginnings of Civilization. While there are earlier settlements of 'incipient agriculturalists', as at the Mesolithic hamlet of circular huts at Einan (map p. 94), the beginnings of town life, or civilization (as it is usually called) are best recognizable at the very early stage of culture known as the Neolithic, in that remarkable oasis, 600 feet below sea level, where some thousands of years later stood the ill-fated city of Jericho. Here 9,000 years ago or more, beside a copious perennial spring, a community of early food-growers built the first walled settlement known to history. Irrigation was the secret of their success. It enabled them in the balmy winters and burning summers of the valley to produce in abundance, and near to their own hearths, food for themselves and their animals at a time when most of their contemporaries were still forced to move periodically in search of a living. The early inhabitants of Jericho learnt also to collaborate in the discipline of citizenship: they built houses, lived together beside their spring, and shared the labour of building a wall round their settlement. They were thus among the pioneers of a revolution which turned stone-age man from a hunter, parasitic on wild nature, to a producer, taming it.

Some 4,000 years later in the Nile and Euphrates valleys another revolution occurred, also based on irrigation. In each of these fertile areas inexhaustible supplies of water offered rich rewards to any group of people capable of collaborating to exploit them. Here for the first time in history, about 3000 B.C., men submitted themselves and their labour to centralized political powers, recognizing in them the permanent authority and sanction of divinity. These were the first dynastic rulers, the first organizers of society on a big scale; and their ascendancy was a social

revolution. It was associated with another: writing. Men submitting to central organization like to get fair shares; fair shares depend on proving services rendered; and writing was a device for recording things said and done, and so placing the measure of service and reward beyond dispute. It was an essential instrument of civilization.

The Bronze Age. From the discovery of writing, shortly before 3000 B.C., city life evolved with accumulating technical knowledge, interrupted by intervals of depopulation and decline. The pattern recurs with marked consistency in Persia, Mesopotamia, Anatolia, Syria and Egypt. Thus it is possible to speak in broad terms of a 'Bronze Age' extending from about 3100 B.C. to 1200 B.C., which roughly applies to all those regions. It was broken by two periods of recession, about 2100 and 1550 B.C., into three phases, called

Early, Middle, and Late Bronze Age. The Early Bronze Age saw the great pyramids built in Egypt, and the Sumerian civilization flourishing in Iraq, which in modern times became famous when the royal tombs were discovered at Ur. The Middle Bronze Age was that of the lawgiver Hammurabi, of the earliest Hittite rulers in Anatolia, Indo-Europeans by speech, and of a brilliant and enigmatic culture in Crete. It was within this time that the Hebrew patriarchs were raising humble sheep on the desert fringes of Canaan. The Late Bronze Age was dominated in Egypt by the warrior Pharaohs of the Eighteenth Dynasty, of whom Tutankhamun, of recent fame, was one of the least. In Anatolia, a great Hittite empire rose and fell; in Mesopotamia the Hurrian Mitannians, also ruled by Indo-Europeans, built another powerful state. It was an age of commerce, widespread literacy, and polished craftsmanship.

Amongst the sea-faring peoples who thronged the coastlands and islands appeared the first known Greek-speaking adventurers and colonists, the Achaeans.

The Iron Age. For the Greeks history began with the siege of Troy. The sack of that city on the north-west coast of Anatolia was but one episode in a cataclysm which throughout western Asia brought the Bronze Age to a sudden end. New populations then occupied many of the ancient cities, the Israelites amongst them. Thereafter for biblical students the scene contracts; and the story of Israel is enacted on the narrower stage represented by the map on p. 94–95 (see also p. 98). Blurred and uncertain at first, the narrative acquires precision with the foundation of David's monarchy, about 1000 B.C. It was the renewal of settled and politically organized life, from 1200 B.C., known as the Iron Age.

Palestine
Archaeological sites
(excavated or partly
excavated, 1973)

T. Tell (Arabic),Tel (Hebrew): mound; city site
Kh. Khirbet (Arabic): ruin
W. Wadi: watercourse

Biblical names when known are given first and
Arabic names are then bracketed.
Hebrew names, when given, follow the Arabic name.

Miles
Kilometres

W   **X**   **Y**   **Z**

Tyre
(es-Sur)

Zarephath
Sarepta,
(Sarafand)

33° 33' N
Sidon (Saida)

•Dan
(T. el-Qadi,
T. Dan)

T. et-Taba'iq

•el-Basseh

Achzib
(ez-Zib, T. Akhziv)

Nahariyeh

•Qal'at el-Qurein

Tarshiha

Suhmata

•Yiron
(Yarun)

•Kedesh
(T. Qades)

Einan•

•Kafr Bir'im
el-Jish
(Gischala)

•Kh. en-Nabratein

Merom (Meirun)

Hazor (T. el-Qedah, T. Hazor)

T. es-Sumeiriyeh

el-Buqei'a•

•Kh. et-Tuleil Kh. Shema'

•Chorazin (Kh. Kerazeh)

•Capernaum (Talhum)

Chinnereth
(T. el-'Ureimeh)
prehistoric caves

Kh. el-Minya•

Acco
(T. el-Fukhkhar)

Achshaph•
(T. Keisan)

•Cabul (Kabul)

Arbela (Kh. Irbid)•

Kh. el-'Asheq, (En-Gev)

Hippos (Qal'at el-Husn)

Beth-yerah (Kh. el-Kerak)•

•el-Hammeh

•Gadara (Umm Qeis)

Sea of
Galilee

Tiberias•

Ubeidiya•

Sycaminum
(T. es-Samak)

T. Abu Hawam•

T. Harbaj•

•'Isfiyeh
T. el-'Amr•

Beth She'arim
(Sheikh Abreiq)

R. Kishon

Umm el-'Amad•

Sepphoris•
(Saffuriyeh)

Nazareth•

Japhia•
(Yafa)

Mt. Tabor•
(Jebel et-Tur)

'Affuleh•

•Beth Hashitta

•Beth Alpha (Beit Alfa)
Beth-shan Scythopolis
(T. el-Husn)

Mugharet Abu Usba• Nahal
'Athlit Oren
Castle
(Pilgrims

W. el-Mughara•
(prehistoric caves)

Dor (Tantura)•

Mugharet el-Kebara•

•T. el-Mubarak

Megiddo•(T. el-Mutesellim)

Taanach•
(T. Ta'annak)

•Dothan
(T. Duthan)

•Meser

Caesarea•

Hadera•

Migdal•
(T. edh-Dhurur, T. Zeror)

Samaria
Sebastiyeh

Tirzah
T. Far'a

•Zarethan
(T. es-Sa'idiyeh)

Jordan

Pella (Kh. Fahil)•

•Qal'at er-Rabad

Ramoth-gilead•
(T. Ramith)

Gerasa•
(Jerash)

Rihab•

34° 30'

35°

36°

35° 30'

32° 30'

2

3

3

4

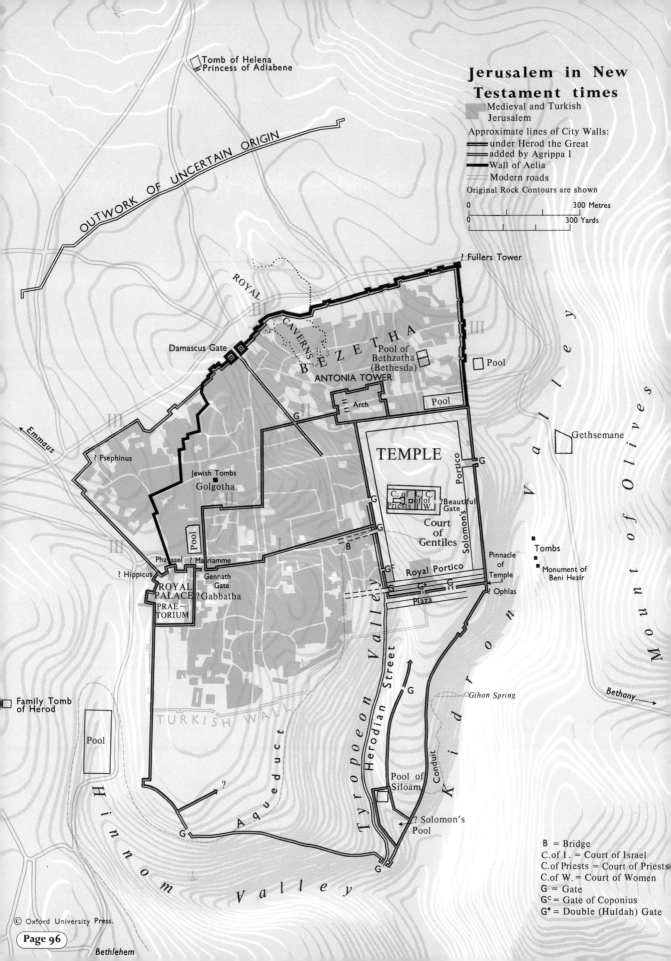

Jerusalem in New Testament times

Medieval and Turkish Jerusalem

Approximate lines of City Walls:
— under Herod the Great
— added by Agrippa I
— Wall of Aelia
— Modern roads

Original Rock Contours are shown

0   300 Metres
0   300 Yards

Tomb of Helena
Princess of Adiabene

OUTWORK OF UNCERTAIN ORIGIN

ROYAL

CAVERNS

B E Z E T H A

? Fullers Tower

III

Pool

Damascus Gate

Pool of
Bethzatha
(Bethesda)

ANTONIA TOWER

Pool

Emmaus

III

? Psephinus

Arch

G

II

Gethsemane

Jewish Tombs
Golgotha

TEMPLE

Portico

G

III

Pool

C. of
Priests

C.
C. of
W.

? Beautiful
Gate

Court
of
Gentiles

Solomon's

Tombs

Monument of
Beni Hezir

Phasael

? Mariamme

? Hippicus

Gennath
Gate

ROYAL
PALACE
PRAE-
TORIUM

? Gabbatha

B

Gc

Royal Portico

Pinnacle
of
Temple

G*

G

Plaza

? Ophlas

Mount of Olives

Family Tomb
of Herod

TURKISH WALL

Tyropoeon Valley

Herodian Street

G

Gihon Spring

Bethany

Pool

Aqueduct

?

Conduit

Kidron

Pool of
Siloam

? Solomon's
Pool

G

Hinnom

Valley

G

Bethlehem

© Oxford University Press.

B = Bridge
C.of I. = Court of Israel
C.of Priests = Court of Priests
C.of W. = Court of Women
G = Gate
Gc = Gate of Coponius
G* = Double (Huldah) Gate

Jerusalem in New Testament times

Herod the Great. The New Testament period opens in the reign of Herod (30–4 B.C.). We may infer from Josephus's account of his works that Jerusalem was transformed by Herod from an unpretentious, though populous, religious centre to one of the most brilliant of Roman provincial cities in the east. It acquired a hippodrome, amphitheatre, theatre, baths, and other public buildings. Above all, its temple was reconstructed on a gigantic scale in an enlarged precinct which overhung the Kidron and Tyropoeon (Cheese-makers') valleys on retaining walls of incomparable workmanship and dizzy height. Remains of these walls (p. 118) enable the precinct to be placed on the map exactly, with some of its gates; but the inner courts and the temple building itself have utterly disappeared and can only be drawn conjecturally from brief accounts left by Josephus and later Jewish writers. Herod enlarged and converted the old Maccabean castle, or 'Baris', into a fortified residence for himself, which he named the Antonia Tower. (Here, probably, St. Paul was later taken by the captain of the cohort in Acts 22.) Herod also built another and much larger royal palace on the western hill, and added three gigantic towers, Hippicus, Phasael and Mariamme, to defend it, in the old city wall, which it adjoined. Phasael still partly stands, and helps to identify the site of the palace, in the north-west corner of the Maccabean city, and there are excavated traces of the other two. Outside the western wall of the city, across the Hinnom Valley, is the four-chambered tomb with rolling stone, built by Herod for his own family's use, and referred to by Josephus. It was discovered in 1892.

Excavations in the area outside the southwest corner of the temple precincts have revealed numerous features of the Herodian city, including the course of the Herodian street as it ran adjacent to the wall along the lower west side and along the southern side of the precincts. On the south it adjoined a 'plaza' where pilgrims could gather before entering the temple gates, and before the Double (Huldah) Gate there was a monumental staircase. The southernmost of the two passageways across the Tyropoeon Valley had but a single supporting arch with 50-foot span (Robinson's Arch), approach being by steps and a ramp on the roof of adjoining buildings. The eastern arch of the upper bridge (Wilson's arch) and adjacent constructions, below present street level, are of relatively easy access now. On the spur of the western hill overlooking the temple the ruins of a pretentious building of the Herodian and Hasmonean periods have been excavated. The southern wall of the city which ran directly across the Tyropoeon Valley is reported as demonstrably belonging to Agrippa I.

Biblical Sites. Of the sites mentioned in the New Testament itself, we can locate only a few. Pilate's praetorium (Matt. 27. 27), also called 'palace' (Mark 15. 16 RSV) we assume to be identical with Herod's palace. The Pavement, called Gabbatha (John 19. 13), must therefore have been a paved open space on the western hill (perhaps just within the Gennath Gate), not to be identified with the famous stone pavement still accessible on the site of the Antonia Tower, where a Roman triple arch of the second century A.D., popularly called the Ecce Homo Arch, now stands. That pavement belonged to the central court of the Antonia Tower, and the arch to Hadrian's Roman city, Aelia Capitolina.

The site of Golgotha (John 19. 17) is a slight elevation of rock authenticated by local tradition since the fourth century, in an area containing ancient Jewish tombs, one of which is venerated as the Holy Sepulchre.

Within the temple the gate called 'Beautiful' (Acts 3. 10) was probably the main east entrance to the Court of the Women; and Solomon's Porch or Portico (John 10. 23; Acts 3. 11; 5. 12) formed one side of this court, or the east side of the outer court as a colonnaded ambulatory.

The pools of Bethzatha (RSV) or Bethesda (John 5. 2) and Siloam (John 9. 7) can both be located by extant remains; and the other large pools that are shown in various parts of the town were all probably in existence.

City Walls. The map shows in red the wall lines assumed to have existed in the time of Herod the Great and in blue those of Herod Agrippa I, who added a third, northern, wall in the principate of Claudius (A.D. 41–54). All these lines are partly conjectural. The northernmost (III) is much disputed. We have made it coincide with the existing Turkish wall for two strong reasons: (1) The Damascus Gate (in the Turkish wall) is known to stand on the foundations of an older gate built in the same style as the Temple enclosure; that may well have belonged to Agrippa's wall; (2) Josephus states clearly that the northernmost wall passed 'through the royal caverns'. The only caverns which exist on the northern side of Jerusalem are the great quarry-caves known as King Solomon's Caves; and the Turkish wall passes precisely through the middle of them. Agrippa's wall was thoroughly destroyed by the Romans in A.D. 70, and, except at the Damascus Gate, and in some re-used stones seen elsewhere in the Turkish wall, nothing can be seen of it today. Somewhere at its north-west corner, on high ground, stood the tower Psephinus, originally an octagon of great height.

Much of the oldest masonry visible in the Turkish wall line today belongs to a reconstruction made in the third or fourth century A.D., when Jerusalem was still a Roman city and named Aelia Capitolina. This reconstruction began at the tower Phasael and passed to the Damascus Gate by a shorter line than Agrippa's wall. This we have coloured black. At the gate itself the restorers re-used many fine stones taken from the Herodian structure, and placed part of their new gate on what remained of the old. The unattached double line near the northern edge of the plan indicates a rough but massive foundation which some scholars believe is Agrippa's wall. But no 'royal caverns' lie on or near its path, and its poor materials conflict with Josephus's description. It has been suggested that it is part of the perimeter of the headquarters of the Xth Legion Fretensis (see p. 117) left by Titus after A.D. 70, or part of the wall of circumvallation of Titus during the siege of the city. Recent excavations do not support a second-century date. The wall marked II is described by Josephus as beginning at the Gate Gennath and ending at Antonia Tower. Its line is partly authenticated by some rock scarps and masonry now deeply buried.

Palestine:
Archaeological Sites

(See map, pp. 94–95)

The association of history, especially religious history, with topography, is a very old one in Palestine. The Israelites and their predecessors linked the periodical manifestations of deity attested in their traditions with ancient landmarks and rustic altars. The earliest Christians commemorated in piously identified localities, which they adorned with churches, the historical events on which their faith was founded. And one of the oldest maps in the world, on the floor of an early church at Madaba, depicts in mosaic the chief cities and sacred places, of Old or New Testament interest, on both sides of the River Jordan.

The modern idea of extracting history from purely material remains has given a new interest to biblical topography. An archaeological map of Palestine can now draw on many years of work directed to that end. It began in 1871, when Captains Kitchener (later Field-Marshal) and Conder, of the Royal Engineers, were sent by the Palestine Exploration Fund to make a survey of the country and collect geographical, archaeological, and natural-historical data relevant to the narratives of the Bible. Not only did they map the whole country west of the Jordan but they also plotted the positions, recorded the names, and described the visible remains of some thousands of ancient sites, many of which were successfully identified with the places familiar from the Old and New Testaments.

It was a natural sequel to Kitchener's and Conder's survey to carry exploration below the ground. In this quest the year 1890 became something of a landmark; for in that year Flinders Petrie for the first time in biblical archaeology applied to a Palestinian site, Tell el-Hesi, his theory of the stratified formation of an ancient city mound.

Thereafter the principle of stratigraphy gained general recognition, and its practice was progressively improved. In the present century the first large-scale excavation was undertaken in 1902 at Gezer, a Canaanite city known from 1 Kgs. 9. 16 as Pharaoh Shishak's wedding present to Solomon. Since then excavations large and small have followed, all the way 'from Dan [Tell el-Qadi, Tel Dan in modern Hebrew] to Beer-sheba [Tell es-Seba', Tel Beer Sheva in modern Hebrew]', including these two recent major archaeological sites. What was in the first edition of this book a decade ago a single-page map, 'Palestine: Archaeological Sites', has become a two-page spread. More than four-score years of progress in archaeological science lie between Sir Flinders Petrie's epoch-making excavations at Tell el-Hesi and today's excavations there under the sponsorship of the Albright Institute of Archaeological Research, supported by a consortium of academic institutions, including Oberlin College. There is an understandable differential between the pioneer excavations at Gezer, Jerusalem, Shechem, and Taanach and those of today at the same sites under Hebrew Union College–Jewish Institute of Religion Biblical and Archaeological Institute, The British School of Archaeology, Hebrew University, and the Albright Institute. There has been progress in pottery analysis, in the use of various aids from the physical and biological sciences, and in stratigraphic field analysis as developed by Kathleen M. Kenyon, G. Ernest Wright, and others, involving meticulous attention to 'balks', the sides of the excavation squares which reveal the levels of rebuilding and filling. The full understanding of the ecology of an ancient site now entails the collection and analysis of all types of scientific data, sometimes involving the use of a computer.

Today's academic practices and educational philosophy have encouraged the use of Volunteer Staffs composed primarily of students, who engage in excavating and bring to the 'dig' variant useful talents and backgrounds of knowledge. Their participation under strict admission requirements and professional guidance becomes for the students a rich educational experience, for which academic credit is often given. The excavations at Caesarea, Gezer, Tell el-Hesi, Beer-sheba, Shechem, Heshbon, Jerusalem, and elsewhere, involve Volunteer Staff programs. (*See frontispiece and p.* 99) The extensive scope of archaeological activity today makes it impossible for any published map to keep abreast with the latest results, and it is right that this edition of the *Atlas* should indicate only the latest available information, with the reminder that much work was in progress at the date of closing for press.

Archaeology and the Bible

Sources of Information

THIS is a Bible Atlas; but the maps it contains presuppose much information which could not be found in any of the books of the Bible. Where does that information come from?

Until the last century the Bible was acknowledged as the oldest historical document in the world; even for those who might question its divine inspiration it was the sole historical source for events which had happened before the Greek historians came on the scene.

The Bible is still in this twentieth century an historical source of respectable age incorporating contemporary or nearly contemporary records of events which preceded the earliest Greek historians by five centuries or more. But it no longer stands alone, nor anywhere near the beginnings of history. The decipherment during the nineteenth century of documents written in the Egyptian hieroglyphic and Mesopotamian cuneiform scripts pushed the frontiers of historical knowledge back to an age preceding the earliest chapters of the Bible by nearly two thousand years. In the time span of human records the Old Testament stands to the earliest Egyptian and Mesopotamian writings as our twentieth-century literature does to the books of the New Testament.

If we turn from the Bible as a document of history to the peoples and places it describes, we find that they, too, occupy a middling position, less prominent on the stage and less ancient in the family tree than would have been assumed in earlier days. Far from dominating the contemporary scene or heading the human pedigree, the heroic characters of the Old Testament prove to have lived about half way along the scale of history before Christ and to have played a part in world events too obscure, and too remote from the centres of civilization, to receive more than the rarest and most cursory mention in the chronicles of their time. Palestine

Student Volunteer Staff and Supervisors working at the excavations of Tell el-Hesi, biblical Eglon (Josh. 10.3, 34, 35). Note excavation squares, balks, and archaeological equipment. See p. 98 and frontispiece.

above: 'The great pool which is in Gibeon' (Jer. 41.12; 2 Sam. 2.13) is 37 ft. in diameter, 82 ft. deep. At the bottom of the pool the stairs continue in a stepped tunnel to a water chamber to reach the receding water table, 45 ft. below the floor level of the pool. This is a part of Gibeon's complex of water works.

One of the stamps on jar-handles found at Gibeon: the design was impressed on the clay when soft, and the Hebrew words mean (top) 'to the king' and (bottom) 'Socoh'.

A similar stamp on a portion of a jar-handle from another site, reading (top) 'to the king' and (bottom) 'Memshath'. For others and their significance, see p. 72.

Tell el-Husn, the mound which covers the ruins of Beth-shan: the name of Beth-shan is preserved in that of modern Beisan which is near by. In foreground, fallen columns from Roman-period city of Scythopolis.

was a broken and narrow land which served as a precarious corridor between richer and more populous regions to north and south. Its inhabitants never played a decisive part in history, but owed their survival to frugal living, a secluded terrain, and vassalage to more powerful neighbours. By such means, in such a land, Israelite tribes or the remnants of them preserved their identity for barely fifteen centuries out of the fifty spanned by recoverable history.

The ability to read the records of ancient Egypt and Babylonia has vastly expanded the limits of history; but the surviving texts leave many gaps, and much of what they tell us is irrelevant to the kind of questions we would like to ask. An Atlas seeking to trace the ebb and flow of populations would be compelled to omit many regions and periods altogether if it relied on written records alone. But there are other resources: topography, language, and archaeology, each of which can help to reveal the past.

Topography

Consider topography first: the biblical scene is set in lands where nature has provided no more than is just enough to support life, and where consequently the pattern of settlement is closely linked with natural features. Of all the factors necessary to life in south-western Asia water is the most precious; and many of the questions which the compilation of a Bible Atlas poses are questions which can be answered by observing the water resources. Thus we can rely on a certain continuity in the siting of town and village settlements, clinging to the springs and irrigable valleys; and we

can be sure that the main lines of communication, based on the marching powers of animals and their need to drink so many times a day, have varied little in the three thousand or more years which have elapsed between the domestication of the camel and the coming of steam.

Language

Secondly, language: the Arabic dialect of modern Palestine has preserved many of the old Semitic names, of towns and springs and local worthies, which in the Bible appear in their Hebrew or Canaanite forms.

Many ancient sites can therefore be placed straight on the map by merely studying modern place-names. So the name of biblical Shiloh is preserved in modern Seilun, Bethel in modern Beitin, Gerasa in Jerash, Emmaus in Imwas. But here caution is necessary. It is not simply that some names have been lost or corrupted; so they have, but that merely leaves gaps in our knowledge. Much more deceptive, and often actually misleading, are the many names which though surviving have moved from the places they once designated to others in the neighbourhood. So Anathoth is not to be located at modern Anata, where there are no pre-Roman remains, but at near-by Ras el-Kharrubeh. The ancient name may be completely lost, as at Tell el-Hesi, which Petrie thought Lachish, but which is now generally identified as Eglon.

In these cases archaeology must step in. It has been noted, for example, that many towns which had a long history behind them ceased to be inhabited in Roman times but were replaced in the neighbourhood by new settlements on lower ground, which inherited the ancient names. So New Testament Jericho was at some distance from Old Testament Jericho and neither at the exact site of modern Jericho. The very same thing has happened in modern Israel since 1920. Such new sites masquerading under Canaanite names, and old ones now anonymous or disguised, can be detected by archaeological means. How does archaeology work?

Archaeology

Put in the plainest terms archaeology is the practice of finding out about people from the things they made or used. This seems an obvious method of inquiry, but before the eighteenth century it had hardly occurred to anyone, and even in the nineteenth it was not used very systematically. Now it is an indispensable aid to history.

Confronted with an unfamiliar object made by man, an archaeologist will begin to ask himself certain questions, which he will arrange in a logical order: first, how was this made? Second, how was it used? If he can answer these, he will proceed: what *sort* of person would have made this; and what *sort* of person would have used it? When a sufficient number of questions of that kind have been asked and answered about a sufficient number of objects in a given context, a certain picture of a society will have begun to emerge. But it will be an abstract picture, of little historical relevance, until it has been linked up in some relationship of time or causality with other societies, and ultimately with our own. To do this, archaeology must find out *when* things happened.

Chronology has been and still is a major interest of archaeologists. It is gradually becoming increasingly feasible through scientific devices to measure directly the age of organic or inorganic bodies, and so to date their archaeological contexts.* But archaeology must still principally rely, for dating past events, on the existence of ancient

---

* Carbon 14 (radiocarbon) dating is a method of estimating the age of ancient organic material (wood, leather, etc.) by comparing its surviving radio-active carbon content with that of living specimens (trees, hides, etc.). At Jericho it has indicated a date of around 6850 B.C. for a pre-pottery (not the oldest) Neolithic level, and 7800 B.C. (plus or minus 200 years), for the late Natufian (Mesolithic) Age, while at the Mt. Carmel caves it provided dates of around 40,000 for Mousterian (Middle Paleolithic) cultures. The development of radiocarbon measurements based on bone collagen has facilitated dating human bones. Analysis of pollen grains in soil (palynology) may have import for chronology and ecological studies. There is a thermo-luminescence method of establishing the date of the last firing of ceramic materials useful for determining their authenticity. Science today aids archaeology in many ways, including the use of high sensitivity magnetometers in detecting and outlining subsurface features.

How was it used and what is its date? Stone pillars and 'troughs' found in important building complexes at Megiddo were at first assigned to the time of Solomon and identified as stables for horses (1 Kgs. 9.15; 10.26). Later excavations point to the period of Ahab, and comparison with pillared structures at Zarethan, Hazor, Beer-sheba, and elsewhere has raised questions as to their use. See p. 64.

Fragment of limestone stele of Pharaoh Shishak, found at Megiddo, with drawing of the royal cartouches of the Pharaoh on it. Shishak's invasion of Judah is reported in 1 Kgs. 14.25, 26. On the walls of the temple of Amon at Thebes (Karnak), Shishak lists more than 150 towns conquered by him in Palestine. See p. 68.

societies who have kept count of the years and recorded in writing the intervals between events that interested them.

Israel in Old Testament times was surrounded by powerful rulers who did just that; and such knowledge as we have of the chronology of the Bible is based ultimately on the royal annals of Egypt, Babylonia, and Assyria. In Palestine itself several datable Egyptian monuments have been found—as a stele of Seti I at Beth-shan, a bronze statue-base of Rameses VI at Megiddo, and many other imported objects including scarabs attributable to the reigns of particular Pharaohs. Physical association with such objects often enables chronological values to be assigned to common domestic chattels found with them; and there are today in Near Eastern museums large classes of every-day objects, especially pottery types, which by such association may now be regarded as datable within narrow margins and used as reliable indications of time.

The process of inference by which such chronological relationships are established and gradually extended is tied up with the practice of stratigraphic archaeological excavation. Stratigraphy means deducing the relative ages of buried remains by observing the order in which they lie in the ground. At all periods and in all parts of the Near East it has been a common practice to make buildings of cheap and perishable materials, of mud, mud-brick, or rubble, with lavish and repeated applications of mud plaster to walls and roofs. When a house so contructed collapses, the ruins contain little worth salvaging, and the owner or a newcomer

wishing to rebuild will merely level off the site and begin again, leaving the stumps of old walls buried in the debris. The new house will then stand on slightly higher ground and a perceptible stratification will distinguish its foundations from those of its predecessor. Thus in the course of years is formed a 'tell' or mound, whose superimposed strata preserve a faithful though complex record of the successive buildings and rebuildings that have gone to form it.

Domestic objects of all sorts will be found in such a site, and will display typological variations. The stratification enables these to be placed in a relative time sequence, and the occasional discovery of an inscribed object, say an Egyptian scarab or stele bearing a royal cartouche, may supply a fixed point by which the whole sequence can be dated. Sometimes a conspicuous break in the strata can be linked with a known political event, like Sennacherib's siege of Lachish (c. 700 B.C.), and suggest an absolute date almost as effectively.

Thus the stratified formation of ancient town sites and the evolution of forms and fashions in domestic chattels, if compared over a whole region and correlated with evidences of date from the annals of literate dynasties, can yield an historical picture of society which stretches far beyond the range of written records. So it is that the story of Israel in the Near East is now to be read in a wide and expanding perspective of which the narrative of the Old Testament proves to have given only a partial glimpse.

above: *Tell ed-Duweir, the mound which marks the site of Lachish;* below: *an artist's impression of the probable appearance of Lachish before its destruction by the Assyrians: the walls, towers, large building, etc., are based on evidence of extant remains and the Assyrian reliefs.*

facing page: *Two panels from the Assyrian reliefs showing the assault on Lachish, and (below) an artist's reconstruction of the scene.*
(The four lines of attackers apparently on four separate ramps in the carving are taken to represent, by a form of ancient perspective, four rows of men on one large ramp or 'mound'.) Three battering rams are attacking the wall near the city gate while infantry advance to the assault and archers and slingers keep up a covering fire, to which the defenders reply.

←

above: *Air view of the mound of Megiddo (Tell el-Mutesellim), taken in the course of the Oriental Institute, Chicago, excavations (1926–39) by a camera attached to a balloon. The deep trenches are from the 1903–05 Schumacher excavations. At right* (see arrow) *is the entrance to the shaft of the water system.*

right: *Modern stairs over worn rock-cut steps leading down to spring (water-hole) in a cave at the foot of the tell at Megiddo. The spring could also be reached from inside the city by a great rock-cut vertical shaft, at the bottom of which a sloping passageway and horizontal tunnel led some 155 ft. to the cave. A blocking wall later covered the mouth of the cave. A small cave to the right of the steps was the post of the guard, whose skeleton was found* in situ.

Israel and Archaeology

Let us, then, consider what means exist for fitting the history and expansion of Israel, as the Bible narrates it, into the wider history of Palestine and Egypt as that can be inferred from the monuments.

The first thing that we shall find is that direct and explicit links are singularly rare, and for the earliest phases non-existent. Of all the characters in Israel's history the earliest to be mentioned in any contemporary monument is Omri, king of Israel about 876–869 B.C. Omri is named together with Mesha king of Moab in an inscribed stone monument put up by the latter and found in 1868 at Dhiban in Trans-jordan, the old capital of Mesha's kingdom. This monument is the contemporary account, from the Moabite side, of events described in 2 Kgs. 3. Later, in 841 B.C., the usurper Jehu appears depicted as a vassal of Shalmaneser III on a stele erected by the king of Assyria in Calah (see p. 26). Thereafter Judean and Israelite kings take their places without too much difficulty in the framework of historical and archaeological record. But before Omri, except for a single isolated reference to 'the people Israel' on a stele erected in Egypt by the Pharaoh Merenptah about 1230, all is silent. Not even Solomon, the son-in-law of a Pharaoh, still less Moses, Joseph, or Abraham, has left his name on any of the monuments.

If the persons thus are lost it need not follow that the events too have passed beyond recovery. If such episodes as the migrations of the Patriarchs, the sojourn in Egypt, or the conquest of Canaan really happened, it should be possible to identify at least their approximate periods; for each pre-supposes a particular pattern of society or political situation of which the material traces or historical record, in Canaan or Egypt, may well be still recognizable.

But did these episodes really happen? To that question the answer must be sought in the character of the narratives themselves as compared with independently attested history.

The stele of Mesha, king of Moab, as reconstructed. (After its discovery, the stone was damaged, but the missing parts are here supplied from an impression made before it was broken.)

The Patriarchs

Any reader of the early chapters of Genesis will feel that a change comes over the narrative from the end of the eleventh chapter. The twelfth introduces the story of Abraham, and for the first time we begin to recognize a real world of which archaeology and the records of Egypt and Mesopotamia give a parallel and by no means inconsistent account. Before Abraham the biblical generations are either seen to be personifications of geographical regions or tribes, or they belong to a fabulous world of which the narrative elements, sometimes traceable to the mythologies of Babylonia, have little or no contact with the daily life of the cities and villages as we find them buried in the ground. Yet stratigraphy points to a continuous evolution of society and technology in the Near East from fully historical times back through successive phases of organized town or village

society into the immense duration of Stone Age man. With the appearance of Abraham not only do the characters for the first time engage in actions which seem historically probable, but they themselves bear names which are paralleled or repeated in ancient texts of certain periods; and they move about in regions or between cities which are perfectly familiar in ancient literature, and many of whose ruins are still available for inspection.

Can we then deduce from anything in the story just when Abraham entered on the scene, or what real part he played in the secular history of his time? Abraham had dealings with a Pharaoh; but we cannot tell which Pharaoh that was. In Gen. 14 he was concerned with a league of four kings, who are named; but all attempts to identify these kings with known historical characters have so far failed. We cannot, therefore, yet find any direct link between Abraham and non-biblical recorded history. Nevertheless the Genesis stories depict a society following a mode of life which is perfectly compatible with the evidence of ancient documents from Iraq and Egypt, and can even be placed in approximate relationship with datable material remains.

The Patriarchs were not townsfolk; they lived in tents not houses, and we cannot expect to find material signs of their passage. Excavations at Beer-sheba show no city there in their time. Their wealth lay in livestock and in the possession of wells to water them by. They dealt with the cities presumably as owners and breeders of sheep, and as dealers in livestock, wool, and hides; perhaps, too, they were long-distance carriers, semi-nomadic donkey-riding merchant caravaneers. Being mobile by habit, in times of drought they could move into the Delta regions of Egypt, seeking pasture there with the Pharaoh's consent, or buying grain and returning northwards.

In all this there are particular features, even particular incidents, which find echoes in datable historical documents. The name of Abraham, for example, in slightly varying forms, has been read in cuneiform texts of the first half of the second millennium B.C. Jacob, too, in its full form Jacob-El, occurs in Mesopotamia of the 18th century B.C. and as a place-name in Palestine during the 15th and 13th. Benjamin is a prominent tribal name in Mesopotamia also of the 18th century.

The Patriarchs in Genesis observe particular rules of conduct in such matters as marriage, adoption, inheritance, and the purchase of land. Cuneiform documents of the 14th and 15th centuries which deal with the same matters, reveal the existence of strikingly similar practices amongst the Horites living beyond the Tigris and amongst the Hittites of Anatolia. It is significant therefore that it was from the Hittites that Abraham is said to have bought the cave of Machpelah, and from the Mesopotamian region that the Patriarchs migrated. See p. 54 for Nuzi, Mari, and Ebla texts.

The Pharaoh who employed Joseph invited his brethren to settle in the Land of Goshen, near the Delta of Egypt. An Egyptian relief of the 14th century shows an officer receiving just such a group of Asiatic Semites; and the accompanying text mentions this as a traditional kindness of the Pharaohs.

These parallels and others that could be cited show that the elements composing the patriarchal stories are quite characteristic of real life in the second millennium B.C. Unfortunately they do not reveal the exact periods at which the incidents described took place. Some archaeologists consider the name and manner of life of Abraham and aspects of the episode of warring kings in Gen. 14 and certain archaeological data point to not later than the 18th century, and probably even a century or two earlier, during a later phase of the Amorite invasions which had around 2300 B.C. brought an end to the Early Bronze fortified towns of Canaan. The tale of Joseph could then fall in the 'Second Intermediate' period of Egyptian history, between 1720 and 1580 B.C., when the country was ruled by the Asiatic Hyksos,

and a Semite might well have held the highest office in the land. Other scholars, however, have objected to this reconstruction of events that it thrusts the age of Abraham too far back into the past, and attributes a duration of more than five centuries to a tribal history which later tradition remembered as covering a mere eight generations. They would prefer to see Abraham as a contemporary of the Hyksos, and Joseph a Semitic immigrant to Egypt under one of the eighteenth- or nineteenth-dynasty Pharaohs.

The uncertainties which enshroud the chronology of the Patriarchs derive from their half-nomadic way of life. We reach firmer ground when the Israelites, having completed their wanderings, took to settled life in Canaan, and gradually supplantanted their predecessors in the land. Once established in towns and villages, living in houses and developing village industries, Israel began to leave material traces of its daily life and became for the first time subject to the processes of observation and deduction described above. When did that occur?

Palestine: Bronze and Iron Ages

About 1200 B.C., or a little earlier or later, most of the ancient sites that have been explored by excavation in Palestine and Syria reveal a drastic change in culture, usually accompanied by signs of a widespread and violent destruction. City walls and houses were overthrown; some were abandoned, some replaced by inferior structures. Many items of personal and domestic equipment familiar in the older houses disappear from the ruins at this stage, and are replaced in the subsequent layers of occupation by new types, again usually of inferior technique and artistic quality. Iron in the later contexts tends to replace bronze as the common material for implements of industry, agriculture, and war. The period before this change is commonly called the 'Bronze Age', and that which follows it the 'Iron Age'. The change denoted by these terms was more than a revolution in technology; it was the cultural manifestation of a far-reaching social disturbance involving a movement of populations throughout the Near East.

Egyptian monuments reveal the time of these events as about the close of the 13th century B.C. Just then the stele of Merenptah makes the first mention of the people of Israel. In lyrical style it recites the abasement or desolation of cities and peoples in Palestine, and includes Israel in their number. What really happened is obscure; but it is clear that the stele was written in the context of change and dissolution which the monuments reveal. Somehow Israel was involved, perhaps suffering like the rest, but being able to turn the confusion to advantage. The Jews later forgot Merenptah, remembering only that their ancestors had dispossessed the older inhabitants of Canaan. Whatever the exact truth, it is quite reasonable to see in the settlement of Israel one of the factors which caused the downfall of the Bronze Age cities and the dissolution of their culture.

Paved roadway to and through gateway at Tell Dan, biblical Dan ; period of Israelite occupation (Judg. 18 ; 1 Kgs. 12.29, 30).

What Archaeology Reveals

Culture is a term used in archaeology to denote the sum of things used and made by a given people at a given time. The first practical problem for archaeology in any region is to identify the cultures represented in the ruins and establish their chronological sequence. This is a necessary stage at the beginning of exploration, and one on which the efforts of the earliest pioneers were largely concentrated. It involves the systematic and laborious observation and classification of artefacts in all their material details, so that material, shape, method of manufacture, and decoration may serve to identify the societies employing them and to date their rise and fall.

Much of the information gathered in this way has little interest in itself; but the trouble of acquiring it is still justified if the material objects classified can help to identify the characters on the stage. In fact, the sequence of cultures encountered in Palestinian sites is now fairly well established, and the current task of archaeology is to gather evidence for the more elusive and interesting aspects of ancient man—his intellectual, moral and artistic capacities, and their reflection in the organization of society, forms of religion, and embellishment of ancient cities and homes. It is in these more advanced fields of interest that archaeology is now striving to reconstruct and amplify the historical background of the Bible. Ecological studies have also become the concern of the archaeologist.

Written Records

As we have already suggested, the bulk of the finds with which archaeology has to deal relate more directly to technology and every-day life than to the finer or profounder activities of the mind. We can follow in innumerable town and village sites the evolution of technical processes, without gaining much insight into the mental equipment of the people who developed them. Yet from time to time fortune rewards the archaeologist with some discovery which throws direct light on the inner workings of society, on religion, kingship, commerce, or even the individual mind. The discovery which contributes more than anything else to a knowledge of these things is that of written texts. The world in which the Patriarchs and their descendants moved was a literate world. Kings communicated with each other and with their servants in writing; they recorded their acts and their conquests on written tablets of stone or clay or wax. The records of commerce, dealings in real estate of all kinds, private contracts, and judicial decisions were attested and preserved in writing. Priests and diviners had inscribed on tablets the rules, omens, rituals, hymns, and epic lays pertaining to their professions. Schoolmen in Egypt and Babylonia wrote down for the instruction of their pupils the salutary tales or precepts they thought proper to education. Such literature offers for our inspection as it were a direct view of the mind of ancient man.

Outstanding discoveries of documents of these kinds have

The Prism of Sennacherib: one of the many examples of written records from the great empires with whom the Israelites were in contact. This prism contains the annals of the king, including his account of his attack on Jerusalem in 701 B.C., in the time of Hezekiah.

yielded more information than it has yet been possible to publish fully or assimilate. Thus in the 1930s the ruins of a gigantic palace at Mari, an Amorite city on the Euphrates, yielded more than 20,000 clay tablets inscribed with the diplomatic, administrative, and commercial archives of one of the greater states of Mesopotamia of the 18th century B.C.

In these documents, many of which are letters exchanged between the king and his servants or diplomatic envoys, we can read the names of villages and tribes within the wide territories of Mari, and of the independent cities with which he maintained commercial or diplomatic relations; we learn the names of administrative officers, and their responsibilities for the maintenance of security, labour supply, irrigation, harvesting, commissariat for the palace, police and settlement work, and in short all the day-to-day affairs of a loosely knit but autocratic state. Early Israelite institutions of covenant making, prophecy, and judgeship are illuminated. The tone of the letters, spontaneous and personal, sounds a direct echo from the speech and thought of dwellers great and small in the land about the time when the patriarchs pastured their flocks between the desert and the city lands.

We associate Israel pre-eminently with a religion and a code of laws; a religion which became in time a strict monotheism, and a law which popular belief accepted as a direct mandate from the deity. Neither of these two national traditions was evolved from nothing; the cult of Yahweh was not intrusive in the Canaanite world, but grew out of it; the Mosaic code was neither an unfamiliar nor an unprecedented document, but one of many analogous compilations, credited with divine authority, in which the customary laws of Sumerian, Semitic, or Hittite peoples had from time to time in the past been codified. Of these law codes the most complete which has survived, but not the most ancient, is the Babylonian code of Hammurabi (18th century B.C.), of which a master text engraved on a diorite stele was found at Susa early in this century. At the head of it the king stands as a worshipper before the enthroned Shamash, the Sun God. Similar but distinct codifications, some older, some more recent, have survived in varying states of fragmentariness, written on clay tablets which have been recovered from the soil in Mesopotamia and Anatolia.

The religion of Israel, no less than its laws, was a natural product of its time. Both the practical side of the cult as the Old Testament reveals it, the High Places and the sacrifice, and also the poetical imagery in which the idea of God was expressed, and which the psalms and prophetic books have preserved, sprang from a common heritage of feeling and imagination in which the Israelites and their Semitic neighbours fully shared. On that heritage of religious thought and practice a flood of light has been thrown by a series of documents discovered since 1929 at Ugarit, a capital city of the Canaanites at the northern end of the Phoenician coast.

The texts of Ugarit consist of clay tablets inscribed in a cuneiform alphabet and in the Canaanite language with a series of poetical compositions describing in near-biblical language the loves and wars of multitudinous gods and goddesses and the trials and adventures of human heroes.

Remote as these fabulous mythologies may appear from the restrained theophanies of the Old Testament, they reveal a background of imagination, obsessed with the presence and power of nature personified, from which in later years the genius of Israel derived its more refined but still anthropomorphic concept of Yahweh, the Lord of Hosts. The archives at Ebla in Syria promise further light on Israelite-Canaanite origins.

Divine Images

The strict practice of Israel allowed no physical emblem of their God. Still, most ordinary people amongst them, and most of their rulers until nearly the time of the Exile, liked to have some tangible evidence of the divine presence before which they might lay their offerings, a graven or molten image, a pillar, or a sacred pole called the *Asherah*. In the Bronze Age ruins of Canaan some of these objects have been found—rare and doubtful traces of the *Asherah* (too perishable to survive), but good examples of the pillars and images. Such things reveal the mode of expression, abstract or explicit, which served the varying moods and purposes of the Semitic mind.

The material symbol, image or pillar, could mark the

place where God was to be found. At Gezer, the Middle Bronze shrine with its alignment of ten monoliths (*masseboth*) has been re-excavated; covenant-making associations have been suggested (cf. Josh. 24. 26–27; see illustrations, pp. 111, 112. At Hazor, the chief Canaanite city of Galilee, there were ten stone slabs, 9 to 26 inches high, behind an offering table in the niche of a 14th-century one-room shrine. Were they commemorative or votive, or symbolic of the presence of deity? Nine of the slabs were just plain basalt stelae with rounded tops; but one was rudely carved with two uplifted hands in flat relief, and above them the moon's disc in a crescent. At one end of the row, beside these abstract emblems, there was placed a more explicit sculptured representation of the god as a human being seated on a chair. Such were those 'other gods' forbidden to Israel, made in the likeness of things in heaven above or on the earth below, and engraved in stone. A crude cult stele from Tell Arad (ca. 2500 B.C.), depicts the goddess and her dead grain-god consort. At Ugarit excavations in and about one of the temples of the city brought to light four carved stone reliefs in which gods and a goddess were shown in human form, the goddess winged, the finest of the gods a warlike figure treading the mountain tops and brandishing a thunderbolt. At Beth-shan the local god Mekal was depicted as a bearded ruler with a horned helmet on his head, a sceptre in his hand, and a robed goddess for his partner. Other images of smaller scale have been found in bronze or

The so-called 'high place' at Gezer, first excavated in 1901, and again more recently with improved techniques. Ten monolithic pillars or standing stones (masseboth) and a large square stone 'socket'. See Gen. 28.18 (Bethel), Josh. 4.19–24 (Gilgal), Josh. 24.26 (Shechem), 2 Kgs. 18.4 (Israel), etc.

The sacred pillar at Shechem in front of ruins of the temple of Baal-berith (El-berith). Possibly 'the great stone' of Josh. 24.26; cf. 'the oak of the pillar' in Judg. 9.6. See also Judg. 8.33; 9.46.

bronze gilt, molten images, in which gods and goddesses are seen as warriors brandishing their weapons, or as nursing mothers, or as rulers enthroned. Such figures varied in artistic quality from utmost crudity to sophisticated elegance. Along the Phoenician coast traditional ties with the Pharaohs taught the Sidonians to admire and affect the fashions of Egypt, as their descendants have adopted those of France. So Ahab's citadel in Samaria, built by Phoenician craftsmen of Jezebel's own country, contained delicately carved and inlaid furnishings on which the gods and goddesses of the country were depicted as Horus and Isis, and the cherubim as winged sphinxes. This was the style, Semitic in thought, Egyptian in manner, that King Solomon, employing Sidonian craftsmen, chose for the decoration of Yahweh's temple in Jerusalem (2 Kgs. 6–7).

The Earliest Writing

We have touched on the importance of written documents for our knowledge of the past. For the organization and stability of society itself the contribution of writing is incalculable; its invention has been the pre-eminent technological achievement of man. Writing developed on parallel but independent lines in Egypt and Sumer from about the end of the fourth millennium. At that time the inhabitants of Canaan were totally illiterate, and were to remain so for many centuries. But later they, too, had a contribution to make. About the middle of the second millennium experiments were afoot in some of the cities of Canaan in the practical problem of finding an easy visual notation to express not the syllables nor the meanings of speech, as hitherto, but its elementary component sounds. This was the beginning of that incalculable simplification of writing which we call the alphabet. The essential sounds of Semitic speech can be rendered by less than three dozen signs, within the capacity of anyone to learn. Thus a system of writing based on simple sounds could make every man his own scribe, and in a literate society set him on the road to enfranchisement. Whatever Canaanite, therefore, first thought of isolating and classifying the ultimate component sounds of words, independently of their meanings, was not only a true scientist but also a notable if unwitting philanthropist.

Excavations in Palestine and Syria have revealed traces of several parallel attempts to establish an alphabet; we may mention two. In the north, the people of Ugarit devised a notation using wedge-shaped marks, which they used in the 14th and 15th centuries to write out the mythological poems mentioned above and other classes of documents. At about the same time, in the south, an entirely different set of semi-pictorial signs, but with similar phonetic values, was being used in some of the cities of Palestine and Phoenicia. This southern notation was to become the basis of the system later inherited, through the Greeks and Etruscans, by the Western world. Among the earliest experiments yet discovered in this script were short inscriptions engraved by Semitic workmen employed by Pharaohs of the eighteenth dynasty in the turquoise mines of Serabit el-Khadim in Sinai. (See illustration, p. 20.) Other short texts with similar letters have been found scratched or painted on pottery vessels of the Late Bronze Age in Lachish and other Canaanite cities. Three 12th-century copper arrowheads from near Bethlehem are inscribed 'arrow of Abd-lebaat.'

Alphabetic writing was thus established in time for the Israelites to adapt it to their own use when settlement and urbanization gave them cause to become literate. The earliest known Israelite text is a doggerel list of months of the year in relation to farming operations engraved on a baked clay pendant in what may now be called Hebrew characters; this was found in Gezer, a Canaanite town given by the Pharaoh Shishak to King Solomon in the 10th century (1 Kgs. 9. 16), when the text may have been written. Thereafter Hebrew documents have been found in various contexts. Some of them are brief notes of tax or revenue receipts written in ink

right: *The 'Lachish ewer': a jar found at Lachish dating from the 13th century B.C. with a painted inscription on the shoulder in ancient Semitic characters. This begins with a word for 'gift' and is probably a dedication.*

Part of one of the Lachish Letters. These are documents written in ink on potsherds (ostraca) found in the ruins of Lachish: the conclusion of Letter IV, referring to the signals from Lachish and from Azekah (see p. 72).

on potsherds; others the names of citizens elegantly engraved on personal seals; others official marks stamped on pottery jars destined to hold royal stores (compare p. 100).

Of monumental inscriptions none has been found on the Israelite side of the Jordan to equal in length or interest the stele of Mesha King of Moab; but several of the Aramaean kings of states in the north of Syria have left stone stelae engraved with historical texts of great interest: and in Judah there has survived the inscription carved by Hezekiah's masons on the wall of the tunnel that brought water through the hill of Zion from Gihon to the king's new reservoir (2 Kgs. 20. 20; see illustration, p. 17, and pp. 80–81).

A very different type of written document, taking us to the heart of Judean history, is represented by a batch of letters written in ink on potsherds which were discovered amid the ashes of Lachish. These letters had passed between the governor of Lachish and an officer in one of his watchposts during the anxious years about 590 B.C. before Jerusalem fell to Nebuchadrezzar, the king of Babylon.

These unique documents not only reveal the authentic style and language in which men of Judah thought, wrote, and spelt in the days of Jeremiah, but also throw independent and parallel light on events recorded in the pre-exilic chapters of the Old Testament—a contemporary commentary many centuries older than the earliest existing Hebrew manuscripts of the Bible.

The Lachish letters (p. 113) and others from Tell Arad belong to the final scene of the monarchy founded by David four centuries earlier. The capture of Jerusalem by Nebuchadrezzar, and the succeeding Babylonian Exile, marked the beginning of a new age, not only for the Jews but for the Mediterranean world. The burden of civilization was passing from Asia to the West. The arts of empire and literacy were no longer the monopoly of Egypt and the Semitic nations. Babylon in 538 fell to Cyrus the Persian; Egypt became a Persian province; and in 490 B.C., just a century after the desolation of Jerusalem, the armies of Darius himself were beaten by Greeks on the field of Marathon. Thereafter we are accustomed to regard Greece and her historians, philosophers, and poets as the literary exponents of civilization and the first source of our knowledge of the contemporary world.

As the biblical scene moves forward into the New Testament the contribution of archaeology changes perceptibly. We no longer rely on synchronisms with Assyria or Egypt to establish the chronology of events. Greek and Latin literature and epigraphy brilliantly illuminate the Hellenistic and Roman empires. The cities of

'Pan niches' at Baniyas (Greek Paneas), near the easternmost sources of the Jordan. Here the Greeks worshipped Pan. Herod the Great built here a temple in honour of Augustus, and his son Philip the tetrarch rebuilt the city and named it Caesarea Philippi (Mark 8.27).

Petra; one of the rock-hewn facades in Hellenistic-Roman style with which the Nabataean rulers and merchants embellished their desert city.

the eastern world, conquered or created by Alexander of Macedon, assumed a new Hellenizing aspect, transforming and renewing the heritage of their oriental environment. From Seleucia on the Tigris, the historical heir of Babylon, to Alexandria at the Nile mouth (see pp. 82–83), Greek names, Greek social and political forms, Greek town-planning and architecture (or hybrid adaptations of these) contributed to a half-European, half-oriental world, acquisitively progressive, politically and spiritually half-caste, direct ancestor of many elements in Near-Eastern urbanism today. Outside the cities a hard and patient peasantry laboured, and still labours, with perpetual endurance to win grain and milk from the dry earth, a peasantry as timeless and unchanging as the land and the climate itself.

On this new half-Hellenized scene, to which the New Testament belongs, archaeology throws a less indispensable but still welcome light. The terrible destruction which Jewish fanaticism brought upon Jerusalem in A.D. 70 has almost obliterated what must have been, under Herod's despotic rule, nearly the most brilliant city in western Asia (see also pp. 96–97). The gigantic towering enclosure of the Temple and some strangely hybrid sepulchral monuments still reflect the exotic twist that a Semitic landscape and people could give to Grecian forms. In Nabataean Petra the same transformation can be seen displayed in the piled-up rock-hewn facades of royal tombs and banqueting rooms. Jerusalem and Petra were the capitals of autonomous, independent or semi-independent, Semitic kinglets never properly Hellenized. The Greek way of life was more nearly reproduced in the older Macedonian foundations, like Antioch and Alexandria, though little remains of their architecture to prove it. There is more to see in Baalbek (Heliopolis), Gerasa (Antioch on the Chrysorhoas), the best preserved city of the Decapolis, and in Palmyra, the half-Arab, half-Aramaean metropolis of the Syrian desert. In that oasis city the measured, stable, forms of Greek architecture are seen curiously adapted to the exotic yet fastidious manners of princely Arabian camel-merchants and caravan-traders.

The colonnaded streets, temples, theatres, and public baths which survive in varying stages of ruin in these Syrian cities, and in others round the coasts and in the interior of Asia Minor, some partly excavated (pp. 92–93), others still hidden in the scrub of wild hill-sides, help to define the life and bustling preoccupations of the people to whom St. Paul addressed his letters—cities whose Greek or Graecized names give a note of pagan glamour to the pages of Acts and Revelation. The names and public services of their citizens survive in innumerable civic decrees, inscribed on stone with the mention of their benefactions, in dedications at temples, and in countless epitaphs. In Jerusalem itself many

above: Ossuary inscribed in Hebrew (reading from R. to L.) 'Maryam' 'Johanna'; (below) the name 'John' (Ioanes) in Greek on another ossuary. (Both from the neighbourhood of Jerusalem.)

left: Inscription discovered in 1961 in the theatre at Caesarea (p. 40), the first found bearing the name of Pontius Pilate, prefect (governor) of Judea, A.D. 26–36. In Latin, the language of imperial Rome, its three lines read: Tiberieum . . . [Pont]ius Pilatus . . . [Prae]fectus Iuda[icae]. The term 'procurator' was not applied to the Roman military governors before the time of Emperor Claudius, and the use of this title for Pilate by the Roman historian Tacitus (c. A.D. 115) is probably anachronistic. The New Testament calls Pilate, Felix, and Festus by the Greek word hegemon, governor (see p. 43).

The warning inscription from Herod's Temple: written in Greek (the language of the Gentile world) it gives warning of the death penalty for any Gentile who enters the court of Israel (compare Acts 21. 28).

right: Part of a commemorative stele found near the Jaffa Gate at Jerusalem, bearing the name of the Tenth Legion (LEG[IO] X FR[ETENSIS]). Although this stone dates from c. A.D. 200, the Tenth Legion had a long association with Palestine and served there also in A.D. 66–70.

ordinary contemporaries of Jesus and his earliest followers have achieved a certain immortality in their familiar names Simon, Mary, Martha, Judas, Salome, Matthias and many others—scrawled, in family tombs of the 1st century A.D., on the humble stone boxes which received their bones after the flesh had decayed. These ossuaries are common objects, and the names read on them are common Jewish names.

A few other isolated inscriptions further revive the New Testament scene. The Temple, where the earliest Christians spent much time, was built, as the historian Josephus tells us, by Herod the Great. Within the vast enclosure, of which great stretches still stand, the outer spaces were accessible to Gentiles; but the inner court they might not penetrate. The strong feeling of the Jews in such matters is recalled in two inscribed fragments of stone notices found in Jerusalem which warned foreigners in the Greek language that they would enter at the peril of their lives.

left: *Recently excavated paved Herodian street with stairs alongside the south wall of the temple enclosure, leading to the double (Huldah) Gate, with debris from the destruction of the Temple in A.D. 70. The typical large blocks of fine Herodian masonry are shown on the wall. See p. 97.*

right: *Excavations below the level of the Damascus Gate at Jerusalem revealed the first arch of a triple gateway, and an inscribed stone above it shows the rebuilding of it belonged to Hadrian's Aelia Capitolina, whose wall here followed the line of the wall of Herod Agrippa I (A.D. 41–45). See p. 97.*

Such minor objects may illustrate the extent to which common archaeological finds give topical substance and definition to the scenes of daily life depicted in the New Testament. Of all such discoveries the most sensational in recent years have been made by bedouin Arabs, who were followed by archaeologists, in the desolate valleys of the Judean wilderness. Since 1947 there have been recovered, at first accidentally, later by systematic search, innumerable fragments of parchment and papyrus writings inscribed during the first two centuries before and after Christ, by Jews who for one reason or another had taken refuge in those inhospitable wastes from the turbulent scenes of their contemporary life. We can imagine the stir which would be caused in 20th-century England if archaeologists were to recover a letter or some personal relic of Cymbeline or Caratacus, British heroes of the 1st century A.D. A comparable discovery was made in the Judean desert in 1951, when there was found high in the cliff face of Wadi Murabba'at (p. 95) a scrap of papyrus inscribed in Hebrew, an order from Simon ben Kosibah (Bar Kokhba), last prince and leader of the Jews in the Second Jewish Revolt, to one of his commanders. This forshadowed the dramatic discovery by Israeli archaeologists of a bundle of papyri containing the dispatches of Simon ben Kosibah in an almost inaccessible cave to the south in Wadi Hever in 1960, in Aramaic and Hebrew.

Not many miles away from Wadi Murabba'at but in caves further north in the vicinity of Khirbet Qumran (p. 95), a large series of manuscripts of an earlier date has been recovered since 1947 from the library of a Jewish sect (the Essenes), whose monastic stronghold centre here was sacked in the war of 66–70 A.D. In the remnants of this library the texts of the Old Testament are revealed as they were copied by the Jews of Palestine a thousand years before the oldest known Hebrew manuscripts. There are among other texts also commentaries and sectarian documents. The ruins of this community centre at Khirbet Qumran (in which the refectory/meeting-hall, the scriptorium in which the texts were copied, cisterns, and other features were disclosed) and the graves where the scribes and leaders were buried,

Papyrus letters, dispatches from Simon ben-Kosibah (bar-Kokhba), leader of the Second Jewish Revolt: Above: *letter found in a cave in Wadi Murabbaʻat (see map p. 95), signed with his name, concerning certain Galileans who had come to Judea;* below: *unopened papyrus, one of a bundle of letters found in a cave in Wadi Hever in 1960 (see text).*

are visible monuments of a reforming or dissident movement in the religion of Jewry with which Jesus must well have been acquainted (see illustrations, pp. 36–7). The most recent Qumran Scroll acquired (1967), the longest of all (about 28 feet), Herodian in date, is the Temple Scroll, so-called because its main concern is the new temple presaging the new age.

It is clear that in such written documents as those just described the mind of ancient man is revealed with a clarity not to be hoped for from the ordinary material evidence of archaeology.

Archaeology and Maps

To return briefly to the making of this Atlas. The fields of archaeology and map-making touch at many points; we cannot reconstruct the life of early man without studying his physical surroundings and communications; conversely we cannot plot the areas of habitation on the globe without knowing something of the tribes and peoples who have moved across it. The particular aim of this Atlas is to illustrate in maps the scene of events recorded in the Bible. Archaeology alone can determine the moments and time at which many sites have been occupied and what places if any they should consequently occupy on the maps. But archaeology itself is a newcomer in the field, and there are many gaps in our knowledge, which only guesswork can fill. Guesses can play a respectable part even in the strict sciences; archaeology is a method of historical inquiry which need not be too mistrustful of them, provided that its limitations and relevance are understood. It is partly with that intention that the foregoing pages have been written.

Notes on Gazetteer

Abel } All names, whether ancient or modern, are shown thus in the alphabetical list. (Biblical names, unless otherwise
Battir } indicated, in the form found in the RSV.)

They may be followed by other names, given thus:

(Abel-beth-maacah): alternative Biblical or other ancient names.

Bethir: biblical (or other ancient) name of place listed under its modern name.

T. Abil: modern name (Arabic, Turkish, etc.) identifying the location of place listed under its Biblical or ancient name. Those enclosed in [ ] are Hebrew names, but in the transliteration used in modern Israeli publications, which often differs from that used in the English Bible or in tradition. (E.g. **Joppa**—English Bible form derived from Heb. through Lat. and Gk. 'Ioppē'; *Jaffa*—traditional English name for same place; *Yafa*—English transliteration of Arabic name; [*Yafo*]—Israeli transliteration of Hebrew name.)*

Biblical references: where *no* biblical references are given the name does not occur in the Bible; where *one* reference is given the name occurs once only in the Bible; where two or more references are given the name occurs twice or more in the Bible; for names occurring frequently a representative selection of references is given.

NOTE: some places are included in this Gazetteer though not located in the maps: this is done to distinguish different places of the same name, or to give a cross-reference or other information.

ABBREVIATIONS

ASV	American Standard Version (generally = RV)	NEB	New English Bible (N.T., 2nd ed. 1970, O.T. and Apocr. 1970)
c.	(Lat. *circa*) about	nr.	near
cap.	capital	N.T.	New Testament
cf.	(Lat. *confer*) compare	O.T.	Old Testament
conj. loc.	conjectural location	*prov.*	province
Gk.	Greek	*q.v.*	(Lat. *quod vide*) which see
illus.	illustration(s)	*qq.v.*	(Lat. *quae vide*) which (*plural*) see
ins	inset to map	*reg.*	region
isl.	island	*riv.*	river
Heb.	Hebrew	Rom.	Roman
Kh.	*Khirbet*, i.e. ruin	RSV	Revised Standard Version (O.T. 1952, Apocr. 1957, N.T., 2nd ed. 1971)
KJV	King James ('Authorized') Version	RV	(English) Revised Version (generally = ASV)
Lat.	Latin		
lit.	literally		
mod.	modern	*T.*	*Tell*, i.e. mound covering ancient site
MSS	manuscripts	*V.*	Valley
mt(s).	mountain(s)	*W.*	Wadi, i.e. watercourse, often dry in dry season

For abbreviations used for biblical books, see p. 8

* It should be noted that some modern places in Israel are not on the same site as the Biblical place of the same name, e.g. the modern village called *Benei Beraq* is not at the Biblical **Bene-berak** (located here at site called in Arabic *Ibn Beraq*).

Reference System

The italic figures (from *49* to *96*) in the Gazetteer refer to pages of the Atlas on which the maps are found. The bold letters and figures (**X6** etc.) refer to the 'squares' indicated by the marginal letters and figures on the maps, defined by lines of latitude and longitude: on the Palestine maps these are at intervals of half a degree (30 minutes) and in the other maps they are at larger intervals according to the scale. (Note: the reference system for Palestine maps is not identical with that in the first edition.)

Gazetteer

Abana: *Nahr Barada ; riv.,*   49, 69 **Z1**
'river of Damascus', 2 Kgs. 5. 12
Abarim, Mts. of: 49, 57, 63 **Y5**
also 'Mts. of Moab', Num. 27. 12; 33. 47, 48; Deut. 32. 49
Abdon: *Kh.ʿAbdeh*   61, 62 **X2**
in Asher, Josh. 21. 30; 1 Chr. 6. 74. Same as Ebron. Josh. 19. 28
Abel (Abel-beth-maacah, Abel-maim): *T. Abil*
    49, 57, 62, 65, 69 **Y2**
in David's Kingdom, later taken by Ben-hadad and Tiglath-pileser, 2 Sam. 20. 14, 15; 1 Kgs. 15. 20; 2 Kgs. 15. 29
Abelane: *Abil el-Qamh*   86 **Y2**
Roman period city succeeding Abel-beth-maacah
Abel-beth-maacah: *see* Abel
Abel-keramim: *Naʿur*   61, 63 **Y5**
Judg. 11. 33 (RV Abel-cheramim; KJV 'plain of the vineyards')
Abel-meholah: *Kh. T. el-Hilu*   61, 62, 65, 69, 73 **X4**
Judg. 7. 22; 1 Kgs. 4. 12
Abel-shittim (Shittim): *T. el-Hammam*   57, 63 **Y5**
Num. 33. 29; Josh. 2. 1; 3. 1; Mic. 6. 5
Abila: *T. Abil*   77, 85, 86 **Y3**
city of Decapolis, *q.v.*
Abilene: *reg.*   85 **Z1**
    91 **G4**
tetrarchy of Lysanias, Luke 3. 1
Abu Simbel   67, 92 **F6**
Abydos (in Egypt): *ʿArabet el-Madfuneh*   54, 78, 92 **F5**
Abydos (on Hellespont): nr. *Çanakkale*   91 **E3**
Greek harbour city
Accaron (Ekron): *Kh. el-Muqannaʿ*   87 **W5**
Gk. name of Ekron, 1 Macc. 10. 89 (KJV)
Acchabare: *ʿAkbaria*   86 **X3**
rock, fortified by Jews against Romans (Josephus, *Jewish War*)
Acco (*see* Acre, Ptolemais): *T. el-Fukhkhar*
    49, 57, 61, 62, 65, 69, 73, 77, 94 **X3**
    55, 67,71 **X4**
Phoenician city, Judg. 1. 31
Acco, Plain of   49 **X3**
Achaea: *reg.*   82 **D3**
Achaemenian Empire: the Persian empire founded by Cyrus: see *pp. 78–79*
Achaia: *Rom. prov.*   89, 91 **D3**
Acts 18. 12; in 2 Cor. 9. 2 name refers to the churches of the province
Achmetha (KJV) (Ecbatana): *Hamadan*   79 **H4**
see Ecbatana
Achor, V. of: *el-Buqeʿa*   49, 61, 69 **X5**
Josh. 7. 24–26
Achshaph: *T. Keisan*   57, 61, 62, 94 **X3**
Canaanite city, Josh. 11. 1; 12. 20
Achzib: *ez-Zib*   49, 57, 61, 62, 73, 77, 94 **X4**
    93 **G4**
in Asher, Josh. 19. 29; Judg. 1. 31. *See* ez-Zib
Achzib (Chezib): *T. el-Beida*   63, 73 **W5**
in Judah, Josh. 15. 44; Mic. 1. 14
Acrabbein (Akrabatta): *ʿAqraba*   87 **X4**
headquarters of toparchy of Acrabittene (Akrabattene) (Josephus)
Acre: 51 **X2**
medieval and European name of Ptolemais, *q.v.*, successor of Acco, *q.v.*
Actium: 88 **D3**
scene of naval victory of Octavian over Antony, 31 B.C.
Adab: *Bismaya*   93 **J4**
Babylonian city

Adadah (Aroer) *ʿArʿarah*   61 **W6**
Josh. 15. 22; same as Aroer (in Negeb)
Adam: *T. ed-Damiyeh*   61, 63, 73 **Y4**
Josh. 3. 16; Hos. 6. 7. (RSV) *See also* Admah (NEB ref.)
Adamah: *Abu esh-Shiba*   62 **X2**
in Naphtali, Josh. 19. 36
Adami-nekeb: *Kh. Damiyeh*   62 **X3**
in Naphtali, Josh. 19. 33
Adana (Seyhan): *Adaniya*   67 **G3**
Turkish city: also approximate site of ancient city
Adasa: *Kh.ʿAddasa*   77 *ins*
    87 **X5**
1 Macc. 7. 40, 45
Adhaim: *riv.*   53, 71, 75 **H4**
Ader   95 **Y6**
excavated site in Moab; Chalcolithic and Bronze Age. Menhirs.
Adiabene; *reg.*   89 **H3**
in Roman times, client kingdom; its Queen Helena was Jewish convert
Adida: *el-Haditheh*   87 **W5**
1 Macc. 12. 38: same as Hadid, *q.v.*
Adithaim: *Kh. el-Hadatheh*   63 **X4**
in Judah, Josh. 15. 36
Admah: *conj. loc.* 57 **X6**
one of the Cities of the Plain, Gen. 10. 19; 14. 2; Deut. 29. 23; Hos. 11. 8 (Hos. 6. 7 NEB). *See also under* Siddim, Valley of.
Adora: *Dura*   85, 87 **X5**
1 Macc. 13. 20: same as Adoraim, *q.v.*
Adoraim: *Dura*   63, 69, 77 **X5**
2 Chr. 11. 9: same as Adora, *q.v.*
Adramyttium: *Edremid*   89, 91 **E3**
Acts 27. 2. Greek city, seaport of Mysia
Adria, Sea of: 88 **C3**
the Adriatic and also the waters south of it, Acts 27. 27
Adulis: *Massawa*   67 **G8**
trading port founded by the Ptolemies
Adullam: *T. esh-Sheikh Madhkur*
    57, 61, 63, 65, 69, 73, 77 **X5**
Canaanite city, Gen. 38. 1; Josh. 12. 15; in Judah, Josh. 15. 35; David's place of refuge, 1 Sam. 22. 1; &c.
Adummim: *Talʿat ed-Damm*   63 **X5**
Josh. 15. 7; 18. 17
Adura: *Dura*   57, 62 **Y3**
mentioned in Amarna letters as city hostile to prince of Pehel (Pella)
Aegean Sea   52, 78, 82, 89, 91 **D3**
Aelana (Aila): *ʿAqaba*   89 **F5**
Roman period port, successor of biblical Elath, *q.v.*
Aelia, Wall of: 96
Aelia Capitolina was Roman colony planted by Hadrian in A.D. 130 on site of Jerusalem, which had been destroyed A. D. 70
Aenon (? *springs N. of Kh. Umm elʿUmdan*   86 **Y4**
John 3. 23
Aetolia: *reg.*   82 **D3**
a backward part of Greece in classical times but later organized as a League of cities
'Affuleh   94 **X3**
site inhabited since prehistoric times, sometimes identified with Ophrah of Judg. 6. 11 etc.
Africa: *Roman prov.*   88 **B4**
former Carthaginian territory in mod. Tunisia, conquered and Romanized, with coastal extension E-wards: civilized and Latin-speaking.
Agade: *T. Abu Ghubar* (?)   55 **H4**

capital of Akkad in 3rd millennium B.C.
Agrigentum: *Girgenti*   88 **B3**
Greek colony, city of Roman prov. of Sicily
Agrippa's Wall: 96
a third north wall of Jerusalem built by Herod Agrippa I (*see p. 97*)
Agrippias (Anthedon): *el-Blahiyeh*, *nr. Teida*   85, 87 **V5**
Greek city of Anthedon rebuilt by Herod the Great and renamed in honour of Emp. Augustus's minister Agrippa
Agrippina: *Kaukab el-Hawa*   86 **Y3**
fortress and signal station
Ahlab: *Kh. el-Mahalib*   61, 73 **X2**
Judg. 1. 31: same as Mahalab, Josh. 19. 29
Ahnas: Heracleopolis, *q.v.*   92 **F5**
Ai: *et-Tell*   57, 61, 63, 69, 95 **X5**
    77 *ins*
Canaanite city, captured by Joshua, Josh. 7–8; also Gen. 12. 8; Ezra 2. 28; (in Jer. 49. 3 'Ai' is a scribal corruption)
Aialon: *Kh. Halyan*   87 **X5**
same as Aiath, *q.v.*
Aiath: *Kh. Halyan*   73 **X5**
    77 *ins*
Isa. 10. 28; same as Avvim, *q.v.*
Aijalon: *Yalo*   49, 57, 61, 63, 69 **X5**
in Dan, Josh. 19. 42; Levitical city, Josh. 21. 24; fortified by Rehoboam, 2 Chr. 11. 10; *see also* Elon (1 Kgs. 4. 9)
Aijalon: *Kh. el-Lon*   62 **X3**
in Zebulun, Judg. 12. 12
Aijalon, Valley of: *W. Selman*   49 **W5**
Aila (Aelana): nr.ʿ*Aqaba*   89 **F5**
see Aelana
Ain: *see* En-rimmon
'Ain ed-Duyuk: 95 **X5**
site of ancient cemetery and ruined synagogue
'Ain el-Maʿmudiyeh: 95 **X5**
ruins of a church associated in tradition with John the Baptist
'Ain Feshkha   95 **X5** *and ins*
spring, near which excavations show buildings of same period as those at Kh. Qumran, *q.v.* Probably same as En-eglaim, *q.v.*
'Ain Karim   95 **X5**
ancient site, traditionally identified with Beth-haccherem, *q.v.*, and with home of Zechariah and Elizabeth (Luke 1. 39)
Ain-rimmon (En-rimmon): *Kh. Umm er-Ramamim*
    63 **W6**
Neh. 11. 29 (En-rimmon). In Josh. 15. 32 'Ain-rimmon' should probably be read for 'Ain, and Rimmon'.
Akhetaton: *Tell el-Amarna*   54, 67 **F5**
    58 **P5**
capital of Egypt under Pharaoh Akhenaton; *see p. 55*; *illus. pp. 22, 23*
Akkad: *reg.*   55, 75 **J4**
country N. of Sumer, with Sumer forming Babylonia: *see pp. 54–55*
Akrabatta (Akrabattene): *ʿAqraba*   77 **X4**
1 Macc. 5. 3; *see also* Acrabbein
Akrabbim, Ascent of: *Naqb es-Safa*   49, 57, 61 **X7**
Judg. 1. 36; Josh. 15. 3
Alaça Hüyük   93 **F2**
ancient site: Hittite remains
Alalakh: *Tellʿ Atshana*   67, 93 **G3**
ancient site, capital of Syro-Hittite kingdom in time

of Egyptian Middle Kingdom

Alashiya: 67 F3
  ancient capital of Cyprus. *See also* Enkomi

Alashiya (Kittim, Cyprus): *isl.*   55 F3

Alborz (Elburz) Mts.   53 K3

Alema: *'Alma*   77 Z3
  Greek name of Helam, *q.v.*; 1 Macc. 5. 26

Alemeth: *Kh. 'Almit*
  in Benjamin, 1 Chr. 6. 60; 7. 8; same as Almon, *q.v.*

Aleppo: *Haleb, Halab*   55, 71, 78, 82, 93 G3
  see also Beroea

Alexandria (in Egypt): *Iskandariyeh*
     52, 82, 89, 90, 92 E4
  city founded by Alexander the Great, in which he was
  buried; capital of Egypt under Ptolemies; seaport and
  large city, mainly Greek, with strong Jewish community. Acts 18. 24; 27. 6; 28. 11

Alexandria (in Syria): *Alexandretta*   82, 91 G3

Alexandria (in Carmania): *Gulashkird*   83 L5

Alexandria (Antiochia Margiana): *Mary*   83 M3
  chief city of Bactria-Sogdiana, founded by Alexander,
  renamed Antiochia Margiana, later *Merv*, now *Mary*

Alexandria Arachōsiōn: *Ghazni*   83 N4
  Alexandria 'of the Arachosians'

Alexandria Ariōn (Artacoana): *Herat*   83 M4
  Alexandria 'of the Arians'

Alexandria Kapisa   83 N3

Alexandria Troas: 89, 91 E3
  full name of city called in N.T. 'Troas', *q.v.*

Alexandrium: *Qarn Sartabeh*   85, 87 X4
  fortress built by Alexander Jannaeus and restored
  under Herod the Great

Alexandropolis: *Kandahar*   83 N4

Alishar (Ališar Hüyük): Ankuwa   93 G3
  excavated Hittite site; the god of Ankuwa is mentioned in Hittite texts

Almon: *Kh. Almit*   63 X5
  In Benjamin, Josh. 21. 18; same as Alemeth, *q.v.*

Almon-diblathaim (Beth-diblathaim): *Khirbet Deleilat*
esh-Sherqiyeh   63 Y5
  Num. 33. 46–47

Alulos: *Halhul*   87 X5
  mentioned by Josephus

Amalek: *people*   65 W6
  Gen. 36. 16; Exod. 17. 8 ff.; 1 Sam. 15. 2 ff.

Amanus Mts.   52, 71 G3

Amarna, *see* Tell el-Amarna

Amasea: 89, 91 G2
  Hellenistic city

Amastris: 91 F2
  Hellenistic city

Amathus (in Palestine): *T. 'Ammata*   85, 86 Y4

Amathus (in Cyprus):   78, 93 F4
  city, originally Phoenician colony

Amida: *Diyarbakr*   67 H3

Amisus: *Samsun*   89, 91 G2
  Greek city-state

Amman: 95 Y5
     93 G4
  modern city, capital of Kingdom of Jordan, on site of
  ancient Rabbah, *q.v.*, chief city of Ammon. *See also*
  Philadelphia

Ammathus: *Hammam Tabariyeh*   86 Y3
  Hellenistic city, former Hammath, *q.v.*

Ammon: *reg.*   57, 61, 63, 65, 69, 73, 77
     67, 71, 75, 78 G4
  country of the Ammonites (Gen. 19. 38), bounded by
  R. Jabbok (Deut. 3. 16); Judg. 10 7 ff.; 2 Sam. 10. 1 ff.;
  11 1 ff.; Amos 1. 13

Ammon (Siwa), Oasis of: 66, 82 E5
  site of temple and oracle of the god Zeus (Jupiter)
  Ammon

Amorites: *people*   57 Y5
  Gen. 10. 16; Num. 21. 13; Judg. 1. 34 ff.

Amorium: 91 F3
  city in Phrygia

Amphipolis: *Neochori, Amfipolis*   90 D2
  Greek city, Acts 17. 1

Amu Darya (Oxus): *riv.*   53 M2

Anab: *Kh. 'Anab es-Saghireh*   61, 63 W6
  in hill country of Judah, Josh. 11. 21; 15. 50

Anaharath: *en-Na'ura*   57, 62 X3
  in Issachar, Josh. 19. 19

Ananiah: *el-'Azariyeh*   63 X5
     77 ins
  Neh. 3. 23; 11. 32; later Bethany, *q.v.*, i.e. Beth-
  ananiah, Greek Bethania

Anat: *'Ana*   75 H4

Anathoth: *Ras el-Kharrubeh*
     61, 63, 65, 69, 73, 77 *and ins*, 87 X5
  in Benjamin, Levitical city, Josh. 21. 18; home of
  Jeremiah, Jer. 1. 1; Neh. 7. 27

Anathu Borcaeus: *Kh. Berqit*   87 X4
  mentioned by Josephus

Anatolia *reg.*   52, 92 F3
  geographical name for the peninsula of Asia Minor,
  q.v., derived from Greek 'anatolē', 'east', since it was
  eastern frontier district of Byzantine empire

Ancona: *Ancona*   88 B2
  Roman city

Ancyra: *Ankara*   82, 89, 91, 93 F3
  capital of Rom. prov. of Galatia, where Augustus set
  up inscription commemorating achievements of his
  reign: *see also* Ankara

Andros: *isl.*   92 D3

Anim: *Kh. Ghuwein et-Tahta*   63 X6
  in hill country of Judah, Josh. 15. 50

Ankara: 93 F3
  mod. capital of Turkey, ancient Ancyra, *q.v.*

Ankuwa: *Ališar Huyuk, Alishar, q.v.*   55 G3

Anshan (in Persia): *city and reg.*
  original home of Cyrus (*see text, p. 78*); unlocated

Antalya: 92 F3
  site of ancient Attalia, *q.v.*

Anthedon (Agrippias): *el-Blahiyeh, just N. of Teida*
     77, 85, 87 V5
  see Agrippias

Anti-Lebanon: *mts.*   49 Y1

Antioch (in Syria): *Antakiyeh (Antakya)*
     82, 89, 91, 93 G3
  city founded by K. Antiochus I; cap. of Seleucid
  empire, then of Rom. prov. of Syria. 1 Macc. 6. 63;
  Acts 11. 19 ff.; 13. 1; 14. 26 etc.; Gal. 2. 11

Antioch (in Pisidia): *Yalvaç*   89, 91, 92 F3
  Hellenistic city, then Rom. colony. Acts 13. 14; 14. 19,
  21; 2 Tim. 3. 11

Antioch (Gerasa)   77 Y4
     82 G4
  also 'Antioch on the Chrysorhoas'

Antiochia-Margiana (Alexandria): *Mary*
  see Alexandria   83 M3

Antiochus, Kingdom of: 91 F3
  territory comprising Commagene, with Cilicia
  Trachea, *q.v.*, ruled by Antiochus as client king under
  early Rom. empire

Antipatris (Pegai): *Ras el-'Ain*   85, 87 W4
  former Aphek, called in Gk. 'Pegai' (springs), rebuilt
  by Herod the Great and renamed in honour of Antipater his father. Acts 23. 31

Antium: *Anzio*   88 B2
  Rom. city and port

Antonia Tower (Jerusalem):   96
  see text, p. 97

Apamea (in Syria): *Famiya, Qal'at Mudiq*   89, 91 G3

Apamea (in Phrygia):   82, 91 F3
  Graeco-oriental city, also called Celaenae

Apennine Mts.   52, 88 B2

Aphairema: *et-Taiyibeh*   77, 87 X5
  Gk. form of name Ophrah, *q.v.*, 1 Macc. 11. 34, same
  as Ephraim in John 11. 54

Aphek- *Ras el-'Ain*   49, 57, 61, 63, 77, 95 W4
  in coastal plain, Josh. 12. 18; site of Philistine camp,
  1 Sam. 4. 1. Excavations. *See also* Antipatris

Aphek (Aphik): *T. Kurdaneh*   61, 62 X3
  in Asher, Josh. 19. 30; Judg. 1. 31

Aphek: *Fiq*   62, 69, 94 X3
  in Transjordan, in half-tribe of Manasseh, 1 Kgs. 20.
  26 ff. Or at *En-Gev, p. 94* Y3

Aphek: *Afqa*
  in Phoenicia, Josh. 13. 4

Aphek, Tower of: *Majdal Yaba*   87 W4
  Gk. 'Aphekou Pyrgos', mentioned by Josephus

Aphekah: *Kh. Kana'an*   63 X5
  in Judah, Josh. 15. 53

Aphik: *see* Aphek

Apollonia (Sozusa): *Arsuf*   77, 85, 87 W4

Apollonia (in E. Macedonia): *Pollina*   90 D2
  Acts 17. 1

Apollonia (in W. Macedonia, on Adriatic)   88 C2

Appia: 91 F3
  Gk. city, earlier Hittite Appawiya

Appian Way: 88 C3
  main road from Rome to Brundisium, and thence via
  Egnatian Way, *q.v.*, to the East

Apii Forum (Forum of Appius):   88 C2
  small Italian town ('forum'=market), Acts 28. 15

Aqaba, Gulf of: 52 F5
     59 U4

Aqar Quf   93 H4

Ar: *el-Misna*   57, 63, 73 Y6
  town of Moab, Deut. 2. 9 ff.; Isa. 15. 1

Arab: *Kh. er-Rabiyeh*   63 X6
  in Judah, Josh. 15. 52

Arabah, the: *el-Ghor*   49, 57, 61, 63, 65, 69, 73 Y4
     52 G2
     59 U2
  the rift valley in which the Jordan and the Dead Sea
  lie, from the Sea of Galilee to the head of the Gulf of
  Aqaba. Deut. 2. 8; 4. 49; Josh. 11. 2

Arabah, Sea of the (Dead Sea, Salt Sea):
     49, 57, 61, 63, 65, 69, 73
  Deut. 3. 17; Josh. 3. 16; 2 Kgs. 14. 25

Arabia: *reg.*   55, 67, 71, 78, 82, 93
  1 Kgs. 10. 15; Ezek. 27. 21. *See also* Arabs, Nabataean
  Kingdom

Arabian Desert   53, 89

Arabs: *people*   75 G4
  2 Chr. 17. 11; 21. 16; Neh. 4. 7

Arachosia: *reg.*   79, 83 M4

Arad: *T. 'Arad*   63, 65, 69, 95 X6
     59 U1
  in records of Shishak, 'Great Arad'. Solmonic and
  later. Excavations

Arad: *T. el-Milh* (?)   57, 61, 69, 95 X6
     59U1
  perhaps Canaanite Arad, or possibly name of a petty
  kingdom (ARAD, pp. 60–61). Num. 21. 1, Josh. 12. 14;
  Judg. 1. 16. In Shishak's list perhaps 'Arad of Beth-
  yeroham'

Arad: *reg. See Arad (Tell el-Milh)*

Arad of Beth-yeroham: *see* Arad (Tell el-Milh)

Aradus: Gk. name of Arvad, *q.v.*
  1 Macc. 15. 23

Araks (Araxes): *riv.*   53 J3

Aral Sea   53 L2

Aram (Syria):   57, 65, 69, 73 Z2
  'Aram' is name of ancestor of the Syrians, Gen. 10.
  22 ff., and Hebrew for 'Syria'. Num. 23. 7; 2 Sam.
  8. 6; Hos. 12. 12. (Hence 'Aramaic' is the Syrian
  language, 2 Kgs. 18. 26; Ezra 4. 7)

Araq el-Emir   63, 77, 95 Y5
  site of castle and tomb of post-Exilic period

Ararat (Urartu): *reg.*   55, 67, 71, 75 H3
  Gen. 8. 4; 2 Kgs. 19. 37; Jer. 51. 27. As 'Urartu' known
  from extra-Biblical sources; roughly equals later
  Armenia, *q.v.*

Aras (Araks, Araxes): *riv.*   53 J3

Araxes (Araks, Aras): *riv.*   53, 79, 83, 89 J3

Arbatta: *reg.*   77 W3
  1 Macc. 5. 23

Arbela (in Galilee): *Kh. Irbid*   49, 77, 86, 94 X3
  1 Macc. 9. 2

Arbela (in Transjordan): *Irbid*   49, 77, 86 Y3
  Gk. name of Beth-arbel, *q.v.*

Arbela (in Assyria): *Erbil (Arbil)*   67, 71, 78, 82, 89 H3
     89, 91 G4

Arca: *reg.*   77 X5

Archelais (in Judea): *Kh. 'Auja et-Tahta*   85, 87 X5
  place founded by Archelaus, son of Herod the Great,
  tetrarch of Judea 4 B.C.–A.D. 6

Archelais (in Cappadocia):   89, 91 F3
  Rom. colony, and capital of K. Archelaus of Cappadocia

Areius: *Heri Rud: riv.*   79, 83 M4

Areopolis (Rabbath-moab): *Kh. er-Rabba*   87 Y6

Argob: *reg.*   57, 65 Z3
  Deut. 3. 4, 13 f.; 1 Kgs. 4. 13

Argos: 54, 92 D3
  Greek city, important in Bronze Age and in classical
  times

Aria: *reg.*   79, 83 M4

Ariha (mod. Jericho):   95 ins
  Arabic form of 'Yeriho' (Eng. Jericho), but site is
  slightly different from those of both O.T. and N.T.
  cities

Arimathea (Rathamin): *Rentis*   87 X4
  Matt. 27. 57 &c., same as Ramathaim-Zophim, *q.v.*

Ariminum: *Rimini*   88 B2

Aristobulias: *Kh. Istabul*   87 X6

Armenia: *reg.*   53, 78, 82, 89, 93 H3
  thirteenth satrapy of Darius I's empire; later kingdom
  on frontier of Rom. empire

Armenia, Lesser: 89 G2
  part of Armenia within the frontier of Rom. empire

Arnon: *Wadi Mojib: riv.*   49 &c., 95 Y6

Num. 21. 13, 24; Deut. 3. 8; Jer. 48. 20

Aroer (in Moab): *'Ara'ir*
           49, 57, 61, 63, 65, 69, 73, 95 **Y6**
allotted to Reuben, Josh. 13. 16; 2 Sam. 24. 5; Jer.
48. 19; excavations

Aroer (in Negeb): *'Ar'arah*   57, 61 **W6**
1 Sam. 30. 28; same as Adadah, *q.v.*

Aroer (near Rabbah):
boundary of Gad, Josh. 13. 25; Judg. 11. 33; unlocated

Arpad: *T. Erfad*   71, 75, 78 **G3**
2 Kgs. 18. 34; Isa. 10. 9; Jer. 49. 23

Arrapkha: *Kirkuk*   69, 71, 75, 78 **H3**

Arretium: *Arezzo*   88 **B2**

Arslan Tash: 93 **G3**
site of Assyrian frontier-town of Hadatu, with palace of
Tiglath-pileser III

Artacoana (Alexandria Ariōn): *Herat*   79 **M4**

Artaxata: *Ardashir*   89 **H2**
capital of kingdom of Armenia

Arubboth: *'Arrabeh*   57, 62, 65 **X4**
in Solomon's third district, 1 Kgs. 4. 10

Arumah: *Kh. el-'Ormeh*   61, 63 **X4**
Judg. 9. 31, 41

Aruna: *T. 'Ara*   57, 62 **X4**
Canaanite and Israelite city mentioned in Egyptian
records

Arus: *Haris*   87 **X4**
mentioned by Josephus

Arvad: *Erwad, Ruwad*   55, 67, 71, 75, 78 **G4**
Phoenician city-state, later Aradus. Ezek. 27. 8, 11

Arzawa: *reg.*   54 **F3**
Anatolian territory conquered by Hittites and incorporated in their empire (location conjectural)

Asagarta *see* **Sagartia**

Ascent of Beth-horon: 61 **X5**
road between Lower and Upper Beth-horon: *see*
Beth-horon. Josh. 10. 10 f.

Ascalon: Gk. form of Ashkelon, *q.v.*

Ascalon, Baths of (Maiumas Ascalon)   77 **W5**

Ashan
in Judah, Josh. 15. 42; unlocated

Ashan: *Kh. 'Asan*   61, 62 **W6**
in Simeon, Josh. 19. 7

Ashdod (Azotus): *Isdud*
        49, 57, 61, 63, 65, 69, 73, 95 **W5**
        78 **F4**
        59 **T1**
Philistine city, Josh. 13. 3; 1 Sam. 5. 1 ff.; Neh. 13.
23 f.; Jer. 25. 20; later Azotus, *q.v.*; excavations

Asher: *tribe*   61, 65, 69, 73 **X2**
Josh. 19. 24–30; Judg. 1. 31; 1 Kgs. 4. 16

Ashkelon (Ascalon): *'Asqalan* [*Ashqelon*]
    49, 57, 61, 65, 69, 73, 77, 85, 87, 95 **W5**
        67, 75 **F4**
Philistine city, Josh. 13. 3; Judg. 14. 19; 1 Sam. 6. 17;
Jer. 25. 20. Later, called Ascalon, Greek city-state

Ashnah: *Idhna*   63 **W5**
in Judah, Josh. 15. 43

Ashnah (near Zorah): *'Aslin*   63 **X5**
in Judah, Josh. 15. 33

Ashtaroth: *T. 'Ashtarah*   49, 57, 61, 62, 69, 73 **Z3**
city of Bashan, Deut. 1. 4; allotted to half tribe of
Manasseh, Josh. 13. 31; 1 Chr. 6. 71

Ashteroth-karnaim:
see text p. 56 and Gen. 14. 5

Asia: *reg.*   89, 91 **E3**
western part of Anatolia, *q.v.*, bordering Aegean Sea;
name possibly derived from Assuwa, *q.v.*; under Rom.
empire an important and wealthy province; Acts 2. 9;
6. 9; 19. 10 ff.; Rom. 16. 5; 1 Pet. 1. 1; Rev. 1. 4

Asia:
in wider sense than above, refers to the Seleucid
empire, 1 Macc. 8. 6; 11. 13. *Cf.* modern name of
continent.

Asia Minor: *reg.*   52 **F3**
modern geographical name for western peninsula of
continent of Asia between Black Sea, Aegean, and
Mediterranean; *see also* Anatolia

Asochis (Shihin): *Kh. el-Lon*   77, 86 **X3**
Gk. name, used by Josephus, for Shihin, *q.v.*; earlier
Aijalon (in Zebulun), *q.v.*

Asor: *Yazur*   61, 62, 73 **W4**
Assyrian Azuru: possible reading in Josh. 19. 45,
following Septuagint (Gk.) version (in place of Heb.
Jehud)

Azor: Gk. form used in Septuagint for 'Hazor' at 1
Macc. 11. 67 (some MSS, and KJV, have 'Nasor'):

see Hazor

Asphaltitis, Lake: 77, 87 **X5**
Greek name for Dead Sea

Asshur: *Qalat Sherqat* 55, 67, 71, 75, 78, 93 **H3**
leading city of Assyria, *q.v.* Ezek. 27. 23

Assos: *Behramköy*   89, 91, 92 **E3**
Greek city and seaport. Acts 20. 13, 14

Assuwa: *reg.*   54 **E3**
country in western Anatolia mentioned in Hittite
records. *See also* Asia

Assyria: *reg.*   55, 67, 71, 75, 78 **H3**
Gen. 2. 14; 10. 11; home of warlike people who conquered great empire, *see pp. 68–71*; 2 Kgs. 15. 19 ff.;
16. 7 ff.; 17. 3–6; 18. 9 ff.; 18. 13 ff.; 19. 36; Isa. 7. 17;
10. 5; 20. 1 &c. Conquered by the Babylonians, Nah.
3. 18. Later ninth satrapy in empire of Darius I. *See
text pp. 70–71, and Introduction*

Astrabad (Gorgan):   79, 83 **K3**
site of ancient city

Ataroth: *T. Mazar*   61, 63 **X4**
on border of Ephraim, Josh. 16. 7

Ataroth: *Kh. 'Attarus*   57, 63, 69, 73 **Y5**
Num. 32. 3, 34

Ataroth:
Josh. 16. 2: same as Ataroth-addar, *q.v.*

Ataroth-addar: *Kefr 'Aqab*   63 **X5**
on border of Ephraim and Benjamin, Josh. 16. 5; 18.
13

Athens: 52, 54, 66, 74, 78, 82, 89, 90 **D3**
leading city of Greece, important especially in 5th
cent. B.C.; under Rom. empire still an intellectual
centre. Acts 17. 15 ff.; 1 Thess. 3. 1.

'Athlit (Pilgrims' Castle):   94 **W3**
site of ancient Phoenician settlement: *see also* Pilgrims' Castle, *and* Bucolōn Polis

Athribis: *T. Atrib*   58 **Q2**
      71 **F4**
cap. of tenth nome of Lower Egypt

Atrax: *riv.*   55 **L3**

'Atshana (T. Atshana) (Alalakh)   93 **G3**
site of important excavations: *see also* Alalakh

Attalia: *Antalya*   89, 91 **F3**
city and seaport, Acts 14. 25

Auja el-Hafir: *see* Nessana   91 **X6**

Auranitis: *reg.*   85 **Z3**
part of the territory of Herod the Great, allotted to his
son Herod Philip the tetrarch; Gk. name of Hauran,
q.v.

Avaris (Rameses, Tanis, Zoan): *San el-Hagar* 54 **F4**
      58 **Q2**
Hyksos capital in Egypt: *see text pp. 58–59, also*
Rameses, Zoan

Avva: *T. Kefr 'Aya*
2 Kgs. 17. 24, 31; on River Orontes

Avvim: *Kh. Haiyan*   73, 77 **X5**
same as Aiath, *q.v.*, Josh. 18. 23

Avvim: *people*
Deut. 2. 23; Josh. 13. 3 (not a place in these references)

Axius: *riv.*   90 **D2**

Ayia Triada (Hagia Triada):   92 **D3**
site of Minoan remains

Azekah: *T. Zakariyeh* 49, 61, 63, 69, 73, 77, 95 **W5**
      59 **T1**
Josh. 10. 10 f.; in Judah, Josh. 15. 35; 1 Sam. 17. 1;
Jer. 34. 7 (*and see text p. 72*); Neh. 11. 30

Azmaveth: *Hizmeh*   77 **ins**
Ezr. 2. 24; Neh. 12. 29; cf. Beth-azmaveth, Neh. 7. 28

Azmon: *Qeseimeh*   59 **T2**
Num. 34. 4; border of Judah, Josh. 15. 4

Aznoth-tabor: *Kh. Umm Jubeil*   62 **X3**
border of Naphtali, Josh. 19. 34

Azotus (Ashdod): *Isdud*   82 **F4**
      77, 85, 87 **W5**
Gk. form of Ashdod, 1 Macc. 5. 68; 10. 77 ff.; Acts
8. 40

Azotus Paralius: 87 **W5**
Gk. name ('Azotus-on-Sea') for coastal settlement
near Azotus

Azov, Sea of   52 **G1**

Baalah (in Negeb): *Kh. Abu Tulul*   63 **W6**
in Simeon, Josh. 15. 29; 19. 3

Baalah (Kiriath-jearim): *T. el-Azhar*   61, 63 **X5**
Josh. 15. 9; 1 Chr. 13. 6; *and see* Kiriath-jearim

Baalah, Mount: *see* **Mount Baalah**

Baalah: *Qatra*   61, 63, 65, 69, 73 **W5**
in Dan, Josh. 19. 44; fortified by Solomon, 1 Kgs.
9. 18; 2 Chr. 8. 6

Ba'albek   93 **G4**
the ancient Heliopolis, *q.v.*, with impressive extant
Rom. remains

Baal-gad: *Hasbaiya*   61 **Y2**
Josh. 11. 17; 12. 7; 13. 5

Baal-hazor: *T. 'Asur*   63, 65, 69 **X5**
2 Sam. 13. 23

Baal-meon (Beth-meon, Beth-baal-meon, Beon): *Ma'in*
      57, 63, 69, 73 **Y5**
Num. 32. 38; 1 Chr. 5. 8; Ezek. 25. 9

Baal-peor (Beth-peor): *Kh. esh-Sheikh Jayil* 63, 69 **Y5**
Deut. 4. 3; Hos. 9. 10; *see* Beth-peor

Baal-perazim: *Sheikh Bedr* nr. Jerusalem
2 Sam. 5. 20; same as Mount Perazim, Isa. 28. 21

Baal-shalishah: *Kefr Thilth*   61, 63, 69 **X4**
2 Kgs. 4. 42: *cf.* 'land of Shalisha', 1 Sam. 9. 4

Baal-tamar (N. of Jerusalem): perhaps *Ras et-Tawil*
Judg. 20. 33

Baal-zephon: *T. Defenneh*   58 **R2**
Exod. 14. 2, 9; Num. 33. 7. *See text p. 58*

Bab ed-Dra':   95 **Y6**
Bronze-Age fortified town and cemetery

Babylon (in Egypt): *Fostat*   89 **F5**

Babylon (in Mesopotamia):
    53, 55, 67, 71, 75, 78, 82, 89, 93 **H4**
ancient city, cap. of first Babylonian empire (*see pp.
54–55*) later in Assyrian empire (2 Kgs. 17. 24); then
cap. of Neo-Babylonian empire which conquered
Assyria (*see pp. 74–75*) and sacked Jerusalem in 586
B.C., carrying Jews into Exile in Babylonia (2 Kgs.
24. 1 ff.; 25. 1 ff.; 25. 27 f.; Ezr. 2. 1; Ezek. 12. 13;
17. 16. Conquered by Cyrus in 538 B.C., then in
Persian empire till conquered by Alexander, 331 B.C.;
then in Seleucid, then Parthian, empire. From time of
Exile onward contained strong Jewish colony. *See
text, pp. 74–75, and Introduction*

Babylon:
in 1 Pet. 5. 13 probably stands for Rome (the heathen
city where God's people are living); in Rev. 17. 5 and
18. 2, 9 also probably Rome (the heathen persecuting
power)

Babylonia: *reg.*   55, 67, 71, 75, 78, 82 **J4**
Ezra 1. 11 &c. *See also* Chaldaea, Shinar, Sumer

Baca, valley of:
Ps. 84. 6; unlocated; perhaps figurative meaning
('baca' = name of a tree of unknown species, related to
verb meaning 'to weep'(?)

Baca: *el-Buqei'a*   86 **X3**
site in Upper Galilee with remains of (post-biblical)
synagogue

Bactra: *Balkh*   79 **N3**
capital city of Bactria, also named Alexandria Bactra

Bactria: *reg.*   79, 83 **M3**
twelfth satrapy in empire of Darius I; reached by
Alexander in his conquests; later under Graeco-
Asiatic kings

Badari: 92 **F5**
excavated site

Bahnasa: *see* Oxyrhynchus   89, 92 **F5**

Balikh: *riv.*   53, 71, 75 **G3**

Balikhu: *T. Djigle*   75 **G3**
city captured by Nabopolassar, mentioned in Babylonian Chronicle; later Rom. Dabana

Balkan Mts.   52 **D2**

Baluchistan: *reg.*   53 **M5**

Bamoth:
Num. 21. 19 f.: same as Bamoth-baal, *q.v.*

Bamoth-baal: near *Kh. el-Quweiqiyeh*   63 **Y5**
Num. 22. 41; allotted to Reuben, Josh. 13. 17

Baris: *fort* (in Jerusalem)   81
see text, p. 80

Bashan: 49, 57, 61, 62, 65, 69 **Y3**
      67 **G4**
kingdom of Og, conquered by Israelites, Num. 21.
33–35; allotted to half tribe of Manasseh, Josh. 13. 29;
fertile and wooded, Isa. 2. 13; Ezek. 27. 6; 39. 18

Baskama: *el-Jummeizeh*   77 **Y3**
1 Macc. 13. 23

Batanaea: *reg.*   85, 86 **Y3**
Gk. name of region corresponding to Bashan, *q.v.*;
part of tetrarchy of Philip, with Ituraea and Trachonitis, *qq.v.*

Bathyra: *Basir*   85 **Z2**
founded by Herod (Josephus, *Antiq.* xvii. 11. 1–3)

Battir: *Bethir*   95 **X5**
small fortified town commanding SW. approach to
Jerusalem; *see* Bethir

Bawit   92 **F5**

Bealoth (in Negeb):
in Judah, Josh. 15. 24; unlocated
Bealoth (in N. Israel):
1 Kgs. 4. 16: with Asher forming Solomon's ninth district; otherwise unlocated
Beautiful Gate, the (in Jerusalem) 96
Acts 3. 2, 10; *and see text, p. 97*
Beer: *el-Bireh* 61, 62 X3
Judg. 9. 21
Beer (in Moab):
Num. 21. 16; unlocated
Beeroth (in Benjamin): *Ras et-Tahuneh*
61, 63, 65, 77 X5
Josh. 9. 17; 18. 25; 2 Sam. 4. 2 f.; Ezr. 2. 25; Neh. 7. 29. *See also* Berea
Beeroth (Bene-jaakan): *Birein* 59 T2
Deut. 10. 6
Beer-sheba: *T. es-Seba'*
49, 57, 61, 63, 65, 69, 73, 77, 85, 87, 95 W6
55 F4
59 T1
site visited by Abraham, Isaac, and Jacob, Gen. 21. 31–33; 22. 19; 26. 23, 33; 28. 10; 46. 1; in Negeb of Judah, Josh. 15. 28; allotted to Simeon, Josh. 19. 2; southern extremity of Israel's territory, Judg. 20. 1; 1 Kgs. 4. 25; renowned as sanctuary, Amos 5. 5; 8. 14. *See also* Bersabe
Beersheba: *mod. city* 51 W6
lies further W. than ancient Beer-sheba
Beer-sheba, Valley of: *Wadi Bir es-Seba'* 49 W6
Beerzeth (Berzetho): *Bir Zeit* 77, 87 X5
place figuring in Maccabean war ('Berea' in 1 Macc. 9. 4, but correctly named by Josephus)
Behistun (Bisitun): 79, 93 J4
site of monumental inscription of Darius I: *see text pp. 78–79 and illus. p. 30*
Beisan: 51 X3
mod. city near site of Beth-shan, *q.v.*
Beit Alfa: *see* Beth Alpha
Beitin: 96 X5
site of ancient Bethel, *q.v.*, partly explored by excavation
Beit Jibrin: *see* Beth Gubrin
Beit Jimal: 95 W5
site of Byzantine church (5th–6th cent. A.D.)
Beit Nattif: 95 W5
site of Bethletepha, *q.v.*
Belus (Kedron): *Nahr Rubin: riv.* 49, 87 W5
Bemesilis: *el-Meseliyyeh* 86 X4
Bene-berak: *Ibn Beraq* 62, 73 W4
in original territory of Dan, Josh. 19. 45; mentioned in Sennacherib's annals as taken in 701 B.C.
Benei Berak: 95 W4
mod. Israeli village with nearby site of ancient settlement and cemetery
Benei Hezir, Monument of (in Jerusalem) 81, 96
Bene-jaakan (Beeroth): *Birein* 59 T2
Num. 33. 31 f.; Deut. 10. 6; *see* Beeroth
Beni-hasan: 54, 92 F5
58 P5
site of Egyptian tomb with wall-painting of Semitic nomads
Beneventum: *Benevento* 88 B2
Benjamin: *tribe* 61, 65, 69 X5
Gen. 35. 18; Josh. 18. 11–28; Judg. 1. 21; 1 Kgs. 4. 18; Neh. 11. 31; Rom. 11. 1
Benjamin, Gate of (in Jerusalem) 81
Jer. 17. 19; 20. 2; Zech. 14. 10
Beon (Baal-meon, Beth-baal-meon, Beth-meon): *Ma'in*
57, 63 Y5
Num. 32. 3; *see also* Baal-meon, &c.
Beracah, Vale of: *Wadi Ghar* 49, 69 X5
2 Chr. 20. 26
Berea (in Palestine): *el Bireh* 87 X5
Gk. form of name of Beeroth, *q.v.*; 1 Macc. 9. 4; *but see* Beerzeth
Berea (in Greece): *see* Beroea
Berea (in Syria): *see* Beroea
Berenike: 67 G6
port on Red Sea, so named by Greeks but existing from earlier period
Beroea (in Greece): *Verria* 89, 90 D2
Gk. town in Rom. prov. of Macedonia; Acts 17. 10, 13; 20. 4 (KJV Berea)
Beroea (in Syria): *Aleppo, q.v.*
2 Macc. 13. 4 (KJV Berea)
Bersabe (in Idumea): 85, 87 W6
Graeco-Roman period town corresponding to Beer-

sheba, *q.v.*
Bersabe (in Galilee): *Kh. Abu esh-Sheba'* 86 X3
village on boundary of Upper and Lower Galilee
Berytus: *Beirut* 55, 67, 71, 82, 89, 91 G4
Phoenician seaport city
Berzetho (Beerzeth): *Bir Zeit* 77, 87 X5
see Beerzeth
Besara: *Kh. Bir el-Beidar* 86 X3
Besor, Brook: *Wadi Ghazzeh [Habesor]*
49, 61, 63, 69, 73, 87 V6
1 Sam. 30. 9, 10
Beten: *Kh. Ibtin (Abtun)* 62 X3
in Asher, Josh. 19. 25
Beth Alpha (*Beit Alfa*) 94 X3
site of Jewish village, with remains of 6th-cent A. D. synagogue
Beth-anath: *el-Ba'neh* 57, 61, 62 X3
in Naphtali, Josh. 19. 38; Judg. 1. 33
Beth-anoth: *Kh. Beit 'Anun* 63 X5
in hill country of Judah, Josh. 15. 59
Bethany: *el-'Azariyeh* 85, 87, 95 X5
N.T. (English) name of 'Bethania', Gk. form of Beth-ananiah, i.e. O.T. Ananiah, *q.v.* Home of Martha, Mary, and Lazarus (hence mod. Arabic name), and of Simon the Leper, Matt. 26. 6; Jesus lodged there, Matt. 21. 17; scene of the Ascension, Luke 24. 50
Betharamphtha (Livias, Julias): *T. er-Rameh* 85, 87 Y5
Rom. period city, renamed in honour of Livia (later, by adoption, Julia) of imperial family; head of toparchy
Beth-arbel: *Irbid* 62, 69 Y3
Hos. 10. 14; *see also* Arbela
Beth-aven (Bethel): *Beitin* 69 X5
Josh. 7. 2; 1 Sam. 13. 5; in Hos. 4. 16 refers to calves set up in Bethel, *q.v.*, and Dan by Jeroboam (1 Kgs. 12. 28 f.)
Beth-azmaveth: *see* Azmaveth
Beth-baal-meon (Baal-meon, Beth-meon, Beon): *Ma'in*
61, 63 Y5
allotted to Reuben, Josh. 13. 17; *see also* Baal-meon, &c.
Beth-bamoth (*p. 68*): *see* Bamoth
Beth-basi: *Kh. Beit Bassa* 77, 87 X5
1 Macc. 9. 62, 64
Beth-dagon (in Shephelah of Judah): *Kh. Dajun*
49, 57, 61, 62, 73 W5
Josh. 15. 41
Beth-dagon (in Asher):
on border of Asher, Josh. 19. 27; unlocated
Beth-diblathaim (Almon-diblathaim): *Kh. Deleilat esh-Sherqiyeh* 63, 69, 73 Y5
Jer. 48. 22
Beth-eden (Bit-adini): *reg.* 71 G3
between Euphrates and Balikh rivers; Bit-adini in Assyrian records; Amos 1. 5; same as Eden, 2 Kgs. 19. 12; Isa. 37. 12; Ezek. 27. 23
Beth-eglaim: *T. el-'Ajjul* 95 V6
important city of patriarchal period, site of excavations
Bethel (Luz, Beth-aven); *Beitin*
49, 57, 61, 63, 65, 69, 73, 77 *and ins*, 87, 95 X5
associated with Abraham and Jacob, Gen. 12. 8; 28. 19; on border of Benjamin, Josh. 18. 13; Judg. 1. 22 ff.; 1 Sam. 7. 16; calf set up there by Jeroboam, 1 Kgs. 12. 29; Amos 3. 14; high place destroyed by Josiah, 2 Kgs. 23. 15; its people, Ezra 2. 28; Neh. 7. 32; excavations
Beth-emek: *T. Mimas* 62 X2
on border of Asher, Josh. 19. 27
Bethesda (Beth-zatha), Pool of, in Jerusalem: 96
John 5. 2. The name is variously given in the MSS: Beth-zatha RSV, Bethesda KJV, NEB
Beth-ezel: *Deir el-Asal* 63, 73 W6
Mic. 1. 11
Beth-gamul: *Kh. ej-Jumeil* 63, 77 Y6
Jer. 48. 23
Beth-gilgal (Gilgal): *Kh. el-Mefjir* 63, 77 X5
Neh. 12. 29: same as Gilgal, *q.v.*
Beth Gubrin (*Beit Jibrin*) 95 W5
site of Rom. period town, called Eleutheropolis after 200 A.D.
Beth-haccherem: *Kh. Salih* 63, 73, 77, 95 X5
Jer. 6. 1; Neh. 3. 14. Not to be identified with *'Ain Karim, q.v.*, but very near *Ramat Rahel*
Beth-haggan (En-gannim): *Jenin* 57, 62, 69 X4
mentioned in Middle Bronze Age sources as Beth-haggan; *cf.* 2 Kgs. 9. 27
Beth-hanan: *Beit 'Anan* 63, 65 X5
in 1 Kgs. 4. 9 'Elon, Beth-hanan' should be read as

separate names; both in Solomon's second district
Beth-haram (Beth-haran): *T. Iktanu* 63 Y5
allotted to Gad, Num. 32. 36; Josh. 13. 27
Beth Hashitta [*Beit Hashitta*] 94 X3
mod. Israeli village, site of excavations. (Not same as Biblical Beth-shittah)
Beth-hoglah: *'Ain Hajlah* 63 Y5
on border of Judah and Benjamin, Josh. 15. 6; 18. 19; but included in Benjamin, Josh. 18. 21
Beth-horon (*see below*): 49, 57, 69, 77 X5
near border of Benjamin, Josh. 18. 14; Levitical city, Josh. 21. 22; 1 Chr. 6. 68; 1 Chr. 7. 24. Comprised Upper and Lower cities.
Beth-horon, Lower: *Beit 'Ur et-Tahta*
61, 63, 65, 87 X5
Josh. 16. 3; 18. 13; fortified by Solomon, 1 Kgs. 9. 17; 2 Chr. 8. 5
Beth-horon, Upper: *Beit 'Ur el-Foqa*
61, 63, 65, 87 X5
Josh. 16. 5; 2 Chr. 8. 5
Bethir: *Battir* 95 X5
in hill country of Judah, Josh. 15. 59 (Septuagint)
Beth-jeshimoth: *T. el-'Azeimeh* 57, 61, 63 Y5
Num. 33. 49; Josh. 12. 3; 13. 20; Ezek. 25. 9
Bethlehem (Ephrath) (in Judah): *Beit Lahm*
49, 57, 61, 63, 65, 69, 73, 77, 85, 87, 95 X5
associated with Rachel, Gen. 35. 19 (*cf.* Matt. 2. 18); in Judah, Judg. 17. 7; home of Ruth, Ruth 1. 1 &c.; of David, 1 Sam. 17. 2; 2 Sam. 23. 15; Mic. 5. 2; Ezr. 2. 21; Neh. 7. 26; birth-place of Jesus, Matt. 2. 1 ff.; Luke 2. 4 (*cf.* John 7. 42)
Bethlehem (in Galilee): *Beit Lahm* 61, 62 X3
in Zebulun, Josh. 19. 15
Bethletepha: *Beit Nattif* 87, 95 W5
Rom. period city, devastated by Vespasian
Bethmaus: *T. Ma'un* 86 X3
Beth-meon (Baal-meon, Beth-baal-meon, Beon): *Ma'in*
63, 69, 73 Y5
city of Moab, Jer. 48. 23; *see also* Baal-meon &c.
Beth-nimrah: *T. el-Bleibil* 57, 61, 63 Y5
in Gad, Num. 32. 36; Josh. 13. 27
Beth-pelet:
in Negeb of Judah, Josh. 15. 27; Neh. 11. 26; unlocated
Beth-peor (Baal-peor): *Kh. esh-Sheikh Jayil* 61, 63 Y5
Deut. 3. 29; 4. 46; Josh. 13. 20. Moses buried 'opposite' it, Deut. 34. 6
Bethphage: *Kefr et-Tur* 87 X5
on Mt. of Olives, Matt. 21. 1 &c.
Beth-rehob: *Banias* 61, 62, 65 Y2
Beth-rehob: *reg.* 65 Y2
Judg. 18. 28; inhabited by Syrians, 2 Sam. 10. 6
Bethsaida-Julias: *el-'Araj* 85, 86 Y3
Rom. period fishing village on Sea of Galilee: new city built there by Philip the tetrarch and named Julias after Rom. imperial family; Matt. 11. 21; Mark 6. 45; John 1. 44; prob. a Greek-speaking place, *cf.* John 12. 20 f.
Beth-shan (Beth-shean, Scythopolis): *T. el-Husn* near *Beisan* [*Beit Shean*] 49, 57, 61, 62, 65, 73, 77, 94 Y4
Bronze-Age city (important excavations); allotted to Manasseh, Josh. 17. 11 (*cf.* 1 Chr. 7. 29); held by Canaanites, Josh. 17. 16; by Philistines, 1 Sam. 31. 10; in Solomon's fifth district, 1 Kgs. 4. 12. *Cf.* 1 Macc. 12. 40. *See also* Scythopolis. (*For illus. see p. 101*)
Beth She'arim: *Sheikh Abreiq [Beit She'arim]* 94 X3
post-Biblical Jewish village, site of excavations of catacombs and synagogue
Beth-shemesh (in Egypt):
Jer. 43. 13 (KJV), same as Heliopolis, *q.v.*
Beth-shemesh (in Judah): *T. er-Rumeileh*
57, 61, 63, 65, 69, 73, 95 W5
on border of Judah, Josh. 15. 10; a Levitical city, Josh. 21. 16; 1 Sam. 6. 9 ff.; in Solomon's second district, 1 Kgs. 4. 9; 2 Kgs. 14. 11; 2 Chr. 28. 18
Beth-shemesh (in Issachar): *Kh. Sheikh esh-Shamsawi*
62 X3
Josh. 19. 22
Beth-shemesh (in Naphtali): *Kh. T. er-Ruweisi* 62 X2
Josh. 19. 38; held by Canaanites, Judg. 1. 33
Bethsura (Beth-zur): *Kh. Tubeiqa* 87 X5
fortified place taken from Syrians by Maccabees, 1 Macc. 4. 61; 6. 7; besieged and retaken, 1 Macc. 6. 31, 49; taken by Simon, 1 Macc. 11. 65
Beth-tappuah: *Taffuh* 63 X5
in hill country of Judah, Josh. 15. 53
Bethul (Bethuel): *Kh. er-Ras* 61, 63 W6
in Simeon, Josh. 19. 4; 1 Chr. 4. 30. In 1 Sam. 30. 27, 'Bethel' should probably be Bethuel, or Bethul

Beth-yerah (Philoteria): *Kh. el-Kerak*
57, 62, 77, 86, 94 Y3
mentioned in Middle Bronze Age sources, site of important excavations

Beth-zaith: *Beit Zeita* 77, 87 X5
1 Macc. 7. 19; also called Bezeth (KJV) and Beth-Zita

Beth-zatha: 96
reading in some texts for Bethesda, *q.v.*

Beth-zechariah: *Kh. Beit Sikariya* 77, 87 X5
1 Macc. 6. 32 f.

Beth-zur (Bethsura): *Kh. Tubeiqa [Beit Tsur]*
61, 63, 69, 77, 87, 95 X5
in Judah, Josh. 15. 58; 2 Chr. 11. 7; Neh. 3. 16; *see also* Bethsura

Betogabri: *Beit Jibrin* 85, 87 W5
name of place later enlarged and renamed Eleutheropolis: *see* Beit Jibrin

Betonim: *Kh. Batneh* 61, 63 Y5
Josh. 13. 26

'between the walls' (in Jerusalem) 81
Isa. 22. 11; *and see text, p.* 80

Beycesultan: 92 E3
site of ancient city, perhaps cap. of Arzawa in Hittite period

Beyond the River: *reg.* 78 G4
'Abar-Nahara', the fifth satrapy of Darius I's empire, including Syria, Phoenicia, Palestine, and Cyprus. Ezr. 4. 10 &c., Neh. 2. 7 &c.

Bezek: *Kh. Ibziq* 61, 62 X4
1 Sam. 11. 8

Bezek: *Kh. Bezqa*
Judg. 1. 4 f.; NE. of Gezer

Bezer (Bozrah): *Umm el-'Amad* 57, 61, 63, 69, 73 Y5
city of refuge and Levitical city in Reuben, Deut. 4. 43; Josh. 20. 8; 21. 36. *See also* Bozrah

Bezeth: *see* Beth-zaith

Bezetha: 96
district of Jerusalem

Bileam: same as Ibleam, *q.v.*

Bishapur: 93 K4

Bisitun: *see* Behistun

Bismaya: *Adab* 93 J4

Bit-adini (Beth-eden): *reg.* 71 G3
see Beth-eden

Bithynia and Pontus: *reg.* 89, 91 F2
neighbouring Rom. provinces administered as one. Acts 16. 7; 1 Pet. 1. 1

Black Sea: 52, 55, 71, 75, 78, 82, 93 F2
Gk. and Lat. 'Euxine Sea' (Pontus Euxinus)

Boğazköy (Hattusa): 93 F2
site of ancient city and archives (tablets), city being Hattusa, *q.v.*, capital of Hittite empire. 'Boğazköy tablets' are important source of information on Hittite history

Bokhara: 79 M3

Bononia: *Bologna* 80 B2

Borim: *Kh. Burin* 62, 69 X4
In Thutmose III and Shishak lists

Borsippa: *Birs Nimrud* 55, 71, 78, 93 H4
important city of Babylonia, conquered by Ashurbanipal

Bosor: *Busr el-Hariri* 77 Z3
1 Macc. 5. 26, 36

Bosora (Bozrah): *Busra eski-Sham* 77 Z3
1 Macc. 5. 26, 28: same as Bostra, *q.v.*

Bosphorus: 52, 89, 91 E2

Bosporan Kingdom: 89 G1
named after the 'Cimmerian Bosphorus (Bosporos)', i.e. Straits of Kertch at entrance to Sea of Azov

Bostra (Bozrah, Bosora): *Busra eski-Sham* 91, 93 G4
oasis city and trading post on edge of desert

Bozkath: *Dawa'imeh* 63, 73 W5
in Shephelah of Judah, Josh. 15. 39; 2 Kgs. 22. 1

Bozrah (in Edom): *Buseirah* 59 U2
Gen. 36. 33; Isa. 34 6; 63. 1; Jer. 49. 13, 22; Amos 1. 12

Bozrah (Bezer) (in Moab): *Umm el-'Amad*
63, 69, 73, 77 Y5
Jer. 48. 24; *see also* Bezer

Bozrah (Bosora): *Busra eski-Sham* 67 G4
77 Z3
see also Bosora *and* Bostra

Brundisium: *Brindisi* 88 C2
seaport on usual route between Rome and the East

Bubastis (Pi-beseth): *T. Basta* 58, Q2
82 F4
cap. of eighteenth nome of Lower Egypt

Bucolōn Polis: *'Athlit* 86 W3

Gk. name ('cattlemen's town') of site of former Phoenician settlement

Buhen: 67 F6

Busiris: *Abu Sir* 58 K2
78 F4
important Delta city, cap. of ninth nome of Lower Egypt; the god Osiris was called 'Lord of Busiris'

Busra eski-Sham: 91, 93 G4
mod. Arabic name of ancient Bozrah (Bosora), also 'Bostra'

Buto: *T. el-Far'ain* 58 P1
cap. of nineteenth nome of Lower Egypt

Buz: *reg.* 67 G5
Jer. 25. 23 (*cf.* Gen. 22. 21)

Byblos (Gebal): *Jebeil* 52, 71, 82, 93 G4
see Gebal

Byzantium: *Constantinople, Istanbul* 78, 82, 89, 91 E2
Greek city, originally less important than Calchedon, *q.v.*; in 4th cent. A.D. made capital of Rom. empire by Constantine and renamed Constantinople

Cabbon: 63 W5
in Judah, Josh. 15. 40

Cabul: *Kabul* 61, 62, 65, 94 X3
in Asher, Josh. 19. 27; ceded by Solomon to Hiram king of Tyre, 1 Kgs. 9. 10–13

Cadasa: *Qadas* 86 Y2
Tyrian village sacked by Jews in war against Rome (A.D. 66–70)

Caesarea (in Palestine): *Qeisariyeh [Qeisari]*
49, 85, 86, 94 W3
89, 91 F4
city founded by Herod the Great on the site of former coastal station called Strato's Tower: harbour, theatre, &c.; a port and administrative centre throughout Roman period. Acts 8. 40; 10. 1 &c.; 18, 22; 23. 23, 33; 25. 6, 13. *Illus. pp.* 40, 116

Caesarea (in Cappadocia): *Kayseri* 89, 91 G3
former Mazaca, renamed in 12–9 B.C. by Archelaus king of Cappadocia; from A.D. 17 cap. of Rom. prov. of Cappadocia

Caesarea Philippi (Paneas): *Baniyas* 85, 86 Y2
89, 91, G4
capital city founded by Philip the tetrarch, son of Herod the Great. Matt. 16. 13; Mark 8. 27

Calah (Kalkhu): *Nimrud* 55, 67, 71, 75, 93 H3
Assyrian royal city, Gen. 10. 11 f.

Calchedon (Chalcedon): *Kadiköy* 82, 91 E2
Greek city on Bosphorus. (The spelling Calchedon is the original; in later Church history better known as Chalcedon)

Callirrhoe: *Zarat* 85, 87 Y5
hot springs ('Callirrhoe', Gk. = 'beautifully flowing'); Biblical Zareth-shahar, *q.v.*

Calneh: *Kullanköy*
Amos 6. 2; *see* Calno

Calno: *Kullaköy* 71 G3
Isa. 10. 9; same as Calneh, *q.v.* By some identified with Canneh in Ezek. 27. 23

Cana: *Kh. Qana* 86 X3
John 2. 1; 4. 46; 21. 2

Canaan: *reg.* 55 F4
57
59 T1
land inhabited by the Canaanites, who were reckoned as descendants of Ham, Gen. 9. 18 &c.; Abraham migrated there, Gen. 11. 31 &c. (*cf.* 12. 1; 15. 7); promised to the Israelites, Exod. 6. 4; Num. 35. 10; entered, Josh. 5. 10; allotted among the tribes, Josh. 14. 1 ff.; fighting against Canaanites, Judg. 4. 1 ff. *See pp. 56–57 and 60–61; also Introduction, p.* 9

Canea: *Khanea* 52 D3

Canneh: *Qana, Bir 'Ali* 67 J8
trading post in Arabia, called in Gk. and Lat. sources Cana; possibly the Canneh of Ezek. 27. 23, though others locate that in area of Haran and Beth-eden, *qq.v. See also* Calno.

Canopus: *Abukir-Taufikiyeh* 89, 91 F4

Canusium: 88 C2

Capar Ganaeoi: 86 Y2
village in Plain of Hazor

Caparorsa: *Kh. Khoreisa* 87 X6

Capernaum: *Talhum [Kefar Nahum]* 49, 85, 86, 94 Y3
Matt. 4. 13 &c.; Mark 1. 21 &c.; Luke 4. 31 &c.; John 2. 12; Gk. and Lat. 'Capharnaum', Heb. Kefar Nahum; mentioned in Jewish sources; ruins of synagogue, built *c.* A.D. 200: *see illus. p.* 46

Capharsaba: *Kh. Sabyeh* 87 W4

village which figured in war of Alexander Jannaeus against Antiochus XII

Capharabis: *Kh. el-Bis* 87 W5
place taken by Vespasian in Jewish War (A.D. 68)

Capharsalama: *Kh. Irha* 77 ins, 87 X5
1 Macc. 7. 31

Caphartobas: *et-Taiyibeh* 87 X5
Heb. Kefar Turban (?). Sacked by Vespasian in Jewish War

Caphtor (Crete): 54, 66, 70, 74 E3
same as Egyptian Keftiu (Crete); homeland of the Philistines, Amos 9. 7; Jer. 47. 4; *cf.* Caphtorim, Gen. 10. 14; Deut. 2. 23; 1 Chr. 1. 12

Capitolias: 86 Y3
former Nabataean city, later in Decapolis; declared autonomous by Trajan, A.D. 97–98

Cappadocia: *reg.* 78, 82, 89, 91 G3
Old Persian 'Katpatuka', Gk. Kappadokia, Lat. Cappadocia; in Persian empire; from *c.* 255 B.C. an independent kingdom; from A.D. 17 a Rom. prov.; Acts 2. 9; 1 Pet. 1. 1

Capparetaea: *Kh. Kufr Hatta* 87 W4
home of Menander, disciple of Simon Magus (according to Justin Martyr)

Capreae: *Capri*: *isl.* 88 B2

Capua: *Santa Maria di Capua Vetere* 88 B2
chief city of Campania, region of W. Italy S. of Rome

Carchemish: *Jerablus* 55, 67, 71, 75, 82, 89, 93 G3
Syro-Hittite capital on Upper Euphrates; captured by Assyrians, Isa. 10. 9; site of battle between Neco of Egypt and Nebuchadrezzar of Babylon, 605 B.C., 2 Chr. 35. 20; Jer. 46. 2; excavated

Caria: *reg.* 74, 78, 82, 91 E3
part of first satrapy of Darius; a district (1 Macc. 15. 23), later in Rom. prov. of Asia

Cariathiareim: *Deir el-Azhar* 87 W5
village and road station in Rom. times

Carmania: *reg.* 79, 83 L5

Carmel: *Kermel* 49, 63, 65, 69 X6
in hill country of Judah, Josh. 15. 55; • Sam. 15. 12; 25. 2 &c.

Carmel, Mt.: *Jebel Mar Elyas*
49, 57, 61, 62, 65, 69, 73, 77, 85, 86 X3
Josh. 19. 26; 1 Kgs. 18. 20 ff.; Amos 9. 3; Jer. 46. 18 &c.

Carnain (Carnion): *Sheikh Sa'd* 77 Z3
1 Macc. 5. 26; 2 Macc. 12. 21; same as Karnaim, *q.v.*

Carpathos: *Scarpanto*: *isl.* 52, 92 E3

Carrhae: *Harran* 89 G3
Gk. and Lat. name of Haran, *q.v.*; scene of defeat of Roman army under Crassus by Parthians, 53 B.C.

Carthage: 88 B3
chief Punic city (a Tyrian colony) of N. Africa, historic rival of Rome, defeated and finally destroyed, 146 B.C. Later cap. of Rom. prov. of Africa

Casphor (Caspin, Chaspho): *Khisfin* 77 Y3
1 Macc. 5. 26, 36; 2 Macc. 12. 13

Caspian Sea (Hyrcanian Sea, Mare Caspium)
55, 59, 67, 71, 75 79, 93

Caspin (Casphor, Chaspho): *see* Casphor

Catana: *Catania* 88 G3
Gk. city; under Augustus became Rom. colony

Cataract, First 52 F6

Caucasus Mts. 53, 78 H2

Cauda (Gaudos): *Gavdos*: *isl.* 89, 90 D4
Acts 27. 16

Cedron: 'brook'
John 18. 1 (KJV): *see* Kidron

Cedron:
1 Macc. 15. 41 (KJV): *see* Kedron

Celaenae (Apamea): *Famiyeh* 82 F3
see Apamea

Cenchreae: *Kechries* 89, 90 F4
harbour town of Corinth, Acts 18. 18; Rom. 16. 1

Central (Cheesemakers') **Valley, Jerusalem** *see*
Cheesemakers' Valley 81

Cephalonia: *Kefallinia*: *isl.* 52 D3

Ceyhan (Jeyhan): *riv.* 52, 93 D3
Turkish name of ancient Pyramos, *q.v.*

Chabulon: *Kabul* 86 X3
Gk. form of name of Cabul, *q.v.*

Chagar Bazar 99 H3

Chalcedon: *see* Calchedon

Chalcidice: 90 D2
triple peninsula in NE. Greece

Chalcis (in Greece): 66 D3
city-state important in Gk. colonization and trade

Chalcis: *reg.* 91 G4

petty principality (city and environs) of which Herod Agrippa II was made king (A.D. 50–53) by Emperor Claudius

Chaldea (Babylonia): *reg.*   75 J4
Ezek. 23. 15 &c.; Babylon is the chief city of Chaldea; 'Chaldeans' is more frequently used in the Bible than 'Babylonians' for the people, *cf.* Gen. 11. 28 &c., 2 Kgs. 24. 2 ff., Jer. 21. 4 ff.; *cf.* Ezek. 23. 23

Charachmoba: *el-Kerak*   87 Y6
Gk. form of name of place in Moab now *el-Kerak*; Biblical Kir-haresheth, *q.v.*, Kir-heres, Kir of Moab

Chaspho (Casphor, Caspin): *see* Casphor

Cheesemakers' Valley, Jerusalem: *el-Wad*   81
the central valley of the site of Jerusalem, commonly called by the Gk. form of name 'Tyropoeon Valley' (Tyropoeōn = 'of cheesemakers')

Chephar-ammoni: *Kafr 'Ana*   63 X5
in Benjamin, Josh. 18. 24

Chephirah: *T. Kefireh*   61, 63, 77 ins X5
city of the Gibeonites, Josh. 9. 17; in Benjamin, Josh. 18. 26; its people, Ezra 2. 25; Neh. 7. 29

Cherith, Brook: *Wadi Yabis*   49, 51, 69, 86 Y4
1 Kgs. 17. 3, 5

Chersonesus: near *Sevastopol*   92 F2
Gk. city so named from standing on a peninsula (Gk. 'chersonesos'). (The Chersonesus proper = *Gallipoli* peninsula.)

Chesalon: *Kesla*   63 X5
Josh. 15. 10 (KJV, RSV)

Chesulloth (Chisloth-tabor): *Iksal*   62 X3
in Issachar, Josh. 19. 18, adjoining Zebulun, Josh. 19. 12

Chezib (Achzib): *T. el-Beida*   59, 63 W5
Gen. 38. 5 (Chezib): same as Achzib in Judah, *q.v.*

Chinnereth: *T. el-'Ureimeh*   51, 61, 62, 69, 94 Y3
Deut. 3. 17; Fortified city in Naphtali, Josh. 19. 35

Chinnereth, Sea of (Sea of Galilee):   49, 57, 61, 62, 65, 69, 73 Y3
Num. 34. 11; Josh. 13. 27

Chinneroth: *see* Chinnereth
so spelled, Josh. 11. 2; 12. 3; 1 Kgs. 15. 20

Chios: *isl.*   52, 66, 89, 91, 92 E3
Acts 20. 15

Chisloth-tabor: *see* Chesulloth

Chitlish: *Kh. el-Maqhaz*   63 W5
in the Shephelah of Judah, Josh. 15. 40 (RSV)

Chittim (KJV): *see* Kittim

Chorasmia: *reg.*   79, 83 L3
medieval *Khwarizm*

Chorazin: *Kh. Kerazeh*   86, 94 Y3
Matt. 11. 21; Luke 10. 13

Cilicia (Kizzuwatna, Khilakku): *reg.*   55, 93 G3
    70, 78, 82 F3
area known to Hittites as Kizzuwatna, *q.v.*, in Assyrian records Khilakku, Gk. 'Kilikia' (Lat. and Eng. Cilicia), O.T. Kue, *q.v.*; fourth satrapy of Darius's empire. Comprised flatter eastern part, Cilicia Pedias (Gk. 'lowland', containing cities of Tarsus &c., and mountainous western part, Cilicia Trachea (Gk. 'rugged'), *q.v. See also* 'Cilicia and Syria', *and* 'Antiochus, Kingdom of.

Cilicia and Syria: *reg.*   89, 91 G3
Rom. prov. of Syria which in N.T. times included Cilicia Pedias (*see* Cilicia) Acts 15. 23, 41; Gal. 1. 21

Cilician Gates: *pass*   89, 91 G3
narrow defile on route between Syria-Cilicia and interior of Asia Minor, where it crosses Taurus Mts.

Cilicia Trachea: *reg.*   91 F3
mountainous eastern part of Cilicia, forming part of Kingdom of Antiochus, *q.v.*

Cimmerians: *people*   78 F3
see also Gimarrai

Citium: *Larnaka*   78, 82, 91, 93 F4
Gk. 'Kition', *cf.* the name 'Kittim', *q.v.*: Phoenician city in Cyprus

City of Moab: *see* Moab, City of

City of Salt: *see* Salt, City of *and* Kh. Qumran

Claudiopolis (in Bithynia):   91 F2
city named after Emperor Claudius (A.D. 41–54)

Claudiopolis (in Cilicia): *see* Kirshu

Cnidus: nr. *Cape Krio*
Acts 27. 7: Greek city

Cnossus: *see* Knossos

Coa: NEB rendering of Hebrew name given as 'Kue' in RSV. *See* **Kue.**

Coele-Syria: *reg.*   82 G4
Gk. 'Hollow Syria'; in contrast to northern Syria (Antioch area); used in Hellenistic period for Syria

---

between Lebanon and Anti-Lebanon Mts., *qq.v.*, and also for Palestine generally: but application of name varied at different periods. 1 Esd. 4. 48; 7. 1 (used by Gk. writer, though referring to Persian period); 2 Macc. 8. 8 (Hellenistic period).

Colchi: *people*   78 H2

Colchis: *reg.*   81 H2

Colonia Amasa: *Qaloniyeh*   87 X5
village where settlement ('colonia') of ex-soldiers was placed by Romans: believed by some to be the Emmaus mentioned in Luke 24. 13: *but see* Emmaus

Colophon: 92 E3
Greek city

Colossae: near *Khonai*   89, 91 E3
Col. 1. 2; the churches of Colossae, Laodicea, *q.v.*, and Hierapolis, *q.v.*, formed a group, probably evangelized at the same time: *see* Col. 4. 12–16

Comana Pontica (in Galatian Pontus)   89, 91 G2

Comana Cappadociae (Cataoniae)   91 G3

Commagene (Kummukhu): *reg.*   71, 78, 82, 89, 91 G3
border-region between Asia Minor and the Euphrates valley; in N.T. times a client kingdom of Roman empire under Antiochus, who also ruled Cilicia Trachea

Coptos: *Kuft*   78 F5

Corcyra: *Corfu:* *isl.*   52, 88 C3

Coreae: *T. el-Mazar*   87 X4

Corfu (Corcyra): *isl.*   52 C3

Corinth: 66, 74, 78, 82, 89, 90 D3
Greek city, important from early times: sacked by Romans, 146 B.C.; refounded by Julius Caesar; most important city of Rom. prov. of Achaia, *q.v.*; Acts 18. 1–18; 1 Cor. 1. 2; 16. 5–6; 2 Cor. 1. 1; 1. 23; 12. 14; 13. 1; 2 Tim. 4. 20. From apostolic times there was here an important Christian community

Corsica: *isl.*   88 A2

Coruh: *riv.*   53 H2

Cos. *isl.*   91 ins. 92 E3
Acts 21. 1

Cotiaeum: 91 E3

Crete (Caphtor):   52, 54, 66, 70, 74, 78, 82, 89, 90, 92 D3
a highly-developed Minoan civilization flourished in Crete, *c.* 2000–1400 B.C. (*see* Knossos); later it was part of Mycenaean world (*see* Mycenae); Heb. Caphtor, *q.v.* In classical times Crete was unimportant and backward; *cf.* Tit. 1. 12; as part of Rom. empire formed one province with Cyrene. Acts 2. 11; *cf.* Acts 27. 7–21; Tit. 1. 5

Crimea (Cimmerian Chersonese)   52 F1

Crocodilon Polis: *T. el-Malat*   86 F5
lit. 'City of Crocodiles': place in territory of Caesarea mentioned by Rom. writers

Crocodilopolis: *Medinet el-Fayum*   46, 82 F5
lit. 'Crocodile-city': Gk. name for chief city of the Fayum

Croton: 88 C3
Greek city in S. Italy

Ctesiphon: 82, 89, 93 H4
on east bank of Tigris, opposite Seleucia, *q.v.*; Hellenistic foundation, but later in Parthian empire, of which it was leading city; remains of hall of Parthian kings extant

Cunaxa:
in NW. Babylonia: *see text p. 79*

Curium   93 F4

Cush (Ethiopia):   54, 67, 78 F6
Gen. 2. 13; 10. 6–8; 1 Chr. 1. 8–10; Ezek. 38. 5. 'Cush' is the usual designation of territory on the Upper Nile, south of Egypt; it is usually translated 'Ethiopia', but is not mod. Ethiopia (= Abyssinia)

Cuthah: *T. Ibrahim*   55, 71, 75 H4
a centre of the cult of Nergal. 2 Kgs. 17. 24, *cf.* 17. 30

Cyclades: *isls.*   52 D3
the island group, roughly circular (Gk. cyclos (kuklos), circle), in the southern Aegean

Cydonia: *Khania*   82 D3

Cyprus (Alashiya, Iadanana, Chittim, Kittim): *isl.*   52, 55, 67, 70, 74, 78, 82, 89, 91, 93 F3
important from Bronze Age as intermediary between Minoan-Mycenaean worlds and the East. Settled by Greeks, who founded Salamis, Paphos, &c., and by Phoenicians in other places. Conquered by Assyrians 709 B.C.; later generally under Persian control, though Greek forces operated there; fell to Alexander. In RSV, the Heb. name 'Chittim' (KJV) or Kittim, *q.v.*, is rendered 'Cyprus' in Isa. 23. 1, 12, Jer. 2. 10, Ezek. 27. 6. Became Rom. prov. 58 B.C.; Acts 4. 36;

---

11. 19 f.; 13. 4–13; 15. 39

Cyprus: *T. el-'Aqabeh:* *fortress*   85, 87 X5
built by Herod the Great, and dedicated to his mother under the name 'Cyprus' (so Josephus)

Cyrene: *Cirene*   78, 82, 88 D4
Greek colony founded *c.* 630 B.C.; annexed by Ptolemy I; in Rom. times centre of civilized area on coast of Libya, and forming a prov. with Crete. Matt. 27. 32; Mark 15. 21; Luke 23. 26; Acts 2. 10; 11. 20; 13. 1

Cyrenaica: *reg.*   52, 82, 88 D4
the region round Cyrene, *q.v.*

Cyropolis (Kura): *Uratube*   79, 83 N3
city established by Cyrus (founder of Medo-Persian empire), hence Gk. name Cyropolis

Cyrus: *Kura:* *riv.*   53, 79, 83 J2

Cythera: *Cerigo, Kithira:* *isl.*   52, 66, 92 D3

Cyzicus: 89, 91, 92 E2
Greek city, colony of Miletus

Dabaloth (Beth-diblathaim): *Kh. Deleilat esh-Sherqiyeh*   77 Y5
see Beth-diblathaim

Dabaritta (Dabira): *Deburiyeh, Kh. Dabur*   86 X3
Gk. name of Daberath, *q.v.*

Dabbesheth: *T. esh-Shammam*   62 X3
border of Zebulun, Josh. 19. 11

Daberath: *Deburiyeh, Kh. Dabur*   62 X3
border of Zebulun, Josh. 19. 12; Levitical city, Josh. 21. 28, 1 Chr. 6. 72, where assigned to Issachar

Dabira: *see* Dabaritta

Dacia: *reg.*   89 D1
in N.T. times barbarian region, though later (under Trajan) occupied by Romans

Dahna: *desert*   53 J5

Dakhla: *oasis*   52 E5

Dali   93 F3

Daliyeh, Wadi
the Samaria papyri were found here in cave Mughret Abu Shinjeh, *q.v.* for location

Dalmanutha (Taricheae): *Mejdel*   86 Y3
Mark 8. 10: apparently same place as Magdala in parallel passage, Matt. 15. 39; both identified with Taricheae mentioned by Josephus &c. Lakeside town, walled on landward side

Dalmatia: *reg.*   88 C2
2 Tim. 4. 10; roughly equivalent to Illyricum, *q.v.*

Damascus: *esh-Sham*
    49, 51, 57, 61, 65, 69, 73, 77, 85 Z1
    55, 67, 71, 75, 78, 82, 89, 91, 93 G4
cap. of kingdom of Syria (Aram), at important junction of trade routes; associated with Abraham, Gen. 14. 15; 15. 2. Frequent conflicts with Israel, 1 Kgs. 11. 24; 20. 1 ff.; 22. 1 ff.; 2 Kgs. chs. 6 ff.; 16. 5 ff.; Isa. 7. 1 ff. Ally of Israel, 1 Kgs. 15. 16 ff.; conquered by Assyrians 732 B.C., 2 Kgs. 16. 9; commercial city, Ezek. 27. 18. In N.T. times contained Jewish inhabitants, Acts 9. 2 ff., and Christianity made early converts there, Acts 9. 10, 19. Although in Rom. prov. of Syria, it was reckoned as belonging to Decapolis, *q.v.*, and an officer of Aretas king of Nabataeans also had authority there, 2 Cor. 11. 32

Damascus Gate (Jerusalem)   96

Damascus Plain   49 Z2

Damghan: *see* Hecatompylus   79 K3

Dan (Laish): *T. el-Qadi*
    49, 57, 61, 62, 65, 69, 73, 94 Y2
northernmost city of Israel, Deut. 34. 1; 1 Kgs. 4. 25; formerly Laish, renamed by tribe of Dan, *q.v.*, Judg. 18. 27–29; shrine established by Jeroboam king of Israel, 1 Kgs. 12. 29, and denounced by prophets, Amos 8. 14

Dan: *tribe*   61 Y2
    61 W5
originally located west of Benjamin on the coast, but later moved to sources of Jordan around Laish (Dan, *q.v.*), Josh. 19. 40–48; Judg. 18. 1 ff., 11 ff., 27 ff.

Dannah: ? *Deir esh-Shemesh or Simya*   63 X6
in hill country of Judah, Josh. 15. 49 (location conjectural)

Danos: *T. el-Qadi*   85 Y2
Gk. name of O.T. Dan, *q.v.*

Danube: *riv.*   52, 88 E2
Gk. Istros, Lat. Danuvius

Daphnae: *T. Dafanneh*
Gk. trading settlement in Egypt: *see* Tahpanhes

Daphne (S. of Dan): *Kh. Dafneh*   86 Y2
mentioned by Josephus

Daphne (Syria):

near Antioch: sacred groves and temples; 2 Macc. 4. 33

Dascylium: 82 E2
(Gk. Daskyleion): Gk. colony founded by Miletus

Dasht-e Kavir: *desert*   53 K4
NW. end of the *Dasht-e Lut, q.v.*

Dasht-e Lut: *desert*   53 L4
the great salt desert of the Iranian plateau

Dathema (Diathema): *T. Hamad*   77 Z3
fortified place, 1 Macc. 5. 9

David, City of (Jerusalem):
see text, p. 80

Dead Sea (Sea of the Arabah, Salt Sea, Lake Asphaltitis): *Bahr Lut*   49, 77, 85, 87, 95 X5
                     52 G4
for Biblical refs. see Arabah, Sea of the, *and* Salt Sea

Debir (in Judah): *T. Beit Mirsim*
     49, 57, 61, 63, 65, 73, 95 W6
Canaanite city taken by Israelites, Josh. 10. 38 f.; 15. 15 (*cf.* Judg. 1. 11); Levitical city, Josh. 21. 15; 1 Chr. 6. 58. Important excavations. Same as Kiriath-sepher

Debir (in Gilead): *Umm el-Dabar*
border of Gad, Josh. 13. 26; same as Lo-debar, *q.v.*

Debir: *Thoghret ed-Debr*   63 X5
on N. boundary of Judah, Josh. 15. 7

Decapolis: *reg.*   85, 86 Y3
                     91 G4
Gk. name for league of approx. ten (deka) Hellenistic or Hellenized cities with their territories, in Rom. times. Besides Scythopolis, W. of Jordan, and those on E. of Perea forming block of territory, they included Dion, Abila, and Damascus. In N.T. figures as largely gentile territory bordering Galilee and Perea: Matt. 4. 25; Mark 5. 20; 7. 31. *See also* Gadara, Gerasa

Dedan: *el-'Ula*   55, 67, 71, 75, 78 G5
an oasis in N. Arabia; Gen. 10. 7; 1 Chr. 1. 9; Jer. 49. 8; Ezek. 25. 13; 27. 20

Dedan: *reg.*   67 G5
the region around *el- 'Ula* (*see above*)

Deir el-Qilt: 95 X5 *and ins*
monastery of St. George in *Wadi Qilt* (*Qelt*)

Deir el-Quruntul: 95 X5 *and ins*
Byzantine monastery on the mountain of Dok, named 'Quarantine' in Middle Ages (from the 'forty days' of Matt. 4. 2; the traditional 'Mount of the Temptation')

Deir Mar Jiryis   95 X5 *and ins*

Deir Tasa   92 F5

Delos: *isl.*   82, 92 E3
island with shrine of Apollo, in Hellenistic and Rom. times a trading centre (slave market)

Delphi: 78, 82, 90, 92 D3
site of temple and oracle of Apollo, Gk. religious and national centre in classical times: excavations

Der: *Bedrai*   75, 78 J4

Derbe: *Kerti Hüyük*   89, 91 F3
visited by Paul, Acts 14. 6, 20; 16. 1; 20. 4 (*see also* Doberus); Derbe was conjecturally located, more probable location adopted in this Atlas, based on inscription recently discovered (*Anatolian Studies*, vol. 7, 1957)

Desert, the (Arabian)   49 Z4

Dhahrat Humraiyeh   95 W5
site of excavation of Middle Bronze Age cemetery

Dhiban (Dibon): *see* Dibon

Diathema: *see* Dathema

Dibon: *Dhiban*   49, 57, 61, 63, 65, 69, 73, 95, Y6
                     59 U2
important Moabite city: here Moabite Stone, monument of King Mesha, was found. Num. 21. 30; 32. 3; 33. 45 f.; claimed by Israelites, Num. 32. 34; Josh. 13. 9; 13. 17; as Moabite city, Isa. 15. 2, 9; Jer. 48. 18, 22; excavations

Dibon (in Judah): Neh. 11. 25; unlocated

Didyma: 82, 92 E3
site of great temple of Apollo, religious centre of Ionian Greeks.

Dilean: *T. en-Najileh*   63 W6
in Shephelah of Judah, Josh. 15. 38

Dilmun: *Bahrain*   55, 67 K5
port on island in Persian gulf

Dinaric Alps   52 C2

Dimnah: *see* Rimmon (in Zebulun)

Dion: *T. el 'Ash'ari*   85, 86 Y3
city of the Decapolis

Diyala: *riv.*   53, 71, 75 H4

Dnieper: *riv.*   52 E1

Dniester: *riv.*   52 E1

Doberus (?nr. *Dojran*)   90 D2

city of Macedonia: in Acts 20. 4 'of Doberus' (Doberaios) is a possible reading in place of 'of Derbe' (Derbaios)

Dodecanese: *isls.*   52 E3
archipelago of approx. twelve (Gk. dōdeka) islands

Dok: *Jebel Quruntul*   77 X5
1 Macc. 16. 15. *See also* Deir el-Quruntul

Don (Tanais): *riv.*   53 H1
reckoned by Gk. geographer Theopompus to mark boundary between Europe and Asia

Dophkah: *Serabit el-Khadim*   59 S3
station of Israelites in the Wilderness, Num. 33. 12 f.; site of copper and turquoise mines, where ancient alphabetic inscriptions were found (*see p.* 20).

Dor (Dora): *et-Tantura*
   49, 57, 61, 63, 65, 69, 73, 77, 85, 86, 94 W3
               55, 67, 82 F4
Canaanite city, Josh. 12. 23; allotted to Manasseh, though in Asher according to Josh. 17. 11, but at first not conquered, Judg. 1. 27; reckoned to Ephraim, 1 Chr. 7. 29. In Hellenistic and Rom. times harbour town. Besieged by Antiochus VII, 1 Macc. 15. 11–14. *See also* Naphath-dor

Dor, Plain of   49 W3

Dora: *Tantura:*   85, 86, 94 W3
               82 F4
Gk. name of Dor, *q.v.*

Doriscus: 78, 91 E2
Persian fortress in campaign against Greece, 480 B.C.

Dorylaeum   89, 91 F3

Dothan: *T. Duthan*   49, 57, 62, 69, 73, 77, 94 X4
Gen. 37. 17; 2 Kgs. 6. 13 ff.

Drangiana: *reg.*   79, 83 M4
prov. or satrapy on Iranian plateau

Drava: *riv.*   52 C1

Dumah: *ed-Domeh*   63 W6
in hill country of Judah, Josh. 15. 52

Dumah (in Arabia): *Dumet ej-Jendal*
Gen. 25. 14; 1 Chr. 1. 30; Isa. 21. 11 f.

Dura-Europos: 82, 89, 93 H4
city on Euphrates, founded by Seleucus I, became frontier city and trading centre between Roman and Parthian empires. Important excavations revealing 2nd-3rd-cent. A.D. city with synagogue and Christian church. Though these are post-Biblical, city was already important in Hellenistic and N.T. period

Dur-sharrukin: *Khorsabad*   71 H3
capital of Assyria under Sargon II

Dyrrhachium: *Durazzo*   89 C2
port on route between Rome and the East

Eastern Desert   52 F5

Eastern Sea (The Lower Sea): *Persian Gulf*   71 K5
Akkadian name for Persian Gulf; mentioned in records of Sargon I &c.

Eastern Sea: *Dead Sea*
Ezek. 47. 18; Joel 2. 20; Zech. 14. 8; here refers to the Dead Sea (on the east of the Holy Land). *See also* Western Sea

Ebal, Mt. *Jebel Eslamiyeh*
   49, 57, 61, 62, 65, 69, 77, 85, 86 X4
Mts. Ebal and Gerizim, *q.v.*, formed pair of summits in centre of Israelite territory. Deut. 11. 29; 27. 4, 13; Josh. 8. 30, 33

Eben-ezer: *Mejdal Yaba, Migdal Aphek*   63 W4
1 Sam. 4. 1; 5. 1

Eben-ezer:
1 Sam. 7. 12: *see* Jeshanah

Ecbatana (Achmetha): *Hamadan*
   53, 55, 67, 71, 75, 79, 83, 93 J4
capital of Media; Persian royal city, Ezra 6. 2; 2 Macc. 9. 3

Ecdippa: *ez-Zib*   86 X2
Gk. name of Achzib, *q.v.*

Eden: *Aden*   67 J8
Ezek. 27. 23. Trading port in Arabia associated with Sheba and Raamah

Eden:
2 Kgs. 19. 12; Isa. 37. 12. Land conquered by Assyrians, same as Bit-Adini or Beth-eden, *q.v.*

Eden, Garden of:
Gen. 2. 8 ff.; Isa. 51. 3, Ezek. 28. 13; 31. 9; 31. 16, 18; 36. 35; Joel 2. 3 (relation to Eden (Bit-Adini) entirely uncertain)

Edessa: *Urfa*   89 G3
see text p. 88

Edfu: 78 F6
the god of Edfu was depicted as the sun disk with

extended wings

Edom: *reg. and kingdom*   49, 57, 61, 65, 69, 73 X7
               67, 71, 75 G4
               59 U2
country of descendants of Esau, Gen. 25. 30; 36. 1, 8, 9; in early period it lay E. of Arabah, whose copper-mines were worked by Edomites; separated from Moab by Brook Zered, Deut. 2. 13 ff.; it lay E. of SE. boundary of Judah, Josh. 15. 1, 21. As kingdom, Gen. 36. 31 ff.; Num. 20. 14 ff.; relations with David and Solomon, 2 Sam. 8. 12, 14; 1 Kgs. 9. 26; 11. 14 ff.; with later kings, 2 Kgs. 3. 8 ff.; 14. 10; 16. 6; prophecies on, Isa. 34. 5 ff., Jer. 9. 26; 25. 21; 49. 7; Ezek. 25. 12; Obad. 1 ff. *See also* Idumaea

Edomites   78 F4

Edrei (in Bashan): *Der'a*   61, 62, 69 Z3
city of Og, king of Bashan, Num. 21. 33; Deut. 1. 4; allotted to Manasseh, Josh. 13. 31

Edrei (in Naphtali):
Josh. 19. 37; unlocated

Eglon: *T. el-Hesi, q.v.*   57, 61, 63, 69, 77, 95 W5
Amorite (Canaanite) city, taken by Joshua, Josh. 10. 3, 34; allotted to Judah, Josh. 15. 39. Excavations: *see* pp. 2, 99

Egnatian Way: 88, 90 D2
Roman road between Adriatic coast and Bosphorus, linking Italy and the East

Egypt: 54, 67, 70, 74, 78, 82, 89, 91, 92 F5
               58
very ancient empire comprising the 'Two Kingdoms' of Upper and Lower Egypt: see pp. 54–55: Gen. 10. 6, 13 (RSV: 'Mizraim' in KJV is Heb. word for Egypt); Gen. 12. 10 ff. Israelite sojourn in, and the Exodus, Gen. 37. 28—Exod. 12. 41 &c., and see pp. 58–59; later relations with, 1 Kgs. 3. 1; 9. 16; 10. 28 f.; 11. 17 ff.; 12. 2; 14. 25; 2 Kgs. 23. 29; Jer. 41. 17; 42. 14 ff. Egypt was conquered by Assyrians under Esarhaddon (670 B.C.) and by Persians under Cambyses (525 B.C.), and became part of sixth satrapy of Darius I; Jews had settled there from before Persian times, *see pp.* 78–79 and Jer. 44. 1 ff.; conquered by Alexander, and became kingdom of the Ptolemies, *see pp.* 82–83 and *cf.* Sirach (Ecclus.), prologue, with mention of Jewish immigration under Euergetes; after battle of Actium (31 B.C.) became personal property of Rom. emperor under a Procurator; Jews had separate quarter in Alexandria, *q.v.*, and *cf.* Acts 2. 10; *see pp.* 88–89 and 90–91

Egypt, Brook of: *Wadi el-'Arish*   59 S1
marked boundary of Palestine on the SE., towards Egypt. Num. 34. 5; Josh. 15. 4, 47; 1 Kgs. 8. 65; 2 Kgs. 24. 7; Isa. 27. 12; Ezek. 47. 19; 48. 28

Egypt, Lower: 52, 54 F4
the Delta region, united with Upper Egypt under the Pharaohs. Under some dynasties Lower Egypt was centre of power, under others, Upper Egypt

Egypt, Upper: 52, 54 F5
the Nile Valley, S. of Memphis: see Egypt, Lower

Egyptian Port: *Merkhah*   59 S3
port (ancient name unknown) used by Egyptians on Gulf of Suez, 17 miles from *Serabit el-Khadim* (Dophkah, *q.v.*)

Einan: 94 Y2
Mesolithic hamlet: excavations

Ekron (Accaron): *Kh. el-Muqanna'*
   49, 57, 61, 63, 65, 69, 73, 77, 87 W5
one of the five cities of the Philistines, Josh. 13. 3; allotted to Judah, Josh. 15. 45 (but *cf.* Josh. 19. 43); in Philistine hands, 1 Sam. 5. 10 ff.; 6. 17; 17. 52; city of the god Baalzebub, 2 Kgs. 1. 2 ff.; prophecies against, Amos 1. 8; Zeph. 2. 4; 25. 20; Zech. 9. 5. In Gk. 'Accaron', *q.v.*

Elah, Valley of: *Wadi es-Sant*   49, 61 W5
1 Sam. 17. 2, 19 ff.

Elam: *Kh. Beit 'Alam*   77 W5
in Judah, Ezra 2. 31; Neh. 7. 34

Elam (Susiana): *reg.*   55, 67, 71, 75, 79, 89 J4
mountainous country E. of Tigris valley. Gen. 10. 22; 14. 9; Isa. 21. 2; 22. 6; Jer. 25. 25; 49. 34–39; Ezek. 32. 24; province in which Susa was, Dan. 8. 2; possibly referred to in Ezra 2. 7; Neh. 7. 2. People from Elam in Jerusalem, Acts 2. 9

Elasa: *Kh. Ilasa*   77 ins
nr. Beth-horon, *q.v.*, 1 Macc. 9. 5

Elath (Eloth, Ezion-geber): *T. el-Khaleifeh*   71, 93 F5
Deut. 2. 8; 1 Kgs. 9. 26; 2 Kgs. 14. 22; 16. 6

el-'Azariyeh:
mod. name of Bethany, *q.v.*

el-Basseh: 94 X2
mod. village with ancient remains and cemetery

el-Buqei'a (Galilee): Baca 94 X3
archaeological site with remains of synagogue (post-Biblical)

Elburz (Alborz) Mts. 53 X3

Elealeh: el-'Al 57, 63, 73 Y5
in Moabite territory, Num. 32. 3, 37; Isa. 15. 4; 16.
9; Jer. 48. 34

Elephantinē (Yeb): Aswan 78 F6
site of Jewish military colony adjacent to Syene, q.v.,
in 6th and 5th cents. B.C., from which come important
Aramaic papyri: see text, pp. 78–79 and illus., pp.
21, 45.

el-Ghazza: Gaza, q.v.

el-Hammeh: Emmatha, Hamath-by-Gadara 94 Y3
ruined town at hot springs, with theatre, baths, and
synagogue of Byzantine period: partly excavated

el-Jib: Gibeon, q.v. 95 X5
excavations revealing great pool &c.: see illus., p. 100

el-Jish: Gischala, q.v. 94 X2
remains of two synagogues (post-Biblical)

el-Jisr: 95 W5
site of ancient settlement with cemetery, partly
excavated, and bridge

el-Kab: Enkhab 54 F5
cap. of third nome of Upper Egypt, city of the goddess
Nekhbet, home and burial place of King Ahmose;
later called in Gk. Eileithyiaspolis

el-Kerak: Kir-hareseth, q.v. 95 Y6
a Crusaders' and Saracenic castle and fortified town,
partly excavated, on site of Moabite capital city

el-Mina: Posidium 93 G3
site of excavations: see also Posidium

el-Mughara, Wadi: 49, 94 W3
valley containing caves with prehistoric remains;
illus., p. 15

el-Murabba'at, Wadi: 49, 87, 95 X5
valley containing inhabited caves, partly explored, and
yielding documents of period of Second Jewish Revolt
(c. A.D. 135); illus., p. 119

Elon: 63, 65 X5
in 1 Kgs. 4. 9 'Elon' and 'Beth-hanan' should be read
as separate names; possibly for 'Elon' read 'Aijalon',
with Gk. versions; this would then refer to Aijalon
(Yalo), q.v.

Elon:
Josh. 19. 43, in original territory of Dan; location
unknown

Elon-bezaanannim see Zaanannim

el-Qubeibeh: 95 X5
ruins of Crusaders' church and monastic buildings;
sometimes identified with Emmaus of Luke 24. 13

el-Quds: Jerusalem, q.v. 95 X5
Arabic name meaning 'the Holy [City]'

Eltekeh: T. esh-Shallaf 62, 69, 73, 95 W5
Josh. 19. 44; in original territory of Dan; Levitical
city, Josh. 21. 23 (Elteke, R.S.V). In Sennacherib's
annals. See text, p. 72

Eltekon: Kh. ed-Deir 63 X5
in the hill country of Judah, Josh. 15. 59

Elymais:
Gk. form of Elam (reg.), q.v.: 1 Macc. 6. 1

Emesa: Homs, q.v.

Emmatha: el-Hammeh 86 Y3
town with temple or fort, hot baths, theatre, &c., in
territory of Gadara in Rom. times

Emmaus (Nicopolis): 'Imwas 77, 87, 95 W5
1 Macc. 3. 40: a well-known city of Hellenistic and
Roman times, in Heb. 'Hamta' and 'Ammaus': headquarters of a toparchy. Some scholars identify with
Emmaus of Luke 24. 13 (where one important MS
reads '160 stadia')

Emmaus (Colonia Amasa): Qaloniyeh 87 X5
village described as 7 miles (60 stadia) from Jerusalem, Luke 24. 13 ff. This distance is less than that of
city of Emmaus (Nicopolis) and place mentioned has
been variously identified, sometimes with Colonia
Amasa. O.T. Mozah, q.v. See also el-Qubeibeh

Enaim:
Gen. 38. 14, 21; between Adullam and Timnah,
qq.v.; not precisely located

Enam: 63 X5
in the Shephelah of Judah; Josh. 15. 34

En-dor: Endor (about 3 miles SSW. of Israeli En-dor)
61, 62 X3
belonged to Manasseh, Josh. 17. 11; home of 'witch'
('medium' RSV), 1 Sam. 28. 7

En-Eglaim: 'Ain Feshkha 95 ins
Ezek. 47. 10. See 'Ain Feshkha

En-gannim (Beth-haggan): Jenin 57, 61, 62 X4
in Issachar, Josh. 19. 21; Levitical city, Josh. 21. 29;
see Beth-haggan

En-gannim:
in Shephelah of Judah, Josh. 15. 34; location uncertain

En-gedi: T. ej-Jurn 49, 61, 63, 69, 77, 85, 87, 95 X6
in the wilderness of Judah, Josh. 15. 62; 1 Sam. 23. 29;
24. 1; Ezek. 47. 10. (In 2 Chr. 20. 2 En-gedi may
indicate general position of Hazazon-tamar relative to
Jerusalem, or may be a gloss identifying (wrongly?)
the two cities)

En-Gev: see Aphek (Fiq)

En-haddah: Hadatha 63 X3
in Issachar, Josh. 19. 21

En-hazor: Hazzur 62 X2
in Naphtali, Josh. 19. 37

Enkomi (Alashiya): 67, 93 F3
site of excavations with tablets in a Cypro-Minoan
script (1500–1100 B.C.); also possible evidence for
invasion of Cyprus by 'Sea People' akin to Philistines

En-rimmon (Ain-rimmon): Kh. Umm er-Ramamin
63, 77 W6
in Simeon, Josh. 19. 7. In Josh. 15. 32 and 1 Chr.
4. 32 'Ain, (and) Rimmon', in Negeb of Judah, should
be read as (one name) 'Ain-rimmon', same as En-
rimmon. See also Neh. 11. 29

En-rogel: Bir Ayyub 81
spring at junction of Kidron and Hinnom valleys at
Jerusalem; Josh. 15. 7; 18. 16; 2 Sam. 17. 17; 1 Kgs.
1. 9

En-shemesh: 'Ain el-Hod 63 X5
spring on boundary of Judah and Benjamin, Josh.
15. 7; 18. 17

En-tappuah: 63 X4
on boundary of Manasseh and Ephraim, Josh. 17. 7.
See also Tappuah

Ephah: 67 G5
trading centre in NW. Arabia; Isa. 60. 6; cf. Ephah
(eldest?) son of Midian, Gen. 25. 4

Ephes-dammim:
'between Soco and Azekah', qq.v., 1 Sam. 17. 1; not
precisely located

Ephesus: 78, 82, 89, 91, 92 E3
leading city of Ionia, with famous temple of Artemis
(Diana); took part in Ionian revolt; in Persian, then
Ptolemaic, empires; cap. of Rom. prov. of Asia, q.v.
Paul's work there, Acts 18. 19–21 (cf. 24–27); 19. 1—
20. 1; 1 Cor. 15. 32; 16. 8; cf. 1 Tim. 1. 3. One of the
seven churches of Asia, Rev. 1. 11; 2 ff. Eph. 1. 1,
KJV, NEB; see RSV note there

Ephraim (Ephron): et-Taiyibeh 63, 65, 87 X5
2 Sam. 13. 23; John 11. 54: see also Aphairema,
Ophrah

Ephraim: tribe 61, 65, 69, 73 X4
together with Manasseh, q.v., formed the Joseph
tribes (Gen. 41. 52; 48. 1, 20); its territory, Josh. 16.
5–10, cf. 17. 14–18; Judg. 1. 29; 'Ephraim' used as
name for Northern Kingdom (Israel as distinct from
Judah), Isa. 7. 2, 9 &c.

Ephraim, Hill Country of: 49, 62 X4
a major division of the central highlands. Josh. 17. 15;
Judg. 7. 24; 1 Sam. 9. 4; Solomon's first taxation
district, 1 Kgs. 4. 8, see pp. 64–65

Ephraim Gate (Jerusalem):
2 Kgs. 14. 13; 2 Chr. 25. 23; Neh. 8. 16; 12. 39. Unlocated, but see pp. 80–81

Ephrath (Bethlehem): Beit Lahm 57 X5
Gen. 35. 16, 18; 48. 7; but a city N. of Jerusalem may
be meant, possibly same as Ephron (Ephraim), later
identified by a gloss with Bethlehem

Ephrathah: same as Ephrath
Ruth 4. 11; Mic. 5. 2

Ephron (Ophrah, Aphairema, Ephraim): et-Taiyibeh
61, 63, 69 X5
on border of Benjamin, Josh. 18. 15; 2 Chr. 13. 19

Ephron (in Transjordan): 77 Y3
1 Macc. 5. 46 ff., 2 Macc. 12. 27 f.

Epiphania: Hama 89, 91 G3
Gk. name of Hamath, q.v., after Antiochus Epiphanes

Epirus: reg. 82, 90 D3
backward region of Greece, in 4th–2nd cents. a kingdom, suppressed by Rome, c. 167 B.C., and incorporated in Rom. prov. of Macedonia 148 B.C.

Erech (Uruk): Warka 55, 71, 75, 78, 93 J4
leading city of Sumer and Babylonia, founded (according to archaeological evidence) c. 4000 B.C.; before 3rd

millennium called 'Kullab'. Its ruler Lugal-zaggisi
defeated by derivation Gk. form of Sargon I, c. 2400 B.C., cf. Gen. 10. 10.
Ezra 4. 9, 10. Finds include early pictographic tablets
and ziggurats. City associated with Gilgamesh and
the god Dumuzi (Tammuz). See Introduction, p. 20

Eridu: Abu Shahrein 55, 93 J4
city of Sumer and Babylonia; in Sumerian king-list
the oldest city of Sumer; site of famous shrine, and of
finding of earliest writing on clay tablets

Erythraean Sea: 79, 83
Gk. name for waters between Iran and Arabia, i.e.
Persian Gulf and N.W. Indian Ocean

Esbus: Hesban 87 Y5
Gk. form of Heshbon

Esdraelon (Great Plain): 86 X3
see Megiddo, Plain of, and Jezreel, Valley of. 'Esdraelon' is by derivation Gk. form of 'Jezreel', used in Gk.
writers (e.g. Judith 1. 8) for general area of Plain of
Megiddo. See illus. p. 10

Eshan: Kh. Sam'a 63 W6
in hill country of Judah, Josh. 15. 52

Eshnunna: T. Asmar, q.v. 67, 78, 93 H4
site of law-maker, King Bilalama: see p. 54

esh-Shaghur, Wadi: 49 X2
marking division between Upper and Lower Galilee

Eshtaol: Eshwa' 63 X5
in the Shephelah of Judah, Josh. 15. 33 but before
Danite migration a centre of the tribe of Dan, Josh.
19. 40; associated with Samson, Judg. 13. 25; 16. 31;
abandoned by Danites, Judg. 18. 2, 11

Eshtemoa: es-Samu' 61, 63, 95 X6
Levitical city, Josh. 21. 14; 1 Sam. 30. 28

es-Samu': Eshtemoa, q.v. 95 X6
village on site of Judean town, with ancient synagogue, partly excavated

es-Sebbeh: Masada, q.v. 95 X6
site of fortress containing palace, built by Herod the
Great; partly excavated. See illus. p. 42.

es-Sela' 93 G5
possible location of Sela, q.v.

Etam: Kh. el-Khokh 61, 63, 69, 87 X5
Judg. 15. 8, 11; fortified by Rehoboam, 2 Chr. 11. 6

Etam:
in Simeon, 1 Chr. 4. 32; unlocated

Etam, Rock of:
Judg. 15. 8, 11; location uncertain

Etham:
on borders of Egypt, Exod. 13. 20; Num. 33. 7; unlocated

Ether: Kh. 'Ater 63 W5
in Shephelah of Judah, Josh. 15. 42

Ether:
in Simeon, Josh. 19. 7; unlocated

Ethiopia (Cush): reg. 52, 54, 67, 70, 74, 78 F6
in O.T. the southern border region of Egypt, S. of
Syene, from which the Pharaoh Tirhaka came (2
Kgs. 19. 9); Isa. 11. 11; 18. 1; 20. 3, 5; Jer. 46. 8 f.;
Ezek. 29. 10; its trade, Isa. 43. 3; 45. 14; limit of
Persian empire, Esth. 1. 1; 8. 9

Etna: mt. 52 C3

et-Tell: Ai, q.v. 95 X5
excavations show early Bronze-Age settlement (c.
3300–2400 B.C.) and then a gap in occupation till
c. 1000 B.C.

Euboea: Evvoia : isl. 52, 90, 92 D3

Euphrates: Shatt el-Furat : riv.
53, 55, 67, 71, 75, 78, 82, 89, 93 H4
Gen. 2. 14; 31. 21; Josh. 24. 2; 1 Kgs. 4. 24; 2 Chr.
35. 20; Jer. 13. 4 ff.; 46. 2, 10; cf. Rev. 9. 14; 16. 10

Europus (Mesopotamia): see Dura-Europus

Europus (Syria): 89 G3
same as Carchemish, q.v.

Euxine Sea (Pontus Euxinus): 89, 91 F2
Gk.–Lat. name for Black Sea

Exaloth: Iksal 86 X3
Gk. name of Chesulloth, q.v.

Ezion-geber (Elath): T. el-Khaleifeh, q.v. 67, 71, 93 F5
59 U3
Num. 33. 35 f.; Deut. 2. 8; port established on the
Red Sea (Gulf of Akaba) by Solomon, 1 Kgs. 9. 26;
22. 48. Important excavations

ez-Zib: Achzib, q.v. 93 G4
94 X2
site covered by modern houses, but over 70 rock-cut
tombs, 8th–6th cents. B.C., have been excavated

Fair Havens: Limenes Kali 90 D4
Acts 27. 8

128

Far'a (Shuruppak) — 93 J4
Farafra Oasis — 52 E5
Farah: *riv.* (in Afghanistan) — 53 M4
Farah, Wadi — 49, 63, 87 X4
Fertile Crescent, the: — 53 H4
modern geographical/historical term for the NE., N., and NW. borders of the Arabian desert where a curve of fertile country connects Mesopotamia with Syria-Palestine and thus with Asia Minor and the Levant
Florentia: *Florence* (*Firenze*) — 88 B2
Forum of Appius (Appii Forum): — 88 B2
small Italian town ('forum'= market); Acts 28. 15
Fullers' Tower (in Jerusalem) — 96

Gabae (Hippeum): *Sheikh Abreiq, q.v.* — 85, 86 X3
settlement of Herod's cavalry veterans (hippeōn = of horsemen)
Gabae: *Isfahan* — 79, 83 K4
Gabaon: *el-Jib* — 87 X5
Gk. form of name Gibeon, *q.v.*
Gabata: *Jaba* — 86 W3
Gabath Saul: *T. el-Ful* — 87 X5
later name of Gibeah, *q.v.*
Gabbatha (in Jerusalem): — 96
place called the Pavement (in Gk. lithostrōtos), John 19. 13; *see text, p.* 97
Gad: *tribe* — 57, 61, 69 Y4
Gen. 30. 11; Num. 32. 1 ff., 33 ff.; Josh. 13. 24–28; 18. 7; 2 Sam. 24. 5; 1 Chr. 5. 11
Gadara (in Perea): *T. Jadur* — 77, 85, 86, 94 Y4
Gadara (of Decapolis): *Umm Qeis* (*Muqeis*) — 77, 85, 86 Y3
— 91 G4
Graeco-oriental city; its territory probably reached beyond Yarmuk to Sea of Galilee, Matt. 8. 28 (*but see RSV note there*)
Galatia: *reg. and Rom. prov.* — 82, 89, 91 F3
reg. of central Anatolia so called after its settlement by Galatae (Gauls), a Celtic people who invaded it from Europe in 2nd cent. B.C. Became Rom. prov. 25 B.C.; later NE. part (Galatian Pontus, *q.v.*) was detached; cap. of prov. Ancyra, *q.v.*, but cities of Pisidian Antioch, *q.v.*, Iconium, *q.v.* Lystra, *q.v.*, and (prob.) Derbe, *q.v.*, were in it, so Acts 13. 14—14. 23 and 16. 1–6 describe Paul's preaching there. Gal. 1. 2; 3. 1; 1 Cor. 16. 1; 1 Pet. 1. 1. *See also* Galatian Phrygia, *and* Gaul
Galatian Pontus: *reg.* — 91 G2
part of Pontus, *q.v.*, which was originally Galatian territory: *see* Galatia
Galatian Phrygia: — 91 F3
Acts 16. 6 ('the region of Phrygia and Galatia' RSV), also 18. 23, might be translated 'the Phrygian-Galatian (or 'Galatian-Phrygian') country, and prob. refer to this border territory, Phrygian territory included in the prov. of Galatia (most of Phrygia being in prov. of Asia)
Galilee: *reg.* — 62, 69, 73, 77, 85 X3
referred to only seven times in O.T.; Josh. 12. 23 (RSV); 20. 7; 21. 32 (= 1 Chr. 6. 76); 1 Kgs. 9. 11; 2 Kgs. 15. 29 (conquered by Assyrians); Isa. 9. 1. Noted for its Gentile inhabitants. Under Hasmonean kings settled by Jews; part of kingdom of Herod the Great; at his death allotted to Herod Antipas as tetrarch. Luke 1. 26; 2. 4; 3. 1; Mark 1.9; 1. 14, 28; Matt. 4. 23; 28. 26; John 7. 1; Acts 9. 31
Galilee, Sea of: *Bahr Tabariyeh* — 49, 85, 86, 94 Y3
in O.T. called Sea of Chinnereth (or Chinneroth), *q.v.*; Matt. 4. 18; 15. 29; Mark 1. 16; 7. 31; John 6. 1; *see also* Tiberias, Sea of, *and* Gennesaret, Lake of. *Illus., p.* 13
Galilee, Lower: *reg.* — 49 X3
the more populous and cultivated part of Galilee
Galilee, Upper: *reg.* — 49 X2
the more hilly and wider part of Galilee. *See illus., p.* 10
Galilee and Perea (Tetrarchy of Herod Antipas): *reg.*; — 86
see text, p. 85
Gallim: *Kh. Ka'kul* — 73 X5
1 Sam. 25. 44; Isa. 10. 30
Gamala: *Ras el-Hal* — 77, 85, 86 Y3
captured by Alexander Jannaeus; besieged and captured by Vespasian A.D. 67
Gandhara: *reg.* — 79, 83 N3
province (part of seventh satrapy of Darius) in extreme E. of Persian empire (mod. Afghanistan–Pakistan)
Gangra — 89, 91 F2

Garis: *Kh. Kenna* — 86 X3
Gath: *T. esh-Sheri'ah* (possibly *Ziklag*) — 57, 61, 63, 65, 69, 73, 77, 95 W6
one of the five Philistine cities, Josh. 13. 3; 1 Sam. 17. 4; 21. 10; 2 Sam. 1. 20; 1 Chr. 18. 1; Amos 6. 2; Mic. 1. 10. Uncertain whether Gath or Gath= Gittaim is intended in 2 Kgs. 12. 17, 2 Chr. 26. 6. Earlier identification with *T. el-Areini* impossible. Excavations. Moresheth-Gath may be intended in 2 Chr. 11. 8.
Gath (Gittaim): *T. Ras Abu Hamid* — 63, 69 W5
1 Chr. 7. 21; 8. 13; *see also* Gittaim
Gath of Sharon: *Jett* — 57, 62 X4
in Thutmose III lists, and in Amarna Letters and Shishak lists (= Gath-pedalla)
Gath-hepher: *Kh. ez-Zurra'* — 62, 69 X3
in Zebulun, Josh. 19. 13; home of Jonah, according to 2 Kgs. 14. 25
Gath-rimmon: *T. el-Jerisheh* — 61, 63, 95 W4
in Dan. Josh. 19. 45; *cf.* Josh. 21. 24, 25; 1 Chr. 6. 69
Gaugamela: — 82 H3
scene of defeat of Persians by Alexander, 331 B.C.
Gaul: *reg.* (*outside NW. edge of p.* 88)
part of Rom. empire corresponding to mod. France and Belgium: southern Gaul (Gallia Narbonensis) was highly civilized and Greek-speaking. Possibly referred to a 2 Tim. 4. 10 (*see RSV and NEB notes*)
Gaulanitis: *Jaulan: reg.* — 77, 85, 86 Y3
region of the city Golan; district-name of N.T. period; part of territory of Philip the tetrarch (Luke 3. 1)
Gaza: *el-Ghazza* — 49, 51, 57, 61, 63, 65, 69, 73, 77, 85, 87, 95 V6
— 55, 67, 71, 75, 78, 82 F4
— 59 T1
one of the five Philistine cities; Gen. 10. 19; Deut. 2. 23; Josh. 11. 22; 13. 3; reckoned to Judah, Josh. 15. 47, *cf.* Judg. 1. 18; but Philistine in Judg. 16. 21, 1 Sam. 6. 17; *cf.* 1 Kgs. 4. 24; 2 Kgs. 18. 8; Jer. 47. 1; in N.T. times independent city; Acts 8. 26
Gazara (Gezer): *T. Jezer* — 77, 85, 87 W5
Gk. form of name 'Gezer'; 1 Macc. 4. 15; stronghold of Simon Maccabeus, 13. 43 ff.
Geba: *Jeba'* — 49, 63, 65, 69, 73, 77 *and ins* X5
in Benjamin, Josh. 18. 24; 1 Sam. 13. 3; 2 Sam. 5. 25; 1 Kgs. 15. 22; 2 Kgs. 23. 8; Ezr. 2. 26
Gebal (Byblos): *Jebeil* — 55, 67, 71, 75, 78 G4
Phoenician seaport city, 1 Kgs. 5. 18; Ezek. 27. 9. Extensive excavations
Gebim: —
N. of Jerusalem, Isa. 10. 31; unlocated
Gederah: *Jedireh* — 63 W5
in Shephelah of Judah, Josh. 15. 36; prob. also 2 Chr. 28. 18 ('Gederoth')
Gediz (Hermus): *riv.* — 52 E3
Gedor: *Kh. Jedur* — 63 X5
in hill country of Judah, Josh. 15. 58
Gedor: —
in Judah (in Simeon), 1 Chr. 4. 18, 39; unlocated
Gedor: —
in Benjamin, 1 Chr. 12. 7: unlocated
Gedrosia (Maka): *reg.* — 79, 83 M5
province in SE. Iran
Gemmaruris: *Kh. Jemrura* — 87 W5
road station of Rom. times
Gennath Gate (in Jerusalem): — 96
the 'Garden Gate', mentioned by Josephus: *see p.* 97
Gennesaret (Ginnesar): *T. el-'Ureimeh* — 85, 86 Y3
on Sea of Galilee, Matt. 14. 34, Mark 6. 53. *See also* Chinnereth
Gennesaret, Lake of: *Bahr Tabariyeh* — 85 Y3
name for Sea of Galilee, Luke 5. 1
Gentiles, Court of the (in Jerusalem) — 96
outer court of the Temple to which Gentiles were admitted
Genua: *Genoa, Genova* — 88 A2
Geoy Tepe — 93 J3
archaeological site
Gerar: *T. Abu Hureira* — 51, 61, 63, 65, 69, 73, 77 W6
— 59 T1
city of the Negeb associated with the patriarchs; Gen. 20. 1, 2; 26. 1, 6 &c.; 2 Chr. 14. 13, 14
Gerasa (Antioch on the Chrysorhoas): *Jerash* — 49, 77, 85, 86, 94 Y4
— 82, 91, 93 G4
city of Gilead, captured by Alexander Jannaeus, 83 B.C.; later independent city of the Decapolis, and an important city of Rom. empire. Its territory prob.

mentioned in Mark 5. 1, Luke 8. 26, 37 as extending to Sea of Galilee, *but see* RSV *note, and see also* Gadara and Gergesa. *Illus., p.* 38
Gergesa: *Kursi* — 86 Y3
city whose territory is mentioned, according to some MSS, in Mark 5. 1, Matt. 8. 28, Luke 8. 26, 37; (*see* RSV *note, also* Gadara *and* Gerasa)
Gerizim, Mt.: *Jebel et-Tur* — 49, 57, 61, 63, 65, 69, 77, 85, 87, 95 X4
Deut. 11. 29; 27. 12; Josh. 8. 33; Judg. 9. 7. *See also* Ebal, Mt. (Gerizim was later the holy mountain of the Samaritans, *cf.* John 4. 20)
Germanicea: *Marash* — 91 G3
Rom. garrison city on E. frontier
Geshur: *reg.* (in Transjordan) — 57, 62 Y2
Josh. 13. 13; 2 Sam. 3. 3; 13. 37; 1 Chr. 2. 23
Geshur (in the Negeb): —
Josh. 13. 2; 1 Sam. 27. 8; unlocated
Gethsemane: — 96
Matt. 26. 36; Mark. 14. 32 (*cf.* Luke 22. 39, John 18.1)
Gezer (Gazara): *T. Jezer* (*T. Abu Shusheh*) — 57, 61, 63, 65, 73, 77, 95, W5
— 93 F4
Canaanite city, Josh. 10. 33; in Ephraim but remained Canaanite, Josh. 16. 10; Levitical city, Josh. 21. 21; taken by Egyptians and presented to Solomon, 1 Kgs. 9. 15–17. Excavations reveal occupation from Chalcolithic to Maccabean periods. City mentioned in Egyptian records and Amarna letters. *See also* Gazara. *See illus., pp.* 16, 111.
Ghazni: *Alexandria Arachōsiōn, q.v.* — 79 N4
Gibbethon: *T. el-Melat* — 61, 63, 69, 73 W5
in original territory of Dan., Josh. 19. 44; Levitical city, Josh. 21. 23; in Philistine hands, Judg. 15. 27; 16. 15, 17
Gibeah: *T. el-Ful* — 61, 63, 65, 73, 95 X5
in Benjamin, Josh. 18. 28; scene of crime and war between Israel and Benjamin, Judg. chs. 19–20; home of Saul, 1 Sam. 10. 26; 15. 34; Isa. 10. 29; Hos. 5. 8; 9. 9; 10. 9. Excavations show city of Judges period (destroyed c. 1100 B.C.), fortress of Saul (destroyed c. 1000 B.C.) and occupation into the Roman period: *see also* Gabath Saul.
Gibeon: *el-Jib* — 57, 61, 63, 65, 77 *and ins,* 95 X5
Canaanite city, Josh. 9. 3, 17; 10. 2, scene of Joshua's victory, Josh. 10. 10; its 'Hivite' (? Horite) inhabitants remained, Josh. 11. 19; in Benjamin, Josh. 18. 25; Levitical city, Josh. 21. 17; its pool, 2 Sam. 2. 13; Jer. 41. 12, excavated (*see illus., p.* 100); high place, 1 Kgs. 3. 4, 5; Neh. 3. 7; 7. 25
Gihon: *'Ain Sittna Miriam: spring* — 81
below Jerusalem in Kidron valley; 1 Kgs. 1. 33, 45; 2 Chr. 32. 30. 14
Gilboa, Mt.: *Jebel Fuqu'ah* — 49, 61, 62, 65 X3
1 Sam. 28. 4; 31. 1; 2 Sam. 21. 12.
Gilead: *reg.* — 49, 57, 61, 63, 65, 69, 73, 77 Y4
— 67 G4
Gen. 31. 23, 25; trans-Jordan tribes settled there, Num. 32. 39; Deut. 3. 12–13, 15; Josh. 17. 1; occupied by Ammonites, Judg. 10. 7, 17; home country of Jephthah, Judg. 11. 1—12. 7; Judg. 20. 1; 2 Sam. 2. 9; in Solomon's sixth and eleventh districts, 1 Kgs. 4. 13, 19; lost to Hazael, king of Syria, 2 Kgs. 10. 33; Amos 1. 3; taken by Assyrians, 2 Kgs. 15. 29
Gilgal (on plain of Sharon): *Jiljulieh* — 63 W4
Josh. 12. 23 (KJV: *see* RSV *note*)
Gilgal (in Ephraim, SW. of Shiloh): *Kh.'Alyata* — 63 X4
Deut. 11. 30; 2 Kgs. 2. 1; 4. 38
Gilgal (Beth-gilgal, nr. Jericho): *Kh. el-Mafjar (Mefjir)* — 57, 61, 63, 65, 69, 73, 77, 95 K5
Josh. 4. 19, 20; 5. 9, 10; 1 Sam. 7. 16; 10. 8. Hos. 4. 15
Giloh: *Kh. Jala* — 61, 63, 65 X5
in hill country of Judah, Josh. 15. 51; 2 Sam. 15. 12; 23. 34
Gimarrai (Gomer): *people* — 71 F3
known from Assyrian records; same as Gk. Kimmerioi (Cimmerians) and to be equated with Biblical Gomer, Gen. 10. 2, 3; *see also* Ezek. 38. 6. Invaders of Asia Minor, an Indo-European group
Gimzo: *Jimzu* — 63, 69, 73 W5
2 Chr. 28. 18
Ginae: *Jenin* — 86 X4
Gk. name of En-gannim, *q.v.*
Ginnesar (Gennesaret): *T. el-'Ureimeh* — 86 Y3
see Gennesaret
Gischala: *el-Jish* — 86, 94 X2
John of Gischala was leader in Jewish revolt (Josephus)
Gitta: *Jett* — 86 X4

village in Narbattene: birthplace of Simon Magus (Acts 8. 9) according to Justin Martyr

Gittaim (Gath): *T. Ras Abu Hamid* 63, 69 **W5**
2 Sam. 4. 3; Neh. 11. 33; *see also* Gath

Gizeh: 92 **F4**
site of the great pyramids, *see illus., p. 21*

Golan: *Sahem el-Jolan* 57, 61, 62 **Y3**
city of refuge, Deut. 4. 43; Josh. 20. 4; Levitical city, Josh. 21. 27; 1 Chr. 6. 71

Golgotha: 96
Matt. 27. 33; Mark 15. 22; John 19. 17

Gomer (Gimarrai): *reg.* 71 **F3**
see Gimarrai

Gomorrah: (*conj. loc.*) 57 **X6**
in valley of Siddim, near Sodom. Gen. 14. 2–11; 18. 20; 19. 24 &c. See Siddim, Valley of

Gophna: *Jiphna* 77, 85, 87 **X5**
mentioned by Josephus; same as Ophni, Josh. 18. 24

Gordion (Gordium) 70, 78, 82, 89, 91, 92 **F3**
city of Phrygia

Gordyene: *reg. (part of Kurdistan)* 89 **H3**

Gorgan (Astrabad) 79, 83 **K3**

Gortyna: 78, 82 **D3**
city in Crete. 1 Macc. 15. 23. Site of inscription, 'Code of Gortyna', important codification of Hellenic laws made *c.* 450 B.C. and containing older elements

Goshen: *ed-Dahariyeh* 61, 63 **W6**
Josh. 10. 41; 11. 16; in Judah, Josh. 15. 51

Goshen: *reg.* (in Egypt) 58 **Q2**
district of Wadi Tumilat; Gen. 45. 10; 46. 28, 29; 47. 1–6, 27; Exod. 8. 22. See Introduction, p. 22

Gozan: *T. Halaf* 67, 71, 93 **G3**
place of deportation of Israelites, 2 Kgs. 17. 6; 19. 12; 1 Chr. 5. 26

Granicus: *riv.* 52, 78, 82 **E2**
scene of Alexander the Great's first victory over Persians in Asia, 334 B.C.

Great Arad: *see* Arad (*T. 'Arad*)

Great Bitter Lake 59 **R2**

Great Plain, The (Plain of Megiddo, Esdraelon): *Merj Ibn 'Amir* 49, 77, 85, 86 **X3**
Hellenistic and Roman name for this plain (Lat. 'Campus maximus Legionis', from Legio, army camp nr. Megiddo). Cf. 2 Chr. 35. 22; Zech. 12. 11; Judith 1. 8

Great Sea, The (Mediterranean Sea) 49 &c.
Biblical name: Num. 34. 6, 7; Josh. 1. 4; 9. 1; 15. 12; 23. 4; Ezek. 47. 10; 48. 28. Assyrian-Babylonian name 'The Upper Sea', 'The Western Sea'; Lat. 'Mare Internum', 'Mare Nostrum'

Greece: 52, 84 **D3**
country called by its own people 'Hellas', by Romans 'Graecia' (after the 'Graioi' a Hellenic people known early in the West). 'Greece' in Dan. 8. 21; 10. 20; 11... 2 = Alexander's empire; cf. Zech. 9. 13. See also Javan. The country, Acts 20. 2 (cf. Achaia)

Greek citadel (in Jerusalem): 81
see text, p. 80

Gulashkird (Alexandria in Carmania) 79, 83 **L5**

Gurbaal (Jagur): *T. Ghurr* 63, 69 **W6**
2 Chr. 26. 7; *see also* Jagur

Gurgum: *reg.* 67 **G3**
district/principality of Hittite empire

Gutium: *reg.* 55 **J3**
barbarian highland country in Zagros mts., land of the Guti (Gutians), in cuneiform records

Habor: *Khabur: riv.* 53, 55, 67, 71, 75 **H3**
2 Kgs. 17. 6; 18. 11; 1 Chr. 5. 26

Hadashah: *Kh. el-Judeideh* 63 **W5**
in the Shephelah of Judah, Josh. 15. 37

Hadera (Khudeirah) 94 **W4**
site of prehistoric ossuary burials

Hadid: *el-Haditheh* 63, 77 **W5**
Ezr. 2. 33; Neh. 7. 37; 11. 24. See Adida

Hagia Triada: *see* Ayia Triada

Halab: *Aleppo, Haleb* 55, 67 **G3**

Halah:
in Assyria; 2 Kgs. 17. 6; 18. 11; 1 Chr. 5. 26 (unlocated: *but cf.* Habor)

Halak, Mt.: *Jebel Halaq*
in the Negeb; Josh. 12. 7 (south of area shown on p. 61 &c.)

Halhul: *Halhul* 63 **X5**
in hill country of Judah, Josh. 15. 58

Halicarnassus: 82, 91, 92 **E3**
Gk. city-state in Caria, later in Rom. prov. of Asia

Halys: *Kizilirmak: riv.*
52, 55, 71, 75, 78, 82, 89, 91, 93 **F3**
chief river of Anatolia: *see note on map, p. 75*

Ham: *Ham* 57, 62, 73 **Y3**
Gen. 14. 5

Hama: *Hamath* 93 **G3**
excavated site: *see also* Hamath

Hamadan (Ecbatana): 93 **J4**
see Ecbatana

Hamath: *Hama* 67, 71, 75, 78, 95 **G3**
city and kingdom, 1 Sam. 8. 9; 2 Kgs. 14. 28; in Assyrian empire, 2 Kgs. 17. 24; 18. 34; 23. 33; Isa. 11. 9; Amos 6. 2; Zech. 9. 2; 1 Macc. 12. 25; renamed Epiphania, *q.v.*

Hamath, Entrance to: 69 **Y1**
northern limit of United Monarchy and of Israel under Jeroboam II. Perhaps near sources of Orontes; possibly to be read as a place-name Lebo-Hamath, mod. *Lebweh*, on the Orontes river. See pp. 9–11

Hammath: *Hammam Tabariyeh* 61, 62 **Y3**
in Naphtali, Josh. 19. 35; later Ammathus, *q.v.* Probably same as Hammoth-dor, Josh. 21. 32. Excavations.

Hammon: *Umm el-'Awamid* 62 **X2**
in Asher, Josh. 19. 28

Hammon:
in Naphtali, 1 Chr. 6. 76; unlocated

Hamun-i-Helmand: *lake* 53 **M1**

Hananel (in Jerusalem): *tower* 81
Neh. 3. 1; 12. 39; Jer. 31. 38; Zech. 14. 10. See p. 80

Hannathon: *T. el-Bedeiwiyeh* 57, 61, 62 **X3**
in Zebulun, Josh. 19. 14

Haran (Carrhae): *Harran* 55, 67, 71, 75, 78, 89, 93 **G3**
halting-place of Abraham, Gen. 11. 31; home of Laban and refuge of Jacob, Gen. 27. 43; 28. 10; in Assyrian empire, 2 Kgs. 19. 12; trading nation, Ezek. 27. 23. See also Carrhae

Harim: *Kh. Horan* 63, 77 **W5**
Ezr. 2. 32; Neh. 7. 35

Harmozeia: 83 **L5**
seaport on Straits of Hormuz, precursor of later *Ormuz*

Harod, Spring of: 68 **X3**
Judg. 7. 1; 2 Sam. 23. 25; 1 Chr. 11. 27. See text, p. 60

Harosheth-ha-goiim: *T. el-'Amr* 61, 62 **X3**
home of Sisera, Judg. 4. 2, 13, 16

Harran (Haran) 93 **G3**

Hassuna 93 **H3**
excavated 'tell' in Mesopotamia disclosing early Neolithic (pre-Tell-Halaf) cultures

Hatra: 93 **H3**
excavated site

Hatti: *reg.* 75 **G4**
in Babylonian chronicles 'Hatti' (the Hittite land, originally) includes both Palestine and Syria

Hatti (Hittite Empire): 55 **F3**
see text, pp. 54–55, and under Hittite Empire

Hattina: *reg.* 71 **G3**
Assyrian name of Syrian Hatti

Hattusa: *Boğazköy* 55, 93 **F2**
capital of Hittite empire: *see* Boğazköy *and* pp. 54–55

Hauran: *el-Hauran : reg.* 49, 69, 73 **Z3**
71 **G4**
NE. limit of Israel in Ezek. 47. 16, 18. Mentioned in Egyptian and Assyrian inscriptions. In Graeco-Roman period Auranitis, *q.v.*

Havvoth-jair: *reg.* 57, 61, 65, 69 **Y3**
towns on border of Gilead and Bashan named after Jair son of Manasseh, Num. 32. 41; Deut. 3. 14; Judg. 10. 4; 1 Chr. 2. 23

Hazar-addar: *Kh. el-Qudeirat* 59 **T2**
Num. 34. 5; probably also to be read for 'Hezron . . . Addar' in Josh. 15. 3

Hazarmaveth: *reg.* 67 **J7**
in Gen. 10. 26, 1 Chr. 1. 20, appears as 'son' of Joktam but represents a region in S. Arabia: *see text, p. 66*

Hazar-shual: *el-Watan* 61, 63, 77 **W6**
in Negeb of Judah, Josh. 15. 28; in Simeon, Josh. 19. 2; 1 Chr. 4. 28; Neh. 11. 27

Hazazon-tamar: *'Ain Husb* 57, 69 **X7**
Gen. 14. 7: evidently near the Cities of the Plain (*cf.* 14. 8) and probably the same as Tamar in Ezek. 47. 18, 19; in 2 Chr. 20. 2 identified with En-gedi, but this is probably a gloss in the MSS

Hazor: *T. el-Qedah, T. Waqqas* 49, 57, 61, 65, 69, 73, 77, 94 **Y3** 55, 67, 93 **G4**
important Canaanite city, Josh. 11. 1, 10–13; Judg.

4. 2; in Naphtali, Josh. 19. 36; fortified by Solomon, 1 Kgs. 9. 15; taken by Assyrians, 2 Kgs. 15. 29; by Babylonians, Jer. 49. 28–30. Important excavations show size and strength of the walls, &c. *Illus. p. 16*

Hazor (in Benjamin): *Kh. Hazzur* 63 **X5**
77 **ins**
Neh. 11. 33

Hazor (in Judah): *el-Jebariyeh*
Josh. 15. 23, where 'Hazor (and) Ithnan' should be read as one name, 'Hazor-ithnan'

Hazor, Plain of: 49, 86 **Y2**
1 Macc. 11. 67

Hazor-hadattah: 63 **X6**
in Negeb of Judah, Josh. 15. 25

Hebron (Kiriath-arba): *el-Khalil*
49, 51, 57, 61, 63, 65, 69, 73, 77, 85 **X5** 55 **G4** 59 **U1**
associated with patriarchs, Gen. 13. 18; 23. 2; 35. 27; visited by Israelite spies, Num. 13. 22; taken by Joshua, Josh. 10. 36; 14. 13–15; in hill country of Judah, Josh. 15. 54; city of refuge, Josh. 20. 7; Judg. 1. 10; David's capital, 2 Sam. 2. 1–3, 11; 5. 5; Absalom there, 2 Sam. 15. 10; fortified, 2 Chr. 11. 10; excavations

Hebron (in Asher):
Josh. 19. 28 (KJV): same as Ebron (RSV); probably an error for Abdon, *q.v.*

Hecatompylus (Damghan) 83 **K3**
city at E. exit from Caspian Gates

Helam: *'Alma* 65 **Z3**
in Transjordan, site of David's victory over Syrians, 2 Sam. 10. 16, 17. Probably same as later Alema, *q.v.*

Helbon: *Halbun* 71 **G3**
trading city, Ezek. 27. 18

Heleph: *Kh. 'Irbada* 62 **X3**
in Naphtali, Josh. 19. 33

Heliopolis (On) (in Egypt): *T. Husn* 54, 67, 71, 74, 78, 82, 89, 92 **F4** 58 **K2**
Gk. name (= City of the Sun) for Egyptian temple city called 'On', *q.v.* Jer. 43. 13 (Beth-shemesh, KJV; Heliopolis, RSV)

Heliopolis (in Syria): *Ba'albek* 91 **G4**
Gk. name (= City of the Sun) for Syrian temple city of Ba'albek, *q.v.*

Helkath: *T. el-Harbaj* 62 **X3**
in Asher, Josh. 19. 25; Levitical city, Josh. 21. 31; and cf. 1 Chr. 6. 75, where Helkath should be read for 'Hukok'

Hellespont: *Dardanelles: strait* 52, 91 **E2**

Hepher: *T. Ifshar* 61, 62, 65 **W4**
Canaanite city, Josh. 12. 17; in Solomon's third district, 1 Kgs. 4. 10

Heraclea: 72, 91 **E2**
Gk. city and seaport, full name Heraclea Pontica

Heracleon: 90 **E3**
Greek city

Heracleopolis: *Ahnes el-Medineh* 54 **F5** 58 **P3**
Gk. name of Egyptian city on right bank of *Bahr Yusuf*, in the *Faiyum*; provided rulers of 9th and 10th dynasties; competitor of Thebes

Hermon, Mt.: *Jebel esh-Sheikh*
49, 57, 61, 65, 69, 73, 77 **Y2**
see pp. 48–49. Prominent mountain on northern border of Israelite territory, Deut. 3. 8–9; Josh. 11. 3; 12. 1 &c.

Hermopolis: *el-Ashmunein* 54, 70, 78, 82 **F5**
Gk. name (City of Hermes) of seat of worship of Egyptian god Thoth (identified with Hermes)

Hermus: *Gediz: riv.* 52, 70, 74, 91 **E3** 85
see text, p. 84

Herod Kingdom of:
see text, p. 84

Herod Agrippa II, Kingdom of 91 **G4**
see text, p. 84

Herodium: *Jebel Fureidis* 85, 87, 95 **X5**
fortress of Herod the Great, and his burial-place. Held out after fall of Jerusalem to Romans, A.D. 70; excavations

Heshbon: *Hesban* 49, 57, 61, 63, 65, 69, 73, 77, 95 **Y5** 59 **U1**
city of Sihon, king of the Amorites, Num. 21. 25–30; Deut. 1. 4; Josh. 12. 2; in Reuben, Josh. 13. 17; Judg. 11. 26; Levitical city, 1 Chr. 6. 86; city of Moab, Isa. 15. 4; 16. 8; Jer. 48. 2, 45; excavations

Hezekiah's Conduit (in Jerusalem) 81
see 2 Chr. 32. 30; 2 Kgs. 20. 20 *and text, p. 80*

Hierakonpolis: *Kom el-Ahmar*   92 F5
Gk. name of Nekhen, prehistoric capital of Upper Egypt: site of excavations

Hierapolis: 91 E3
Col. 4. 13. Colossae, Laodicea, and Hierapolis formed a group of cities all evangelized at same time

High Place (perhaps at *Nebi Samwil*)   65 X5
at Gibeon, *q.v.*; 1 Kgs. 3. 4

Hindush: *reg.*: (W. part of Indian sub-continent)   79, 83 N5
20th satrapy in empire of Darius I; *see also* India

Hinnom Valley (at Jerusalem): *Wadi er-Rababeh*   81, 96
see text, pp. 80, 97

Hippeum (Gabae): *Sheikh Abreiq*   85, 86 X3
see Gabae

Hippicus (in Jerusalem): *tower*   96
part of Herodian fortifications; *see p.* 97

Hippos (Susitha): *Qal 'at el-Husn*   77, 85, 86, 94 Y3
city of Decapolis

Hittite Empire (Hatti):   55 F3
predominant power in Anatolia, in 16th and in 14th–13th cents. B.C.; Hittite documents discovered at Boğazköy, *q.v.* (Hattusa), reveal its relations with Egypt, &c., and names of kings, deities, &c. 'Hittites' in Bible are people from this race settled in Syria-Palestine after fall of empire, e.g. Gen. 15. 20; Gen. 23. 2, 10; 1 Kgs. 10. 29

Hittites: 67 G3
see above and cf. 1 Kgs. 10. 29

Holon (in Judah): *Kh. 'Alin*   63 X5
in hill country of Judah, Josh. 15. 51; Levitical city, Josh. 21. 15

Holon (in Moab):
Jer. 48. 21; unlocated

Homs (Emesa)   67, 94 G4
NE. of Kadesh-barnea. Num. 20. 22 &c.; unlocated

Hor, Mt.:

Horeb (Sinai), Mt.   59 S4
Exod. 3. 1; 17. 6; 33. 6; Deut. 1. 2 &c.; Deut. 4. 10 ff. equates Horeb with Mt. Sinai of Exod. 19. 11 &c. Possible identifications: (1) *Jebel Musa*, (2) *Jebel Helal. See text, p.* 58

Horem: *Kh. Qatamun*   62 X2
in Naphtali, Josh. 19. 38

Horites: *people*   67 G3
name of early inhabitants of Seir in Gen. 14. 6; Deut. 2. 12, 22; also same as Hurrians known from non-Biblical sources in Mitanni in N. Mesopotamia, perhaps same as Hivites

Hormah: *T. el-Mishash*   57, 61, 63, 77 W6
    59 T2
Num. 14. 45; 21. 3; Deut. 1. 44; Josh. 12. 14; in Negeb of Judah, Josh. 15. 30; in Simeon, Josh. 19. 4; according to Judg. 1. 17 formerly Zephath; 1 Sam. 30. 30

Hormuz, Straits of   53 L5

Hosah:
in Asher, Josh. 19. 29; possibly same as Uzu, *q.v.*

Hukkok: *Yuquq*   62 X3
in Naphtali, Josh. 19. 34; *cf.* 1 Chr. 6. 75

Hukok:
1 Chr. 6. 75; *see* Helkath

Huleh (Semechonitis), *lake*   49 Y2

Husban, Wadi   49 Y5

Hyrcania: *Kh. Mird*   85, 87 X5
Hasmonean and Herodian fortress

Hyrcania: *Gurgan*: *reg.*   79, 83 K3
in Achaemenian empire; conquered by Alexander

Hyrcanian Sea: *Caspian Sea*   79, 83 K3
called after Hyrcania, where Greeks first reached it, and believed (e.g. by Alexander) to be possibly a gulf of the outer Ocean

Iadanna (Cyprus)   70 F3
name for Cyprus in 8th–7th cent. B.C. Assyrian records

Ialysus: 92 E3
site of Minoan colony *c.* 1600–1425 B.C., later Greek city

Iamnitarum Portus (Jamnia Harbour): *Minet Rubin*   87 W5

Ibleam: *T. Bel'ameh*   49, 57, 61, 62, 69, 73 X4
belonged to Manasseh, Josh. 17. 11; *but see* Judg. 1. 27; 2 Kgs. 9. 27; 15. 10 (RSV): same as 'Bileam' in 1 Chr. 6. 70

Iconium: *Qoniyah*   89, 91 F3
city on borders of Phrygia and Lycaonia, included from 25 B.C. in Rom. prov. of Galatia. Acts 14. 1 ff.;

16. 2 (*cf.* 16. 4); 2 Tim. 3. 11

Ida, Mt.   52, 78 E3

Idumea: *reg.*   77, 85, 87 W6
Gk. name of country on southern borders of Judea inhabited by Idumeans (Edomites) who had moved north in post-Exilic period when Nabataeans occupied former Edom; 1 Macc. 4. 61; 5. 3; Mark 3. 8. (In Isa. 34. 5, Ezek. 35. 15; 36. 5, KJV, 'Idumea' stands for Edom, *q.v.*)

Ije-abarim
Num. 21. 11; 33. 44 (KJV): *see* Iye-abarim

Ijon: *T. ed-Dibbin*   57, 69 Y2
in Naphtali, captured by Ben-hadad of Damascus, 1 Kgs. 15. 20, and by Tiglath-pileser III, 2 Kgs. 15. 29

Ilium (Troy): *Hisarlik*   54, 82 E3

Illyricum: *Rom. prov.*   88 C2
Rom. 15. 19: this was at that time the official Roman name of the province though Dalmatia, *q.v.*, was alternative name, later official

Ilon: *Beit Illo*   87 X5
mentioned in apocryphal Jewish literature (Bk. of Jubilees)

Imbros: *Imros*: *isl.*   91, 92 E2

'Imwas (Emmaus)   95 W5
mod. name of Emmaus (Nicopolis): *see under* Emmaus

India (Hindush):   79 N5
see Hindush, *and cf.* Esth. 1. 1; 8. 9

Indus: *riv.*   79, 83 N5
see Hindush, *and cf.* Esth. 1. 1; 8. 9

Ionia: *reg.*   78, 82, 91 E3
country of the Ionians, or Eastern Greeks, who settled in Asia Minor in Gk. history. Etymologically equivalent to Heb. 'Javan', *q.v.*

Ionian Sea: 52 C3
between Italy and Greece (name Iōnian Sea is not connected with Iōnia)

Iphtah: *Tarqumiyeh*   63 X5
in Shephelah of Judah, Josh. 15. 43 (KJV 'Jiphtah')

Iphtah-el: *Wadi el-Melek*: *valley*   62 X3
on border between Zebulun and Asher, Josh. 19. 14, 27

Ipsus: 82 F3
town in S. Phrygia, where Antigonus was defeated, 301 B.C., by Seleucus I, Ptolemy I, and Lysimachus

Iran (Persia):   53 K4
geographically Iran is the great plateau between Mesopotamia and Baluchistan, and between Caspian Sea and Persian Gulf; also mod. kingdom in this area, commonly called 'Persia', which really denotes smaller area in SW. Iran. *See also* Persia

Iron (KJV) same as Yiron, *q.v.*

Irq el-Ahmar (*Umm Qatafa*)   95 X5
prehistoric caves near *W. el-Murabba'at*

Isin: *Ishan Bahriyat*   55 J4
city in Mesopotamia, seat of rule of Lipit-Ishtar, pre-Hammurabi lawgiver (*see text, pp.* 54–55)

Isfahan (Gabae)   79 K4

'Isfiyyeh   94 X3

Israel: *reg. and kingdom*   62, 65, 69, 73
    67, 71 G4
geographically, (1) the area settled by the people of Israel (the twelve tribes descended from the sons of Jacob) (Gen. 32. 28); it extended from Dan to Beer-sheba, Judg. 20. 1; 1 Sam. 3. 20; David and Solomon were kings of all Israel (2 Sam. 8. 15); but owing to importance and separateness of Judah, *q.v.*, Israel often referred only to (2) the northern tribes and their territory, distinct from Judah (2 Sam. 3. 10; 19. 41 ff.); on death of Solomon this became separate kingdom (1 Kgs. 12. 16) though 'Israel' as a nation could still include Judah (1 Kgs. 12. 17). Kingdom of Israel reached its greatest extent under Jeroboam II (2 Kgs. 14. 25); overthrown by Assyrians, 721 B.C. (2 Kgs. 17. 6 ff.)

Israel, Court of (in Jerusalem)   96
part of Temple precinct reserved for Israelites, Gentiles being excluded on pain of death (*cf.* Acts 21. 28)

Israel, Hill Country of: 57, 61 X4
central upland region of Israel, N. of Jerusalem

Issachar: *tribe*   61, 65, 69, 73 X3
Gen. 35. 23; Josh. 19. 17–23; Solomon's tenth district, 1 Kgs. 4. 17; 2 Chr. 30. 18

Issus: 78, 82, 91 G3
Plain of Issus was the scene of crucial battle between Alexander and Darius III, 333 B.C.

Istria: *penins.*   52 B1

Istros: 89 E2
town near mouth of Danube (Istros)

Itabyrium (Tabor): *Jebel et-Tur*   86 X3
Greek and Latin name of Mt. Tabor; fortified by Josephus against Romans, *c.* A.D. 66

Italy: *reg.*   52, 88 B2
Acts 27. 1, 6; Heb. 13. 24

Ituraea: *reg.*   85 Y2
territory of Ituraeans, the Jetur of Gen. 25. 15, 1 Chr. 1. 31, in the *Beqa'*; after death of Herod the Great, part of tetrarchy of Philip, Luke 3. 1

Izalla: *reg.*   75 H3
in N. Mesopotamia, on border of Urartu, scene of campaigns of Nabopolassar and Nebuchadrezzar

Iye-abarim:
on border of Moab, Num. 21. 11; 33. 44. (*text, p.* 58)

Iyyon
NEB spelling of Ijon, *q.v.*

Jabbok: *Nahr ez-Zerqa*: *riv.*   49, 57, 61, 63, 65, 73, 77, 85, 87, 95 Y4
Gen. 32. 22; marked N. boundary of kingdom of Sihon, Num. 21. 24; Deut. 2. 37; boundary between trans-Jordan tribes of Israel and the Ammonites, Deut. 3. 16; Josh. 12. 2; Judg. 11. 13, 22

Jabesh-gilead: *T. Abu Kharaz & T. Meqbereh*   61, 62, 65, 73 Y4
Judg. 21. 8 ff.; 1 Sam. 11. 1 ff.; 31. 11 f., 2 Sam. 2. 4 f.; 31. 11

Jabneel: *T. en-Na'am*   62 Y3
in Naphtali, Josh. 19. 33

Jabneel (Jabneh, Jamnia): *Yebna*   49, 61, 63, 73, 77 W5
in Judah, Josh. 15. 11; same as Jabneh, *q.v.*

Jabneh (Jabneel, Jamnia): *Yebna*   69, 73 W5
2 Chr. 26. 6: same as Jabneel in Judah, *q.v.*; later Jamnia, *q.v.*

Jaffa (Joppa): *Yafa* [*Yafo*]   95 W4
see Joppa

Jagur (Gurbaal): *T. Ghurr*   63 W6
in Negeb of Judah, Josh. 15. 21; *see also* Gurbaal

Jahaz: *Kh. et-Teim*   63, 69, 73 Y5
Num. 21. 23; Deut. 2. 32; in Reuben, Josh. 13. 18; Levitical city, Josh. 21. 36; in Moab, Isa. 15. 4; Jer. 48. 34

Jair, towns of: *see* Havvoth-jair

Jalo Oasis   52 D5

Jamneith: *Kh. Benit*   86 Y3
Rom. period fortress mentioned by Josephus

Jamnia (Jabneh, Jabneel): *Yebna*   77, 85, 87 W5
Greek form of 'Jabneh', 1 Macc. 4. 15; detached from Herod's kingdom and given to Empress Livia, wife of Augustus, *c.* A.D. 10

Jamnia Harbour (Iamnitarum Portus): *Minet Rubin*   87 W5
mentioned by geographer Ptolemy

Janoah: *T. en Na'meh*   63, 69 X2
conquered by Tiglath-pileser III; 2 Kgs. 15. 29. To be placed here, or at *Yanuh*, SE. of Achzib

Janoah: *K. Yanum*   63 X4
on border of Ephraim, Josh. 16. 6, 7

Japhia (Japha): *Yafa*   57, 62, 86, 94 X3
in Zebulun, Josh. 19. 13 (19. 12 KJV); still existed in Rom. period; fortified by Josephus *c.* 66 A.D. Excavations

Jarmu: 93 H3
prehistoric site

Jarmuth: *Kh. Yarmuk*   61, 63, 77 W5
Canaanite city, Josh. 10. 3ff; in Shephelah of Judah, Josh. 15. 35

Jarmuth: *Kokab el-Hawa*   62 Y3
Levitical city in Issachar, Josh. 21. 29; same as Remeth, Josh. 19. 21 and Ramoth, 1 Chr. 6. 73, *qq.v.*

Jattir: *Kh. 'Attir*   61, 63 X6
in hill country of Judah, Josh. 15. 48; Levitical city, Josh. 21. 14; 1 Sam. 30. 27

Javan: *reg.*   66, 70 E3
Heb. term for Greece, especially Ionia, *q.v.*; the reference varies in different passages: *see* Gen. 10. 2, 4; Isa. 66. 19; Ezek. 27. 13. *See also* Greece

Jaxartes: *Syr Darya*: *riv.*   53 N2

Jazer: *Kh. Jazzir*   57, 63, 65, 73, 77 Y4
marked boundary of the Ammonites, Num. 21. 24, 32; occupied by tribe of Gad, Num. 32. 1, 3, 35; Josh. 13. 25; Levitical city, Josh. 21. 39; 1 Chr. 26. 31; extreme limit of Moab, Isa. 16. 8; Jer. 48. 32; 1 Macc. 5. 8. Explorations show occupation *c.* 1200–600 B.C.

Jebeil: Byblos, Gebal, *q.v.*   93 G4

Jebel et-Tur: Gerizim, Mt., *q.v.*   95 X4

Jebel et-Tur: Tabor, Mt., *q.v.*   *95* X3
Jebel Fureidis: Herodium, *q.v.*   *95* X5
Jebel Helal: *mt.*   *59* S2
   one possible identification for Mt. Sinai, *q.v.*
Jebel Jermaq: *mt.*   *49* X2
Jebel Shifa: *mt.*   *52* G5
Jebel Tuwaiq: *mt.*   *53* J6
Jebus   *61* X5
   Josh. 18. 28; 19. 10–11; captured by David, 2 Sam. 5. 6. *See* Jerusalem
Jekabzeel (Kabzeel): *Kh. Hora*   *63, 77* W6
   Neh. 11. 25; same as Kabzeel, *q.v.*
Jemdet Nasr: *93* H4
   excavated site in Babylonia, after which the latest pre-Dynastic cultural period (*c.* 3200–2800 B.C.) is called
Jenin: En-gannim, Ginae, *qq.v.*   *51* X3
Jerash: Gerasa, *q.v.*   *94* Y4
Jericho: *T. es-Sultan*   *49, 51, 57, 61, 63, 65, 69, 73, 77, 95* X5
    95 ins
    55, 93 G4
    59 U1
   very ancient city, where excavations disclose many Neolithic levels reaching back to 7th millennium, including a pre-pottery phase and the earliest known city fortifications. No houses or walls of the time of Joshua (13th cent.) remain on the tell; *see* Josh. 6. 1–26; on border of Ephraim, Josh. 16. 7; rebuilt, 1 Kgs. 16. 34; 2 Kgs. 2. 4 ff.; Ezra 2. 34; Neh. 3. 2. *Illus.* p. 15
Jericho: *Tulul Abu el-'Alayiq*   *85, 87* X5
    95 ins
   Herodian (N.T. period) city of Jericho revealed by excavations a little S. of *T. es-Sultan*, where Wadi Qilt opens into Jordan plain. Herod's winter capital, equipped by him with fine buildings. Matt. 20. 29; Luke 10. 30; 18. 35; 19. 1
Jericho: *Ariha*   *95* ins
   mod. city on slightly different site from both the above
Jeruel, Wilderness of: *49* X5
   2 Chr. 20. 16; between Tekoa and En-gedi
Jerusalem: *el-Quds*   *49, 51, 57, 61, 63, 65, 69, 73, 77 and ins, 85, 87, 95* X5
    52, 55, 67, 70, 75, 78, 82, 89, 91, 93 G4
    59 U1
    plans of: pp. 81, 96
   called Urusalim in Amarna Letters (*see* p. 55); probably same as Salem (Shalem) in Gen. 14. 18; Canaanite (Jebusite) city, Josh. 10. 1 ff.; 15. 8, 63; 18. 28; Judg. 1. 8; taken by David, 2 Sam. 5. 6 ff., and became capital of kings of Judah, 2 Sam. 20. 3; 1 Kgs. 2. 36; 3. 1; 9. 10; 10. 27; 2 Kgs. 14. 13; threatened by Assyrians, 2 Kgs. 18. 35; taken and sacked by Babylonians, 2 Kgs. 24. 10 ff., 25. 1 ff.; restoration, Ezra 1. 2 ff.; 7. 7, 15; Neh. 2. 11 ff.; Zech. 2. 2 ff. &c. Attacked by Antiochus Epiphanes, 1 Macc. 1. 29 ff.; cleansed by Maccabees (*see* 1 Macc. 4. 36–60) 1 Macc. 6. 7, but Greek citadel remained, 1 Macc. 10. 7 ff.; Hasmonean capital, 1 Macc. 10. 10 ff.
   City of Herod the Great, Matt. 2. 11; and religious centre of Judea in Rom. times, Luke 2. 41 ff.; John 2. 13 ff.; Matt. 21. 1 ff.; Acts 1. 4 ff.; 15. 2 ff.; Gal. 1. 18; 2. 1 &c. *See* texts, pp. 80, 97; *illus.*, pp. 45, 116, 117, 118
Jeshanah: *Burj el-Isaneh or el-Burj*   *63, 69* X4
   1 Sam. 7. 12; 2 Chr. 13. 19
Jeshua: *T. es-Sa'wa*   *63, 77* W6
   Neh. 11. 26
Jetur: *see* Ituraea
Jezreel (in Judah): *Kh. Tewana*   *61, 63* X6
   in hill country of Judah, Josh. 15. 56; 1 Sam. 25. 43
Jezreel: *Zer'in*   *49, 61, 63, 69* X3
   city at head of Valley of Jezreel, in Issachar, Josh. 19. 18; in Solomon's fifth district, 1 Kgs. 4. 12; 18. 45; Ahab had palace there, 1 Kgs. 21. 1 ff.
Jezreel, Valley of: *Nahr Jalud*   *49, 61, 62, 65, 69, 86* X3
   descending from watershed E-ward to Jordan. W. of watershed is Plain of Megiddo, to which later the Greek form of name 'Jezreel', i.e. Esdraelon: some scholars include it in O.T. term 'Valley of Jezreel'. Josh. 17. 16; Judg. 6. 33; Hos. 1. 5. *Illus.*, p. 10
Jezzine: *51* Y1
Jiphtah (KJV): same as Iphtah, *q.v.*
Jogbehah: *Jubeihat*   *49, 57, 61, 63* Y4
   in territory of Gad, Num. 32. 35; Judg. 8. 11
Jokdeam: *Kh. Raqa'*   *63* X6
   in hill country of Judah, Josh. 15. 56
Jokmeam: *see* Jokneam

Jokneam (Jokmeam): *T. Qeimun*   *57, 61, 62, 65, 69* X3
   Canaanite city, Josh. 12. 22; Levitical city, in Issachar, near border of Zebulun, Josh. 19. 10; 21. 34; in Solomon's fifth district, 1 Kgs. 4. 12
Jokshan: Gen. 25. 2; *see* text, p. 66
Joktan: *reg.*   *67* H6
   in Arabia, Gen. 10. 25, *and see* text, p. 66
Joppa: *Jaffa, Yafa [Yafo]*   *49, 57, 61, 63, 65, 69, 73, 77, 85, 87, 95* W4
    53, 55, 67, 89, 91 F4
   Josh. 19. 46; seaport, 2 Chr. 2. 16; Ezra 3. 7; Jon. 1. 3; Acts 9. 36 ff.; 10. 5 ff. Excavations.
Jordan: *esh-Sheri'ah el-Kebireh:* *riv.*   *49, 57, 61, 63, 65, 69, 73, 77, 85, 87, 94* Y4
    52 G4
   Gen. 13. 10; 32. 10; Num. 13. 29; Josh. 3. 1 ff.; 13. 23 ff.; 2 Kgs. 5. 10 ff.; Jer. 12. 5; Matt. 3. 5; &c. *Illus.*, p. 14
Jotapata: *Kh. Jefat*   *86* X3
   Rom. period name of Jotbah, *q.v.*; in Jewish War of A.D. 66–70 fortified against Romans
Jotbah: *Kh. Jefat*   *62, 73* X3
   2 Kgs. 21. 19; same as Jotapata, *q.v.*
Judaea: *village : el-Yehudiyyeh*   *87* W4
   possible reading in 1 Macc. 4. 15 (with some Gk. MSS; others read Idumea—so KJV, RSV, NEB). The reading 'Judaea' as name of a village (*cf.* mod. name) is perhaps correct
Judah: *tribe*   *61, 65* X5
   Gen. 29. 35; 35. 23; Josh. 15. 1–63; Judg. 1. 2–20; 1 Kgs. 12. 20, 23
Judah: *reg. and kingdom*   *61, 63, 69, 73, 77*
    67, 71, 75, 78 F4
   southern part of Israelite country 'from Geba to Beersheba' (2 Kgs. 23. 8); in this sense 'Israel and Judah' denoted the whole nation, 1 Sam. 17. 52; David was king over Judah, 2 Sam. 2. 4, 10; then 'over Israel and over Judah', 2 Sam. 3. 10; *cf.* 5. 5; 12. 8; after Solomon's death his descendants reigned over Judah alone, 1 Kgs. 12. 17, i.e. the tribe of Judah, with Benjamin, 1 Kgs. 12. 21–23, until its fall to the Babylonians, 586 B.C., 2 Kgs. 24. 12—25. 21; some people remained in the land, 2 Kgs. 25. 22, and others returned, Ezra 1. 5; 4. 1; they became known as Jews (i.e. Judahites), Neh. 1. 2, and their land was called in Gk. and Lat. 'Judea', *q.v.*
Judah, Hill Country of: *49, 57, 61* X5
   the highland area of Judah between the Hill Country of Ephraim and the Negeb, bordered on W. by the Shephelah, on E. by Wilderness of Judah. Josh. 11. 21; 15. 48–60; 20. 7; 2 Chr. 21. 11; 27. 4; Luke 1. 39
Judah, Wilderness of: part of Judah E. of Hill Country, descending to Dead Sea. Josh. 15. 61–63; Matt. 3. 1. *Illus.*, p. 11
Judea: *reg.*   *77, 85, 87*
    89, 91 G4
   Gk. and Lat. form of 'Judah', 1 Macc. 6. 12 (KJV); 1 Macc. 10. 38; hence the Hasmonean kingdom of which Judah was the nucleus, and the kingdom of Herod the Great, Luke 1. 5; but also, geographically, the land of Judah (southern Israel), Matt. 2. 1; on death of Herod, this (with Samaria, *q.v.*) became kingdom of Archelaus, 4 B.C.–A.D. 6, Matt. 2. 22, after which it was placed under Roman administration through governors (Luke 3. 1). *See* pp. 84–87
Judea, Wilderness of: *see* Judah, Wilderness of
Julias (Betharamphtha): *T. er-Rameh*   *87* Y5
   see Betharamphtha
Juttah: *Yatta*   *59* U1
    61 X6
   in hill country of Judah, Josh. 15. 55; Levitical city, Josh. 21. 16

Kabul (Cabul): *see* Cabul
Kabul: Ortospana   *83* N4
   capital of modern Afghanistan
Kabzeel (Jekabzeel): *Kh. Hora*   *61, 63, 65* W6
   in Negeb of Judah, Josh. 15. 21; 2 Sam. 23. 20; 1 Chr. 11. 22
Kadesh: *T. Nebi Mend*   *55, 71, 75, 93* G4
   city on Orontes; 2 Sam. 24. 6 (RSV, NEB, with some Gk. MSS)
Kadesh (in Negeb): *see* Kadesh-barnea
   called 'Kadesh', Gen. 20. 1; Num. 13. 26; 20. 16
Kadesh-barnea: *'Ain Qedeis*   *55* F4
   (*possibly Kh. el-Qudeirat*)   *59* T2
   Num. 32. 8; 34. 4; Deut. 1. 2; Josh. 15. 3; *see also*

Kadesh, Meribath-kadesh
Kafr Bir'im: *94* X2
   site of important post-Biblical synagogue (3rd–4th cent. A.D.)
Kain: *Kh. Yaqin*   *63* X6
   Num. 24. 22; in hill country of Judah, Josh. 15. 57
Kalkhu (Calah): *Nimrud*   *75* H3
   Assyrian name of Calah, *q.v.*
Kamon: *Qamm*   *61, 62* Y3
   burial-place of Jair the Gileadite, Judg. 10. 5
Kanah: *Qanah*   *57, 62* X2
   in Asher, Josh. 19. 28
Kanah, Brook of: *Wadi Qanah*   *49, 63, 87* W4
   on border of Ephraim and Manasseh, Josh. 16. 8; 17. 9
Kandahar: Alexandropolis, *q.v.*   *79, 83* N4
Kanish: *Kültepe*   *55, 67* G3
   Hittite city, excavated
Kara: *riv.*   *53* G3
Kara-Bogaz-Gol: *inlet*   *53* K2
Kara Kum: *desert*   *53* L2
   meaning 'Black Sands'
Karatepe: *93* G3
   site of important excavations: finds of Hittite period include bilingual inscription in old Phoenician and Hittite Hieroglyphic
Karduniash (Babylonia) *see* text, p. 71
Karnaim: *Sheikh Sa'd*   *49, 57, 62, 69, 73* Z3
   sister city of Ashtaroth, Amos 6. 13; *cf.* Ashteroth-Karnaim, Gen. 14. 5
Karkor: *Qarqar*   *55* G4
    61 Z6
   place of encampment of Midianites, Judg. 8. 10
Kartah: Levitical city, in Zebulun, Josh. 21. 34; unlocated
Kartan: Levitical city, in Naphtali, Josh. 21. 32; prob. same as Kiriathaim in Naphtali, *q.v.*
Kassites: *93* G3
   mountain people inhabiting region of modern Kurdistan; invaded and ruled Babylonia *c.* 1650–1100 B.C.
Kayseri: *Caesarea Mazaca, q.v.*   *93* G3
Kebera: *see* Mugharet el- Kebara
Kedar: *people and reg.*   *55, 71, 75, 78* G4
    67 G5
   Gen. 25. 13; Isa. 21. 16–17; 42. 11; 60. 7; Jer. 2. 10; 49. 28; Ezek. 27. 21. Inscriptional evidence indicates Geshem of Neh. 2. 19 and 6. 1 ff. was king of Kedar. Assyrian 'Qidri'.
Kedemoth: *ez-Za'feran*   *57, 61, 63* Y5
   Deut. 2. 26; in Reuben, Josh. 13. 18; a Levitical city, Josh. 21. 37
Kedesh (in Naphtali): *T. Qades, T. Qedesh*   *49, 57, 61, 62, 69, 73, 77, 94* Y2
   a Canaanite city, Josh. 12. 22; in Naphtali, Josh. 19. 37; city of refuge and Levitical city, Josh. 20. 7; 21. 32; home of Barak, Judg. 4. 6, 10; captured by Tiglath-pileser III, 2 Kgs. 15. 29
Kedesh (in Issachar):   Levitical city, 1 Chr. 6. 72 (in Josh. 21. 28 called 'Kishion'; location uncertain: *T. Qisan* at foot of Mt. Tabor has been suggested
Kedesh (in Judah):   Josh. 15. 23; same as Kadesh-barnea, *q.v.*
Kedron: *Qatra*   *77, 87* W5
   1 Macc. 15. 41 (Cedron KJV)
Kedron (Belus): *Nahr Rubin : riv.*   *49, 87* W5
   the (unnamed) stream referred to in 1 Macc. 16. 5–10
Keilah: *Kh. Qila*   *57, 61, 63, 77* X5
   in the Shephelah of Judah, Josh. 15. 44; associated with David, 1 Sam. 23. 1–13; Neh. 3. 17–18
Kelkit: *riv.*   *52* G4
Kenath: *see* Nobah
Kenites: *tribe*   *67* F4
   a tribe of smiths, perhaps incorporated into the Midianites; Gen. 15. 19; Num. 24. 21; Judg. 1. 16; 4. 11 ff.; 1 Sam. 15. 6; 27. 10; 30. 29
Kerioth: *Saliya*   *63, 73* Y6
   city of Moab; Jer. 48. 24; Amos 2. 2
Kerioth (KJV):   in Josh. 15. 25, 'Kerioth-hezron' should be read
Kerioth-hezron: *Kh. el-Qaryatein*   *63* X6
   in Negeb of Judah, Josh. 15. 25
Kerman: *79* L4
   city in Iran, important in Achaemenian period: for name, *cf.* ancient Carmania, *q.v.*
Kesalon   Josh. 15. 10 (NEB): *see* Chesalon

Midas City *92* **F3**

55, 67, 75, 93 **G4**
fortified city where pass across Mt. Carmel enters Plain of Esdraelon (Plain of Megiddo). Captured by Thutmose III; opposed Joshua and remained in Canaanite hands, Josh. 12. 21; 17. 11; Judg. 1. 27; in Solomon's fifth district, 1 Kgs. 4. 12; fortified by Solomon, 1 Kgs. 9. 15; *cf.* 2 Kgs. 9. 27; 23. 29. Scene of important excavations showing occupation from early fourth millennium to *c.* 350 B.C. *Illus., pp. 12, 102, 103, 106*

Megiddo, Plain of: *49, 62, 73* **X3**
same as Plain of Esdraelon; 2 Chr. 35. 22; Zech. 12. 11

Meidum: *92* **F5**
site of necropolis, pyramid, and temple of first king of 4th Dynasty, Snefru

Meirun: Merom *94* **X3**
mod. village with remains of ancient synagogue and other buildings and tombs. *See also Merom*

Melid (*Malatya*): *67, 93* **G3**
cuneiform Meliddu, Gk. Melitene, *q.v.*

Melita (Malta): *isl.* *88* **B3**
Acts 28. 1 (KJV): Gk. and Lat. form of Malta

Melitene (Milid, Melid, *Malatya*):
71, 78, 82, 89, 93 **G3**
frontier town between Cappadocia and Armenia: attacked by Romans 69 B.C.; base of operations against Armenia and under Titus a legionary garrison-town

Melos: *isl.* *66, 92* **D3**

Memphis (Noph): *Mit Rahneh*
54, 67, 70, 74, 78, 82, 89 **F5**
58 **Q3**
Hos. 9. 6 (Heb. 'Moph'); also Isa. 19. 13; Jer. 2. 16; 44. 1; 46. 14, 19; Ezek. 30. 13 (RSV; in these latter passages KJV and NEB retain the Hebrew name 'Noph'). Capital of Lower Egypt; some Judeans settled there in 586 B.C.

Memshath:
along with Hebron, Ziph, and Socoh the name 'Memshath' appears on stamped jar-handles of the late 7th cent. B.C., indicating perhaps location of royal potteries or storehouses. 'Memshath' is possible allusion to Jerusalem.

Menderes (Maeander): *riv.* *52, 92* **E3**

Menzaleh, Lake *58* **Q1**

Meribah (Kadesh-barnea): *'Ain Qedeis* *59* **T2**
Exod. 17. 7; Num. 20. 13; 27. 14; same as Meribath-kadesh, Deut. 32. 51; Ezek. 47. 19

Meroe: *67* **F7**
at sixth cataract of Nile, ⅜ mile north of *Kabushiyeh*; ancient royal city of Ethiopia (Cush)

Merom: *Meirun* (*Meiron*) *49, 55, 61, 62, 65, 69, 94* **X3**
see Waters of Merom, *and Meirun*

Merom, Waters of: *49, 61, 62* **X3**
Josh. 11. 5, 7; perhaps the *Wadi Meiron–Wadi Leimun* watercourse

Meronoth: *Beit Unia* *77 ins*
1 Chr. 27. 30; Neh. 3. 7

Meroth *86* **X3**
later name of Merom

Mersin: *95* **F3**
site of important excavations

Mesad-hashavyahu *95* **W5**
Judean fort, late 7th cent. Excavations

Mesembria: *91* **E2**
Gk. city

Meser *94* **X4**
excavated site, Chalcolithic period

Meshech (Mushki, Moschi): *67, 70* **F3**
78 **G2**
people and territory of Asia Minor, associated with Tubal, *q.v.* Gen. 10. 2; the Mushki of Assyrian records, beginning *c.* 1100 B.C.; in conflict with Sargon II; Gk. 'Moschoi'; a trading people, Ezek. 27. 13; *cf.* Ezek. 32. 26; 38. 2; 39. 1

Mesopotamia: *53, 89, 93* **H3**
Heb. Aram-naharaim (Aram of the two rivers); Gk. (='between the rivers'), Lat., and mod. geographical name for land between Tigris and Euphrates. Gen. 24. 10; Judg. 3. 8; 1 Chr. 19. 6; Acts 2. 9; 7. 2

Messana: *Messina* *88* **C3**
Gk. city, formerly Zancle, refounded *c.* 490 B.C.; from *c.* 227 B.C. a leading city of Rom. prov. of Sicily, controlling straits

Michmash: *Mukhmas* *49, 61, 63, 73, 87* **X5**
77 ins
location of Philistine encampment, 1 Sam. 13. 2, 5, 11; 14. 5; occupied by returning exiles, Neh. 7. 31; residence of Jonathan Maccabeus, 1 Macc. 9. 73

Middin: *Kh. Abu Tabaq* *61, 63, 69, 95* **X5**
in Wilderness of Judah, Josh. 15. 61

Midian: *people and reg.* *55, 67* **G5**
11 **U3**
Gen. 25. 2, 4; 36. 35; Moses stayed there, Exod. 2. 15 ff.; enemies of Israel, Num. 22. 4, 7; 25. 17; 31. 3 ff.; Judg. 6. 1 ff.; 8. 28; the land, 1 Kgs. 11. 18; Isa. 60. 6; Hab. 3. 7. Midianites as traders, Gen. 37. 28, 36. *See also p. 66*

Migdal: *T. edh-Dhurur, T. Zeror* *57, 62, 94* **W4**
In Thutmose III's list. Excavations

Migdol: *T. el-Heir* *70, 74* **F4**
Judean refugees there after 586 B.C., Jer. 44. 1; with Syene, *q.v.*, marked limits of Egypt, Ezek. 29. 10; 30. 6 (RSV)

Migdol:
Exod. 14. 2; Num. 33. 7: perhaps a military post; location unknown

Migron: *T. Miriam* *63, 73* **X5**
1 Sam. 14. 2; Isa. 10. 28

Miletus: *78, 82, 89, 91, 92* **E3**
a leading city of Ionia, founded by Ionian Greeks in 10th cent. B.C.; under rule of Lydia and, from 546, of Persia; leader in Ionian revolt, sacked as punishment; tributary ally of Athens; taken by Alexander; city of Rom. prov. of Asia; Acts 20. 15, 17; 2 Tim. 4. 20

Milid (Melitene): *Malatya* *71* **G3**
see Melitene

Millo (in Jerusalem): *81*
possibly refers to terraces on eastern slope of Ophel, or to fortified tower; *see p. 80;* 2 Sam. 5. 9; 1 Kgs. 9. 15, 24; 11. 27; 2 Kgs. 12. 20; strengthened by Hezekiah, 2 Chr. 32. 5.

Minni (Mannai): *people* *71, 75* **J3**
see Mannai

Minoans: *people* *54* **E3**
inhabitants of Crete whose civilization (called Minoan after legendary king Minos) flourished *c.* 2000–1400 B.C., in Crete and southern Aegean, with splendid palace at Knossos; in Gk. tradition 'Minos' ruled a sea-empire (thalassocracy) in this period

Mishna (in Jerusalem): *81*
the 'Second Quarter' (RSV, NEB) of Jerusalem where the prophetess Huldah dwelt, 2 Kgs. 22. 14; 2 Chr. 34. 22 (KJV 'the college'); Zeph. 1. 10 (KJV 'the second')

Mishrefeh: *see* Qatna *67, 95* **G4**

Misrephoth-maim: *Kh. el-Musheirefeh* *61, 62* **X2**
Josh. 11. 8; 13. 6

Mitanni: *reg.* *55* **H3**
Horite kingdom, with Indo-Iranian rulers, in N. Mesopotamia *c.* 15th–14th cents. B.C.

Mitylene (Mytilene): *93* **E3**
chief city of island of Lesbos, Acts 20. 14

Mizpah: *T. en-Nasbeh* *49, 61, 63, 69, 73, 77, 95* **X5**
same as Mizpeh in Benjamin, Josh. 18. 26; an early sanctuary site; Judg. 20. 1 ff.; associated with Samuel, 1 Sam. 7. 5, 15; 10. 17; fortified by Asa king of Judah, 1 Kgs. 15. 22; seat of Gedaliah's government after fall of Jerusalem, 586 B.C., 2 Kgs. 25. 23; Jer. 40. 6 ff.; re-occupied after exile, Neh. 3. 17. Excavations reveal Asa's fortifications &c.

Mizpeh (in Gilead): *Jal'ud* *63* **W5**
place of pillar called Mizpah (RSV) by Laban, Gen. 31. 49; associated with Jephthah, Judg. 10. 17; 11. 29, 34 (Mizpeh, KJV). *See also* Ramath-mizpeh

Mizpeh of Moab:
1 Sam. 22. 3; not located

Moab: *reg. and kingdom*
49, 57, 61, 63, 65, 69, 73, 77 **Y6**
67, 71, 75, 78 **G4**
59 **U1**
country of Moabites (*cf.* Gen. 19. 37), Exod. 15. 15; Num. 21. 13, 15, 26; 22. 1; enemy of Israel, Num. 22. 3 ff., Josh. 24. 9; Judg. 3. 12–30; home of Ruth, Ruth 1. 1, 4 ff.; conquered by David, 2 Sam. 8. 2; its king Mesha, 2 Kgs. 3. 4 ff. (his inscription, *see p. 107*); Isa. 15. 1—16. 13; Jer. 48. 1 ff.; Amos 2. 1 ff.

Moab, City of: *Kh. el-Medeiyineh* *57, 63, 73* **Y6**
Num. 22. 36; same as 'city that is in [the middle of] the valley', Deut. 2. 36; Josh. 13. 9, 16; 2 Sam. 24. 5

Moab, Plains of: *49, 57* **Y5**
E. of Jordan, opposite Jericho, Num. 26. 3 &c.; 33. 49; Josh. 13. 32

Modein (Modin): *el-Arba 'in* *77, 87* **X5**
home of Mattathias, father of the Maccabees, 1 Macc. 2. 15, 23, 70; 9. 19 &c.

Moeris, Lake: *Birket Qarun* *58* **P3**
in the Fayyum

Moesia: *Rom. prov.* *89* **D2**
constituted 29 B.C. as part of Augustus's policy of securing empire up to Danube frontier

Moladah: *Khereibet el-Watan* *63, 77* **W6**
in Negeb of Judah, Josh. 15. 26; in Simeon, Josh. 19. 2; re-occupied after Exile, Neh. 11. 26

Mons Casius: *Ras Qasrun* *59* **S1**
traditional (Lat.) name of site near *el-Gals* suggested by some scholars as location of Baal-zephon, *q.v.*

Montfort: *Qal'at el-Qurein* *94* **X2**

Morava: *riv.* *52* **D2**

Moreh:
sacred oak near Shechem, Gen. 12. 6; 35. 4; Deut. 11. 30; Judg. 9. 37 (RSV)

Moreh, Hill of: *Nebi Dahi* *49, 61* **X3**
Judg. 7. 1; at E. end of Plain of Esdraelon, known as 'little Hermon'

Moresheth-gath: *T. Judaiyideh* *63, 73, 95* **W5**
home of Micah, Mic. 1. 1, 14; Jer. 26. 18; 'Morasthite' (KJV)='of Moresheth' (RSV)

Moschi (Meshech): *people* *78* **G2**
Gk. form of Meshech, *q.v.*

Mount Baalah: *Mughar* *61, 63, 69, 73* **W5**
on border of Judah, Josh. 15. 11

Mozah: *Qaloniyeh*
Josh. 18. 26. *See* Emmaus (Colonia Amasa)

Mugharet Abu Shinjeh *95* **X4**
cave in which the Samaria papyri were found, *see p. 32*

Mugharet Abu Usba' *94* **W3**
prehistoric cave settlement, excavated

Mugharet el-Kebara *94* **W3**
prehistoric cave settlement, excavated

Mugharet Shuqba: *see* Shuqba

Mukellik, Wadi *95 ins*

Murabba'at, Wadi *49, 87, 95* **X5**
See el-Murabba'at, Wadi

Murat: *riv.* *53* **H3**

Murrar, Wadi *95 ins*

Mushki: *see* Meschech *70* **F3**

Musri: *reg.* *71* **G3**
NE. of Kue, *q.v.*, and mentioned with it in Assyrian records; perhaps Musri should be read instead of Misraim (Egypt) in 1 Kgs. 10. 28

Musyan *93* **J4**

Muza: *Mocha* *67* **H8**
S. Arabian port named by Gk. and Lat. authors

Mycale: *cape* *78* **E3**
scene of Athenian victory over Persians, 479 B.C.

Mycenae: *54, 92* **D3**
leading city of Bronze-Age Greece, with tombs of Achaean kings; gives its name to 'Mycenaean civilization' which spread over Aegean after fall of empire of Minoans, *q.v.*, reaching Rhodes, Asia Minor, &c.

Myos Hormos *67* **F5**
port on Red Sea named by Gk. and Lat. authors

Myra: seaport in Lycia, Acts 27. 5 *43, 45* **F3**

Mysia: *reg.* *91* **E3**
district of Asia Minor; with Lydia formed second satrapy of Darius I's empire; later in Rom. prov. of Asia; Acts 16. 7, 8

Mytilene: older spelling of Mitylene, *q.v.* *78, 82* **E3**

Naamah: *Kh. Fered*
in the Shephelah of Judah, Josh. 15. 41

Naarah: *Kh. el-'Ayash, nr. Kh. 'Auja Tahta* *61, 63* **X5**
on E. border of Ephraim, Josh. 16. 7; same as Naaran, 1 Chr. 7. 28

Nabataeans, Nabataean Kingdom *77, 85, 87* **Y6**
82, 89, 91 **G4**
an Arabian people, occupying Edom, southern Trans-jordan, and SE. Syria, with capital at Petra; 1 Macc. 5. 25; a client-kingdom of Rome, 1st cent. B.C.-1st cent. A.D. under kings who were rivals of the Herods, including Aretas (2 Cor. 11. 32)

Nafud: *reg.* *53* **H5**

Nag Hammadi *83* **F5**
site of discovery of Coptic papyri (4th cent. A.D.)

Nahal Hever: *valley* *95* **X6**

Nahal Oren: *94* **W3**
Mesolithic and Neolithic cultures. Excavations

Nahaliel: *Wadi Zerqa Ma 'in: riv.* *49, 57, 65, 69, 87* **Y5**
Num. 21. 19

Nahalol: *T. en-Nahl* *61, 62* **X3**
in Zebulun, but remained Canaanite, Judg. 1. 30

Nahariyeh: *94* **X2**

site of Canaanite Bronze-Age shrine and other later remains, partly excavated

Nain: *Nein*   86 X3
Luke 7. 11–17

Nairi: *reg.*   71 H3
in Upper Tigris area, below Ararat; mentioned in Assyrian records

Naissus: *Nish*   89 D2
city of Moesia

Napata: at foot of *Jebel Barkal*   67 F7
royal city of Egyptian 25th (Nubian) dynasty, on Nile below 4th Cataract

Naphath-dor: *reg.*   61 W3
Josh. 11. 2 (Naphoth-dor, RSV); 12. 23; in Solomon's 4th district, 1 Kgs. 4. 11. Perhaps region around Dor, including foothills of Mt. Carmel, 'heights of Dor'

Naphtali: *tribe and reg.*   61, 65, 69, 73 X3
(Gen. 30. 8; 35. 25); Josh. 19. 32–39; Judg. 1. 33; formed Solomon's 8th district, 1 Kgs. 4. 15; conquered by Syrians, 1 Kgs. 15. 20; by Assyrians, 2 Kgs. 15. 29; Isa. 9. 1; Matt. 4. 13, 15

Naqada   92 F5

Narbata: *Kh. Beidus*   77, 86 X4

Nasor: see Asor

Natanya: *mod. city*   51 W4

Naucratis: *en-Nibeira*   67, 89, 91 F3
originally Gk. trading settlement, established *c.* 610 B.C.; favoured by Pharaohs before Persian conquest; later, Hellenistic city

Naxos: *isl*   92 E3

Nazareth: *en-Nasireh*   49, 85, 86, 94 X3
home of Jesus, Matt. 2. 23; 4. 13; Luke 1. 26; 4. 16

Neapolis (in Palestine): *Nablus*   85, 87 X4
Rom. period city (Colonia Julia Neapolis) near Shechem, *q.v.*

Neapolis (in Macedonia): *Kavala*   89, 90 D2
port of Philippi, on Paul's route, Acts 16. 11

Neapolis (in Italy): *Naples, Napoli*   88 B2

Neara: *Kh. el-'Ayash*
according to Josephus adjacent to place where Archelais was founded, part of water-supply of Neara being diverted to it; same as O.T. Naarah (Naaran), *q.v.*

Nebaioth: *people and reg.*   67 G4
Arabian people reckoned among descendants of Ishmael: Gen. 25. 13–16; Isa. 60. 7. (Not to be identified with Nabataeans, *q.v.*)

Neballat: *Beit Nabala*   63, 77 W5
a village of Benjamin after the Exile, Neh. 11. 32

Nebo (in Judah): *Nuba*   63, 77 X5
ancestral home of some of returning exiles, Ezr. 2. 29; Neh. 7. 33

Nebo (in Moab): *Kh. el-Mekhaiyet*   63, 69, 73, 77 Y5
allotted to Reuben, Num. 32. 3, 38; 1 Chr. 5. 8; Moabite city, Isa. 15. 2; Jer. 48. 1, 22

Nebo, Mt.: *Jebel en-Nebu*   49, 57, 61, 63 Y5
   59 U1
in mountains of Abarim, *q.v.*, place of death of Moses, Num. 33. 47; Deut. 32. 49 ff.; 34. 1 ff.; the mountain's lower summit to the N.W. is *Ras es-Siyagha*, probably Mt. Pisgah

Negeb, The: *Negev, reg.*   49, 57, 61, 65, 69, 73 W6–7
   59 T2
(in KJV translated 'south', but the word is the name of a definite region; *cf.* Deut. 34. 3.) Desert to the S. of Palestine, particularly S. of the Beersheba—Valley of Salt depression, though it might include areas N. of Beersheba (*see* pp. 48–49; area of wanderings of the Patriarchs, Gen. 12. 9; 13. 1 ff.; 20. 1; 24. 62; inhabited by Amalekites, Num. 13. 29; Canaanites, Num. 21. 1; settled by Calebites, Josh. 15. 19; included territory of Simeon (Josh. 19. 1–8); *cf.* 1 Sam. 27, 10; 30. 11, 14; 2 Sam. 24. 7; Isa. 21. 10; 30. 6 &c.

Neiel: *Kh. Ya'nin*   62 X3
in Asher, Josh. 19. 27

Nekhen: see Hierakonopolis

Nephtoah, Waters of: *Lifta*   63 X5
Josh. 15. 9; 18. 15

Nessana: *'Auja el-Hafir*   93 F4
in the Negeb, border post on caravan route from Aila to Gaza in Nabataean and Byzantine times

Netophah *Kh. Bedd Faluh*   63, 65, 73, 77 X5
in Judah, home of two of David's officers, 2 Sam. 23. 28–29; ancestral home of some of returned exiles, Ezra 2. 22; Neh. 7. 26

Nezib: *Kh. Beit Nesib*   63 X5
in Shephelah of Judah, Josh. 15. 43

Nibshan: *Kh. el-Maqari*   61, 63, 69, 95 X5
in Wilderness of Judah, Josh. 15. 62

Nicaea: *Isnik*   82, 91 E2
Graeco-Roman city in Bithynia

Nicephorium   89 G3

Nicomedia: *Izmit*   89, 91 E2
Graeco-Roman city in Bithynia

Nicopolis: 88, 90 D3
city founded by Augustus in 31 B.C. to commemorate victory (Gk. 'nikē') of Actium; Tit. 3. 2

Nicopolis (Emmaus): *'Imwas*   85, 87 W5
   58 Q3
see Emmaus: 'Nicopolis' was new name given to Emmaus in 3rd cent. A.D.

Nicosia: 52 F3
mod. capital of Cyprus

Nile: *riv.*   52, 54, 67, 70, 74, 78, 82, 89, 92 F3
the great river on which Egypt's life has always depended. Gen. 41. 1 ff.; Exod. 7. 17 ff.; Isa. 19. 5 ff.; 23. 10; Jer. 46. 7 f., Ezek. 29. 3; Nah. 3. 8 (RSV). *Illus., p. 21*

Nile Delta: 52 F4
cf. 'the branches of Egypt's Nile', Isa. 19. 6 (RSV)

Nimrim, Waters of: *Wadi en-Numeirah*   49, 69, 73 Y6
in Moab, Isa. 15. 6; Jer. 48. 34

Nimrud: *Calah, q.v.*   93 H5
site of Assyrian royal city

Nimrud Dagh: 93 G3
site of sanctuary of Antiochus I of Commagene, excavated

Nineveh: *T. Quyunjiq and T. Nabi Yunus*   53, 55, 67, 71, 75, 78, 93 H3
capital of Assyria; Gen. 10. 11; 2 Kgs. 19. 36; Jon. 1. 2 ff.; Nah. 1. 1; destroyed in 612 by combined onslaughts of Babylonians and Medes, *cf.* Nah. 2. 8; 3. 7; Zeph. 2. 13. Excavations have revealed many cuneiform texts from Ashurbanipal's royal library. *Illus., p. 24*

Ninus: 89 H3
Gk. and Lat. name of Nineveh

Nippur: *Nuffar*   55, 67, 71, 75, 78, 82, 93 J4
religious and cultural centre of Sumer, founded *c.* 4000 B.C., and important down to Parthian times; excavated

Nisibis: *Nisibin, Nuseybin*   75, 82, 89 H3
Assyrian city (Nisibina) in NE. Mesopotamia; reached by Nabopolassar, in his conquest of Assyria, 612 B.C. Roman frontier fortress

No (Thebes): *Karnak, Luxor*   54, 67 F5
in Heb. called No and No-amon; hence 'No' in KJV. Jer. 46, 25; Ezek. 30. 14–16; Nah. 3. 8; ('multitude of No' and 'populous No' in KJV should read 'Amon (god) of No' and 'No-amon', *see* RSV note at Nah. 3. 8). Capital of the Two Lands, Upper and Lower Egypt, first in Middle Kingdom, then under 18th Dynasty &c. Important extant remains—temples, etc.

Nob: *et-Tor*   63, 73 X5
in Benjamin; city of priests, successor to Shiloh, 1 Sam. 21. 1; 22. 9, 16; Isa. 10. 32; Neh. 11. 32

Nobah:
in Gad, Judg. 8. 11; nr. Jogbehah, *q.v.* (In Num. 32. 42 alternative name for Kenath, mod. *Qanawat*, in the Hauran)

Noph (Memphis): *Mit Rahneh*   54, 67, 70, 74 F5

see **Memphis**

Novae: 89 E2
Roman frontier station

Nubian Desert   52 F6

Nuzi: *Yoghlan Tepe*   55, 67, 93 H3
centre of Hurrian (Horite) settlement, founded in prehistoric times, which flourished in mid-2nd millennium B.C. Tablets found there throw light on customs of patriarchal period

Oboth: *'Ain el-Weiba?*   59 U2
stopping-place of Israelites in Exodus journey, Num. 21. 10, 11; 33. 43, 44

Odessus: *Varna*   89 E2
Gk. city founded *c.* 560 B.C.

Oea: *Tripoli* (Libya)   88 B4
Roman city, former Sidonian colony

Oescus: *Gigen*   89 D2
Roman frontier station

Old Conduit (in Jerusalem)   81

Old Pool (in Jerusalem)   81
Isa. 22. 11: see text, p. 80

Olympia: 82, 92 D3
ancient sanctuary and site of Olympic games; excavated

Olympus: *mt.*   52, 90 D3
Greek sacred mountain

Olynthus: 92 D2
Greek city: site of excavations

Oman, Gulf of: 53 L6

On (Heliopolis): *T. Husn*   54, 67, 70, 74 F4
   58 Q2
in Lower Egypt: centre of sun-worship, hence Greek form Heliopolis; home of Joseph's Egyptian wife, Gen. 41. 45, 50; called 'the City of the Sun' (RSV), Isa. 19. 18, 'Heliopolis' (RSV) Jer. 43. 13 (Bethshemesh, KJV)

Ono: *Kefr 'Ana*   57, 62, 73, 77 W4
in Benjamin, 1 Chr. 8. 12; ancestral home of some of the returned exiles, Ezr. 2. 33; *cf.* Neh. 6. 2; 7. 32; 11. 35

Ophel (in Jerusalem):   81
site of original Jebusite settlement, captured by David; its fortifications improved by Jotham, 2 Chr. 27. 3; outer wall built by Manasseh, 2 Chr. 33. 14; *cf.* Neh. 3. 26, 27; 11. 21

Ophir: Mahd edh-Dhahab? (Cradle of Gold), *q.v.*   55, 67, 71 H6
source of gold in Arabian peninsula, and place from which Solomon received gold. Gen. 10. 29

Ophlas (in Jerusalem):   96
Gk. form of Aramaic 'Ophla, same as Heb. Ophel; in Josephus, a quarter of the city in close proximity to the sanctuary

Ophni:
in Benjamin, Josh. 18. 24. ? same as Gophna, *q.v.*

Ophrah (Ephron): *et-Taiyibeh*   61, 63 X5
in Benjamin, Josh. 18. 23; 1 Sam. 13. 17. Greek name Aphairema, *q.v.*

Ophrah:
in Manasseh, home of Gideon, Judg. 6. 11, 24; 8. 27, 32; and Abimelech, Judg. 9. 5. See also 'Affuleh

Opis:
on R. Tigris below Baghdad; *text, p. 75*

Orontes: *Nahr el-'Asi: riv.*   52, 55, 67, 71, 75, 89, 91 G3
chief river of Syria

Ortospana: *Kabul*   83 N3
Graeco-Bactrian city

Osroëne: *reg.*   89 G3

Ostia: 88 B2
harbour city of Rome at mouth of Tiber; excavations show flourishing city in 1st cent. A.D.

Oxus: *Amu Darya: riv.*   53, 79, 83 M3

Oxyrhynchus: *Bahnasa*   89, 92 F4
Gk. name of Egyptian village where important discovery of papyri was made

Paddan-aram: *reg.*   55 G3
same as Aram-naharaim, *q.v.*, i.e. Mesopotamia. Gen. 25. 20; 28. 5–7; 21. 18; 33. 18

Paestum: 88 B2
Gk. city (with notable temples still extant)

Palace (in Jerusalem)   81
see text, p. 80

Palaikastro: 92 E3
site of Minoan remains

Palestine, reg.   52, 93 G4
the modern name is derived from the Gk. 'Syria Palaistinē', i.e. Syria of the Philistines or Southern Syria, the Philistine settlements on the coast being known to the Greeks before the interior

Palmyra (Tadmor): *Tudmur*   82, 89, 93 G4
oasis in desert between Syria and Iraq. Perhaps O.T. Tadmor (Tamar), *q.v.* Important trading city

Pamphylia: *reg.*   78, 82, 89, 91 F3
coastal region settled in Bronze Age by Achaeans, and Greek-speaking; later in first satrapy of Darius I; Rom. prov., Acts 2. 10; 13. 13; 14. 24; 15. 38

Paneas (Caesarea Philippi): *Baniyas*   49, 85, 86 Y2
   82 G4
at one of the sources of the Jordan: renamed by Herod Philip who took it as his capital; *see* Caesarea Philippi. *Illus., p. 114*

Pannonia: 88 C2
Rom. prov.

Panormus: *Palermo*   88 B3
Phoenician commercial colony and harbour city, later Roman

Paphlagonia: *reg.*   78, 82, 91 F2

Paphos: *Baffo*   *82, 89, 91* **F4**
Hellenistic-Rom. city. Acts 13. 6–13. (By N.T. times this new city had replaced Old Paphos, which was on different site at *Kouklia, q.v.*)

Paraetonium: *82* **E4**
Gk. colony, later Hellenistic-Rom. settlement (also called Ammonia). (With Pelusium, *q.v.*, called 'horns of Egypt' as guarding frontiers.)

Parah: *Kh. el-Fara* (? *T. Qurein*)   *63* **X5**
in Benjamin, Josh. 18. 23

Paran, Wilderness of: *59* **T3**
south of Canaan, and north of Sinai: Kadesh-barnea and Wilderness of Zin seem to have been in it, and it reached Elath. Cf. El-paran, Gen. 14. 6; home of Ishmael, Gen. 21. 21; in Israelites' wanderings, Num. 10. 12; 12. 16; 13. 3, 26; *cf.* Deut. 1. 1; 33. 2; David's refuge, 1 Sam. 25. 1; *cf.* 1 Kgs. 11. 18; Hab. 3. 3

Paros: *isl.*   *92* **E3**

Parsagarda (Pasargadae):   *79, 83* **K4**
near Persepolis, *q.v.*, first capital of the Persians, site of park and palaces of Cyrus

Parthia: *reg.*   *79, 83* **L3**

Parthian Empire: *89* **H3**
around middle of 2nd cent. B.C. Parthians secured independence from Seleucid rulers: their empire extended from Euphrates to Indus, and remained independent of Rome. Cf. Acts 2. 9, *and text, p. 88*

Pasargadae (Parsagarda):   *79* **K4**
see Parsagarda

Patara (Pasargada):   *89, 91* **E3**
Acts 21. 1

Pathros: *reg.*   *74* **F5**
Upper Egypt, Isa. 11. 11; Jer. 44. 1, 15; Ezek. 29. 14; 30. 14. *See also text, p. 71*

Patmos: *isl.*   *91* **E3**
island to which, acc. to tradition, John was banished, and where he saw visions recorded in Revelation, Rev. 1. 9

Patrae: *Patras*   *90* **D3**
harbour city in Achaea

Pattala: *Hyderabad* (Pakistan)   *79, 83* **N5**
place where Alexander reached R. Indus and established harbour and docks for his fleet (on old course of Indus)

Paturisi (Pathros): *see text, p. 71*

Pazarli: *93* **F2**
archaeological site

Pegai (Antipatris): *Ras el-'Ain*   *87* **W4**
Gk. name ('springs' for O.T. Aphek, *q.v.*, renamed Antipatris, *q.v.*)

Pehel (Pella): *see* Pella   *57, 94* **Y4**

Pekod (Puqudu): *reg. and people*   *71* **J4**
Assyrian 'Puqudu'. An Aramaean tribe living east of R. Tigris, mentioned in records of Tiglath-pileser III, Sargon, and Sennacherib. Jer. 50. 21; Ezek. 23. 23

Pella (Pehel): *Kh. Fahil*   *57, 61, 77, 85, 86, 94* **Y4**
Canaanite Pehel, mentioned in early Egyptian inscriptions and Amarna records; rebuilt by Greeks under Greek name Pella; city of Decapolis; after A.D. 70 centre of Christian community, refugees from Judea; excavations

Pella (in Macedonia):   *82* **D2**
capital of Macedonian kings, i.e. family of Alexander the Great; excavations

Peloponnese (Peloponnesus): *reg.*   *52, 78* **D3**
lit. 'Island of Pelops', the peninsula south of Isthmus of Corinth

Pelusium: *T. Farama*   *70, 74, 78, 82, 89, 91* **F4**
    59 **R1**
fortress east of Nile Delta, guarding approach to Egypt; Hebrew name 'Sin'. Ezek. 30. 15, 16 (RSV; 'Sin' in KJV; in NEB, Heb. 'Sin' is rendered 'Syene' (*q.v.*) with Septuagint)

Penuel (Peniel): *Tulul edh-Dhahab*   *55, 61, 63, 69, 73* **Y4**
place of Jacob's wrestling, Gen. 32. 30; sacked by Gideon, Judg. 8. 8, 9, 17; fortified by Jeroboam I, 1 Kgs. 12. 25

Perea: *reg.*   *85, 87* **Y5**
the territory beyond the Jordan (Gk. 'peran', beyond), with Galilee forming tetrarchy of Herod Antipas. In N.T. called 'beyond the Jordan' ('peran tou Iordanou'), Mark 3. 7

Perga: *Murtana*   *82, 89, 91, 92* **F3**
city of Pamphilia visited by Paul, Acts 13. 13, 14; 14. 25

Pergamum: *Bergama*   *67, 82, 89, 91, 92* **E3**
former capital of Attalid kingdom, city of Rom. prov. of Asia, and centre of emperor-worship (Rev. 2. 13);

---

its church one of the 'seven churches' of Asia, Rev. 1. 11, 2. 13 ff.

Persepolis: *Takht-i-Jamshid*   *53, 79, 83, 93* **K5**
from time of Darius I capital of Persia, in succession to Parsagarda; burned by Alexander. Spectacular remains and important excavations. *Illus., pp. 29, 31*

Persia (Persis): *Fars*   *53, 75, 79, 93* **K4**
Persian 'Parsa', original home of Persians in SW. Iran *Cf.* Ezek. 27. 10; 38. 5

Persian Empire: *78–79*
usual name for the Medo-Persian or Achaemenian empire founded by Cyrus: 2 Chr. 36. 20; Ezra 1. 1; 4. 5, 7; note 'Media and Persia', Esth. 10. 2; Dan. 8. 20. *See text, pp. 78–79, and Introduction, pp. 29–31*

Persian Gulf (Lower Sea)   *53, 55, 67, 75, 79, 83* **K5**

Persis (Persia): *reg.*   *79* **K5**
Gk. form of Parsa (mod. *Fars*) i.e. Persia, *q.v.* ('Persis' used for the limited area, a satrapy of the empire, in contrast to 'Persia' for the empire itself)

Perusia: *Perugia*   *88* **B2**

Pessinus   *89, 91* **F3**

Petra: *82, 89, 93* **G4**
desert city amid rock-cliffs, capital of Nabataean kingdom: area includes the rocky height which is probably Sela, *q.v. Illus., p. 115*

Phaistos (Phaestus):   *54* **D3**
centre, with Knossos, of Minoan civilization; palace and other remains, including 'Phaistos disk', clay disk inscribed in non-Greek script

Pharathon (Pirathon): *Far'ata*   *77, 87* **X4**
Gk. name for Pirathon, 1 Macc. 9. 50

Pharos: *67* **E4**
island where port existed before foundation of Alexandria, *q.v.*; later site of lighthouse (called 'pharos') marking harbour of Alexandria

Pharpar: *Nahr el-A'waj : riv.*   *49, 69, 73* **Z2**
river of Damascus, 2 Kgs. 5. 12

Phasael: *fort*   *96*
one of the towers of Herodian Jerusalem: *see text, p. 97*

Phasaelis: *Kh. Fasa'yil*   *85, 87* **X4**
named after Phasael of Herodian royal family: its palm groves mentioned by Pliny

Philadelphia (Rabbah): *Amman*   *77, 85, 87, 95* **Y5**
    82, 91, 93 **G4**
city of Decapolis: former Rabbah, Rabbath-ammon, captured by Ptolemy II (Philadelphus) and renamed: became Hellenized

Philadelphia: *Alashehir*   *89, 91* **E3**
city founded by Attalus Philadelphus; its church one of the 'seven churches' of Asia, Rev. 1. 11; 3. 7 ff.

Philippi: *Filibedjik*   *82, 89, 90* **D2**
rebuilt by Philip II of Macedon; a Roman colony, visited by Paul, Acts 16. 12 ff.; 20. 6; 1 Thess. 2. 2; Phil. 1. 1 ff.; 4. 15

Philippi, Caesarea: *see* Caesarea Philippi

Philippopolis: *Plovdiv*   *89, 90* **D2**
city established by Philip II of Macedon

Philistia: *reg.*   *63, 69, 73* **W5**
southern maritime plain of Palestine, named after the Philistines. Exod. 15. 14; Ps. 60. 8; Joel. 3. 4

Philistia, Plain of   *49* **W5**

Philistines: *61, 65* **W5**
people, prob. immigrants from Mediterranean region (Caphtor, *q.v.*) settled in maritime plain especially in five cities, Gaza, Ashkelon, Ashdod, Gath, and Ekron. 'Peleset' or 'Pulesat' mentioned as raiders attacking Egypt and eastern Mediterranean coasts in early 12th cent. B.C.; *cf.* Gen. 10. 14; Amos 9. 7. Met by Israelites on settlement in Canaan, Judg. 3. 3; enemies of Israel, Judg. 3. 31; 10. 7; 13. 5 ff.; 1 Sam. 4. 1 ff.; 13. 3 ff.; 17. 1 ff.; 31. 2 ff.; David's campaigns against them, 2 Sam. 3. 18; 5. 17–25; 8. 1; 21. 15 ff.; defeated by Hezekiah, 2 Kgs. 18. 8; Isa. 9. 12; Jer. 47. 1 ff.; disappeared from history after Babylonian conquest

Philistines, Land of the: *77* **W5**
former territory of the Philistines, Obad. 1. 19; Zeph. 2. 5; 1 Macc. 3. 24; 4. 22

Philoteria (Beth-yerah): *Kh. el-Kerak*   *77, 86* **Y3**
fort, with aqueduct and bridge, where Jordan flows out of Sea of Galilee. *See also* Beth-yerah

Phoenicia: *reg.*   *62, 73, 77, 86* **X2**
    78, 94 **G4**
coastal territory from Mt. Carmel, or from Acco, north to *Nahr el-Kebir* (R. Eleutherus) inhabited by Phoenicians; chief cities Tyre and Sidon. (Phoenix, plur. Phoenices in Gk. means 'purple': *see Introduction, p. 9*.) Obad. 1. 20 (RSV); Acts 11. 19; 15. 3; 21. 2

Phoenicia, Plain of   *49* **X2**

Phoenix: *Porto Loutro*   *89, 90* **D3**
harbour city in Crete, Acts 27. 2

Phrygia: *70, 78, 82, 91* **F3**
territory settled by Phrygians who invaded Asia Minor from Thrace, overthrowing Hittite empire; in Lydian, then Persian empires; district mainly in Rom. prov. of Asia, Acts 2. 10. Acts 16. 6 and 18. 23 prob. refers to Phrygian country in prov. of Galatia: *see p. 90*

Pibeseth (Bubastis): *T. Basta*   *58* **K2**
    74 **F4**
in Lower Egypt, Ezek. 30. 17

Pighades: *93* **F3**
archaeological site

Pi-hahiroth:
on border of Egypt, Exod. 14. 2, 9; Num. 33. 7, 8; *see text, p. 58*

Pilgrims' Castle ('Athlit   *94* **W3**
ruins of a Templar castle (Castrum Peregrinorum) built A.D. 1218 for protection of Christian pilgrims; on site of ancient Phoenician settlement

Pindus Mts.   *52* **D2**

Piraeus: *90* **D3**
harbour city of Athens

Pirathon: *Far'ata*   *61, 63, 65, 69, 77* **X4**
in Ephraim: Judg. 12. 15; 2 Sam. 23. 30; 1 Chr. 11. 31; 27. 14; *see also* Pharathon

Pirindu: *reg.*   *75* **F3**
western Cilicia (Cilicia Trachea), which had been under Assyrian domination, and was reached by K. Neriglissar of Babylon in 557/6 B.C.

Pisgah, Mt: *Ras Siyagha*   *49, 57, 61, 63, 95* **Y5**
see under Nebo, Mt. Num. 21. 20; 23. 14; Deut. 3. 17, 27; 34. 1; Josh. 12. 3; 13. 20

Pisidia: *reg.*   *82, 89, 93* **F3**
the hinterland of Pamphylia, on Anatolian plateau; in N.T. times part of prov. of Galatia. Acts 13. 14; 14. 24

Pithom: *T. er-Retabeh*   *58* **Q2**
    92 **F4**
store city built by Israelites in Egypt, Exod. 1. 11. *See also* Tell Rutabeh

Pitusu: *isl.*   *75* **F3**
fortified island off coast of Pirindu, *q.v.* (Modern *Kargincik Adasi* or *Manavat*)

Plain, The: *el-Beqa*   *49* **Y2**
in the valley between Lebanon and Anti-Lebanon Mts.

Po: *Padus: riv.*   *88* **B2**

Pola: *Pulj*   *88* **B2**

Polatli: *92* **F3**
archaeological site

Pompeii: *88* **B2**
Rom. city destroyed by eruption of Vesuvius in A.D. 79

Pontus: *reg.*   *88* **G2**
southern coastal region of Black Sea (Pontus Euxinus), east of Bithynia; in 1st cent. B.C. a kingdom under K. Polemo, then part incorporated in prov. of Galatia, part united with Bithynia, *q.v.*, to form province. Acts 2. 9; 18. 2; 1 Pet. 1. 1

Pontus Euxinus (Euxine Sea): *Black Sea*   *89, 91* **F2**

Portus Veneris: *Portovenere*   *88* **A2**
at SW. point of Gulf of Spezia (according to legend visited by St. Peter)

Posidium: *el-Mina*   *67, 93* **G3**
Greek trading centre (Gk. Poseideïon, after Poseidon, god of the sea) on coast of Syria; excavated

Post-exilic Jewish tombs (in Jerusalem)   *81*

Pre-exilic Jewish cemetery (in Jerusalem)   *81*

Priene: *92* **E3**
city of Ionia; fine temple, &c., excavated

Prusa: *Bursa*   *89, 91* **E2**

Prut: *riv.*   *52* **E1**

Psephinos (in Jerusalem):   *96*
tower in city wall: *see text, p. 97*

Pteria: *Boğazköy*   *78, 82* **F3**
Greek name of site of former Hittite capital, Hattusa (?), *q.v.*; scene of battle between Cyrus and Croesus, 547 B.C. (Placed by some at mouth of R. Halys)

Praetorium (at Jerusalem)   *96*
Matt. 27. 27 (RSV); Mark 15. 16; John 18. 28 ff. (RSV)

Ptolemaic Empire: *82*
set up by Ptolemy (Ptolemaeus), Alexander's general, who became king of Egypt and was succeeded by kings, all named Ptolemy, until Cleopatra, on whose death (30 B.C.) Egypt was annexed by Rome. *See text, pp. 82–83, and Introduction, pp. 32–33, 35*

Ptolemais (in Egypt): *el-Menshiyeh*   *82* **F5**
autonomous Gk. city founded by Ptolemy I

Ptolemais (Acco): *Acre* 49, 77, 85, 86, 94 X3
82, 89, 91 G4
Hellenistic city and port, corresponding to former Acco, founded in time of Ptolemaic rule over Palestine. 1 Macc. 5. 22; 11. 22, 24; 12. 45, 48; Acts 21. 7

Punon: *Feinan* 59 U2
halt of Israelites in wilderness, Num. 33. 42, 43. It lay in copper-mining area of Edom

Punt: *reg.* 67 H8
in Egyptian records, fabulous land on east coast of Africa, source of myrrh; included present Somaliland, perhaps also coast of Arabia

Puqudu (Pekod): 71 J4
see Pekod

Pura: *Fahraj* 79, 83 M5
halting-place of Alexander's army in Gedrosian desert

Put: *reg.* 54, 66 D4
Cyrenaica i.e., Libyan region west of Egypt. Gen. 10. 6; 1 Chr. 1. 8; Jer. 46. 9; Ezek. 27. 10; 30. 5; associated with Libyans, Nah. 3. 9

Puteoli: *Pozzuoli* 88 B2
port where Paul landed in Italy, Acts 28. 13

Pylos: *Ano-Englianos*, nr. *Navarino* 54, 92 D3
Mycenaean city with palace (associated in Homer with king Nestor); important excavations including tablets in Mycenaean script and Greek language, earliest known Greek writing

Pyramos: *Ceyhan*: *riv.* 91 G3

Qal'at el-Husn (Hippos): 94 Y3

Qal'at el-Qurein: 94 X2
ruins of a Crusaders' castle (Montfort), partly excavated

Qal'at er-Rabad: 94 Y4
Saracenic castle

Qantir:
in Lower Egypt, identified by some with Rameses, *q.v.* (here placed at *San el-Hagar*)

Qarqar: *Kh. Qarqur* 71 G4
on Orontes, site of battle between Shalmaneser III and twelve kings including Ahab of Israel, 853 B.C.

Qarun, Lake (*Birket Qarun*): 52 F5
ancient Lake Moeris, *q.v.*

Qaryat el-'Inab (*Abu Ghosh*) 95 X5
mod. village containing Crusaders' church, built over a spring. Excavated remains of earlier caravanserai adjoining. In 12th cent. A.D. identified with Emmaus because 60 stadia distant from Jerusalem (Luke 24. 13)

Qasr el-Hayr: 93 G4
archaeological site

Qatna: *T. el-Mishrifiyeh* 67, 93 G4
site of extensive excavations

Qattara Depression: 52 E5
marshy depression below sea level, in western desert of Egypt

Qau 92 F5

Qeshm: *isl.* 53 L5

Qezel: *riv.* 53 J3

Qidri (Kedar), *reg.* 71 G4
Akkadian form of name Kedar, *q.v.*

Qilt, Wadi: 95 ins
valley with perennial stream flowing near Jericho into Jordan: N.T. (Herodian) Jericho was on its banks

Qubeiba, Wadi: 49 W5
transverse valley and route from coastal plain through the Shephelah, dominated by Lachish

Qumran, Wadi: 95 ins
valley in Wilderness of Judea running past *Kh. Qumran. Illus., p. 37*

Qumran: *see under Kh. Qumran*

Quramati: *Qala 'at Ja 'bar* 75 G3
involved in Nabopolasar's campaigns of 605–604 B.C.: *see text, p. 74*

Qurna (Theban cemetery) 92 F5

Raamses: *see* Rameses
Rabbah: *Amman*
49, 57, 61, 63, 65, 69, 73, 77, 85, 87, 95 Y5
59 U1
capital of Ammon (also Rabbath-ammon), Deut. 3. 11; Josh. 13. 25; taken by David's forces, 2 Sam. 11. 1; 12. 26 ff.; 1 Chr. 20. 1; Jer. 49. 2, 3; Ezek. 21. 20; 25. 5; Amos 1. 14. *See also* Philadelphia

Rabbah: ? nr. *Suba* 63 X5
in Judah, Josh. 15. 60

Rabbath-ammon (Rabbah): 65 Y5

('Rabbah of Ammon': *see* Rabbah, and KJV, Deut. 3. 11; Ezek. 21. 20)

Rabbath-moab (Areopolis): *el-Misna* 87 Y6
later name for Ar, *q.v.*, in Moab; excavations

Raga: *see* Rhagae

Rages: *see* Rhagae

Rakkath: *T. Eqlatiya* 62 X3
Josh. 19. 35

Ramah: *er-Ram* 49, 61, 63, 69, 73 X5
77 ins
in Benjamin, Josh. 18. 25; fortified by Baasha, K. of Israel, but demolished by Asa of Judah, 1 Kgs. 15. 17–22; Babylonian internment camp after fall of Jerusalem, 586, Jer. 40. 1; its people after Exile, Ezra 2. 26. Associated with Rachel, the mother of Joseph and Benjamin, Jer. 31. 15; Matt. 2. 18

Ramah: *Rentis*
same as Ramathaim-zophim, *q.v.* Home of Samuel, 1 Sam. 1. 19; 2. 11; 7. 17; 8. 4

Ramah: *Ramieh* 62 X2
on boundary of Asher, Josh. 19. 29

Ramah: *er-Rameh* 62 X3
in Naphtali, Josh. 19. 36

Ramah: *T. Ramith*
same as Ramoth-gilead, *q.v.*

Ramat el-Khalil: 95 X5
traditional site of Abraham's Oaks of Mamre (*see* Mamre); pottery evidence of occupation from 9th cent. B.C.; enclosure wall of Herod the Great, and remains of well. After A.D. 330 Christian church built.

Ramathaim-zophim (Rathamin): *Rentis* 61, 63, 77 X4
in Ephraim, home of Samuel, 1 Sam. 1. 10; otherwise known as Ramah; in N.T. times Arimathea, *q.v.*

Ramath-mizpeh: *Kh. Jel'ad* 63 Y4
in Gad, Josh. 13. 26; same as Mizpeh of Gilead: *see under* Mizpeh

Ramat Rahel: Beth-haccherem 95 X5
mod. village in Israel containing ruins (*Kh. Salih*) identified with Beth-haccherem. Extensive excavations

Rameses (Raamses) (Zoan, Tanis, Avaris): *San el-Hagar* 58 Q2
built by Israelites in Egypt, Exod. 1. 11 (Raamses); also Exod. 12. 37; Num. 33. 3, 5. *See also* Qantir

Ramoth (Remeth, Jarmuth): *Kokab el-Hawa* 62 Y3
Levitical city, in Manasseh, 1 Chr. 6. 73

Ramoth-gilead: *T. Ramith*
49, 57, 61, 62, 65, 69, 73, 94 Z4
city of refuge in Gad, Deut. 4. 43; Josh. 20. 8; Levitical city, Josh. 21. 38; centre of Solomon's sixth district, for northern trans-Jordan, 1 Kgs. 4. 13 (*see p.* 65); scene of defeat of Israel by Syrians, under Ahab, 1 Kgs. 22. 3, 29 ff.; and under Joram, 2 Kgs. 8. 28; 9. 1 ff.; excavations

Raphana (Raphon): *er-Rafeh* 85 Z3
city of Decapolis (in enclave of territory in Batanaea): *see also* Raphon

Raphia: *Rapha* 69, 77, 85 V6
55, 71, 82, 91 F4
59 T1
on route between Palestine and Egypt, mentioned in Egyptian and Assyrian records, and involved in Ptolemaic-Seleucid wars

Raphon (Raphana): *er-Rafeh* 77 Z3
1 Macc. 5. 37; *see also* Raphana

Ras Shamra (Ugarit): 93 G3
site of Canaanite-Phoenician city of Ugarit, mentioned in Amarna letters; important excavations producing 14th-cent. Canaanite temple library and royal archives in alphabetic cuneiform

Ras Siyagha: Mt. Pisgah, *q.v.* 95 Y5

Rathamin (Ramathaim, Arimathea):
61, 63, 77, 87 X4
1 Macc. 11. 34 (RSV; Ramathem, KJV; Ramathaim, RV): same as Ramathaim-zophim, *q.v.*

Ravenna 88 B2

Red Sea: 52, 55, 67, 71, 75, 78, 82, 89, 93 G5
59 T5
In Exodus narrative the Heb. term (lit. 'Sea of Reeds') applies to part of Lake Menzaleh (*see pp.* 58, 59), Exod. 13. 18; 15. 22; elsewhere it refers to Gulf of Aqaba and what is today known as the Red Sea; Exod. 23. 31; 1 Kgs. 9. 26 &c.

Red Sea Hills: 52 F5

Rehob: *T. es-Sarem* 57, 62 X4
place south of Beth-shan, mentioned in Egyptian records, in stele of Seti 1 from Beth-shan, and in a tablet from Taanach

Rehob: *Kh. el-'Amri* (?) 62 X2
on border of Asher, adjoining Phoenicia, Josh. 19. 28

Rehob: *T. el-Gharbi* 61, 62 X3
in Asher, by Aphek, Josh. 19. 30; Judg. 1. 31; Levitical city, Josh. 21. 31; 1 Chr. 6. 75

Rehob: *see also* Beth-rehob
Num. 13. 21; 2 Sam. 10. 8, *cf.* 10. 6

Rehoboth: *Ruheibeh* 57 W6
on the way to Shur, SW. of Beer-sheba, Gen. 26. 22

Remeth: *see* Ramoth

Rephaim, Valley of: *el-Buqei'a*
valley near Jerusalem, Josh. 15. 8; 18. 16; scene of Philistine approach to city, 2 Sam. 5. 18, 22; *cf.* Isa. 17. 5. *See text, p.* 64

Reuben: *tribe* 57, 61 Y5
Gen. 29. 32; Num. 32. 1 ff., 33, 37; Josh. 13. 15–23; 18. 7; Judg. 5. 15 f.

Reza'iyeh (Urmia), Lake 53 J3

Rezeph: *Rezzafeh* 71 G3
captured by Assyrians, 2 Kgs. 19. 12; Isa. 37. 12

Rhagae: *Rey (Rayy)* 79, 83 K3
Gk. form of Old Persian Raga, in Media; later Europus; same as 'Rages' in Media, Tobit 1. 14; 5. 5; 6. 10 &c.

Rhegium: *Reggio* 88 C3
Acts 28. 13

Rhodes: *isl. and city*
52, 54, 66, 70, 74, 78, 82, 89, 91 (and ins), 92 E3
the island controls the entry into Aegean Sea from the SE. and was a focal point of trade in early times; settled by Minoans and Mycenaeans, then by Dorian Greeks; supported by Alexander with naval forces and was important in Hellenistic age. Ezek. 27. 15; Acts 21. 1.

Rhodope: *mts.* 52 D2

Riblah: *Ribleh* 71, 75 G4
'in the land of Hamath', i.e. north of Israel in Syria; Ezek. 6. 14; place of punishment by Babylonians of captured kings of Judah, 2 Kgs. 23. 33; 25. 6, 20; Jer. 39. 5; 52. 9, 26

Riblah:
Num. 34. 11: possibly same as above, but possibly a corruption in text

Rihab: 94 Z4
excavated site: occupied from Roman times (therefore prob. not Beth-rehob, which is sometimes placed here)

Rimmon: *Rammun* 61, 63, 73 X5
same as Rock of Rimmon, Judg. 20. 45 ff.; Isa. 10. 27 (RSV)

Rimmon: *Rummaneh* 61, 62 X3
in Zebulun, Josh. 19. 13; same as Rimmono, Levitical city, 1 Chr. 6. 77 (RSV; Rimmon in KJV). (In Josh. 21. 35 'Rimmon' should prob. be read in place of 'Dimnah')

Rimmon: *Kh. Umm er-Ramamin*
same as En-rimmon, *q.v.* (Josh. 15. 32; *cf.* Josh. 19. 7; 1 Chr. 4. 32)

Rishpon 95 W4
excavated site

Rogelim: *Bersynia* 62, 65 Y3
2 Sam. 17. 27; 19. 31

Roman Empire: 88–89
see text, p. 88; 1 Macc. 8. 1–32; 12. 1–4; 15. 16 ff.; Luke 2. 1; 3. 1; John 11. 48; Acts 16. 37; 22. 25 ff.

Rome: 52, 88 B2
1 Macc. 7. 1; 8. 17, 19; 12. 1; 15. 15; Acts 2. 10; 18. 2; 19. 1; 28. 14 ff.; Rom. 1. 7, 15; 2 Tim. 1. 17. *See also under* 'Babylon'. *Illus., p.* 44

Royal Caverns (at Jerusalem) 96

Royal Palace (Praetorium) (at Jerusalem) 96
Mark 15. 16; *see also* Praetorium

Royal Portico (at Jerusalem): 96

Rumah: *Kh. Rumeh* 62, 69, 73, 86 X3
2 Kgs. 23. 36

Rub' al-Khali: *desert* 53 K6

Rusapu 75 H3

Saab: *Sha'b* 86 X3
village mentioned by Josephus

Sabaeans: people of Saba, *q.v.*

Saba (Sheba): *reg.* 71 G6
see Sheba

Sabastiyeh: Samaria 94 X4
see Samaria

Sabratha: *Sabratah* 88 B4
Rom. city on site of former Phoenician colony

Safad: *Sepph, q.v.* 51 X2
Illus., p. 10

Saffariyeh: Sepphoris, *q.v.*   94 **X3**

Safid: *riv.*   53 **J3**

Sagartia: *reg.*   79 **K4**
Gk. form of Persian 'Asagarta'; part of 14th satrapy of empire of Darius I

Sahara Desert   88

Saida: Sidon, *q.v.*

Sais: *San el-Hagar*   71, 78, 82, 89, 91 **F4**
city of the Delta, capital of 26th Dynasty

Saka (Scythians): *people and reg.*   79, 83 **N2**
see Scythians: Saka was Persian name for region and people called by Greeks 'Skythia' and 'Skythai'

Sakarya (Sangarius): *riv.*   52, 92 **F2**

Sakçe Gozu   93 **G3**
archaeological site

Salamis: N. of *Famagusta*   78, 82, 89, 91 **F3**
Greek city in Cyprus, Acts 13. 5

Salamis: *isl.*   78, 92 **D3**
famous for Gk. naval victory, 480 B.C., over Xerxes' invasion fleet

Salecah: *Salkhad*   71 **G4**
in east of Bashan; city of King Og, Deut. 3. 10; Josh. 12. 5; in territory allotted to trans-Jordan tribes, Josh. 13. 11; on border of Gad, 1 Chr. 5. 11

Salem (Jerusalem ?)   57 **X5**
Ps. 76. 2 and ancient Jewish tradition identified Salem and Jerusalem; but Salem of Gen. 14. 18 is uncertain: some identify with Salim

Salim: *Umm el-'Amdan*   86 **Y4**
place mentioned in John 3. 23

Sallat: *Salate*   75 **H4**
Babylonian city plundered by Assyrians in 625 B.C.

Sallune: *Selindi*   74 **F3**
western Pirindu, *q.v.*; K. Neriglissar of Babylon laid waste area from Sallune to Lydian border, B.C. 557

Salmone (Sammanion): *Cape Sidheros*   89, 91 **E3**
promontory in E. of Crete, Acts 27. 7

Salonae: *Split*   88 **C2**

Salt, City of: *Kh. Qumran*   63, 69 **X5**
in Wilderness of Judea, Josh. 15. 62; identified with *Kh. Qumran*, *q.v.*

Salt, Valley of: *Wadi el-Milh*   49, 65, 69 **W6**
2 Sam. 8. 13; 2 Kgs. 14. 7; 1 Chr. 18. 12; 2 Chr. 25. 11

Salt Sea (Sea of the Arabah, Dead Sea):
    49, 57, 61, 63, 65, 69, 73 **X5**
    59 **U1**
called 'the Salt Sea' in Gen. 14. 3; Num. 34. 3, 12; Deut. 3. 17; Josh. 3. 16; 12. 3; 15. 2; 15. 5; 18. 19; see also Arabah, Sea of the

Samal: *Zinjirli*   67, 71 **G3**
Aramaean city of N. Syria; its king Panammu II paid tribute to Tiglath-pileser III of Assyria; controlled Yaudi, *q.v.*; important excavations

Samaga: *es-Samik*   77 **Y5**
involved in Maccabean wars in time of John Hyrcanus

Samaria: *Sebastiyeh*   49, 62, 69, 73, 77, 85, 86, 94 **X4**
    67, 71, 78, 82, 89, 91, 93 **G4**
founded by Omri as capital of Israel (northern kingdom), 1 Kgs. 16. 24; 2 Kgs. 3. 1 &c.; Isa. 7. 9; 8. 4; taken by Assyrians, 2 Kgs. 17. 5–6; foreigners placed there, 2 Kgs. 17. 24, and despised by people of Judah for heathenism, 2 Kgs. 17. 29. Capital of Assyrian, and then Persian, province; Ezra 4. 17; rebuilt by Herod the Great and re-named Sebaste, *q.v.* (Perhaps referred to in Acts 8. 5, reading 'the city' as KJV, *but see below.*) *Illus., pp. 17, 41*

Samaria: *reg.*   73, 77, 85, 86 **X4**
    75 **G4**
the region around, or ruled from, Samaria, Amos 3. 9; Jer. 31. 5; Obad. 1. 19; *cf.* 1 Kgs. 13. 32; 2 Kgs. 17. 26; 23. 19; after 721 name of Assyrian province, and thereafter name of region (between Judah and Galilee) until Rom. times. Ezra 4. 17; 1 Macc. 3. 10; 10. 30; Luke 17. 11; John 4. 4; Acts 1. 8; 8. 1; 9. 31; 15. 3. (In Acts 8. 5 true reading is prob. 'a city of Samaria', not 'the city, Samaria', referring to the region as in John 4. 5 &c.)

Samarra   95 **H4**

Samos: *isl. and city*   52, 66, 78, 82, 91, 92 **E3**
island of Ionia, settled by Achaean Gks.; active in colonization and trade. Acts 20. 15

Samosata: *Samsat*   89 **G3**
capital of Commagene in Rom. times

Samothrace: *isl.*   90, 92 **E2**
Acts 16. 11

San el-Hagar (in E. of Nile Delta): *see* Tanis
San el-Hagar (in W. of Nile Delta): *see* Sais

Sangarius (Sakarya): *riv.*

    52, 54, 70, 74, 78, 82, 89, 92 **F2**

Sankara: *see* Larsa   93 **J4**

Sansannah: *Kh. esh-Shamshaniyat*   63 **W6**
in Negeb of Judah, Josh. 15. 31

Sappho: *Saffa*   87 **X5**
village mentioned by Josephus

Saqqarah: site E. of Memphis   54, 92 **F5**
    58 **Q3**
tomb and pyramid area, including stepped pyramid of Djoser

Sardica: *Sofia*   89 **D2**

Sardinia: *isl.*   88 **A2**

Sardis: *Sart*   67, 70, 74, 78, 82, 89, 91, 92 **E3**
capital of Lydia (O.T. Lud, *q.v.*), and referred to as Sepharad, Obad. 1. 20. Under Rom. empire capital of prov. of Asia containing one of the 'seven churches', Rev. 1. 11; 3. 1 ff.

Sarepta: 85 **X2**
Greek form of Zarephath, *q.v.*, found in Luke 4. 26 (Gk., also KJV, NEB); RV and RSV have O.T. form Zarephath

Sarid: *T. Shadud*   62 **X3**
on boundary of Zebulun, Josh. 19. 10, 12

Saros: *riv.*   91 **G3**

Sarvistan   93 **K5**

Sattagydia: *reg.*   79 **N4**
with Gandhara and nearby areas part of seventh satrapy in empire of Darius I

Sava: *riv.*   52 **C2**

Scodra: *Shkoder* (formerly *Scutari*)   88 **C2**

Scopus, Mt.:   49, 87 **X5**
highest and most northerly of three summits of Mt. of Olives

Scupi: *Skopje*   88, 90 **D2**

Scyros: *isl.*   92 **D3**

Scythians (Saka):   79, 83 **N2**
see Saka

Scythians: 89 **F1**
to Gks. and Romans the Scythians were best known as barbarian (i.e. non-Greek, non-Roman) people N. of Black Sea, on extreme edge of civilized world: *cf.* Col. 3. 11

Scythopolis (Beth-shan): *T. el-Husn*
    49, 77, 85, 86, 94 **Y4**
Greek name of former Beth-shan, *q.v.*, in use from Hellenistic period ; Judith 3. 10 ; 2 Macc. 12. 29–30. (But in 1 Macc. 12. 40 Heb. name Beth-shan is used.) In N.T. times a city of Decapolis, walled, with hippodrome, theatre, pagan temples, &c.

Sealand: *reg.*   67 **J5**
alluvial region at head of Persian Gulf

Sebaste (Samaria): *Sebastiyeh*   85, 86 **X4**
    91 **G4**
'Sebastē' is fem. of Gk. 'Sebastos' which equals Lat. 'Augustus': name given by Herod the Great to his rebuilt city of Samaria in honour of Augustus. See Samaria

Secacah: *Kh. es-Samrah*   61, 63, 69 **X5**
in Wilderness of Judah, Josh. 15. 61, in Valley of Achor

Second Quarter (Jerusalem): *see* Mishnah

Seilun: Shiloh, *q.v.*   95 **X4**
ruins of Bronze and Iron Age settlements, also of Rom. and Christian periods

Seir: *reg.*   67 **G4**
the mountainous country E. of Arabah chiefly inhabited by Edom. Gen. 32. 3; 36. 9; Deut. 2. 5; 33. 2; Judg. 5. 4

Sela: *Umm el-Bayyarah*   67, 71, 78 **G4**
    59 **U2**
capital of Edom, Judg. 1. 16; 2 Kgs. 14. 7; Isa. 16. 1; 42. 11: see also Petra. Another possible location is es-Sela', NW. of Bozrah.

Selame: *Kh. Seilame*   86 **X3**
village mentioned by Josephus

Seleucia (in Gaulanitis): *Seluqiyeh*   77, 86 **Y2**

Selencia (in Mesopotamia):   82, 89 **H4**
on R. Tigris at mouth of *Nahr el-Malik*; founded in 312 B.C. by Seleucus I; replaced Babylon in importance; mixed Greek and Babylonian population with Jewish colony; an outpost of Hellenism in the East

Seleucia (in Cilicia): *Silifke*   89, 91 **F3**
founded by Seleucus I; under Rom. empire a free city (i.e. not in prov. of Cilicia)

Seleucia Pieria: *Seluqiyeh*   91 **G3**
port of Antioch, founded *c.* 300 B.C., 1 Macc. 11. 8; Acts 13. 4

Seleucid Empire: 82–83

---

founded by Alexander's former general Seleucus who became king (Seleucus I) in 312 B.C. and after 301 B.C. secured Syria, setting up capital at Antioch. See *Introduction, pp. 32–35* and text, pp. 82–83

Selo (Shiloh): *Seilun*   87 **X4**
see Shiloh

Semechonitis, Lake: *Lake Huleh*   49, 62, 86 **Y2**
Greek name of the lake called in Rabbinic literature Sea of Samcho (Simchu)

Senaah: *Kh. 'Auja el-Foqa*   77 **X5**
village represented among returning exiles, Ezra 2. 35; Neh. 7. 38

Senir (Mt. Hermon):   57 **Y2**
alternative name for Mt. Hermon, *q.v.*, Deut. 3. 9; *see also* 1 Chr. 5. 23; S. of Sol. 4. 8; *Ezek.* 27. 5

Senkereh, Sankara: *see* Larsa

Sepharad (Sardis):   70 **E3**
Heb. name for Sardis, *q.v.* Obad. 1. 20

Sepharvaim: nr. Hamath, *q.v.*
2 Kgs. 17. 24

Sepph: *Safad*   86 **X3**
fortress involved in Jewish Revolt

Sepphoris: *Saffuriyeh*   49, 85, 86, 94 **X3**
important city of Lower Galilee in N.T. times, rebuilt by Herod Antipas

Serabit el-Khadim: *Dophkah*   55, 93 **F5**
    58 **S3**
site of ancient mining settlement where earliest alphabetic inscriptions found: *see Introduction, p. 20*. See also Dophkah

Sevan, Lake   53 **J2**

Seyhan: *see* Adana

Seyhun : *Saros*, *q.v.*

Shaalbim: *Selbit*   61, 63, 65 **W5**
held by Amorites, Judg. 1. 35; later in Solomon's second district, 1 Kgs. 4. 9; same as Shaalabbin in Dan, Josh. 19. 42

Shabwa: 67 **J7**
incense trading centre in South Arabia; called Sabota by Pliny

Shaghur, Wadi esh-:   49 **X3**
marking division between Upper and Lower Galilee

Shah Tepe: 93 **K3**
archaeological site

Shalisha: *see* Baal-shalisha

Shamir: *el-Bireh*   63 **W6**
in hill country of Judah, Josh. 15. 48

Shamir:
Judg. 10. 1; possibly same as later Samaria, *q.v.*

Sharon, Plain of: 49, 57, 62, 65, 69, 73, 85, 86 **W4**
fertile coastal plain. 1 Chr. 5. 16; 27. 29; S. of Sol. 2. 1; Isa. 33. 9; 35. 2; Acts. 9. 35

Sharuhen: *T. Fa'ra*   57, 63, 69, 73, 95 **V6**
in Simeon, Josh. 19. 6

Shaveh-kiriathaim:
a plain in Moab near Kiriathaim, *q.v.*

Sheba (Saba): *reg.*   67, 71 **H8**
region in S. Arabia, Gen. 10. 7, 28; 25. 3 (*and cf. text, p. 46*), whose queen visited Solomon, 1 Kgs. 10. 1 ff.; source of gold, Ps. 72. 15, and incense, Jer. 6. 20; *cf.* Isa. 60. 6; Ezek. 27. 22; 38. 13

Shechem: *T. Balata*
    49, 57, 61, 63, 65, 69, 73, 77, 95 **X4**
    55, 67 **G4**
associated with Abraham and Jacob, Gen. 12. 6; 33. 18; 37. 12; city of refuge, Josh. 20. 7; Levitical city, Josh. 21. 21; burial-place of Joseph, Josh. 24. 32; city of the judge Abimelech, Josh. 9. 1 ff.; place of assembly for Israel. 24. 1; 1 Kgs. 12. 1; fortified by Jeroboam I, 1 Kgs. 12. 25, and first capital of kingdom of Israel, Hos. 6. 9. *Illus., pp. 19, 112*

Sheikh Abreiq (Beth She'arim)   94 **X3**
site of ruined town overlooking Kishon valley, with synagogue and extensive Jewish necropolis; identified with Beth She'arim, residence of the Sanhedrin after A.D. 135; others place Gabae (Hippeum) here

Shema: *Kh. el-Far*   63 **W6**
in Negeb of Judah, Josh. 15. 26; *cf.* 1 Chr. 2. 43

Shephelah, The (The Lowland)
    49, 57, 61, 65, 69, 73 **W5**
the foothill region between hill country of Judah and plain of Philistia; in older versions the Heb. word is translated 'lowland', but in RSV and NEB retained as geographical name of region: 1 Kgs. 10. 27; 1 Chr. 27. 28; 2 Chr. 26. 10; 28. 18; Jer. 17. 26; Obad. 1. 19

Shihin (Asochis): *Kh. el-Lon*   77, 86 **X3**
Heb. name of place called in Gk. Asochis, mentioned in Talmud

Shihor-libnath: *Wadi Zerqa : riv.*   *49, 62* **W3**
on border of Asher, Josh. 19. 26

Shikkeron: *T. el-Ful*   *61, 63, 69, 73* **W5**
on border of Judah, Josh. 15. 11

Shiloh: *Seilun*   *49, 61, 63, 65, 69, 73, 77, 87, 95* **X3**
assembly-place of Israel, Josh. 18. 1 ff., and sanctuary,
18. 10; Judg. 18. 31; 21. 19; 1 Sam. 1. 3 ff.; 1 Kgs.
14. 2 ff.; its destruction referred to, Ps. 78. 60; Jer.
7. 12

Shimron: *T. Semuniyeh*   *57, 61, 62* **X3**
Canaanite city, Josh. 11. 1; also Shimron-meron,
Josh. 12. 20; in Zebulun, Josh. 19. 15

Shinar: *reg.*
the territory of Sumer and Akkad (Babylonia, q.v.).
Within it lay the cities of Babylon (Babel), Erech, and
Akkad (Gen. 10. 10). See Gen. 11. 2; 14. 1, 9; Isa. 11. 11;
Dan. 1. 2. See pp. 25, 26 and map p. 55

Shittim (Abel-shittim):   *57, 61, 63, 73* **Y5**
    59 **U4**
camping-place of Israelites before invasion of Canaan,
Num. 25. 1; Josh. 2. 1; 3. 1; Mic. 6. 5

Shunem: *Solem*   *57, 61, 62, 69* **X3**
in Issachar, Josh. 19. 18; 1 Sam. 28. 4; associated with
Elijah, 2 Kgs. 4. 8 ff.

Shuqba: *95* **X5**
site of prehistoric settlement (*Mugharet Shuqba*)

Shur: *reg.*   *59* **S2**
    67 **F4**
Gen. 16. 7; 20. 1; 25. 18; Exod. 15. 22; 1 Sam. 15. 7;
27. 8

Shuruppak (*Far'a*):   *93* **J4**
home of flood hero in Sumerian and Babylonian tales

Shushan (Susa): *Shush*   *71, 79* **J4**
KJV form, following Hebrew, of Susa, q.v. Neh. 1. 1;
Esth. 1. 2 &c.; Dan. 8. 2 (KJV)

Shutu: ancient name of Moab; *see text p. 56*

Sibmah: *Qurn el-Kibsh*   *63, 73* **Y5**
in Reuben, Num. 32. 38; Josh. 13. 19; a city of Moab,
Isa. 16. 8; Jer. 48. 32

Sichar: *see Sychar*

Sicily   *52, 88* **B3**

Siddim, Valley of   *57* **X6**
Gen. 14. 3, 8, 10. In Gen. 14. 3 with explanatory note,
'that is, the Salt Sea.' In this area on the southeast side
of the Dead Sea, were 'the Cities of the Plain,' Sodom,
Gomorrah, Admah, Zeboiim, and Zoar, perhaps to be
associated with *Bab ed-Dra'* and four sites between the
Waters of Nimrin (q.v.) and the lower part of the Dead
Sea depression, *Numeira, es-Safi* (by the Brook Zered),
Feifa, and *Khanazir*.

Side (in Pontus)   *89, 91* **G2**

Side (in Pamphylia):   *92* **F3**
Greek colony founded *c.* 750 B.C.; excavations

Sidon: *Saida*   *49, 57, 61, 65, 69, 73, 77, 85, 94* **X1**
    52, 55, 67, 71, 75, 78, 82, 89, 91, 93 **G4**
chief city of Phoenicia, Judg. 1. 31; 1 Kgs. 17. 9; Isa.
23. 2, 4, 12; Joel 3. 4–8; Matt. 11. 21; Acts 27. 3. ('The
Great Sidon', including the suburbs and outskirts,
Josh. 11. 8; 19. 28)

Sidonians: *people*   *65, 69* **X2**
not merely the people of Sidon but the Phoenicians;
Deut. 3. 9; Judg. 3. 3; 10. 12; 1 Kgs. 5. 6 (people of
Hiram, K. of Tyre); 11. 1, 33; 16. 31 (Ethbaal was K.
of Tyre)

Sigoph: *'Uyun esh-Sha'in* (?)   *86* **X3**
fortified village mentioned by Josephus

Siloam (at Jerusalem):   *81, 96*
Luke 13. 4; John 9. 7, 11

Simeon: *tribe*   *61, 69* **W6**
Gen. 29. 33; 46. 10; the territory of Simeon was
included within that of Judah, Josh. 19. 1–9; Judg.
1. 3, 17; the tribe of Simeon had virtually no independent history (but *cf.* 2 Chr. 15. 9; 34. 5)

Simonias: *Semuniyeh*   *86* **X3**
village fortified by Josephus in Jewish Revolt

Sin (Pelusium): *T. Farama*   *59* **R1**
city on E. edge of Nile Delta called by Gks. Pelusium

Sin, Wilderness of: ? *Debbet er-Ramleh*   *59* **S3**
Exod. 16. 1; 17. 1; Num. 33. 11; in Sinai Peninsula
but location uncertain

Sinai, Mt.: possibly *Jebel Musa*   *59* **S4**
or *Jebel Helal*   *59* **S2**
the holy mountain where the Law was given, Exod.
19. 1, 11 ff.; 19. 20 &c., and so in later tradition, Ps.
68. 8, 17; Neh. 9. 13; Acts 7. 30; Gal. 4. 24, 25
('Arabia' in Paul's time included Sinai Peninsula);
traditionally *Jebel Musa* in the S. of the Peninsula, but
Jebel Helal is a possible alternative. *See also* Horeb

Singidunum: *Belgrade (Beograd)*   *88* **D2**
Rom. frontier station and garrison

Sinope: *Sinop*   *78, 82, 91, 93, 95* **G2**
Greek colony founded 770 B.C., active in trade in
Black Sea

Siphtan: *Shufah*   *62, 69* **X4**
in Thutmose III Lists, Amarna Letters and Samaria
ostraca

Sippar: *Abu Habbah*   *55, 71, 75, 78, 95* **H4**
in Babylonian king-list; temple restored by Nebuchadrezzar; captured by Cyrus; excavations (many
cuneiform tablets)

Sirbonis, Lake: *Sabkhet Bardawil*   *59* **S1**

Sirhan, Wadi: *see also text, p. 48*   *52* **G4**

Sirion (Mt. Hermon):   *57* **Y2**
alternative name for Mt. Hermon, q.v., Deut. 3. 9;
4. 48; Ps. 29. 6; Jer. 18. 14

Sirmium: *Sremska Mitrovica*   *88* **C2**
Rom. frontier fortress

Siscia: *Sisak*   *88* **C1**

Sistan: *reg.*   *53* **M4**

Siut (Assiut): *Lycopolis*   *70* **F5**

Siwa (Ammon), Oasis of   *66, 82* **E5**
oasis with temple and oracle of Egyptian god Amon-
Re, called by Gks. Zeus Ammon; Alexander visited it
and, like the Pharaoh, was saluted as son of the god,
i.e. semi-divine ruler of Egypt

Siyalk   *93* **K5**

Skudra (Thrace): *reg.*   *78* **E2**
Persian satrapy (including Macedonia) under Darius I

Smyrna: *Izmir*   *67, 89, 91, 92* **E3**
city of Ionia, later of Rom. prov. of Asia, containing
one of the 'seven churches' of Asia, Rev. 1. 11; 2. 8 ff.

Socoh: *T. er-Ras (Kh. Suweikat)*   *57, 61, 62, 65, 69* **X4**
in Solomon's third district, 1 Kgs. 4. 10 (Soco, RSV;
Sochoh, KJV). In Thutmose III, Amenhotep II, and
Shishak records

Socoh: *Kh 'Abbad*   *57, 61, 63, 69 73* **W5**
in Shephelah of Judah, Josh. 15. 35; 1 Sam. 17. 1;
2 Chr. 28. 18 (Soco, RSV; Socoh, Shochoh, or
Shocho, KJV)

Socoh: *Kh. Suweikeh*   *63* **X6**
in hill country of Judah, Josh. 15. 48 (Soco, RSV;
Socoh, KJV)

Sodom (possible location):   *57* **X6**
Gen. 10. 19; 14. 2 ff.; its destruction, Gen. 19. 24;
Isa. 13. 19; Matt. 10. 15 &c. *See also* Siddim

Sogane: *Sakhnin*   *86* **X3**
in Galilee, mentioned by Josephus and Talmud

Sogane: *el-Yehudiyeh*   *86* **Y3**
in Gaulanitis, fortified by Josephus and allotted to
Agrippa

Sogdiana: *reg.*   *79, 83* **N3**
part of 16th satrapy in empire of Darius I

Soli (in Cyprus): *Aligora*   *78* **F3**
Gk. city taken by Persians in 498 B.C.

Soli (in Cilicia): *Mezetlu*   *82, 91* **F3**
Gk. city; visited by Alexander before battle of Issus;
restored by Pompey and for short time called Pompei-
opolis

Solomon's Pool: *Birket el-Hamra* ?   *96*
mentioned by Josephus. Same as King's Pool, Neh.
2. 14?

Solomon's Portico (at Jerusalem)   *96*
'porch' (KJV) or (more correctly) 'portico' (RSV and
NEB) (Gk. 'stoa') reputed to have been built by
Solomon, in Temple area: John 10. 23; Acts 3. 11;
5. 12; *see text, p. 97*

Sorek: nr. *Kh. es-Sureik*   *61, 63, 65* **W5**

Sorek, Valley of: *Wadi es-Sarar* [*Soreq*]   *49* **W5**
Judg. 16. 4

Sparta: *52, 78, 82, 88, 90, 92* **D3**
see under Lacedaemon: the Spartans in 6th-4th cents.
B.C. were a leading power of Greece: withstood
Persians at Thermopylae, 480 B.C., conquered
Athens in Peloponnesian War ending 404 B.C.;
forced to submit to Macedon, but retained their
kings as late as 2nd cent. B.C.; 1 Macc. 12. 2, 5–23
(RSV, NEB)

Strato's Tower (Caesarea):   *77, 85* **W3**
former name of Caesarea, q.v.

Strymon: *Struma: riv.*   *90* **D2**

Subartu: *reg.*   *55* **H3**
inhabitants defeated by Sargon I and Hammurabi

Subeita: *Isbeita*   *93* **F4**

Succoth: *T. Deir 'Allah*   *57, 61, 63, 65, 73, 95* **Y4**
in the Arabah. Gen. 33. 17; Josh. 13. 27; Judg. 8. 4 ff.;
1 Kgs. 7. 46; Ps. 60. 6

Succoth (in Egypt): *T. el-Mashkuta, q.v.*   *58* **B2**
on Exodus route, Exod. 12. 37; 13. 20; Num. 33. 5, 6

Suez, Gulf of   *52* **F5**
    59 **R3**

Suhmata: *94* **X2**
village containing excavated remains of an early
church with mosaic floors

Sukhu: *reg.*   *75* **H4**
in Babylonian Chronicles

Sumer: *reg.*   *55* **J4**
Lower Mesopotamia, below Akkad; with Akkad
formed Babylonia: on Sumerian civilization, *see text,
p. 54*

Susa (Shushan): *Shush*   *55, 67, 71, 75, 79, 83, 93* **J4**
capital of Persian empire under Darius I and
successors; taken by Alexander 331 B.C. 'Susa' is Gk.
form, commonly used by historians, and in RSV,
Ezra 4. 9; Neh. 1. 1; Esth. 1. 2 ff.; Dan. 8. 2 (KJV
'Shushan', following Hebrew)

Susiana (Elam):   *79, 83* **J4**
region round Susa, Ezr. 4. 9 (RSV); 8th satrapy in
empire of Darius I

Susitah (Hippos): *Qal 'at el-Husn*   *77, 85* **Y3**
a city of Decapolis. (Susithah, the Aramaic name of
place, was translated into Gk. as 'Hippos', both
meaning 'horse')

Sycaminum: *T. es-Samak*   *86, 94* **W3**
road station in Rom. times

Sychar: *'Askar*   *87* **X4**
place containing Jacob's well, John 4. 5 (some MSS
read 'Sichar')

Syene: *Aswan*   *54, 67, 70, 74, 78, 82* **F6**
southernmost place in Egypt, on border of Cush
(Ethiopia). Ezek. 29. 10; 30. 6; RSV and NEB
reading in Isa. 49. 12 (Sinim, KJV): *see also* Elephantine

Syracuse: *88* **C3**
a leading city of Sicily, originally Gk. colony; Acts
28. 12

Syr Darya (Jaxartes): *riv.*   *53* **M2**

Syria (Aram): *reg.*   *57, 65, 69, 73* **Z1**
   52, 55, 71, 75, 82 **G4**
the region N. and NE. of Israelite territory, as far as
the Euphrates, Judg. 10. 6; chiefly figures in O.T. as
the kingdom centred on Damascus, 1 Kgs. 15, 18;
often at war with Israel under the monarchy, and
once allied with Israel against Judah: fell to Assyrians in 740; 1 Kgs. 20. 1; 2 Kgs. 8. 28; 16. 5 ff., *cf.*
Isa. 7. 1 ff. Later the Seleucid empire, q.v. (capital
Antioch), 1 Macc. 3. 13; 7. 39

Syria, Province of: *85, 86*
    89, 91 **G3**
Rom. province which included, or was joint province
with, Cilicia (Pedias), q.v.; its governor had authority
over Galilee and Judea as superior to the client kings,
tetrarchs, and/or governors of Judea. Luke 2. 2; Matt.
4. 24; (*cf.* Mark 7. 26); Acts 15. 23, 41; Gal. 1. 21

Syrian Desert   *52, 93* **G4**

Syrtis, Greater: *bay*   *88* **C4**

Syrtis, Lesser: *bay*   *88* **B4**
Acts 27. 17

Taanach: *T. Ta'annak*   *49, 57, 61, 62, 65, 69, 73, 94* **X3**
Canaanite city, Josh. 12. 21; in Manasseh, Josh. 17. 11;
Levitical city, Josh. 21. 25; held by Canaanites, Judg.
1. 27; *cf.* Judg. 5. 19; in Solomon's fifth district,
1 Kgs. 4. 12. A large mound (tell); important excavations

Tabal (Tubal): *reg.*   *71* **G3**
see Tubal

Tabbat el-Hammam   *93* **G4**

Tabbath: *Ras Abu Tabat*   *61, 62* **Y4**
Judg. 7. 22

Tabor, Mt.: *Jebel et-Tur*   *49, 61, 62, 69, 94* **X3**
Josh. 19. 22; Judg. 4. 6, 12, 14; Ps. 89. 12; Jer. 46. 18

Tabor:
Levitical city, 1 Chr. 6. 77; unlocated

Tabor (Itabyrium)   *86* **X3**
see Itabyrium

Tabriz   *67* **J3**

Tadmor (Tadmar, Palmyra):   *55, 67, 71, 78, 93* **G4**
its building ascribed to Solomon, 2 Chr. 8. 4, but this
is either an error, or refers to a different place, prob.
Tamar, q.v. Tadmor, caravan city in desert, became
Palmyra, q.v.

Tahpanhes: *T. Dafanneh*   *70, 74, 78* **F4**
Jer. 2. 16; Jeremiah there with Jewish refugees, Jer.
43. 7 ff.; 44. 1; 46. 14. Later, Gk. trading settlement

of Daphnae established there

Talhum (*T. Hum*): Capernaum   94 **Y3**
Arabic name for the well-preserved ruins of 3rd cent. A.D. synagogue, generally identified with Capernaum, *q.v.*

Tamar: *'Ain Husb*   65 **X7**
place built (i.e. fortified) by Solomon, 1 Kgs. 9. 18 (RSV reading; Tadmor, KJV; *see* Tadmor), Ezek. 47. 18, 19; 48. 28. *See also* Hazazon-tamar

Tanis (Rameses, Avaris, Zoan): *San el-Hagar*   58 **Q2**
       70, 74, 92 **F4**
see Rameses

Tantura (Dor):   94 **W3**
ruins of Hellenistic and Rom. harbour town, on a more ancient mound identified with Canaanite city of Dor, *q.v.*

Tappuah (Tephon): *Sheikh Abu Zarad*
     61, 63, 69, 77 **X4**
Canaanite city, Josh. 12. 17; in Ephraim, close to Manasseh, Josh. 16. 8; 17. 8; 2 Kgs. 15. 16 (RSV). *See also* Tephon

Tappuah:
in Shephelah of Judah, Josh. 15. 34

Taralah: *Kh. Irha*   63 **X5**
in Benjamin, Josh. 18. 27

Taranto, Gulf of   52 **C3**

Tarentum: *Taranto*   88 **C2**
Gk. city and seaport of Italy

Taricheae (Magadan, Dalmanutha): *Mejdel*
     77, 85, 86 **Y3**
Gk. name of place called in Heb. Migdal (Magdala, *q.v.*): from 'taricheuein' to smoke or preserve fish. *See* Dalmanutha

Tarracina: *Terracina*   88 **B2**

Tarshiha: 94 **X2**
village on ancient site

Tarsus: 67, 78, 82, 89, 91, 93 **F3**
city dating from Mycenaean period, patronized by Alexander, and afterwards Hellenized; home of apostle Paul, Acts 9. 11, 30; 11. 25; 21. 39; 22. 3

Taurus Mts.   52, 55, 91 **F3**

Taurus: *Beit Jabr et-Tahtani*   87 **X5**
Herodian fortress

Tavium: *Nefezköy*   89, 91 **F3**

Tekoa: *Tequ'*   63, 65, 69, 73, 77, 87 **X5**
in Judah, 2 Sam. 14. 2 ff.; fortified by Rehoboam, 1 Chr. 2. 24; home of Amos, Amos 1. 1; Jer. 6. 1. Nearby was Wilderness of Tekon, 2 Chr. 20. 20; 1 Macc. 9. 33

Tel Akhziv: Achzib   94 **X2**
Tel Dan: Dan   94 **Y2**
Tel Hazor: Hazor   94 **Y2**
Tell Abu Hawan: 93 **G4**
     94 **X3**
ruins of an oversea-trading city of late Bronze Age onwards: deserted before Rom. period

Tell Abu Matar: 95 **W6**
one of several excavated sites in neighbourhood of Beersheba. Chalcolithic period

Tell Abu Shahrein: *see* Eridu   55, 93 **J4**
Tell Abu Shusheh: Gezer   95 **W5**
site of Gezer (Gazara), *qq.v.*; also called *Tell Jezer*. Excavated: finds include 'Gezer calendar', and Solomonic gateway. *Illus.*, pp. 16, 111, *q.v.*

Tell Ahmar: Til-barsip, *q.v.*   93 **G3**
Tell Ashara: Tirqa, *q.v.*   67, 93 **H3**
Tell Asmar: Eshnunna, *q.v.*   93 **H4**
Tell Atshana: *see* Atshana
Tell Balata: Shechem, *q.v.*   95 **X4**
excavations reveal occupation from Chalcolithic through Bronze and Iron Ages to Hellenistic period; fortifications of patriarchal period, and temple of Baal-berith

Tell Basta: Pibeseth, Bubastis   92 **F4**
Tell Beit Mirsim: Debir, *q.v.*   93 **F4**
     95 **W6**
ruins of Bronze and Iron Age city: important excavations

Tell Brak   93 **H3**
excavated site with cultures from Tell Halaf period (*see p. 54*) to Hurrian level (c. 1700–1400 B.C.)

Tell Dafanneh: Tahpanhes, *q.v.*   92 **F4**
Tell Duthan: Dothan, *q.v.*   94 **X4**
Tell ed-Duweir: Lachish, *q.v.*   95 **W5**
Bronze and Iron Age walled city, with temple &c.; finds include 'Lachish Letters', Hebrew writing on potsherds from time of Babylonian invasion of Judah. *Illus.*, pp. 104, 105, 113

Tell el-'Ajjul: Beth-eglaim   93 **F4**
     95 **V6**
ruins of Bronze-Age coastal city, the site of Ptolemy's defeat of Demetrius in 312 B.C. Called by Eusebius 'Bethagla' or 'Bethaglaim', probable Heb. form Beth-eglaim, *q.v.*

Tell el-Amarna: Akhetaton   54, 67, 92 **F5**
     58 **P5**
see Akhetaton and text, p. 55: illus., pp. 22, 23

Tell el-'Amr: Harosheth-ha-goiim, *q.v.*   94 **X3**
Iron Age city mound guarding a crossing of River Kishon

Tell el-'Areini: 95 **W5**
can no longer be identified with Gath, though name 'Tell Gath' still in use. *See* Gath

Tell el-Asawir   62 **X4**
formerly identified with Yehem

Tell el-Fukhkhar: Acco, *q.v.*   94 **X2**
ancient city mound and cemetery now 1½ miles from sea due to silting

Tell el-Ful: Gibeah, Gabath Saul, *qq.v.*   95 **X5**
ancient city mound with ruins of stone-built citadel; occupied first in 13th–12th cents. B.C.; destroyed by Babylonians; rebuilt in Hellenistic and Rom. times

Tell el-Hesi: Eglon   95 **W5**
remains of Bronze and Iron Age city, partly excavated; prob. indentification Eglon. (Rom. period ruin in vicinity called 'Ajlan) pp. 2, 99

Tell el-Husn: Beth-shan, Scythopolis [*Beit Shean*]
     94 **Y4**
ancient city mound; inscriptions give evidence of Egyptian suzerainty and nearby cemeteries possibly indicate Philistine garrison. Rom. period remains of Scythopolis include theatre and city walls extending far beyond area of Beth-shan. *Illus.*, p. 101

Tell el-Jerisheh: Gath-rimmon   95 **W4**
Bronze and early Iron Age settlement

Tell el-Khalaifeh: Ezion-geber, Elath   93 **F5**
founded by Solomon; remains of copper-smelting (refineries), and seal of king Jotham found

Tell el-Kheidar: Tell Mor   95 **W5**
Tell el-Mubarak: 94 **W3**
Rom. mausoleum on an artificial mound, partly excavated

Tell el-Mutesellim: Megiddo   94 **X3**
Chalcolithic, Bronze and Iron Age city mound strategically sited at junction of *Wadi 'Ara* with the Plain of Megiddo. *See* Megiddo. Site uninhabited from Rom. times when its military functions were transferred to new legionary camp further south called Legio (*Leijjun*). *Illus.*, pp. 12, 103, 106

Tell el-Qadi: Dan   94 **Y2**
Tell el-Qasileh: 95 **W4**
harbour town with temple, founded by Philistines; perhaps referred to in 2 Chr. 2. 16

Tell el-Qedah (*Tell Waqqas*): Hazor   94 **Y2**
walled Bronze and Iron Age settlement commanding descent from Galilee to Lake Huleh: see Hazor

Tell el-'Ubeid: 93 **J4**
see also text, p. 54

Tell el-'Ureimeh: Chinnereth
remains of Bronze Age settlement on small hill overlooking Sea of Galilee: part of Egyptian royal stone found on the tell

Tell el-Yahudiyeh: 58 **Q2**
     92 **F4**
site where fortified camp of the Hyksos (*see text, p. 55*) was discovered

Tell en-Nasbeh: Mizpah   95 **X5**
Iron Age walled town on rocky summit commanding approach to Jerusalem from north. Extant walls and gateway probably those of king Asa (1 Kgs. 15. 22)

Tell er-Ras   95 **X4**
site of Samaritan, and also Hadrianic, temple on Mt. Gerizim (*cf.* John 4. 20)

Tell er-Rumeileh: Beth-shemesh   95 **W5**
Bronze and Iron Age city mound on western approach to Jerusalem: occupied by Canaanites, Israelites, and Philistines. Nearby Byzantine ruins called '*Ain Shams* (*cf.* 'Beth-shemesh')

Tell er-Ruqeish: 95 **V6**
Iron Age cemetery among coastal sand-dunes; a few burials possibly from lost Phoenician settlement

Tell esh-Sheri'ah: Gath, *q.v.*   95 **W6**
Tell es-Safi: Libnah   95 **W5**
Bronze and Iron Age settlement partly excavated. Crusader castle of 'Blanche Garde' or 'Monteler' at same site preserves meaning of Heb. name ('white')

Tell es-Samak: Sycaminum   94 **W3**
ruins of a small coastal settlement

Tell es-Sultan: Jericho   95 **ins**
occupied from the earliest Neolithic times (earliest walled city known: notable Neolithic finds) to Iron Age. Extensively excavated. On this site was O.T. Jericho; but association of any extant remains with city taken by Joshua is doubtful. *See also Tulul Abu el-'Alayiq. Illus.*, p. 15

Tell es-Sumeiriyeh: 94 **X3**
ancient settlement on coastal road containing many excavated tombs

Tell et-Taba'iq   94 **X2**
Tell Far'a: Sharuhen, *q.v.*   95 **V6**
city mound on *Wadi Ghazzeh* of Bronze and Iron Ages

Tell Far'a: Tirzah, *q.v.*   94 **X4**
ancient city mound commanding descent fromt Shechem to the Jordan, extensively excavated

Tell Halaf: Gozan, *q.v.*   55, 93 **G3**
Tell Harbaj: Helkath, *q.v.*   94 **X3**
Bronze and Iron Age city mound, commanding approach to Acco from Jezreel

Tell Harmal   93 **H4**
Tell Jemme: *Yurza*   95 **V6**
excavated site: *see* Yurza

Tell Judaiyideh (*Judideh*): Moresheth-gath   95 **W5**
ancient city mound, partly excavated

Tell Judeideh: 93 **G3**
Tell Keisan: Achshaph   94 **X3**
ancient city mound in plain of Acco)

Tell Makmish   95 **W4**
Iron Age excavations

Tell Maskhuta: Succoth (in Egypt)   92 **F4**
Tell Mor: *T. el-Kheidar*   95 **W5**
excavated Bronze Age site

Tell Nebi Mend: *see* Kadesh (on Orontes)   93 **G4**
Tell Qades: Kedesh   94 **Y2**
Tell Qudadi: 95 **W4**
ruins of Iron Age fortified site at mouth of R. Yarkon

Tell Ras el-'Ain: Aphek, Antipatris, *qq.v.*   95 **W4**
Bronze Age city mound, partly excavated, at source of R. Yarkon: later the site of Antipatris, and still later fortified by Crusaders

Tell Ramith: Ramoth-gilead, *q.v.*   94 **Z4**
Tell Rutabeh: Pithom, *q.v.*   92 **F4**
Tell Sandahanna: Mareshah, Marisa, *qq.v.*   95 **W5**
ruined city mound, partly excavated, with Hellenistic rock-hewn painted tombs in vicinity

Tell Sukas   93 **G3**
Tell Ta'annak: Taanach, *q.v.*   94 **X3**
city mound, partly excavated

Tell Waqqas (Tell el-Qedah): Hazor   94 **Y2**
see Tell el-Qedah, also Hazor

Tell Zakariyeh: Azekah   95 **W5**
city mound, with remains of citadel

Telloh: *Lagash*   93 **J4**
see Lagash

Tema: *Teima*   52, 55, 67, 71, 75, 78, 89 **G5**
city in Arabia, reckoned among sons of Ishmael, Gen. 25. 14; Job. 6. 19; Isa. 21. 14; Jer. 25. 23

Teman: *Tawilan*   59 **U2**
     75 **G4**
in Edom (*cf.* Gen. 36. 31–34; 42); Jer. 49. 7; Ezek. 25. 13; Amos 1. 12; Obad. 1. 12; in Jer. 49. 20, Hab. 3. 3, the 'poetic' equivalent of Edom

Temple (in Jerusalem):   81, 96
1 Kgs. 6. 1–37; 2 Kgs. 24. 13; 25. 13 ff.; Hag. 1. 1–14; Zech. 4. 9; 1 Macc. 1. 54; 4. 36–59; rebuilt by Herod, John 2. 20; Acts 3. 2; 4. 1 &c.

Temple, Pinnacle of   96
probably refers to corner of the Temple area where there is sheer drop from parapet to Kidron Valley below. Matt. 4. 5; Luke 4. 9

Tenos: *isl.*   92 **E3**
Tepe Gawra: 93 **H3**
important site for prehistoric cultures, beginning with Tell Halaf period (*see text, p. 54*)

Tepe Giyan   93 **J4**
Tepe Hissar   93 **K3**
Tephon (Tappuah): *Sheikh Abu Zarad*   77, 87 **X4**
1 Macc. 9. 50: *see also* Tappuah

Terebinthus (Mamre): *Ramat el-Khalil*   87 **X5**
Gk. and Rom. name of Mamre, *q.v.*, where grew the 'oaks' (Gk. 'terebinths', *see* RV and RSV notes) of Abraham (Gen. 13. 18)

Tesmes: *Mashad*   79 **L3**
see Mashad

Tetrarchy of Philip: *reg.* 86 Y2
Luke 3. 1

Thamna (Timnath): *Kh. Tibneh* 85, 87 X4
Gk. name of Timnath, 1 Macc. 9. 50 (Thamnatha, KJV; called Thamna in Pliny): in Rom. times head-quarters of a toparchy

Thapsacus: *Dibseh* 78, 82 G3
Gk. name of Tiphsah, *q.v.*

Thapsus: 88 B3
city of Rom. prov. of Africa, where Julius Caesar defeated Pompeians, 46 B.C., and finally consolidated his power

Thasos: *city and isl.* 82, 92 D2
early Phoenician settlement; later Greek colony; famed for gold mines

Theban cemetery (Qurna): 92 F5
the cemetery of Thebes, *q.v.*, in Egypt

Thebes (No) (in Egypt): *Luxor, Karnak, Medinet Habu, &c.* 54, 67, 70, 74, 78, 82, 92 F5
capital of Upper Egypt, city of the god Amon, with temples, royal tombs &c. Jer. 46. 25; Ezek. 30. 14–16; Nah. 3. 8. *See* No

Thebes (in Greece): 78, 82, 90 D3
chief city of Boeotia: rival of Sparta in 4th cent. B.C., defeated by Macedon, 338 B.C.

Thebez: *Tubas* 61, 62, 65 X4
Judg. 9. 50; 2 Sam. 11. 21

Thella: *et-Tuliel* 86 Y2
in Rom. times NE. boundary point of Galilee

Thermae (in Lesbos): 92 E3
archaeological site

Thermopylae: *pass* 78 D3
on road to Greece from N., in 490 B.C. a narrow passage between mountains and sea, where Spartans fought to death against Persian advance

Thessalonica: *Salonica (Thessaloniki)* 82, 89, 90 D3
formerly 'Thermae' (hot springs); named after wife of Cassander of Macedon; in Rom. period capital of one of districts of Macedonia; a free city from 42 B.C. Paul's work there, Acts 17. 1–13; 27. 2; Phil. 4. 16; 1 Thess. 1. 1; 2 Thess. 1. 1; 2 Tim. 4. 10

Thessaly: *reg.* 78, 82, 91 D3

Thrace (Skudra): *reg.* 78, 82, 89, 91, 92 E2
non-Gk. ('barbarian') country N. of Aegean, called Thrace by Gks. and Skudra by Persians: overrun by Darius I and Xerxes I and included in Persian empire; under Rom. empire but not a province till Vespasian (A.D. 69–79)

Three Taverns: 88 B2
small place (Lat. Tres Tabernae) on Appian Way, Acts 28. 15

Thyatira: *Akhisar* 89, 91 E3
Gk. city of prov. of Asia, Acts 16. 4; its church one of the 'seven churches' of Asia, Rev. 1. 11; 2. 18 ff.

Tiber: *riv.* 52, 90 B2

Tiberias: *Tabariyeh* 86, 94 Y3
89, 91 G4
city built by Herod Antipas, tetrarch of Galilee, and named in honour of Emp. Tiberius (see *p. 84;* Herod's castle adjoined city. John 6. 1, 23; 21. 1

Tigranocerta: 89 H3
city of Armenia, founded by king Tigranes I, captured by Romans in Armenian campaigns, 70 B.C. and A.D. 59

Tigris: *riv.* 53, 55, 67, 71, 75, 78, 82, 89, 93 H4
same as Hiddekel of Gen. 2. 14; Dan. 10. 4

Til-barsib: *T. Ahmar* 93 G3
near ford on Euphrates: captured by Shalmaneser III

Til-garimmu (Togarmah): 71 G3
see Togarmah

Timna (in S. Arabia): 67 J8
on principal incense trade-route: *cf.* Gen. 36. 12, 22; *also* 36. 40

Timnah: *Tibnah* 57, 61, 63 X5
in hill country of Judah, Josh. 15. 57; Gen. 38. 12–14

Timnah: *T. el-Batashi* 61, 63, 69, 73, 95 W5
on border of Judah near Philistia, Josh. 15. 10; 19. 43; Judg. 14. 1, 5; 2 Chr. 28. 18

Timnath (Thamna): *Kh. Tibneh* 77, 87 X5
1 Macc. 9. 50 (RSV): same as Timnath-serah, *q.v.*

Timnath-serah (Timnah): *Kh. Tibneh* 61, 63 X5
in hill country of Ephraim, burial-place of Joshua, Josh. 19. 50; 24. 30; same as Timnath-heres, Judg. 2. 9

Timsah, Lake: 59 R2

Tipsah: *Dibseh* 67, 71 G3
1 Kgs. 4. 24; later Thapsacus

Tirathana: 87 X4

Tirqa (Tell 'Ashara): 67, 93 H3
capital city of Khana on the middle Euphrates

Tiryns: 54, 92 D3
Mycenaean city with massive fortifications

Tirzah: *T. Far'ah* 49, 57, 61, 62, 69, 75, 94 X4
Canaanite city, Josh. 12. 24; 1 Kgs. 15. 17; capital of kings of Israel from Baasha to Omri, 1 Kgs. 15. 21, 33; 16. 6, 8, 15, 23 (*see also* Samaria); 2 Kgs. 15. 14; excavations

Tishbe: *Listib* 62, 69 Y4
home of Elijah 'the Tishbite', 1 Kgs. 17. 1

Tisza: *riv.* 52 D1

Tjaru (Zilu): *T. Abu Seifeh* 59 R2
see p. 58

Tob: *et-Taiyibeh* 61, 65 Z3
Judg. 11. 3; 2 Sam. 10. 6, 8

Togarmah (Til-garimmu): *Gürün* 71 G3
Gen. 10. 3; 1 Chr. 1. 6

Tombs (at Jerusalem): 81, 96
pre-exilic Jewish cemetery at Silwan (*p. 81*); post-exilic (Hellenistic-Rom.) Jewish tombs in Kidron Valley (*pp. 81, 96*); other tombs of Q. Helena, Herodian family, and at Gethsemane (*p. 96*)

Tomi: 89 E2
city regarded by Ovid (who was exiled there) as utterly remote from cililization (i.e. from Rome)

Topheth (at Jerusalem): 81
2 Kgs. 23. 10; Jer. 7. 31 ff.; 19. 6, 11–14

Trachonitis: *reg.: the Leja, q.v.* 85 Z2
from Gk. trachys, 'rough, rugged', the region of broken country N. of the Hauran (Auranitis) in-habited in N.T. times by turbulent tribes; conquered by Herod the Great and included in Tetrarchy of Philip, Luke 3. 1

Transylvanian Alps: *mts.* 52 D1

Trapezus: *Trebizond, Trabzon* 78, 82, 89, 93 G2
Gk. colony, founded by Miletus, 756 B.C.

Trebizond: 93 G2
Medieval and traditional name of ancient Trapezus (mod. *Trabzon*); important in Byzantine times

Tripolis: *Tarabulus* 82, 89, 91 G4
Hellenistic city formed from three older cities on coast of Syria

Tripolitania: *reg.* 88 B4
region of the three cities of Sabratha, Oea, and Lepcis Magna, *qq.v.*

Troad, The:
region in NW. Asia Minor round Troy, *q.v.*

Troas (Alexandria Troas): 89, 91 E3
Hellenistic-Roman city and port; Acts 16. 8, 11; 20. 5, 6; 2 Cor. 2. 12; 2 Tim. 4. 13

Troy (Ilium): 54, 82, 92 E3
important Bronze Age city controlling routes along and across Hellespont; famous in legend, as shown by Homer's *Iliad*. Excavations show successive cities, one particularly rich (Troy VII A) destroyed about 1200 B.C.

Tseelim, Wadi: 95 X6
valley where some scrolls were found in cave, 1960

Tubal (Tabal): *reg.* 67, 71 G3
Gen. 10. 2; Isa. 66. 19; Ezek. 27. 13; 32. 26; 38. 2 f.; 39. 1; Tabal in Assyrian records; Tabaleans (people) in Gk. (Herodotus)

Tuleilat el-Ghassul: 95 Y5
ruins of Chalcolithic settlements

Tulul Abu el-'Alayiq: 85 X5 *and ins*
site of excavations revealing Herodian (i.e. N.T. period) buildings of Jericho

Turang Tepe (Zadrakarta): 79, 83, 93 K3
capital of Hyrcania, partly excavated

Turkish Wall (at Jerusalem): 81, 96
the wall of the medieval (Turkish) city, still enclosing the 'Old City', but not corresponding entirely with the area of the Biblical city: see *p. 80*

Turushpa (Tuspar): *Van* 71 H3
most important and royal city of Haldia; reached but not taken by Tiglath-pileser III, by-passed by Sargon II

Tuz, Lake: 52 F3

Tyana (Tukhana): *Kizli Hisar* 82 F3
paid tribute to Tiglath-pileser III and Sargon II, conquered by Esarhaddon; on route of Cyrus's advance against Artaxerxes II (401 B.C.; see *p. 79*): in Hellenistic period an urban centre in Cappadocia

Tyre: *es-Sur* 49, 57, 61, 62, 65, 69, 73, 77, 85, 86, 94 X2
52, 55, 67, 71, 75, 78, 82, 89, 91, 93 G4
ancient Phoenician city on island close to coast. Josh.

19. 29; 2 Sam 5. 11; 24. 7; 1 Kgs. 5. 1; 7. 13 f.; 9. 11f.; its wealth depended on trade, *cf.* Isa. 23. 1, 5, 15 ff.; Ezek. 26–28 passim; 29. 18; Amos 1. 9 f.; Zech. 9. 3; taken by Babylonians 573 B.C., and by Alexander, 332 B.C., who joined it to mainland by a mole. Matt. 15. 21; Mark 7. 31; Acts 12. 20; 21. 3. *Illus., p. 32*

Tyre, Ladder of: *Ras en-Naqura* 49, 77 X2
the narrow passage between mountains and sea, southern entrance to Plain of Phoenicia. (Road formerly narrowed here to series of steps cut in rock)

Tyrrhenian Sea 88 B3

Ubeidiya 94 Y3
Lower Palaeolithic Pebble Culture site, see *p. 13*

Ugarit: *Ras Shamra, q.v.* 55, 67, 93 G3

Ulatha: *reg.* 85, 86 Y2
plain north of Lake Huleh (name used by Josephus)

Umm el-'Amad: 94 X3
ruined town in Galilee, with synagogue and tombs

Umm Qatafa: 95 X5
place with prehistoric caves

Upper City (in O.T. Jerusalem): 81
the part of the city on the western hill, so designated by Josephus

Upper Pool (in Jerusalem): 81
2 Kgs. 18. 17; Isa. 7. 3; 36. 2

Upper Sea (Mediterranean Sea): 54, 70, 78 E4
Mesopotamian (Sumerian, Akkadian) term for the Mediterranean: *cf.* text, *p. 54*. See also Great Sea, Western Sea

'Uqeir: 93 H4
archaeological site

Ur: *el-Muqeiyar* 53, 55, 67, 71, 75, 78, 93 J4
Sumerian and Babylonian city, outstanding for rich-ness of objects found in Sumerian royal tombs, striking ziggurat &c.: see text, *p. 54*; illus., *p. 25*; its territory was home of Abraham's family; Gen. 11. 28, 31; 15. 7; Neh. 9. 7

Ura: *Olba* 75 F3

Urartu (Ararat): *reg.* 55, 67, 71, 75, 78 H3
region and kingdom mentioned in cuneiform texts, same as Biblical Ararat, *q.v.*

Urmia, Lake: *L. Reza'iyeh* 53, 55, 71, 78, 82, 89, 93 J3

Uruk (Erech): *Warqa* 55, 71, 75, 78, 82, 93 J4
see Erech

Ushu: *T. Rashadiyeh* 71 G4

Usiana: *Tuz Koi* 71 F3
in Assyrian annals

Utica: 88 B3
city of Rom. prov. of Africa

Uzal: *San'a* 67 H7
Arabian trading centre; *cf.* Gen. 10. 27; 1 Chr. 1. 21; *see also* Ezek. 27. 19

Uzu: *T. Rashidiyeh* 57, 62, 73 X2
the mainland 'suburb' of the city of Tyre; men-tioned in Assyrian and Egyptian records; possibly equals Hosah, *q.v.*

Van: Turushpa, *q.v.* 67, 93 H3

Van, Lake 53, 55, 67, 71, 78, 82, 89, 93 H3

Vesuvius, Mt. 52 B2

Viminacium: *Kostolac* 88 D2
Rom. frontier post and military camp

Volga: *riv.* 53 J1

Vouni: 93 F3
archaeological site

Vounous: 93 F3
archaeological site

Wadi: Arabic word for watercourse (often dry in dry season) and valley containing it. For names so beginning *see under following name*

Warka (Erech, Uruk): 93 J4
see Erech

Water Shaft (in Jerusalem): 81
2 Sam. 5. 8 (RSV): *see* text, *p. 80*

Western Desert (of Egypt): 52 E5

Western Sea (Great Sea): *Mediterranean* 57, 70
Deut. 11. 24; 34. 2; also sometimes so called in Mesopotamian records, where usually 'Upper Sea'

Women, Court of (in Temple, Jerusalem) 96

Xanthus 78, 82, 91, 92 E3

Yafa: Japhia, *q.v.* 94 X3

Yaham: *see* Yehem

Sources of Illustrations

The publishers are very grateful to the following for supplying illustrations for this book:

Aerofilms Ltd: 115 Alinari: 39 (top); Alinari-Mansell: 39 (bottom); Archives Photographiques: 32 (top); Directorate of Antiquities, Baghdad: 25 (top); Bibliotheca Bodmeriana: 47; The Trustees of the British Museum: 20 (bottom), 22 (right), 25 (bottom), 26, 27, 28 (right), 33 (bottom), 34 (top), 100 (bottom right), 105, 110; Brooklyn Museum: 21 (bottom), 45 (top); University of Chicago (Oriental Institute): 103, 106 (top); Professor H. Thomas Frank: frontispiece, 11, 14 (bottom), 15 (bottom), 17 (top), 19, 33 (top), 41, 45 (bottom), 46, 109, 112, 114, 117 (bottom), 118 (top); Professor A. Frova: 116 (left); Giraudon: 34 (bottom); Israel Department of Antiquities and Museums: 17 (bottom), 36, 113 (top), 117 (top), 119; Israel Government Tourist Office: 13, 40, 101, 106 (bottom); Israel Museum: 37 (bottom), 116 (top and bottom right); University of London (Institute of Archaeology): 104 (bottom), 113 (bottom); Musée du Louvre: 32 (top), 34 (bottom), 107; Mansell Collection: 44; Professor Mazar: 118 (left); Metropolitan Museum of Art: 22 (left), 23 (top left and right and bottom right); University of Michigan (School of Oriental Research): 30; University Museum of Pennsylvania: 20 (top); Paul Popper: 10 (bottom), 14 (top), 21 (top), 24, 29, 31; Dr. J. Pritchard: 100 (top and bottom left); Radio Times Hulton Picture Library: 38; Turin Museum: 23 (left), 28 (left); Professor Yigael Yadin: 42.

Other illustrations were kindly supplied by Professor Herbert G. May; the plans on p. 16 were drawn by Miss Christine M. Helms of Oberlin College.